1963

THE PHILOSOPHERS OF CHINA

The Philosophers of China

Classical and Contemporary

By

CLARENCE BURTON DAY, Ph.D.

Former Chairman, Department of Foreign Languages and Instructor in Philosophy, College of Arts in Hangchow University; Member of the North China Branch of the Royal Asiatic Society

THE CITADEL PRESS

NEW YORK

This paperbound edition published 1962 by
The Citadel Press, 222 Park Avenue South, New York 3, N Y.
Manufactured in the United States of America
Library of Congress Catalog Card Number 61-12618

DEDICATION

To The Late W. B. Pettus, President,
The Late Robert F. Fitch, Dean, and
the Civilian Students of the
California College in China
(Peking College of Chinese Studies)
refugeeing during World War II
at the
University of California
in Berkeley,
to whom part of this material
was presented in lecture form.

TABLE OF CONTENTS

PART III

CONFUCIAN AND TAOIST REACTIONS TO BUDDHIST THOUGHT
CONFUCIANISM REASSERTS ITSELF

PART IV

RECONSTRUCTION IN CONTEMPORARY PHILOSOPHY

Confucius

"I will not teach a man who is not anxious to learn, and will not explain to one who is not trying to make things clear to himself. And if I explain one fourth and the man does not go back and reflect and think out the implications in the remaining three-fourths for himself, I will not bother to teach him again."

(–Confucius in the *Lun Yü*)
(Lin Yutang translation)

THE PHILOSOPHERS OF CHINA

PREFACE

In view of the fact that, owing to far-reaching historical developments since World War II, the American public has become increasingly China-conscious and desirous of knowing how the Chinese mind works, it has seemed urgently advisable to prepare an introduction to Chinese philosophy that will throw light on the background of Chinese thinking from ancient times down to the present day. The approach to classical thought has been made through the medium of English translations, preferably the work of Chinese scholars, although in some instances translations by "foreigners" have also been used. Much of their contemporary thinking has been done directly in English by present-day Chinese scholars, who have made that or some other Western language their second language.

Whereas the serious investigator should procure such longer and more comprehensive treatises as Fung Yu-lan's *History of Chinese Philosophy,* the present work aims to present in brief but readable form a selection of materials that will enable the college student or interested layman to follow the main currents of Chinese thought in what may be his or her first approach to the Chinese mind historically considered.

Quotations have been chosen that seem best to preserve the flavor of the Chinese original; free use has also been made of comments and interpretations of the translators, inasmuch as they were inspired by first-hand scanning of the Chinese text. In this way, the reader will be brought as close as possible to the minds of the Chinese philosophers themselves. A special effort has been made to present a fairly accurate picture of the contemporary scene, which has been omitted from Professor Fung's treatment, which does not go beyond the founding of the Republic in 1911-1912, simply because he himself is a leading figure in the contemporary setting.

The writer here wishes to make acknowledgment of special aid received from interested friends and kind critics:

To Dr. Derk Bodde, Chairman, Department of Oriental Studies in the University of Pennsylvania and Fung Yu-lan's translator, and to Dr. Clarence H. Hamilton, formerly of the Oberlin Graduate School of Theology, for their helpful suggestions in the early stages of this project; to Dr. Hu Shih, former Ambassador to the United States and currently President of the *Academia Sinica,* for insistence on a more adequate treatment of the Buddhist philosophy from the Chinese angle; to Dr. Mei Yi-pao, of Iowa State University, for generously supplying valuable outlines and bibliographical material; to Dr. Hsü T'eng-hui, Pastor of the Chinese Presbyterian Church in Toronto, for permission to quote from his Hartford doctoral dissertation, and to Dr. Andrew Tod Roy, Vice-President of Ch'ung Chi College in Hong Kong, for permission to quote from his Princeton doctoral dissertation; to Professor Sheh K'uen-shan and Miss Chin Chao-wen, formerly of Hangchow University, for their meticulous translation of Professor Ho Lin's *Tang-Tai Chung-Kuo Chê-Hsüeh* (Contemporary Chinese Philosophy).

Grateful acknowledgment is made to the Librarians of the University of California, the Low Library of Columbia University, the Case Memorial Library of the Hartford Seminary Foundation, the Princeton University Library, the Library of Congress Division of Orientalia (Chinese Section), and the American University Library in Washington, D. C., for special research privileges; as well as to Dr. R. Pierce Beaver, then Director of the Missionary Research Library in New York City, for personal assistance in obtaining reference materials.

My warm thanks are due to Dr. Arthur W. Hummel, former Director of the Division of Orientalia in the Library of Congress, for reading the whole manuscript; to Dr. Warren Horton Stuart, former President of Hangchow University, for permission to quote from his Yale doctoral dissertation, as well as for his kind reading of parts of the manuscript; to Dr. Ku Tun-jou, former Dean of the College of

Arts in Hangchow University and presently Dean of Arts at Tunghai University, T'aichung, T'aiwan, for reading parts of the manuscript, and to each for making timely suggestions for its improvement. To Dr. Wing-tsit Chan, Professor of Chinese Philosophy and Culture at Dartmouth College, go my very special thanks for his kind scrutiny of the whole manuscript and for making valuable suggestions for its improvement. Only the writer, however, can be held responsible for the errors that will inevitably appear in this book. Finally, to my wife, Ethelwyn Brownell Colson Day, am I indebted most of all for patiently bearing with my extended preoccupation with the ancients and for her encouragement at times when it was most sorely needed.

No one is better aware of the lacunae and other inadequacies in the present undertaking than the present writer himself, who, nevertheless, wishes to share with others the results of his "investigation of things" in the minds of China's philosophers, to the end that another bridge of understanding may be built between West and East.

C. B. D.

"Glenayr Court"
Arlington, Virginia

PART I

CREATIVE INDIGENOUS CHINESE PHILOSOPHY

Chapter 1

Proto-Sinistic Theories of the Chou Period

"The Eight Elements determine all good and evil and the great complexity of life."
—The *Book of Changes* (Appendix I) *

In the long course of their historic quest for the good life, the Chinese people have ever sought the most harmonious adjustment to their environment. From the dawn of their ancient civilization, they have propitiated Earth to encourage its fecundity; they have likewise paid homage to Heaven and its life-sustaining forces. Living as they did very close to Nature, the Chinese early began to theorize about the structure of the cosmos and the ways of its inner working. Later, as life became more complex, the problems of cosmogony, of human nature and government came to the fore. This natural order of the growth of *mores* and ideas from the more primitive to the more complex will guide our investigation of ancient pre-Taoist, and early Taoist theories before proceeding to the Confucian, Mohist, Legalist and Dialectical philosophies.

To discover the sources of Chinese philosophy, we should need to reconstruct a picture of ancient cult practices in the Yellow River Basin in the Shang (Yin) and Chou periods—more especially from the settling of the Shang rulers at Anyang (1300 B.C.) to the removal of the Chou capital from Ch'ang-An in the west to Lo-Yang in the east (770 B.C.)[1] For there are strong indications that out of divination practices associated with the cults of these periods there arose in the diviners'

* Wing-tsit Chan translation.

minds a "Proto-Sinistic" cosmology with which they explained the constitution and operation of the world as they knew it. From his own research, Joseph Needham concludes that the concepts of *macrocosm* and *microcosm* in their spontaneous organizational relations may have been derived from the method of divining future events from the entrails or scapulae of a sacrificial animal.[2] Unfortunately, documentary evidences are lacking for a full reconstruction of the earlier periods mentioned; yet the writings of a later time reflect ideas that had been current for several previous generations. During the overlordship of the House of Chou, and more particularly in the period known as the "Ch'un Ch'iu" (ca. 770–481 B.C.), immediately preceding the Late Chou "Period of the Warring States" (ca. 403-221 B.C.), the long-held theories of an earlier age became crystallized sufficiently to form the matrix of "Classical" traditions on which were built the Taoist and Confucian philosophies.[3]

In their effort to solve the two basic problems of cosmology (or structure of the universe) and cosmogony (or creative origin of the universe), ancient Chinese thinkers had developed two lines of thought which had become well articulated long before the time of Confucius. By the time of the Warring States Period, the ideas of those who were primarily interested in the problem of structure were reflected in the "Grand Norm" (*Hung Fan*) section of the *Book of History* (*Shu Ching*) and also in the "Monthly Commands" (*Yüeh Ling*) section of the *Lü-Shih Ch'un Ch'iu* (both of the late fourth or third centuries, B.C.)[4] Both describe the action of the "Five Elements" (Agents) and make no mention of either the *Yin* or the *Yang* as creative forces in Nature. On the other hand, the ideas of those who had elaborated their theory of the origin of the cosmos are found expressed in the "Appendices" to (or "Amplifications" of) the *Book of Changes* (*Yi-Ching*) (dated ca. third century B.C.), which fully describe the working of the *Yin* and *Yang* but say nothing of the "Five Elements." Thus we have clearly outlined two distinct theories, a "Five Elements" theory and a "*Yin-Yang*" theory.

The fact that early Chinese life was based largely on the cultivation of the soil, and the fact that the chapter on "The Values of Agriculture" in the *Lü-Shih Ch'un Ch'iu* (XXVI, 3) stresses the farmer class as the more dependable "root" occupation (in contrast to the less dependable merchant class labelled as the "branch" occupation) has led Fung Yu-lan to suggest that the physical properties of Nature (soil, water, fire, metal, and wood) would very naturally give rise to a "Five Elements" theory to account for the structure of the visible physical world. This may be taken as the tap-root of the Taoist philosophy (represented in *The Lao-tzu*) that reflected the attitudes of a rural population living close to the soil. On the other hand, the *"Yin-Yang"* theory represented something that may have developed out of the different economic background of the merchant class and formed the tap-root of the Confucianist philosophy (represented in the *Appendices* to the *Book of Changes* dating from the Late Chou period).[5] As the agrarian element in any society usually develops earlier than the mercantile element, it may be safely assumed that the rise of the "Five Elements" theory slightly antedated the rise of the *"Yin-Yang"* theory.

The Five Elements Theory

The theory of the activities of the "Five Elements," as described in the *Hung Fan*,[6] was attributed to the Viscount of Ch'i, a prince of Shang conquered by Wu Wang of the Chou dynasty at the end of the twelfth century B.C., but whose ideas he in turn attributed to the "Great Yü" (traditional founder of the Hsia dynasty, living about 2200 B.C.).[7] It seems fairly certain, then, that the ideas were quite old.

By the time of the Middle or Late Chou periods, however, the theory of the "Five Elements" (Agents or Powers) had become more than a simple explanation of the physical world; it had come to assume an intimate relation between the laws of Nature and human affairs (especially those of the ruling class), and thus became the accepted theoretical basis for the whole science of divination. We turn, then, to certain writings of the Late Chou and Early Han periods for details of the application of the theory.

According to the *Yüeh Ling* (one of the earliest of Chinese almanacs), "each of the Five Elements has its period of ascendancy during the four seasons of the year. Thus the element or power in ascendancy in springtime is *wood;* in summer it is *fire;* in autumn it is *metal;* and in winter it is *water.*" Inasmuch as the *Yüeh Ling* failed to state when the power of *earth* (soil) became ascendant, a later *Yin-Yang* School writer, in the *Huai-nan-tzu,* recorded the third month of summer as the time when earth gains the ascendancy.[8]

The best known early interpreter of the "Five Elements" theory was Tsou Yen (ca. 350-270 B.C., or possibly a decade later),* who lived first in Ch'i and later moved to Yen.[9] To Ssu-ma Ch'ien's *Historical Records* (*Shih Chi,* Chapter 74), dating from the beginning of the Former Han dynasty, we are indebted for our knowledge of Tsou Yen's ideas. In his *Chü Yün* (now lost), Tsou Yen philosophized not only about the earth itself: its topography, fauna, flora, and the products of its soil and waters, but even made conjectures about the nine continents separated by nine seas and all surrounded by an encircling ocean at the horizon.

Tsou Yen's active mind envisaged the course of time and evolved an interpretation of history in accord with the revolutions and changes of the "Five Elements." The rise of the Yellow Emperor was correlated with *earth;* the rise of the Great Yü (Hsia dynasty) correlated with *wood.* The rise of Shang was related to the ascendant power of *metal;* while the House of Chou ruled under the ascendancy of *fire.* Later, the cycle of Nature was completed when the House of Ch'in (succeeding Chou) took *water* as the pattern for its affairs (221 B.C.) and in turn was supplanted by the Han dynasty (207 B.C.–A.D. 220), which took *earth* (soil) as the element on which its power was based.[10]

---

* Yang Hsiang-Kwei dates him ca. 305-240 B.C. *Vide* Note 9.

The thaumaturgists of the time explained the endless cycle of phases of the elements-in-flux thus: earth is overcome by wood, wood by metal, metal by fire, fire by water, which in turn is overcome by earth. In truth the "Five Elements" (*wu hsing*) might better be termed powers, agents, or forces (*tê*), for they were thought of not as static, fixed forms (substances) so much as dynamic processes by which natural evolution is effected.[11]

From Chou times on, all the general affairs of government, as well as all personal details of the running of the imperial household, were rigidly determined according to the elemental power in ascendancy during any particular month of the year. If, perchance, the Sage-King should happen to follow the *Yüeh Ling* incorrectly, his misconduct would immediately begin to affect the seasons and all sorts of strange catastrophes would occur. In the *Hung Fan* there is a passage to the effect that the ruler's gravity, regularity, intelligence, wisdom, and deliberation would bring favorable rain, sunshine, heat, cold, and wind; whereas opposite results could be expected from his madness, insolence, idleness, haste, or ignorance.[12]

The "Five Elements" theory was given still more specific application to government in the later *Kuan-tzu*,* which stated that water is not only the blood of Earth flowing through its muscles and veins, but is also something spiritual flowing through man and affecting all his faculties. Therefore, only the ruler who knows how to interpret its principles can act correctly. The Sage-King who would transform the world must take his cue from water. "When water is pure, the people's hearts are at ease. Men's hearts being upright, their desires do not become dissolute. The people's hearts being upright, their conduct is without evil."[13] As Wing-tsit Chan has aptly observed: "Water is symbolic of reality's purity and goodness. It occupies the low places, yet serves all alike. Its harmony with all about it is natural; so we must attain a natural harmony

---

* Formerly *The Kuan-tzu* was placed in the 7th century, but in its extant form is now dated somewhere in the late 4th century, B.C.

in the ethical sphere by learning to know the Eternal. That is true insight."[14]

The Yin-Yang Theory

Developing more or less contemporaneously with the theory of the "Five Elements," was the theory of the *Yin* and the *Yang* as the two Primary Modes, or creative agents, in the universe. For detailed references, we are, unfortunately, dependent upon rather late writings, such as the "Appendices" to the *Book of Changes,* which are sometimes referred to as the "Ten Wings." In Appendix I, Section 11, for example, it is stated: "The *T'ai Chi* (Great Ultimate) at the beginning of time, engenders the Two Primary Modes of *yin* and *yang,* which in turn engender the Four Secondary Modes or Forms, which in their turn give rise to the Eight Elements, and the Eight Elements determine all good and evil and the great complexity of life."[15]

A slightly varying amplification of the theory is given in Appendix V, where the chief parts of the cosmos are symbolized by the Eight Trigrams or *Pa Kua*:—*Ch'ien* (☰) is Heaven (*Yang,* male or father); *K'un* (☷) is Earth (*Yin,* female or mother). By combining their parts in various ways, they produced other material forms, such as Thunder (represented by the trigram *Chen,* ☳); Wood-and-Wind (*Sun,* ☴); Water-and-Moon (*K'an,* ☵); Fire-and-Sun (*Li,* ☲); Mountain (*Ken,* ☶); and Marsh (Tui, ☱). These in turn were believed to have so combined as to produce all things in the world of Nature (indicated in 64 hexagrams) in a way analogous to the production of all living beings by the intercourse of male and female creatures.[16]

In Appendix III,[17] the trigrams are discussed according to the numbers of those related to Heaven and Earth. Number 1 stands for Heaven (*Yang*), number 2 for Earth (*Yin*) and so on alternately to number 10. By comparing these numbers with the various arrangements of the milfoil stalks, the diviners could find answers to the problems involved in relating the manifold evolutions of Nature to corresponding human affairs.

Since the "Sixty-four Hexagrams" represented fluctuations in Nature that correspond to changes in human life, they, therefore, became models for the conduct of society and government.[18] According to the *Kuo Yü* (*Discussions of the States,* ca. 300 B.C.), "One must make use of the regularities of the *yin* and the *yang,* and comply with the regularities of Heaven and Earth; be soft yet not yielding, strong yet not hard. . . ."[19] It became a matter, therefore, of utmost importance that the early sage-kings and all their vassal lords should become aware of and minutely follow the laws of *yin* and *yang,* or the seasonal demands of Heaven and Earth.

Another reference to the *Yin-Yang* theory in the *Kuo Yü* states that an earthquake in 780 B.C. was explained as resulting from the "concealment" or "repression" of the *yang* and *yin* forces.[20] The *Tso Chuan* commentary on the *Ch'un Ch'iu,* coming from the same period, also mentioned the *yin* and the *yang* as affecting good and bad fortune in the year 644 B.C.[21] These references indicate that the *Yin-Yang* theory was well advanced in the Middle Chou period.

An old tradition placed the invention of the Eight Trigrams (and even the 64 hexagrams) as early as Fu Hsi—legendary ruler before the Yellow Emperor. Modern critics, however, think the whole *Pa-Kua* system was devised by early Chou diviners not only to explain the previous Shang method of auguring from cracks appearing on tortoise shells or scapulae when subjected to heat but also to cover their own interpretations when shuffling stalks of the milfoil plant and finding answers in the trigrams or hexagrams. In fact, Fung Yu-lan finds here a probable origin of the *Book of Changes,*[22] whose alternate name is "Chou I"—meaning "Chou (dynasty) Easy"—(i.e. a more precise way of divining by milfoil stalks and hexagrams rather than by the unlimited patterns of cracks on shells and bones held over fire).[23] At any rate, in the Chou period the "Eight Trigrams" system (or *Yin-Yang* theory) was apparently quite separate from the "Five Elements" system.

Only later, in the Former Han period, were the two taken as one system by Ssu-ma Ch'ien (d. 110 B.C.) in his *Historical Records* (*Shih Chi*) and given the name of The *Yin-Yang* School.[24]

Since there is in the *Hung Fan* the suggestion of the existence of a Supreme Ruler who would be angered by the improper actions of a sovereign on earth and would send down punishments of one kind or another, in the form of harmful phenomena, the question may well be raised as to whether for the ancient Chinese the cosmos was teleologically conceived as influenced by a Supreme Being or was simply a mechanistic *yin-yang* world. Undoubtedly there was a mixture of both in the early Chinese world-view; for, as Fung has pointed out, the *Yin-Yang* School vacillated between the concept of a teleological universe (as indicated in the *Hung Fan*) and that of a mechanistic universe (as indicated in the *Yüeh Ling*).[25]

Pursuing this question a step farther, we find Fung of the opinion that even a very primitive, quasi-scientific, *yin-yang* world-view of the early Chou period was to be preferred to the mixture of polyanimistic, polytheistic, and henotheistic explanations based on a *T'ien* (Heaven), a *Shang Ti* (Upper Ruler), and a host of lesser spirits, passed on by the Hsia and Shang dynasties. "The 'heaven' described (here)", remarks Fung, "is a naturalistic one bearing strong resemblance to that of Lao Tzu, and seems to be a forerunner of Taoist philosophy."[26]

In conclusion, it seems certain that, while the ideas of the so-called "Yin-Yang-and-Five-Elements School," as we have them in written form, were elaborated in the late Chou period, they record theories that had been handed down through many previous generations and were strongly reflected in the *Classics*. Yang Ch'ing-k'un intimates that the acceptance of the *Five Classics* by Confucius and Mencius could be taken as their endorsement of such ancient beliefs enshrined in them as, for example, the concept of heaven as supernatural, fate, divination by portents and other means, along with the theory of the Yin-Yang-and-Five-Elements.[27] He further reminds us that

Confucius himself was known to possess "a well-thumbed copy of the *Yi-Ching,* which he used to ascertain the dictates of fate."[28] Possibly recognized as an independent *Yin-Yang* School as early as the fourth century, B.C., certainly from the beginning of the Han period (ca. 207 B.C.), the *Yin-Yang* theory fused with the "Five Elements" theory gained great credence as a means of discovering the will of Heaven. What is still more significant, they were applied directly to the interpretation of the *Classics,* and colored the thought of Confucianists and Taoists alike, as may be seen in the work of Huai-Nan-Tzu and Tung Chung-shu. Thus the Yin-Yang-and-Five-Elements School, more often referred to as the "Huang-Lao" School, became a radiating center for all medieval Chinese philosophy.[29] In writing of the Han era, Fung Yu-lan concludes: "It makes no difference whether the thinkers of that era regarded themselves as Taoists or as Confucianists; all their viewpoints embodied the viewpoint of the Yin-Yang School and its essential spirit."[30]

Chapter 2

The Ancient School of Taoist Naturalism

"*Tao* invariably does not do, yet there is nothing that is not done."
—Lao Tzu in the *Tao Tê Ching**

"Identify yourself with the Infinite and wander freely in the Unfathomable."
—Chuang Tzu in *The Chuang-tzu***

Lao Tzu and His Philosophy of the Tao

While the farmers of forty centuries ago were busily eking out a meager existence, the thinkers who had had time to meditate on the mysteries of life busied themselves in evolving a cosmology to satisfy their questionings in regard to Nature and how to live in harmony with it. What came to be called the Taoist School grew out of the same matrix of elementary concepts which had become articulate in the Yin-Yang-and-Five-Elements School of thought, whose real origin is lost in the mists of China's ancient past.

If, however, Leopold de Saussure is correct in his opinion that the lunar zodiac of the Babylonians spread across Asia in the third millenium B.C. and became the basis of Chinese astronomy, we have the fruitful suggestion of an astronomical origin not only for early Chinese rituals for divination and

* Fung Yu-lan translation.
** Wing-tsit Chan translation.

sacrifices but for the development of mythology and philosophy to explain the signs derived therefrom:—signs from the celestial lights, from seasonal atmospheric phenomena, as well as signs observed in connection with birds and animals. From his wide studies in this field, elucidated in his *The Hall of Light,* the late William Edward Soothill came to the conclusion: "Astronomy was learning *par excellence* in China's early culture, the key to all wisdom and power."[1]

From their star-gazing, the early Chinese gradually came to think of the Great One (*T'ai Yi*), either in terms of the Five Ti (ancestral spirits of the four cardinal directions, plus the center taken as Earth), or as the impersonal, underlying unity in the universe (called "*Tao*"). Absorption in the Tao by a growing number of thinkers led to their being called "Taoists." In written form, the philosophy of Lao Tzu and his School of Taoism is doubtless much later than the older sinologues supposed. Yet it seems to represent a philosophical tradition older than the ideas propounded by the school of thought which took its name from Confucius. It savors of the ancient, rural recluse who had the quietist point of view and cared little for the amenities of social life, much less for the activist philosophy that inevitably accompanied the rigors and regulations of organized government.

Our knowledge of Lao Tzu and his philosophy of the *Tao* comes chiefly from the work known as *The Lao-tzu,* which some Chinese critics have assigned to the Period of the Warring States (403–221 B.C.). Despite conflicting views, Wing-tsit Chan intimates that critical opinion is swinging back to the traditional early dating in the sixth century B.C.[2] Tradition has ascribed its authorship to one Li Êrh, a historical personage confused with the mythical Lao Tan, whose name very possibly he had used as a pseudonym. The scholars of the Later Han dynasty gave to the book in question the title of *Tao Tê Ching* —*The Canon of Reason and Virtue* (as Paul Carus translated it) or (as Arthur Waley has rendered it) *The Way and Its Power.* Fung Yu-lan is of the opinion that "the *Lao-tzu* as it exists today has suffered changes through the editing and rearranging made by the Han scholars, so that it cannot really be said to be the work of one man." [3]

The Doctrine of the Way and Its Power

(The Meaning of *Tao,* or Way) :– In the first chapter of the *Tao Tê Ching* we read: "The *Tao* that may be called *Tao* (literally that may be *tao*-ed) is not the invariable *Tao.* The names that can be named are not invariable names. Non-Being is the term given to that from which Heaven and Earth sprang. Being is the term given to the mother that rears the ten thousand things (on earth) . . . . These two have issued together but are different in name. The two together we call the Mystery (*hsüan*) . It is the Mystery of Mysteries, the Doorway of all secret essences." [4]

In other words, *Tao* is the eternal, unchanging principle lying behind and in the phenomenal world, the unity underlying all diversity. Under its aspect of Non-Being, or the Undefined, free from all attributes, it is the Great Oneness (*T'ai Yi*) through which all things, beginning with Heaven and Earth, were brought into being. This aspect of Being in the *Tao* spontaneously produced the duality of Heaven or *Yang* (the principle of activity) and Earth or *Yin* (the principle of passive receptivity) . From their harmonious interaction issued the forms and entities which we call objects or events, each of which has its own individuating principle (*Tê*) at work in it.

(The Meaning of *Tê,* or Power):–The principle of individuality in things is *Tê,* so often translated "Virtue," but in reference to inanimate objects better rendered "Efficacy" or "Power." In the *Kuan-tzu,* it has been aptly defined: "*Tê* is the dwelling-place of *Tao.* . . . Living things obtain it so as to function; it is the essence of *Tao.* Therefore, *Tê* is an obtaining." [5] On this Fung comments: "That is, *Tê* is *Tao* 'dwelling' in objects, or in other words, *Tê* is what individual objects obtain from *Tao* and thereby become what they are." [6]

The Doctrine of Effortlessness (Wu-Wei) and Spontaneity

Two important things to note about the working of *Tao-in-Tê* are its effortlessness and its spontaneity. An oft-quoted line from the *Lao-tzu* (*Tao Tê Ching*)—"*Tao* invariably does not do, yet there is nothing that is not done" (*Wu wei êrh wu pu wei*)[7]—was quietism's way of observing Nature's silently producing the myriad forms of plant and animal life, apparently without effort. From this was deduced the doctrine of inaction or letting Nature have its own way, an early *laissez faire* doctrine in human affairs.

Again we read: "Therefore, of the ten thousand things, there is not one that does not honor *Tao* and prize its *Tê*. No one has commanded the honoring of *Tao* and prizing of its *Tê*, but this has been forever spontaneous."[8] That is to say, the energizing power in the universe (like Bergson's *élan vital*) accomplishes its ends by the silent working of the inner law of its being, without any prompting from the outside.

The Doctrine of Reversion or Nature's Equilibrium

Another thing calling for explanation was the way in which Nature keeps a proper balance in all its working. If any activity moves to an extreme in one direction, sooner or later a change occurs to swing it back toward the opposite result. This was styled the "way of reversion" or "returning," expressed in the *Lao-tzu* as, "Vastness means passing on, and passing on means going far away, and going far away means returning" . . . "The movement of *Tao* consists in reversion" . . . "The mysterious *Tê*, so deep, so remote, is to things their reverse. It is from this that there comes the Great Harmonious Accord."[9]

The apparently unsolvable paradoxes of life were to the ancient Taoists simply the natural law of reversion underlying phenomenal changes of all kinds. "It is because of this law that 'a hurricane never lasts a whole morning, nor a rainstorm the whole day.' "[10] A little fire, the dripping of water or a hidden root may crack a great rock. Paradoxical as it may seem, "the world's weakest overcomes the world's hardest."[11] Therefore, the "Old Philosopher" boldly declared: "He who by *Tao* helps a ruler of men, *does not with arms force a conquest of the world, for such things invite a reversal.*"[12]

The Harmfulness of Desire and Knowledge

Early Taoists felt that the fewer desires men had the more easily would they be satisfied. "He who does not prize life, does better than he who prizes life. . . . If we cease to set store by products that are hard to get, there will be no more thieves. . . . If the people never see such things as excite desire, their hearts will not be confused. . . . Being without desires, there comes quiescence and the world, of itself, is at rest."[13] Thinking it was not possible, however, to make men entirely free from desire (as the Buddhists sought to do), the later Taoists aimed simply at making men frugal in all their habits. Elsewhere, the *Lao-tzu* taught: "To rule men and serve Heaven, there is nothing better than frugality." Again, "He who is content suffers no humiliation; who knows where to stop, cannot be harmed. . . . There is no disaster greater than not knowing contentment with what one has; no greater sin than having desire for acquisition."[14]

In the same way, desire for acquiring knowledge was deprecated: "Banish wisdom, discard knowledge, and the people will be benefited a hundredfold. . . . Banish skill, discard profit, and thieves and robbers will disappear. If when these three things are done, they find life too plain and unadorned, then let them have accessories."[15] Knowledge was considered harmful because it enabled men to know more objects of desire and led to discontent. "Because of study, we daily increase (in desire) . . . . Those who rule by giving knowledge are despoilers of the state. Those who rule without giving knowledge are the state's good fortune." In another passage, knowledge was deplored because it brought artificiality into life, thus causing unhappiness:— "When intelligence and knowledge appeared, the Great Artifice began."[16] In fact, the distaste of Taoists generally for all things artificial can hardly be overestimated.

The Way To Be Completely Civilized

Since an infant's desires are few and his knowledge very simple, this was considered the desirable norm for adults; the Taoist ideal for man and society, therefore, was set forth in such epigrammatic maxims as:—"I alone am inert, giving no indication (of activity), like an infant that has not yet smiled." Even a stupid appearance was considered commendably characteristic of a man who had cultivated himself.—"Mine is the heart of a very idiot. So dull am I. So many people are there who shine. I alone am dark. They look lively and self-assured; I alone, depressed." The apparent stupidity of the wise man was, nevertheless, held to be a real achievement; for had not the *Lao-tzu* declared, "The practice of *Tao* consists in subtracting day by day (from knowledge and desire) . . . till one has reached non-activity (*wu wei*)?"[17]

This "Back to Nature" doctrine of Lao Tzu's represented a highly polished civilization, however much it may have looked like a primitive barbarism. This was the philosophy of a breed of men who were content to grow old and die without resorting to war to despoil their neighbors of territory or goods. They did not feel the imperative necessity of surrounding themselves with innumerable things. Simplicity and ingenuousness characterized the Taoist ideal of civilized living. In his *Science and Civilization in China,* Joseph Needham has in passing called attention to this emphasis on humility or "yieldingness" in early Taoist thought.[18]

Taoist Theory of Enlightened Government

The political philosophy revealed in the *Lao-tzu* was simple. To know the general laws of Nature and abide by them was considered the *sine qua non* of a wise ruler:—

'Attain complete emptiness; maintain steadfast quietude. . . . To know the Eternal is called insight. Not to know the Eternal and to act blindly is disastrous. To know the Eternal is to be liberal. To be liberal is to be without prejudice. To be without prejudice is to be comprehensive. To be comprehensive is to be great. To be great is to be like *Tao* (the Way). To be like Tao is to (possess it) forever and not to fail throughout one's lifetime." [19]

The enlightened ruler, therefore, will govern best by governing least. "I act not and the people of themselves are transformed. I love quiescence, and the people of themselves go straight. I concern myself with nothing, and the people of themselves are prosperous. I am without desires, and the people are of themselves of an unwrought simplicity." [20]

In the Taoist mind, too many institutions made for confusion in society. Too many laws made more trouble than they were worth. "The more restrictions and prohibitions there are in the world, the poorer the people will be." [21]

Ambition to rule was considered a dangerous thing. "The empire is a holy vessel, which may not be tampered with. Those who tamper with it, harm it. Those who grab at it, lose it." (And again) "The people are difficult to keep in order because those above them interfere." [22] In short, the wise sage-king who could rule through non-activity would avoid disorders and find nothing that was not ruled well.

The Doctrine of Returning Good for Evil

A well-known commentator has said that Lao Tzu's 'Way of the *Tao*' was epitomized in the words: "Not to act from any personal motive; to conduct affairs without worrying; to account the great as small and the small as great; to recompense injury with kindness." [23] Here was reached the high-water mark of Taoist quietism.

Chuang Tzu, Outstanding Interpreter of Taoist Thought

As Socrates had his Plato and Confucius his Mencius, so Lao Tzu had his Chuang Tzu, as chief commentator, to carry on the Taoist tradition, amplifying and enriching it with his own brand of mysticism. Chuang Tzu (ca. 369-286 B.C.) reputedly held a small magistracy in the state of Sung. Though he and Mencius were contemporaries, neither mentioned the other, probably because each was unsympathetic with the other's point of view. As the chief spokesman for the anti-intellectual movement of the fourth century, B.C., Chuang Tzu expounded Taoist philosophy in a way to make a study of it most rewarding.

TÊ *is constantly in flux*

Chuang Tzu's conceptions of *Tao* and *Tê* are practically the same as those outlined in the *Lao-tzu*. For example, "Form without *Tao* cannot have existence. Existence without *Tê* cannot have manifestation."[24] The forms of things, however, do not remain what they were when they were created, inasmuch as a process of change is going on all the time. "They pursue their course with the speed of a galloping horse. Is it not deplorable?"[25] Or again, "There is no movement through which they do not become modified, no time when they are not changed."[26] This endless cycle of change which Chuang Tzu saw going on in the forms of things, producing the different species, he called *t'ien chün* or the "Evolution of Nature."[27]

Liberty and equality are inalienable rights

Along social and political lines, Chuang Tzu stood for complete freedom of action. Only as men have liberty, he argued, can they follow their own natures and obtain happiness. The correlate of this is that only with complete equality can men fulfill their true relationships. Each person has a right to his own opinion and way of doing things; though there may be differences, yet each may be right and each is good.

According to Chuang Tzu, right and wrong cannot be decided by argument. As all viewpoints may be equally right, there is no need for argument. "Let us forget the distinctions of 'right' and 'wrong,' " he urged. "Let us find enjoyment in the realm of the infinite and remain there."[28] "Therefore, the sage harmonizes the systems of right and wrong and rests in the 'evolution of Nature.' "[29] He sees all things *sub specie aeternitatis*—from the viewpoint of *Tao*. To one and all Chuang Tzu would say: "Identify yourself with the Infinite and wander freely in the Unfathomable."[30]

All values are relative

We should regard all men and all things as having value in a relative way. "From the standpoint of *Tao*," Chuang Tzu continued, "What is valuable? What is worthless? . . . (Things) have no guarantee of permanence. Now empty, now full, they have no set form. . . . Hold all things in your embrace, and then which will leave you? . . . Do not hold to something bigotedly. . . . Do not be one-sided in your conduct, for this would be diverging from *Tao*."[31]

Unity can be found in diversity

For Chuang Tzu, therefore, the way to obtain happiness was for each one to follow his own spontaneous nature, without any thought of distinctions in men. Since people are constructed differently, it is only right that they should remain so. In this way unity can be discovered in difference. The trouble, he said, with political and other social institutions is that leaders decide upon a single good as a standard of conduct and try to make everybody follow this standard. This, he maintained, is to constrain difference to a forced uniformity, resulting only in harm.

Here the Taoist School took violent exception to the teachings of the Confucianists, who, as the Taoists claimed, stressed the desirability of making everyone obey the same laws, as drafted by a governmental bureaucracy. Like Lao Tzu and his fellow-Taoists, Chuang Tzu believed in a *laissez faire* policy of letting people alone, so that good order would result *spontaneously*. As soon as artifice crept in, the happiness derived from 'according oneself with the natural' was lost. "The result was not only poignant unhappiness but a loss of all interest in life as well." [32]

Death is to be neither feared nor mourned

In regard to death and immortality, Chuang Tzu held a somewhat stoical view. He believed in controlling one's emotions and not showing any spirit of mourning at the loss of a loved one. When his own wife died, a friend found him singing while beating out the rhythm on a porcelain bowl. When questioned, he replied: "While she is thus lying asleep in the Great House (the Universe), for me to go about weeping and wailing would be to show myself ignorant of Fate. I therefore refrain." [33]

For Chuang Tzu, death was nothing more than a change from one form of existence to another. It is the natural result of life. To feel undue bitterness against it, therefore, is to show ignorance of natural law and, consequently, to incur the penalty of increased emotional suffering. To hold oneself free from devastating emotion is to be released from bondage in life or death.

Tranquility under strain is a great achievement

Chuang Tzu's teaching on the virtue of maintaining tranquility under all provocation is well summed up in the following passage:

"I kept on speaking to him; after three days, he began to be able to disregard all worldly matters . . . after seven days, he began to be able to disregard all external things . . . I kept on speaking to him; after nine days, he began to be able to disregard his own existence . . . (and) . . . was enlightened. Having become enlightened, he was . . . able . . . to gain the vision of the One . . . (and) . . . was then able to transcend the distinction of past and present . . . (This enabled him) to enter the realm where life and death are no more. Then, to him the destruction of life did not mean death, nor the prolongation of life an addition to the duration of his existence. . . . To him everything was in destruction, everything was in construction. This is called tranquility in disturbance. Tranquility in disturbance means perfection."[34]

In all later generations, few virtues have been held in higher esteem than this lofty Taoist ideal of equanimity of mind in the face of adverse circumstances. Lack of perturbation became the hallmark of the sage.

Identification with the great flux is possible

Such an experience as that described above signified for Chuang Tzu that a person may arrive at a state of pure experience in which he accepts the given presentation of the immediate universe. He becomes *en rapport* with the universe by intuition, as it were, without intellectual process of knowledge. To attain this is to be a True Man. "The less knowledge one has of things, distinctions, and of right and wrong, the more pure is the experience. . . . Therefore, the truly intelligent man avoids all distinctions, and rests in a state of pure experience, in which he is near perfection. . . . At this point one can truly realize that 'Heaven and Earth came into being with me together, and with me all things are one'."[35]

This pure state of experience is further denoted in two other remarkable phrases: one is the 'fast of the mind'; the other, 'sitting in forgetfulness.' For example, in one place the *Chuang-tzu* says: "Maintain the unity of your will. . . . (Listen not only with your ears but also) with the mind . . . (and) . . . with the spirit. . . . But the spirit is an emptiness ready to receive all things. *Tao* abides in the emptiness; the emptiness is *the fast of the mind.*"[36] And again, "I have abandoned my body," said Yen Hui, "and discarded my knowledge, and so have become one with the Infinite. This is what I mean by *sitting in forgetfulness.*"[37]

Chuang Tzu's mysticism was epitomized finally in the maxim: "The Perfect Man is spirit-like."[38] In this state he unites with the universe; he attains a mysterious power through identification with the great flux, which is the normal condition of the Perfect Man. To this, Fung Yu-lan would add: "No place is there where the Perfect Man does not find his way. This is the ultimate of freedom."[39]

Summary

In its appreciation of a great, unseen reality working within the material universe, Taoist philosophy is surprisingly modern. Nor is it incompatible with the attitudes of most modern scientists. While there is a certain following of the line of least resistance, there can also be detected beneath the surface a strong discipline of body and mind—a regimen of life—which must be attended to carefully if the true Taoist would find the vitality that he seeks. Taoist philosophy reveals in the Chinese mind a deep love of Nature, which is reflected so well in Chinese landscape paintings, where the artist seems to have lost all sense of self in a kind of mystic identification with crag and torrent and swirling mist. It was in his exaltation of Nature over against humanism, which became so great an influence in Chinese art, that Wing-tsit Chan believes the true greatness of Chuang Tzu lay.[40]

In stressing simplicity and unobtrusive humility, the Taoist philosophy is closely akin to the Christian, especially as interpreted by the Society of Friends. It seeks to avoid war by restraining the overweening ambitions of men. "With gentle compassion, I can be brave. With economy, I can be liberal. Not presuming to claim precedence in the world, I can make myself a vessel fit for the most distinguished services."[41]

Some would hold that, because Lao Tzu wished to learn the effectual quietness of Heaven, he should be rated higher than Confucius, who did not often lift his eyes to the eternal mysteries of things invisible. In one translation, Lao Tzu is quoted as saying:

"It is almost as though there were a Supreme Being; but the First Cause of all things is far beyond our reach. That there is One from whom I derive this power of motion I believe, but I have never seen his form. He has thoughts and feelings but he has no shape."

In another passage, after contemplating his own bodily preservation, Lao Tzu is said to have exclaimed: "Verily, there is One, Supreme, who holds all this together. . . . I conform to the teachings of Him who had the guiding of my heart. Who indeed is there without such a guide? Why need one understand all about the changes and revolutions of the world? All is clear to the heart that is thus taught and even the simplest and most ignorant are not left without instruction."[42]

With these remarkable quotations, which are rather free renderings of the original, to be sure, we take leave of Taoist quietism to inquire into Confucianism—that other indigenous school of Chinese thought which was fused with Taoism into that broad, basic philosophy of life known as "Sinism." *

---

* Note:—A term used much by H. G. Creel (Cf. his book *Sinism*); the term is also used by J. C. Archer (*Faiths Men Live By*).

Chapter 3

The Formative School of Confucian Morality

"Only after having peaceful repose can one begin to think. Only after one has learned to think, can one achieve knowledge." —Confucius in the *Ta Hsüeh**

"What you do not wish others should do to you, do not do unto them."
—Confucius in the *Chung Yung**

Confucius

Born in 551 B.C., left fatherless at the age of three, and motherless when still in his early twenties, K'ung Chung-ni (or K'ung Ch'iu) was educated by a local magistrate near Chüfu in the state of Lu (modern Shantung). After his marriage at nineteen, he was entrusted with the care of certain government granaries and later placed in charge of some public lands.

By the time the youthful K'ung was twenty-five, he had organized a preparatory school for boys and had become well-known as a strict disciplinarian. Here he taught the rudiments of music, archery, literature, science, and ethics, along with social etiquette and civic propriety. Where Lao Tzu and Chuang Tzu had preferred to be armchair critics of society and government, K'ung Fu-tzu (Teacher K'ung), or Confucius, was anxious to test out his theories in public office,

---

*** Lin Yutang translation.**

where he could gradually gain the practical experience needed for his great work as teacher and reformer. For some ten years he faithfully performed duties in the local government in addition to his teaching. Then he decided to give his whole time to education and further research on the relation of education to government.

In 501 B.C., Confucius again accepted official position—this time as Assistant Superintendent of Public Works for the state of Lu. He is also mentioned as the Chief Justice or, as some have interpreted it, the Prime Minister of Lu. For a time he was apparently quite successful in public administration but after awhile things went wrong and either he was exiled or he resigned and of necessity became a wandering pedagogue. Travelling from state to state, he, with a band of faithful understudies, underwent numerous dangers and privations.

Wherever he could get a hearing, Confucius would preach to kings and vassal lords his doctrines of the functions of the ruler and the duties of the governed. Returning finally to his native state, he spent the remaining three years of his life presumably collating his notes on the subjects he had taught, as well as in editing and interpolating the existing textbook materials which had been used in his classes. This process was traditionally referred to as "expunging and rectifying the Six Classics (Liu Ching)." In 479 B.C., Confucius died a disappointed man, feeling that his life had been a failure. His grave at Chüfu, Shantung, early became a national shrine, and, later, temples to his honor were built in every city of the empire.

The Confucian Books

The Chinese refer to their Confucian literature as the *Ssu Shu, Wu Ching,* or Four Books and Five Classics, although chronologically the Five Classics came first. Western writers have sometimes referred to them as "The Old Testament of Confucianism" and to the *Four Books* as "The New Testament of Confucianism." The *Record of Music* (*Yüeh Chi*), originally one of the "Six Disciplines," (*Liu I*), which formed the basis of education for the nobility, was lost; this accounts for the usual reference to only five *Classics*. All together these books probably have been the subject of more teaching and more written commentary than any other sacred literature in the world, unless it be the Indian Vedas or the Hebrew-Christian Bible.

The *Five Classics* are known traditionally as:—

1. The *Book of Poetry* (*Shih Ching*), containing five Odes of *Shang* dating ca. 1800 (1766) B.C.; eleven Odes of *Chou* from ca. 1100 (1027) B.C., and other Odes of *Chou* as late as 600 B.C. Its archaic language and intimate knowledge of Chou customs mark it as genuinely old.

2. The *Book of History* (*Shu Ching*), containing records, speeches, and state papers dating possibly as far back as 2000 B.C., with some archaisms reflecting early Chou, some reflecting middle Chou (ca. 700 B.C.) style. Some critics find tampering interpolations bearing Han style (from second or first centuries, B.C.).

3. The *Book of Changes* (*I*—or *Yi-Ching*),* a system of nature-philosophy based on Eight Diagrams (*Pa Kua*) or combinations of long and short lines elaborated into Sixty-four Hexagrams, with accompanying oracles attributed traditionally to Wên Wang and his younger brother, Chou Kung, ca. 1000 B.C. At one time regarded as the oldest of the *Classics*. Its *Appendices* (Amplifications) are now presumed to have been added, with Confucian interpretations, in the (late Chou) Period of the Warring States or early years of the Former Han dynasty (ca. fourth or third centuries, B.C.).[1]

4. The *Book of Rites* (*Li Chi*), containing rules for ceremonial etiquette on public and private occasions: a collection of documents and traditions of the *Chou* dynasty, reputedly compiled near the end of the first century, B.C. and re-edited as late as the second century A.D. Its underlying principles and practices, however, are reflections of the Chou, modified in the Ch'in and Han periods.[2]

5. The *Spring-and-Autumn* (*Ch'un Ch'iu*)—or "Annals of Lu"—a chronicle of events in the State of Lu for the years 722–464 B.C. Very condensed in style; based on earlier records; at one time

---

* which E. R. Hughes (*Chinese Philosophy in Classical Times,* p. 8) prefers to call "The Book of Phases."

thought to have come from the pen of Confucius himself, but now regarded as not from his hand. The most noted commentary on this classic is known as the *Tso Chuan.*[3]

The *Four Books,* or Commentaries on the *Classics,* traditionally have been referred to as:—

1. The *Analects of Confucius* (*Lun Yü*), Discourses of the Sage with his disciples; edited by them or collated by their immediate disciples.

2. The *Great Learning* (*Ta Hsüeh*), or Sayings of Confucius, giving his politico-moral philosophy for a ruler. Used as main textbook in the education of princes of the blood or sons of the landed gentry. Collated by Confucius' disciples or (as the later Sung scholars claimed) written by Tsêng Tzu, the youngest disciple of Confucius. Given varyingly as an original chapter (39 or 42) of the *Li Chi;* used separately after Chu Hsi.

3. The *Doctrine of the Mean* (*Chung Yung*), or Conduct of Life, supposed sayings of Confucius on the topic: "The Human Mind in Itself and Its Expression According to the Will of Heaven." Thought by some to have been written by Tsu Ssu, grandson of Confucius and pupil of Tsêng Tzu. Given varyingly as an original chapter (28 or 31) of the *Li Chi.* Part of it may date after Mencius, perhaps second century, B.C.[4]

4. The *Book of Mencius* (*The Mêng-tzu*), containing rules of righteous government; the qualities of a good ruler; notes on human nature, duty, etc., purporting to be the teachings of Mencius (*Mêng Tzu*)—early Confucian commentator. Regarded as fairly authentic, and is dated ca. third century, B.C. Like the other books, it has suffered at the hands of editors and redactors.[5]

Purpose and Method of Confucius' Career

The aim of Confucius was the establishment of a new order in society by straightening out the ideas and habits of leaders and common people on the fundamentals of character-building, social obligations, and decent government. As Hu Shih has described it:— "The age of Confucius . . . was an age of political disintegration, social unrest, and intellectual anarchy. Above all, it was an age of moral disorder. . . . It was natural that the central problem of Confucius should be the reform of society. . . . He, too, was in quest of the *Tao,* of the way of ordering the world. . . ."[6]

Confucius felt the dire necessity, therefore, of bringing order out of chaos by teaching monarchs to take their responsibilities seriously and by instilling into common people the principles of sane human living. He believed the quickest way was to work from the top down, by correcting the mind and heart of the emperor and all his nobles, until they recognized the principle of *noblesse oblige* and made it their aim to become exemplars for their people.

As a first step, Confucius wished to make the actualities of life—things, people, events—correspond to the essence of each which is conveyed in its name. (When) "Tsu Lu said: 'The prince of Wei is awaiting you, Sir, to take control of his administration. What will you undertake first, Sir?' The Master replied: 'The one thing needed is the rectification of names.' "[7] He wanted the ruler to live up to the ideal in the word 'ruler'; the minister to be one who really serves the state. He thought that if each person could get the 'idea' or 'ideal' clear in his mind, he would naturally try to measure up to this norm for his particular role in an orderly society. To the end that names be used judiciously, Confucius instituted the early study of semantics and insisted that his students make precise definitions of terms. He also regarded as essential clearer definitions of the personal virtues.

The Confucian Virtues

If good qualities are to be practiced by everybody, there must be a code of good manners, or *li,* to include not only the rules of personal courtesy but all the best social and governmental usages. As a standard for his theory and a pattern for his practice, Confucius confessedly took the customs and manners of the Kingdom of Chou, in the honest belief that they represented the best culture of the age.[8] In his own personal life, he sought to exemplify those qualities that he so persistently built into his teachings on ethical character as the foundation of all true living. Selecting the greater virtues of the ideal person, he delineated for his pupils a pattern of personality which they could follow if they would.

1. *Uprightness* (*Chih*) – In describing the Superior Man (*chün tzu*), who was fit to rule others in any capacity, Confucius insisted that first of all a man must be upright, deceiving neither himself nor his neighbors. As a woman must first possess an attractive smile and soulful eyes before she can make effective use of powder and rouge, so a man must have a genuinely sincere nature before he may practice public ceremonials acceptably. Without inner integrity of character, fine manners and musical accomplishments become empty artificiality.[9]

2. *Benevolence* (*Jên*) –Another quality to which Confucius most often referred was that of *jên,* which the late Lucius C. Porter of Yenching University once translated as *human heartedness.*[10] Other renderings into English have been: benevolence, morality, virtue, love, and true manhood; in adjectival form it is virtuous, humane, sympathetic. It is the perfect virtue! "The firm of spirit, the resolute in character, the simple in manner, and the slow of speech are not far from *jên.*" . . . "It is to love your fellow men.". . . (or) "*Jên* is the denial of self and response to the right and proper (*li*)." Then there are the oft-quoted lines:

"When abroad, behave as if interviewing an honored guest; in directing the people, act as if officiating at a great sacrifice; do not do to others what you do not like yourself. Then neither in your state nor in your private home will there be any resentment against you." The Great Sage is also quoted as saying:

"For the man of *jên* is one who desiring to maintain himself sustains others, and desiring to develop himself develops others. To be able from one's own self to draw a parallel for the treatment of others: that may be called the way to practise *jên.*"[11]

3. *Conscientiousness* (*Chung*) and *Altruism* (*Shu*) – In the quotation just given, lie hidden two other Confucian virtues:

those of conscientiousness and altruism, the practice of which is likewise the practice of *jên*. On one occasion, Confucius said that his teaching contained one pervading principle and left his disciples to ponder over it. When someone asked Tsêng Tzu what the Master meant, he replied: "Our Master's teaching is conscientiousness and altruism, and nothing else."[12] This inclusion of loyalty to and concern for others in the concept of *jên* led Fung Yu-lan to make the comment: "This is why *jên* is the 'all-pervading principle' of Confucius' teaching, and the center of his philosophy."[13]

4. *Righteousness* (*I* or *Yi*)—One more of the personal character-qualities which Confucius emphasized was that of *yi*, or righteousness. He believed in doing a thing because it was right, regardless of consequences. He never calculated the results of a particular action. One of his pupils is quoted as saying: "The reason why the Superior Man tries to go into office is that he holds this to be right, even though he is well aware that his principles cannot prevail." Of Confucius himself it was said, "Is he not the one who knows he cannot succeed and keeps on trying to do so?" . . . "The Master seldom spoke of what was 'profitable.'"* Occasionally, however, he would say: "The Superior Man is informed in what is right. The inferior man is informed in what is profitable (to himself)."[14]

Righteousness for righteousness' sake was strongly advocated by Confucius and Mencius alike. It formed the basis of their opposition to the utilitarianism of Mo Tzu, in its personal aspect more especially, although both the Confucian and Mohist Schools approved of what was profitable for the people as a whole.

5. *Filial Piety* (*Hsiao*)—In the last analysis, filial piety came to be regarded as the root of all other virtues. In general, it implied the attitude of an individual toward anyone above him in social position, to preserve station and rank. It was concretely expressed in the Five Relationships:—

(1) Subject to Emperor, or citizen to magistrate

* *li*—a different character from the *li* which means 'rules of propriety.'

(2) Son to Father, or daughter to mother
(3) Younger to Elder Brother, or sister to sister
(4) Younger to Older Friend
(5) Wife to Husband

The list could be lengthened, for example, to include the guest-host relationship. The second relationship mentioned above—of children to parents—received extraordinary emphasis in Chinese society.

For Chinese, *hsiao* begins at home, by showing respect to parents while they are alive and by presenting offerings to their spirits after death. Thus, ancestor worship was the only form of religion encouraged by Confucius. "When Tsai Wo suggested that for the three-year mourning period one year would be enough, Confucius said that he lacked *jên*." (Here *jên* carries the meaning of 'filial piety,' as also Mencius implied it when he said: "There never has been a man of *jên* who has neglected his parents."[15]) Here the ideal man is the ideal son, who shows duty to his parents and maintains family solidarity. It is reflected in the *Li Chi* where Tsêng Tzu is quoted as saying: "There are three degrees of filial piety. The highest is the honoring of our parents; the second is not disgracing them; the lowest is being able to support them."[16] In order that this teaching might be crystallized for posterity, the *Book of Filial Piety* (*Hsiao Ching*) was reputedly composed soon after the Sage's death and, as time went on, became very popular.

The Confucian Philosophy

A modern rendering of the salient teachings of the *Four Books* of the Confucian School may be summarized here only briefly under four main topics.

Human Nature and the Cosmic Order

In the *Doctrine of the Mean* (*Chung Yung*), human nature is the starting point of Confucius' philosophizing. As he looked into his own and other men's minds, he found a basic moral law operating, from which no man could escape. Moreover, when he looked outward, he discovered the same moral order controlling the universe and made the natural deduction that when there is harmony within the central self, human beings are moving in the orbit of cosmic or universal harmony. This law of harmony he tried to express in the words peace, truth, integrity, as the essence of the law of man's moral being. It was susceptible of cultivation but never fully realized.

In his rendering of *The Wisdom of Confucius* into modern English, Lin Yutang has recaptured the quintessence of wisdom in Confucius' reflections on the meaning of life as crystallized in words either from his own pen or from those of his disciples. (From the *Chung Yung,* for example) :—

"What is God-given is what we call human nature. . . . The cultivation of the moral law is what we call culture. . . . Wherefore, the moral man watches diligently over his secret thoughts. . . . When the passions . . . have not awakened, that is our central self, or moral being. . . . When these passions awaken and each and all attain due measure and degree, that is harmony or the moral order.[17] To find the central clue to our moral being which unites us to the universal order, that indeed is the highest human attainment. . . ."[18]

"To be patient and gentle, ready to teach, returning not evil for evil. . . . To lie under arms and meet death without regret. . . . How unflinching is his strength of character. . . ."[19]

"Truth does not depart from human nature. . . . When a man carries out the principles of conscientiousness and reciprocity, he is not far from the moral law. What you do not wish others should do to you, do not do unto them. . . . Is it not just this thorough genuineness and absence of pretense which characterizes the moral man? . . . In one word, the moral man can find himself in no situation in life in which he is not master of himself. . . . He complains not against God, nor rails against men."[20]

Thus, in these and many other passages, Confucius made clear his conviction that within the human spirit could be established a 'golden mean' or 'central harmony' which was cosmic in quality and therefore worthy of achievement.

True Manhood and the Social Order

Having established the cosmic quality of human nature, the Confucian philosophy moved on to develop the theme that by being true to his own inner self, man will naturally exhibit those qualities of true greatness on which the social order depends for stability. In the *Chung Yung* we read: "Truth means the fulfillment of our self; and moral law means following the law of our being. . . . Only those who are absolutely their true selves in this world can have pervading influence.[21] . . . Being true to oneself is the law of God."[22] The ideal man who follows the 'golden mean,' will show no pride of self or position, will be neither wily nor garrulous; neither will he worry over material things. . . . "The Superior Man attends to the spiritual things and not to his livelihood."[23] . . . "Do not worry about people not knowing your ability, but worry that you have not got it."[24] . . . "A glib talker with an ingratiating appearance is seldom a gentleman."[25] . . . "Humility is near to moral discipline; loyalty (to others) is near to sincerity of heart; simplicity of character is near to true manhood."[26]

The relation of true manhood to the social order is even more thoroughly discussed in the *Li Chi* (*Book of Rites*). Envisaging each person in his social milieu, Confucius affirmed his task to be the development of mutual respect or courtesy between individuals in every basic relationship of life, beginning first of all in the family as the fundamental social unit. This true relationship he expressed with the word *li,* as the principle of all orderly living to be manifested not only in the home but also in all larger communal life.

"Therefore, human nature is the field cultivated by the sage or saintly ruler. He ploughs it with *li,* sows it with the seeds of duties, weeds it by education and learning, harvests it with true manhood, and enjoys it with music. Therefore, *li* is but the crystallization of what is right."[27]

In like manner, regular sacrifices to the spirits of Heaven and Earth and to the ancestors will denote a desire to maintain a right relationship with the invisible world and so "constitute the embodiment of *li*."[28]

Burdened with the multifarious problems of his own time, Confucius often sighed for the good old days of the Three Dynasties, when the sage-kings ruled a utopian society: "When the great *Tao* prevailed (i.e., in the former Golden Age), the world was a common state (not belonging to any particular ruling family). . . . This was the period of *ta-t'ung*, or the Great Commonwealth."[29]

Yet, quickly reminding himself that an ideal national life must ever rest upon personal integrity, Confucius would continue teaching: "From the emperor down to the common man, all must regard the cultivation of the personal life as the root or foundation."[30] The 'cultivation of the personal life' he then explained as depending on setting one's heart right so as to avoid anger, love-blindness, or anxieties, and thus preserve one's inner balance. 'Making the will sincere' he defined as satisfying one's own conscience, being especially watchful over oneself when alone. "If a man would be sincere toward himself and generous toward others, he would never arouse resentment."[31]

Continuing the stress on the personal, Confucius urged all men not to show those attitudes which they do not like in other people. "This is the principle of the measuring square (or foot-rule)." In regard to acquisitiveness, he would reiterate: "Thus character is the foundation, while wealth is the result. . . . The true man develops his personality by means of his wealth, and the unworthy man develops wealth at the expense of his personality."[32]

The relation between personal and family life is to be cultivated, moreover, so one can see the bad in those whom he likes and see the good in those whom he dislikes, thereby preserving sound judgment. Furthermore, good home training is bound to be felt in the nation's life. This will be true in respect to avarice, as well as in kindness and courtesy; for the power of personal example is tremendous. It is repeated: "The ordering of national life depends on the regulation of one's home life."[33] "It follows, therefore, that when marriage ceremonies are taken lightly or disregarded, then marital relationships become difficult and promiscuity will become rampant. . . . *Li,* or the principle of social order, prevents the rise of moral or social chaos as a dam prevents a flood."[34]

Government by Moral Example

Always, for Confucius, the objective in his training of young men was ability to govern wisely. Because society and government rested upon the five relationships: ruler-subject; father-son; husband-wife; elder and younger brother, and friend-to-friend, every potential ruler must learn the obligations implicit in those relationships. In a word, harmony in each relationship is to be established and maintained only by moral example.

A ruler must be made especially aware of the fact that his people will emulate his example. In one of his aphorisms, Confucius insisted: "When the ruler himself does what is right, he will have influence over the people without giving commands, and when the ruler himself does not do what is right, all his commands will be of no avail."[35] Or again, in the *Chung Yung* we find him saying: "Through sincerity and faithfulness, he (the sovereign) maintains his rule, and through pride and self-indulgent living he loses it." It would be useless for the head of government to aim at gathering wealth, for "the material prosperity (or strength) of a nation does not consist in its material prosperity but in righteousness."[36]

At one point, Confucius defined 'achieving true knowledge' as instilling into people a healthy respect for a magistrate and the law that he represents.[37] Nevertheless, he likewise taught magistrates "to aim so that there should be no lawsuits."[38] To his mind, this spelled good government in simplest terms at the grass-roots level.

At the top level, order in the empire rests squarely upon the shoulders of the emperor. His character and conduct will determine his success or failure. If he will regulate his own conduct, cherish his kindred, honor his ministers, wisely choose worthy advisers, show himself a "father to his people," encourage useful arts, receive foreign visitors with tenderness, and attend to the welfare of the princes of the realm, the emperor's reign will be crowned with honor and success.[39]

For such responsibilities, however, a man must receive thorough preparation. At the beginning of the *Ta Hsüeh,* there is a long statement concerning the ordering of national life by regulating family life and by cultivating personal life, which is accomplished by setting hearts right, by making wills sincere, and by achieving true knowledge, which in turn is accomplished by the 'investigation of things.'[40] In all things, Confucius concluded, the ruler must show wisdom, compassion, and courage. "Love of knowledge is akin to wisdom. Strenuous attention to conduct is akin to compassion. Sensitiveness to shame is akin to courage."[41]

Finally, in order to provide good examples for the rulers of his time, Confucius pointed to the ancient emperor, Wu Wang, and his brother, Chou Kung, as eminently successful, for one reason because they were pious men. They did not neglect the proper ceremonies in their ancestral temple or fail in the seasonal offerings in the Hall of Light (*Ming T'ang*) to Heaven and Earth and the Five *Ti.** It is worthy of note, he said to his students, that "if one only understood the meaning of the sacrifices to Heaven and Earth and the sig-

---

* Wu Wang left his kingdom to his infant son in care of his younger brother, Chou Kung, as regent. When the son became of age and was enthroned as Ch'êng Wang, out of gratitude he honored his uncle by granting him the special privilege of sacrificing to Heaven in his own "Ming T'ang" in his barony of Lu. (Cf. Soothill: *Hall of Light,* p. 97.)

nificance of the services in ancestral worship in summer and autumn, it would be as easy to govern a nation as to point a finger at the palm."[42]

Education the Prime Necessity

Inasmuch as good government implied the acquiring of true knowledge through the investigation of things, Confucius saw the urgent necessity of education and set himself the task of providing it for those who were 'born to rule.' The first requirement was a quiet place in which to study. The true man, he felt, must first have a definite purpose, calmness of mind, and 'peaceful repose.' "Only after having peaceful repose can one begin to think," he reasoned. "Only after one has learned to think, can one achieve knowledge. . . ."[43]

(a) *A Few General Principles*:—

The need for education and its general principles are expounded in the *Book of Rites* (*Li Chi*) in such passages as the following:

"The only way for the superior man to civilize the people and establish good social customs is through education. A piece of jade cannot become an object of art without chiselling, and a man cannot come to know the moral law without education."[44]

"Reading without thinking gives one a disorderly mind, and thinking without reading makes one flighty (or unbalanced)."[45] . . ."Therefore, in the education of the superior man . . . one is given time to digest things, to cultivate things, to rest and to play."[46]

In other words, a student must learn to think things out for himself.

"To know what you know and know what you don't know is the characteristic of one who knows."[47]

But the learning process will depend very much on the spirit and method of the teaching. All important is it, then, that pupils have a wise teacher and that a harmonious personal relationship be established between them.[48] Only thus can they "feel at home at college," "acquire conviction in ideas," and "leave their teachers without turning their backs on their studies. . . ."[49]

Like certain of the Greek sophists, Confucius was the first to offer basic courses in the art of governing wisely. While he gave instruction in practically every branch of learning then known; namely, poetry, history, rites, music, primitive science, archery, and historical biography,* yet his main objective was to prepare graduates to assume the responsibilities of political life. Like Socrates, he laid great stress on man's ethical nature as even more fundamental than his capacity to serve the state.[50] Rather than stress the doctrines of one particular school of philosophy, he preferred to train all-round men who could be useful to the state. For this reason, he sought by induction to frame universal definitions, which he called the "rectification of names," which could serve as standards of human conduct.

A modern student of Confucianism has put into a nutshell Confucius' conviction that "to be kept stable, society must have leaders who can be trusted; that the only leaders to be trusted are men of character; that character is to be developed through education acquired both from others and through self-discipline; that no man is a safe leader who goes to extremes; that the right cultivation of his own character must be the chief concern of every leader; that no parent, teacher, or public officer has the right to take lightly his responsibilities for guiding, through precept, rules, and example, the conduct of those who are under him."[52]

(b) *The Ideal Teacher*

The worthy teacher is one "who goes over what he has already learned and gains some new understanding from it."[53] He is ever a learner dissatisfied with his own knowledge.

---

* According to the modern sinologist, Ch'ien Mu, the curriculum commonly used by ancient *Ju-chiao* scholars comprised the "Six Arts" of ceremonies, music, archery, charioteering, writing (or history), and mathematics. (51)

Through teaching he comes to realize his inadequacy and "one then feels stimulated to improve oneself. Therefore, it is said, 'The processes of teaching and learning stimulate each other. . . . Teaching is the half of learning.' "[54]

The ideal teacher uses four good methods: "prevention" (of bad habits); timely presentation; orderly sequence; "mutual stimulation . . ." (by) "letting students admire the excellence of other students . . ."[55] "A good questioner proceeds like a man chopping wood—he begins at the easier end, attacking the knots last, and after a time the teacher and student come to understand the point with a sense of pleasure."[56]

Confucius criticised the education of his day as not giving students enough chance to develop their own "natural inclinations" and thereby "bring out the best in their talents."[57] He urged the superior teacher, therefore, to guide his students but not pull them along, urge them to go forward and not suppress them, open the way but not take them to the place.[58] He cautioned against "that type of scholarship which is bent on remembering things in order to answer questions (but) does not qualify one to be a teacher. . . . When he sees a student is doing his best but is lost, then he explains it to him, and if after the explanation, the student still does not understand, he may as well leave the matter alone."[59] "Now if the process of learning is made gentle and easy and the students are encouraged to think for themselves, we may call the man a good teacher."[60]

(c) *The Core of Education is* Li *or Harmony*

"Education," declared Confucius, "begins with poetry, is strengthened through proper conduct (*li*) and consummated through music."[61] *Li* is the expression in personal attitudes and behavior of the same harmony that flows through all Nature (Heaven and Earth). Yutse is quoted as saying: "Among the functions of *li,* the most valuable is that it establishes a sense of harmony. . . ."[62] And evidently it was counted a rare attainment, for we read that Confucius commended both Ah Shang and Ah Sze for their independent (or harmonious) thinking and said they were now worthy to study the *Book of Songs* (Odes) with him.[63]

So vital was *li* to his thinking, that Confucius once affirmed: "This *li* is the principle by which the ancient kings embodied the laws of heaven and regulated the expressions of human nature. Therefore, he who has attained *li* lives, and he who has lost it dies."[64] He then stated in detail how the sage-kings taught men how to live, and made them more civilized, with *li*. Its inner working could be seen not only in people as individuals but in the various social groups as well. To quote: "*Li,* the principle of social order, is to a country what scales are to weight and what the carpenter's guide-line is to straightness, and what the square and the compass are to squares and circles. . . ."[65] Or again, "*Li* is the principle of mutual respect and courtesy. . . ."[66] It accounts for affection in the home, piety in public worship, and order in all official circles from village council to imperial court. Hence the reiterated remark of Confucius: "There is nothing better than *li* for the maintaining of authority and the governing of the people. . . ."[67] In fact, Lin Yutang would include religion, the social order, army discipline, historical scholarship, and all etiquette in the philosophy of *li*. "The religious character of *li* cannot be doubted," he affirms, "and the Chinese have actually called Confucianism 'the religion of *li*,' a current term even today."[68]

An Estimate of Confucius

Of himself, Confucius reputedly once remarked: "I merely try to describe (or carry on) the ancient tradition, but not to create something new."[69] Continually learning and unceasingly teaching was the aim of his mature years. He had no patience with a pupil who was not at least "trying to make things clear to himself."[70] In similar vein Chu Hsi once remarked to his students: "If you do not remember the book, study it thoroughly and you will remember it. If the meaning is not clear, think deeply and it will be clear."[71]

His contemporaries said of him: "Confucius taught four things: literature, personal conduct, being one's true self, and honesty in social relationship. . . . (He) was gentle but dignified, austere yet not harsh, polite and completely at ease."[72] In his own personality, he set an example for others to follow, for he was convinced that "unless there be the highest moral character, the highest moral law cannot be realized. . . ."[73] (and further that) "every moral man's example is followed for generations. . . . How simple and self-contained his true manhood! . . . Who can understand such a nature except he . . . who has reached in his moral development the level of the gods?"[74]

It is safe to say that Confucius was, in his own way, a deeply religious man, yet for him worship or reverence was limited to an attitude of courtly respect. In an oft-used epigram,—"Respect the heavenly and earthly spirits and keep them at a distance"—he simply meant to inculcate a healthy respect, fearing that too great familiarity would breed contempt. When asked about death, and the worship of spirits, he replied: "We don't know yet about life (or 'how to serve men'), how can we know about death (or 'about serving the spirits') ?"[75]

His code of ethics was simple: "Repay kindness with kindness, but repay evil with justice (or severity)" . . . "I do not expect to find a saint today, but if I can find a gentleman, I shall be quite satisfied." Or again, "It is easy to be rich and not haughty; it is difficult to be poor and not grumble" . . . "The people who live extravagantly are apt to be snobbish (or conceited), and the people who live simply are apt to be vulgar. I prefer the vulgar people to the snobs."[76]

As the Chinese speak of him, Confucius was first of all a scholar, then a teacher, and finally a statesman. It is, however, as a great Teacher that he is revered and best loved by his countrymen. Although later on, Confucius was deified and reverenced in shrines as China's greatest Sage and Mentor,[77] nevertheless, at the present we contemplate him as the scholar-teacher, for he was primarily an educator. He thought of himself as "striving unwearyingly (in study) and teaching others without flagging."[78]

Confucius created a new profession—worthy of compensation

After likening the activities of Confucius to those of Socrates and the Greek Sophists, Fung Yu-lan went on to say: "Confucius was the first man in China . . . to popularize culture and education. It was he who . . . developed that class of gentleman in ancient China who was neither farmer, artisan, merchant, nor actual official, but was professional teacher and potential official."[79]

Until Confucius' time, book-learning was available only for the "noble élite," but he declared: "From him who has brought his simple present of dried meat, seeking to enter my school, I have never withheld instruction."[80] By giving equal attention to every student, rich or poor, who would pay something for tuition, he opened the way for education to reach the masses.

The establishment of a new class in Chinese society—that of scholar—did not come easily, however, for professional scholar-teachers were openly criticised as parasitic, because they depended entirely upon others for their financial support. This might come from tuitions paid by pupils, from the patronage of a feudal lord, or through accepting public office with its perquisites and emoluments. Although in his earlier years, Confucius did hold small public offices as a primary means of earning his livelihood, yet later on he felt that, as an itinerant dispenser of knowledge to youth and advice to rulers, he was well worth his salt and brought up his pupils to believe that the profession of teaching was in itself worthy of recompense.

For this opinion and practice, Confucius was at times severely criticized by his contemporaries. Once, while Tzŭ Lu was traveling with Confucius, and met an old farmer beside the road, the latter remarked: "You, whose four limbs know not toil, and who cannot distinguish the five grains, who may your Master be?"[81] In the *Shih Chi,* a biographical sketch of Confucius records a noted statesman of the time as saying: "Sophists who travel from place to place begging for loans, they are incapable of directing a state."[82]

In the *Chuang-tzu* may be found another fierce diatribe on Confucius: "You are a mere word-monger, who talks nonsense about Kings Wên and Wu (founders of the Chou dynasty) . . . . You do not sow and yet you are clothed. . . . You make a deceiving show of filial piety and brotherly love, so that by good chance you may secure some fat fief or post of power."[83] Of scholars in general, with their 'dialectical learning,' Han Fei Tzu of the Legalist School (d. 233 B.C.) cynically remarked: "Now if one pursues literary studies and practices the arts of conversation, one has none of the labor of cultivating the soil and has the actuality of possessing riches; one has none of the dangers of war and has the honor of noble position. Who, then, would not do this?"[84]

Despite these criticisms and many more like them, no doubt, Confucius stuck to his guns on the value of a scholar in the community and on what he considered to be a liberal education. Once, when a disciple asked to be taught gardening and agriculture, the Sage replied, "What a little-minded man is Fan Hsü!" Of another student, who had engaged in commercial enterprises, Confucius disparagingly remarked, "Tz'u is not content with his lot, yet his goods increase abundantly. Nevertheless, in his judgment he often hits the mark."[85]

In the *Lun Yü* (*Analects*), the Sage is quoted as saying: "The occupant of office, when his duties are finished, should betake himself to study; the student, when his studies are finished, should betake himself to office."[86] In fact, ever since that time, the scholar class in China usually has been limited to two occupations: that of a teacher in an educational institution of some kind or that of a government official.

In conclusion, Confucius looked upon himself as a preserver of the best culture of the Chou dynasty, as it was then flowering in the state of Lu. He had a sense of mission and could not refrain from laments over the degeneracy of his times. For this reason, he was a conservative, seeing little hope in the future—only a golden age in the past. As for religious beliefs, as already pointed out, Confucius showed respect for Heaven as a purposeful, Supreme Being, whose purpose he called *ming*, or Fate. Toward the lesser spirits, however, he was rather skeptical, advising his pupils "while respecting the spirits, to keep aloof from them," in order the more earnestly to do one's duty to humanity.

As W. T. Chan has expressed it, "the logical foundation of the Confucian system lies, therefore, in moral experience—in being true to oneself and loyal to others. This is the 'central harmony,' or *Chung Yung*. This is the backbone of all Chinese philosophy and life."[87] The social, political, and psychological aspects of Confucius' practical philosophy were left for Mencius and Hsün Tzu to develop after him.

Mencius—Amplifier of Confucian Thought

Mêng Tzu (latinized as Mencius), styled Mêng K'o, was born about 371 and died in 289 B.C. He considered himself the perpetuator of the teachings of Confucius, as recorded in his own words: "From Confucius downward to today there have been one hundred odd years. . . . Under these circumstances is there no one (to transmit his doctrines)?"[88] In the opinion of Lin Yutang, Mencius was "probably the best historical scholar of his day," and "the *Book of Mencius* is incomparably better prose than the Analects."[89]

The Goodness and Rationality of Human Nature

While Mencius and Hsün Tzu considered themselves true disciples of Confucius, they were at the same time quite at variance in many of their interpretations. As leader of the "idealistic wing" of Confucianism, Mencius held the "orthodox" Confucian view that human nature is essentially good, while Hsün Tzu, as leader of the "naturalistic wing,"* viewed it as basically evil. Consequently, the two differed in their approaches to the problem of inculcating proper habits in

* To use Wing-tsit Chan's characterizations (*Outline*, p. 11).

young men. Mencius maintained there was enough universal quality in the human mind on which to base an appeal for unity in human affairs. He felt that if their moral sense could be given full development, men's contacts with one another would bring out their best personalities.[90]

On the other hand, Mencius did not claim that men's natures were entirely good: he believed that men possessed the beginnings of the four cardinal virtues of *jên* (benevolence), *yi* (righteousness), *li* (propriety), and *chih* (wisdom), which when developed could produce a sage-king. "These (virtues) are not fused into us from without," he would say. "We originally are possessed of them. . . . Hence I say, 'Seek and you will find them; neglect and you will lose them.'"[91] The thing that distinguishes man from other animals, he argued, is his Heaven-bestowed mind and faculty of thinking and remembering, which must be developed as he grows. Hence the need for education. The cultivated man has improved his mind and thereby made himself great, for reason is the essence of 'human nature.'

"Human nature follows the good as water seeks the lower level," Mencius said, pointing out that the moral consciousness in different persons differs only in degree, not in kind. Just so, he averred, "the Sages belong to the same species as ourselves. . . . Therefore, I say, there is a common love for flavors in our mouths, a common sense for sounds in our ears, and a common sense for beauty in our eyes. Why then do we refuse to admit that there is something common in our souls also? What is that thing that we have in common in our souls? It is reason and a sense of right."[92]

Believing that all men have a mind which cannot bear to witness the sufferings of others, Mencius reasoned that such a feeling of commiseration could be made the basis of good government:

"If one extend one's kindliness to others, it will suffice to protect all within the four seas. If one does not extend this kindliness, it will be insufficient to protect one's own wife and children."[93]

Where Confucius had limited himself to an exposition of the meaning of such virtues as benevolence, conscientiousness, and mutuality or altruism, as applied to individuals, Mencius extended their application to society and government. In other words, whereas Confucius was chiefly interested in producing the 'Inner Sage,' Mencius wished also to produce the 'Outer King.'[94] He stressed filial piety as the greatest of all virtues, because it made for harmony in all social relationhips. Moreover, by making *jên* the basis of society and *yi* the basis of politics, Mencius gave a psychological basis for humanism which marked a decided advance and influenced all later neo-Confucian thought.[95]

The Cultivation of the Higher Life

As a mountain loses its beauty if all its trees are hacked down, so a human soul may lose its love and righteousness if hacked daily by adverse circumstances until it is reduced to the level of the beasts. Then a person cannot recognize his original, true nature. True character will grow only by adequate, concentrated cultivation. To carry this line of thought still further, Mencius went on to say:

"All people have the common desire to be elevated in honor, but all people have something still more elevated in themselves without knowing it." (meaning that true nobility is not given from without) . . .
"The ancient people cultivated what belonged to God's noblemen and they obtained without conscious effort the ranks of man-made nobility." . . .
(As a man takes care of his body by nourishing it, so he should take care of his mental or spiritual nature) . . . "He who attends to his smaller self becomes a small man, and he who attends to his greater self becomes a great man." . . .
"Charity is the heart of man, and righteousness is the path for men. Pity the man who has lost . . . his heart and does not know how to recover it. . . . There are times when a man would not avoid

danger. . . . All men have this feeling; only the good men have been able to preserve it." . . .
"I love life, but I also love righteousness, and if I can't have both at the same time, I will sacrifice life to have righteousness. I would not have life at any price." . . .[96]

Defense of Freedom of Thought and Spiritual Aspiration

If men are to develop their rational nature, they must, according to Mencius, be given the individual right to use their own minds in an independent way of thinking. Such a theory would almost inevitably bring them into conflict with tradition and its time-honored rules of etiquette. Mencius, therefore, made allowance for changing times and conditions when he said:

"Acts of propriety which are not really proper, and acts of righteousness that are not really righteous, the great man does not do." . . . "The path of virtue should be followed without any bend, and not to seek emolument . . . The Superior Man simply follows the law (of right) and then waits for his Fate."[97]

In some of the sayings of Mencius, there is even a slight suggestion of the mystic speaking, as for example in the passage:

"Wherever the Superior Man passes through, transformation follows; wherever he abides, there is a spiritualizing influence. This flows abroad, above and below together with Heaven and Earth" . . . (Or again) . . . "All things (literally: "the ten thousand things") are complete within us. There is no greater delight than to find sincerity when one examines oneself. If one acts with a vigorous effort at mutuality in one's seeking for benevolence, nothing will be closer to one."[98]

Mencius also taught that those who have attained to the highest state will possess a spiritual force which is 'life-changing,' which is produced by a life-time of righteous deeds, is "nourished by uprightness" and "fills up all between Heaven and Earth."[99]

Promotion of Agrarian Policies

As an agrarian economist, Mencius was well ahead of his time. Since agriculture was practically the only form of production, he advocated an equalization of land distribution and ownership. He sponsored what was known as the 'well-field' system, whereby a square of land was subdivided into nine lots (three rows of three each), each of 100 *mow,* the central lot being the 'state farm.' A family was allotted one of the eight lots and the eight families joined in cultivating the ninth or central lot (with the common well upon it) as their means of paying off the state's land tax.[100] Thus a peaceful, cooperative rural life would be assured and the state tax would not become a burden to anyone. Since the whole concern of government was the contentment and moral uplift of the people, if it failed to insure that, then, according to Mencius, revolution was in order.

That his agrarian policy was acceptable to the nobles is very doubtful, because of the socialistic twist which Mencius gave to the old well-field system. In earlier days, all the land had been thought of as belonging to the nobility, for whom the peasantry farmed as tenants. But Mencius held that the land, being the public property of the state, should be parceled out to the people who actually cultivated it. Thereby, they became freeholders, paying their tax to the state with produce from the public field. In this way he sought to make the rulers feel their responsibility for ensuring economic security to the common people. As the following passages indicate, his mind constantly worked on the problem of livelihood for the rural population.

"If the seasons for farming are not interfered with (by warfare), the grain will be more than can be eaten. If close-meshed nets are not allowed to enter the pools and ponds, the fish and turtles will be more than can be consumed. If axes and bills enter the mountain forests only at the proper time, the wood will be more than can be used. When grain, fish, and turtles are more than can be eaten, and there is more wood than can be used, the people are enabled to nourish their living and bury their dead without any dissatisfaction. This nourishing of the living and burying of the dead without any dissatisfaction marks the beginning of the Kingly Way." [101]

"Let mulberry trees be planted around five-acre home-steads, and persons of fifty years may be clothed with silk. In rearing fowls, pigs, dogs, and swine, do not neglect their times (for breeding), and persons of seventy years may eat meat. Do not take away the time proper for the cultivation of a farm of one hundred acres, and its family of several mouths will not suffer from hunger." [102]

"Let careful attention be paid to education in the schools, with stress on the inculcation of filial piety and fraternal duty, and there will be no gray-haired men on the roads carrying burdens on their backs or heads. There has never been a case of one who did not become a (real) king when (under his rule) persons of seventy wore silk and ate meat, and the common people suffered neither from hunger nor cold." [103]

Denunciation of Graft in Any Form

Mencius noted that whenever men got into positions of power, they almost invariably yielded to a desire for personal glory or private gain. He saw very clearly that this detestable intriguing for material gain was undermining the state. Therefore, in no uncertain terms, he attacked the acquisitive desire which could, if not checked, ruin the whole of society. On the other hand, he fully recognized that "the minimum requirement for moral life is that the livelihood of a man and his family be safeguarded." [104]

Throughout his life, Mencius stoutly defended the thesis that men's nature is potentially good; that education can prevent the beclouding of human nature; that government is primarily for the benefit of the people; and, finally, that a clear distinction is to be made between a kingly ruler (ruling by virtue) and a dictator (ruling by force or cunning).[105]

Hsün Tzu—Moulder of Ancient Confucianism

Hsün Tzu will be understood best if we remember that he lived toward the end of that very troubled Period of the Warring States (403-221 B.C.). Born in the northern state of Chao (modern Hopei) about 320 B.C. (when Mencius was already past middle life), Hsün Tzu may have lived until 238 or possibly 235.[106] According to Homer H. Dubs, the best known Western interpreter of Hsün Tzu, this philosopher elaborated the Confucian philosophy in a more coherent way than had either Confucius or Mencius. As an orthodox follower of Confucius, but indeed superior as a philosopher, Hsün Tzu wrote logical discussions on unified themes which cover the whole ground of the Confucian teaching. "In many matters," writes Dubs, "especially as showing the fundamental authoritarianism of Confucianism, he reveals an attitude more truly Chinese than can be had from a cursory reading of either Confucius or Mencius."[107]

Philosophy of Heaven and Human Nature

Influenced undoubtedly by the Taoists, Hsün Tzu showed a definite naturalistic trend in his thinking about 'Heaven.'

"Heaven has a constant regularity of activity. . . . Respond to it with good government, and success will result. . . . Heaven has its seasons, Earth has its material resources, man has his government. This is what is meant (when it is said that man) is able to form a trinity (with Heaven and Earth)."[108]

Hsün Tzu was content to let Nature's processes run their course, but at the same time was keenly interested in controlling Heaven's seasons and Earth's resources for human interests. Man's part in the trinity seemed to be to put Heaven and Earth to work for him.

"Instead of exalting Heaven and thinking about it, why not heap up wealth and use it advantageously? Instead of obeying Heaven and praising it, why not adapt Heaven's Fate and make use of it? . . . Instead of relying on things to increase of themselves, why not put forth one's ability and develop them?" [109]

Clearly Hsün Tzu here is more interested in mastering than in meditating upon the world of Nature. Whereas Mencius' Heaven was an ethical one, Hsün Tzu's, being naturalistic, contained no ethical principle. We are warned, however, by W. T. Chan not to rank Hsün Tzu among the materialists, as he did not reduce mind to matter or quantity.[110]

Correlatively, Hsün Tzu's theory of human nature, being radically cynical, was diametrically opposite to that of Confucius and Mencius. He was convinced that as the nature of man was fundamentally evil, his goodness had to be acquired by training. This doctrine of 'original depravity' is elaborated in passages like the following:

" (Man's) nature is the unwrought material of the original; what are acquired are the accomplishments and refinements brought about by culture and the rules of proper conduct. . . . Now man, by his nature, loves profit . . . is envious and hateful . . . possesses the desires of the ear and the eye, and likes sound and women. . . . Therefore, to give rein to man's original nature and to follow man's feelings, means inevitable strife and rapacity, together with violations of etiquette and confusion in the proper way of doing things. . . . Therefore, the civilizing influence of teachers and laws . . . (is) . . . absolutely necessary. . . ." [111]

These and many other similar statements indicate how close the premises of Hsün Tzu's philosophy lay to the doctrines of the Legalistic School. Still, there was some hope for man. It was conceivable, in Hsün Tzu's view, that any man might become good. If 'the man in the street,' for example, would only "direct his capacities to learning, concentrating his mind on one object, thinking . . . and investigating thoroughly," he could "add daily to his knowledge" and "accumulate goodness" until he reached a state of "spiritual clairvoyance," thus forming a genuine "trinity with Heaven and Earth."[112]

This loophole of escape from man's depraved tendencies, Hsün Tzu outlined further in the saying:

> "A man who accumulates (practice in) hoeing and ploughing becomes a farmer; who accumulates (practice in) chopping and shaving wood, becomes an artisan; who accumulates (practice in) trafficking in goods, becomes a merchant; who accumulates (practice in) the rules of proper conduct and standards of justice, becomes a Superior Man."[113]

Thus, by the slow process of habit formation does man arrive at his goal of actualizing truth within himself.

As J. Leighton Stuart has phrased it: "The characteristic word in Hsüntze's thinking is 'Nurture' . . . (which) . . . is set in opposition to 'Nature.' Nurture stands for the factors in human development that are distinctly man-made; the influences of training, education, social tradition, established authority. In these latter, Hsüntze found the basis for human improvement. . . . Much of the discussion of Nurture versus Nature suggests modern . . . discussions over the relative significance of heredity and environment in human development. In defense of his views, Hsüntze begins with a careful psychological analysis. He develops the necessity for an external standard by which to guide the processes of training and of education."[114]

A System of Psychology as a Basis for Education

From his thoroughgoing studies of Hsün Tzu, Dubs concludes that he "is the most psychological of all the ancient Chinese philosophers, and the keenness of his insight is shown in the startling modernness of his analyses . . . Hsün Tzu attempts an analysis of the senses which comes close to our present analysis. . . . He also catalogued the emotions, of which there are six: love, hate, joy, anger, sorrow, and pleasure (not mentioning fear) . . . . Yet the distinguishing of them is done by the mind. . . .[115]

"Most remarkable of all," Dubs continues, "is that Hsün Tzu in one place mentions the 'stimulus and response relation,' and 'impulse,' and indeed implies this concept throughout his psychologizing. For him, men are always doing something and being affected by something: pure thought does not exist for him. He does not separate the cognitive faculties from the others; . . . but cognition is for the sake of action. Knowing the right is for the sake of willing and doing the right."[116]

One of the great problems for a moral philosopher in those days was that of desire and how to control it. According to Dubs, Hsün Tzu recognized desire as "a fundamental fact in human nature (that) cannot be removed." Whereas every attempt to abolish desires is bound to fail, nevertheless, without removing or lessening them, as Hsün Tzu claimed, "the mind is the ruler of the body and master of the spirit. It gives commands and all parts of the body obey."[117] Thus Hsün Tzu gave to the mind the power of ruling the whole personality.

On the other hand, urged Hsün Tzu, "we must remember that . . . the mind cannot make choices according to its own view of what is best without grave risk of going astray. . . . Indeed . . . it is only the Superior Man or Sage who can conform to the three conditions of emptiness, concentration (unity), and unperturbedness (or quiescence), and can judge by an inner standard; others must follow the (principles) . . . (worked out by the Sages) . . . in order to avoid prejudice and error. . . ." "Thus," says Dubs, "Hsün Tzu . . . (kept) . . . to his authoritarian standard of conduct."[118]

For Hsün Tzu, this standard was *li,* or 'rules of conduct,' or the 'Confucian Way' of accepted ethics. It was based primarily on the *Tao,* not of Heaven but of Earth, or the Way of Man. It included the old Confucian virtues of benevolence, righteousness, obedience to law, and uprightness (or integrity), all of which were expressed in proper conduct, standards of justice and orderliness. Following this divinely human way, men could live and satisfy their desires in legitimate fashion.[119]

Education Aimed at Character Development

Since the inherent tendency in men is toward evil, and since they must be given a criterion of action by which to choose and act aright, Hsün Tzu, like his predecessors, saw the supreme necessity of promoting a systematic method of education. This was aimed not at developing the natural man but at changing him into a good man. This could best be done by giving him something to study which would help him to learn good habits. Concentration, perseverance, and practice all were considered essential in acquiring the status of sage. How could one begin? . . . "The art begins by reciting the *Classics* and ends in learning the *Rites*. Its purpose begins with making the scholar and ends in making the *Sage*."[120]

As material for instruction, Hsün Tzu, "the outstanding philosopher of education in ancient China,"[121] confirmed the canon of the *Five Classics*. "The *Rites* and *Music*," he declared, "give principles and no false teaching; the *Odes* and *History* tell about the ancients and are not familiar; the teaching of the *Spring and Autumn* is suggestive rather than expressed."[122] In thus exalting the authority of the *Classics*, he represented the attitude of all faithful Confucians.

Hsün Tzu likewise saw the great need for dependable teachers of youth, if the *Classics* were to be taught in an orthodox manner. "In studying there is nothing better than being intimate with a worthy teacher. . . . Familiarize yourself with his teaching; reverence it as universal and common to every age."[123]

In addition to this, thoroughness and comprehensiveness in study were stressed, and above all, practice in virtue, in *li*, in ethical growth of character, which was the aim of all Confucian education. It did not, however, mean overpassing the limits of common sense in the 'investigation of things': "If you wish to exhaust the inexhaustible, to pursue the illimitable . . . to the end of your days, you would not be able to reach your goal."[124]

Stress on the Quality of Sincerity

However much one may criticize Hsün Tzu's authoritarian scheme of education, as allowing insufficient place for individual freedom, which alone makes for creative living, nevertheless one can find a high personal note in his discussion of the virtue of sincerity.

> ". . . With a sincere mind preserve human-heartedness, and it will become tangibly manifested. . . . Alternately to reform oneself and to transform others is to have a virtue like Heaven. . . .
> "He who would skillfully practise the *Tao,* without sincerity cannot have singleness of purpose. . . . The Sage is intelligent, but without sincerity he could not have any effect upon the people. . . . Sincerity is what the Superior Man adheres to, and is the root of government." . . .[125]

Concluding Estimate

In estimating the contribution of Hsün Tzu, Professor Dubs has declared: "This teaching is very modern. It is the nearest that Confucianism came to Christian teaching of the infinite worth of every individual. It shows the fundamental democracy of Chinese thought—that there is no fundamental inequality between human beings, such as Aristotle alleges in the defense of slavery. At the same time, Confucian thought does recognize an inequality in humanity as it has actually developed, but this inequality is not an aristocratic inequality, rather a moral inequality, due to different degrees of moral development. Thus Hsün Tzu in remarkable fashion combined in his doctrine of human nature an extremely idealistic teaching of human equality with a practical recognition of the facts of human life."[126]

Although some of his critics called Hsün Tzu a pessimist because he held that man's original nature was evil, yet it must be granted that he held an optimistic view of the infinite improvability of every man, provided that man avails himself of every opportunity to improve. According to Wing-tsit Chan, it was the appearance of the *Chung Yung* at the end of the fourth century B.C.—in Hsün Tzu's lifetime—that gave to his and later philosophy the metaphysical basis for humanism· In it man's moral being is taken as at one with the law of the universe. Therefore, it is enough to be true to oneself; then all existence will be perfected and 'physical' nature will contribute to the benefit of man.[127]

Chapter 4

The Mohist School of Political Science

"Love only exists when it has reached everybody; love has disappeared the moment it fails to include all; when love is not pervasive, it cannot be called love."
—Mo Ti in *The Mo-tzu**

Mo Ti and his School of Political Science

Mo Ti, or Mo Tzu,** was born probably about 470 and died in 391 B.C. He is thought to have been a native of the state of Lu, later holding office in the state of Sung. Here he established a school for government service and gained a wide reputation, many of his graduates becoming officials in neighboring states as well as in Sung and Lu. Like other philosophers, Mo Tzu also traveled from place to place giving lectures on his favorite topics of frugality, universal love, "peaceful co-existence," and mutual profit. Called a heretic by the orthodox Confucians, he differed from them at certain points, setting what he believed to be a higher standard of character and conduct.

As Chü-tzu, or Leader, of his organization, Mo Tzu exercised a strongly ascetic influence on his disciples. As Hu Shih has described them, Mo Tzu's "followers lived a simple life, wearing coarse clothing, encouraging hard labor, practising self-

---

* Liang Ch'i-ch'ao translation.

** Mo Tzu is also written Motse, Motze, or Micius (whence the adjective Mician); other derivative forms will be found, such as, Moist, Mohist, Moism, and Mohism.

denial, prohibiting singing and music, and abolishing all rituals for burial and mourning."[1] Strangely enough, perhaps because of the exigencies of the times, the students of the 'Mohist' School were trained in the use of arms and military tactics for defense.

As the years passed, the alumni of the Mohist School of Political Science grew in numbers and were organized into a solid body of men loyal to the principles of Mo Ti, whom they acknowledged as their guiding mentor. While, in a way, they were his henchmen, Mo Tzu never used his power over them for political aggrandizement, his one aim being to keep them true to the ideals he had set for them and serve the 'Will of Heaven.'

So ingrained was Mohist sense of duty and loyalty that later when a leader named Mêng Shêng failed in the defense of a small state, eighty-five of his disciples are said to have committed suicide with him.[2] On another occasion, when a Master of the Mohists, Fu Tun by name, learned that his own son had been found guilty of murder, he ordered his summary execution, extenuating his act by saying: "I could not but carry out the laws of the Mohists."[3]

Tenets of the Mohist School

Universal Love—Mo Tzu has been called 'The Philosopher of Universal Love,' because he widely preached it to be the greatest of all virtues:

> "To give peace to the world is the function of the sages. . . . What is the origin of disorders? It is the lack of love for one another. . . . What proceeds from impartiality means universal good; what proceeds from partiality means universal harm."[4]

"Such is the essence of the (Mo Ti) philosophy," wrote Liang Ch'i-ch'ao, "acquisitiveness is the root of all the evils of mankind." He then went on to say that Mo Tzu did not like the Confucians' discrimination in their altruism, letting charity begin at home and extending it out only as far as necessary from there. Moreover, he held their notion of self over against the other fellow to be a source of evil, and boldly asserted: "Love only exists when it has reached everybody; love has disappeared the moment it fails to include all; when love is not pervasive, it cannot be called love." [5]

Mo Ti's views on the universality of love are further expressed in *The Mo-tzu* as follows:

"The purpose of those who are virtuous lies in procuring benefits for the world and eliminating its calamities. Now among all the current calamities . . . I say that the attack on the small states by the large ones . . . oppression of the weak by the strong . . . disdain toward the humble by the honoured . . . (are the most important) . . . We should say that they have arisen out of hate of others and injuring others. . . .

"It is incomprehensible then that people should all object to universality when they hear of it. . . . Suppose there are two men. Let one of them hold to partiality and the other to universality. . . . Therefore, when he (the universal one) found his friend hungry he would feed him, and when he found him cold he would clothe him. In his sickness he would minister to him, and when he was dead he would bury him. Such is the word and deed of the advocate of universality." [6]

It seems clear that in the mind of Mo Tzu the practice of universal love would benefit not only the one who was loved but also the one who loved. By employing the principle of reciprocity, therefore, Mo Tzu was really utilitarian and therein lay the difference between his altruism and the Confucian *jên* or 'human-heartedness.' [7] Fung Yu-lan would intimate here that the Confucian philosopher is on a higher ethical level because his altruism is more disinterested than that of the Mohist, despite the wider range of the latter's application of the law of 'charity for all.'

Mutual Profitableness—Looking more closely at Mo Tzu's principle of mutual profit or 'profitableness,' which some have labelled 'utilitarianism,' we find him laying down three tests for any proposition: namely, its basis on proved historical grounds; its verifiability by the senses of the common people; and its applicability by using it in government and observing its benefits.[8] These are what Y. P. Mei (Mei Yi-pao) has called the "historical argument," the "testimonial argument," and the "pragmatic argument." [9] In the last analysis, usefulness to the majority, or the greatest good to the greatest number, constitutes the final test and furnishes proper motivation for all social and political action.

As a further example of this phase of Mo Tzu's teaching, there is his argument that marriages should be contracted at an early age for the purpose of increasing the total population, not so much to provide cannon fodder, but simply to prevent race suicide by filling up the ranks of the people depleted by the twin scourges of war and disease.[10] Again, we find him exalting frugality and opposing all forms of unnecessary extravagance among the people, such as elaborate funerals and long periods of mourning, which hindered the accumulation of wealth as a distinct asset to the state.[11] For the same reason, Mo Tzu frequently came into conflict with the Confucians because he consistently objected to all demonstration of emotional feeling even in the performance of sacrifices to ancestors or the spirits of Nature. No less strong was his opposition to the use of music on the ground that it was unprofitable, since it contributed only to the immediate personal pleasure of those present and not to the upbuilding of the body-politic.[12]

Thus, Mo Tzu seemed always to be looking for what would be of mutual benefit to all concerned. On this point Liang Ch'i-ch'ao has observed: "While Confucianists, notably Mencius, teach that profit and righteousness are contradictory and mutually exclusive, Motze holds that they are one and the same thing. He says, 'Righteousness is that which yields profit . . . Mutual love produces mutual profit . . . (And again) Love without partiality is that which will yield profit . . . Common good arises from loving and profiting others . . . God must like to see men loving and benefiting one another.' " [13] It is to be noted that in all his stress on the profitable, Mo Tzu had in mind the many or the total group, not merely the few or the individual. For him, mutual profit must include in its range the whole of society.

Mo Tzu's Economic Theories

For Mo Tzu, the ideal state was that in which everyone from the emperor down did his particular kind of work—his fair share of either mental or manual labor that needed to be done for the benefit of all. As Legge has translated him:

> "For the rulers to go to court early and retire late, to listen to lawsuits and attend to government, is their duty. For the gentlemen to exhaust the energy of their limbs and employ fully the wisdom of their minds, to attend to the court within and collect taxes without . . . in order to fill up the granaries and the treasury, is their duty. For the farmers to set out early and come back late, to sow seeds and plant trees in order to produce a large quantity of soybeans and millet, is their duty. For the women to rise up at dawn and retire in the night, to weave and spin in order to produce much silk, flax-linen, and cloth, is their duty."[14]

Here Mo Tzu recognized the value of individual differences in people's capacities for mental as well as manual exertion. On some occasions he, like his predecessors, was compelled to defend himself against those who thought he was a social parasite because he did no productive agricultural work.

The ascetic trend in Mo Tzu's living habits and his advocacy of the simple life for all classes stemmed from his recognition of the fact that an economic balance can be struck only by a strict economy in expenditures. Therefore, he opposed all elaborate funerals, orchestras, and the like, as time and money wasters, spelling poverty for all.[15] Limiting consumption was the only way he could discover of making ends meet for all social groups, until such time as wars should cease and allow for normal increase of population and wealth to meet increasing demands. Anything beyond what is absolutely necessary to maintain life in modest comfort "robs the people of their supplies," said Mo Tzu.

On the other hand, he did not argue that a man should necessarily stop producing as soon as he had enough to satisfy the needs of his own family. "When one has spare energy," he would say, "he should help others; when one has spare wealth, he should distribute it to others."[16] Too often, however, the feudal lords demanded the production of luxuries for themselves and their women-folk, thereby reducing the necessities of life available for the masses. Confronted with this difficulty, Mo Tzu urged the nobles to limit their extravagances, to reduce disorder by finding a fair balance between the demands of society for production and the power of the peasants and artisans to produce.[17]

Mo Tzu's Anti-War Propaganda

Mo Tzu realized clearly that the deplorable economic condition of his age could be traced directly to the political disorganization and destruction caused by war, aggravated by the famines and epidemics which almost invariably followed in the wake of war. By killing off the workers, war created a manpower shortage and, as the devastated fields could not be adequately tilled, famine inevitably ensued. This laid a heavy burden upon those able-bodied men who survived their military service.[18] For these reasons, Mo Tzu inveighed against the evils of warfare which constantly menaced every community:—

"Suppose soldier hosts arise. . . . If it is in spring, it will take people away from sowing and planting, and if in fall it will take them from reaping and harvesting. . . . Innumerable horses and oxen will start out fat and come back lean, or will die and never come back at all. And innumerable people will die because their food will be cut off. . . . Then the army will be lost in large numbers or in its entirety; . . . which means that the spirits will lose their worshipers, the number of these being also innumerable.

"Why, then, does the government deprive the people . . . to such a great extent? It has been answered: 'I covet the fame of the victor and the possessions obtainable through conquest; therefore I do it' . . .
"But when we consider the victory as such, there is nothing useful about it. When we consider the possessions obtained through it, it does not even make up for what has been lost."[19]

Our attention is called to this condemnation of war merely as *unprofitable* in contrast to Mencius' denunciation of war as *unrighteous*. The latter inveighed against "those who are skillful in warfare," arguing that they "should suffer the highest punishment." When Sung K'êng told Mencius that he hoped to turn the kings of Ch'in and Ch'u away from war by showing them how unprofitable it was, Mencius urged him to appeal to these kings on grounds of human-heartedness and righteousness.[20] Many would feel that here Mencius was on higher ethical ground than Mo Tzu.

Although Mo Tzu condemned offensive or aggressive war, saying, "it is not acting in accordance with the *Tao,*" yet he was not a pacifist in the sense of not being willing to see men lift a hand in defense of their homes and cities. He condoned defensive measures, as is shown in the passage:

"When the outer and the inner walls of the city of the small state are in ruin, he (i.e., the just and virtuous ruler) would demand their repair." . . .[21]
"Some small states . . . are well stored with supplies, their outer and inner city walls are in repair, and in them the superiors and the subordinates are harmonious. Therefore, the large states would not want to attack them."[22]

Mo Tzu certainly believed in preparedness.

The story is told of how Mo Tzu himself averted an invasion of Sung by demonstrating to the chief of ordnance of the powerful neighboring state of Ch'u that his (Mo Tzu's) methods of defense would be more than a match for their newfangled 'secret weapon' or 'cloud-ladder.' He let it be known that he had three hundred faithful Mohists waiting on the city-wall of Sung to repel any attack that Ch'u might make. Mo Tzu's slogan of "Be Prepared" evidently had the desired effect, for it is a matter of record that the King of Ch'u, hearing about it, called off his armed forces and postponed his "D-Day" indefinitely.[23]

Besides supporting defensive resort to arms, Mo Tzu justified punitive expeditions, provided they were clearly for the punishment of aggressors and not simply predatory or retaliatory attacks. Clearly Mo Tzu's position, as Yi-pao Mei states it, was that in his age "the wicked rulers were not loving their people and should be removed, peacefully if possible and by force if necessary. Although the punitive expedition itself causes bloodshed and might be said to be a breach of universal love, yet it is a relatively small price to pay to rid (the world) of an evil and to promote the principle of love in the end."[24]

Political and Religious Sanctions in Mo Tzu's Philosophy

In support of his doctrines, Mo Tzu invoked the sanctions of government and religion:

By Appeal to an All-Wise Temporal Ruler—Because of what he calls "a difference in standards" among the people, Mo Tzu took it for granted that centralized rule was needed. His argument runs:

"In the beginning of human life, when there was yet no law and government, the custom was 'Every man according to his own idea' . . . .The disorder in the (human) world was like that among birds and beasts. Yet it was evident that all this disorder was owing to the want of a ruler. Therefore . . . a . . . person . . . who was virtuous and able . . . was established to be Son of Heaven . . . (He) . . . issued a mandate to the people, saying:

'Upon hearing good or evil one shall report it to a superior. What the superior thinks to be right, all shall think to be right. What the superior thinks to be wrong, all shall think to be wrong.' . . .

"Now why is it that the empire becomes orderly? Just because the administration is based on the principle of *Agreement with the Superior* . . . The Emperor will further bring together the ideas of the empire and put them in agreement with Heaven . . ."[25]

At this point, Hsün Tzu criticized Mo Tzu for giving no voice to the people or any room for development of individuality, when he said: "Mo Tzu had vision regarding uniformity, but no vision regarding individuality."[26] The striking similarity has been pointed out between Mo Tzu's political philosophy and that of Thomas Hobbes, who maintained that the state must have "authority equal to God's," if it was to avoid "the poison of seditious doctrines; whereof one is, That every private man is Judge of Good and Evil actions."[27]

By Appeal to Heaven Itself—Appealing to religious sanctions for moral conduct, Mo Tzu taught men to fear the wrath of Heaven and . . . seek its rewards for goodness, since happiness or disaster are the gifts of Heaven in proportion to men's own good or bad conduct:

"Those who obey the Will of Heaven, love universally and benefit others and will then be inevitably rewarded. Those who oppose the Will of Heaven, are partial and unfriendly and harming others and will inevitably incur punishment. . . . Who is it that sends down the calamity? It is Heaven."[28]

Here Mo Tzu appears to conceive of Heaven in a personal way.

By Appeal to the Host of Lesser Spirits—In order further to persuade men to be good, Mo Tzu urged them to heed the influences of a host of supernatural spirits who, like the 'Heavenly Mind,' were able to help good men and harm evil men:

"With the passing of the Sage-kings of the Three Dynasties (Yü—founder of *Hsia,* T'ang—founder of *Shang,* and Wên and Wu—founders of *Chou*), the world lost its righteousness and the feudal lords took might as right. . . . Rulers do not attend diligently to

government. . . . The people practise immorality . . . and become rebellious. Thieves . . . hold up innocent people on the highways . . . to enrich themselves . . ."
"Now what is the reason for this? It is all because of doubt as to the existence . . . of ghosts and spirits. . . . If now all the people in the world could be made to believe that the spirits can reward virtue and punish vice, how could the world be in chaos?"[29]

This firm conviction that rewards and punishments were handed out by Heaven and the spirits accounts for Mo Tzu's strong rejection of the idea of Fate, as being incompatible with his concept of a moral universe.[30] In other words, Mo Tzu took religion to be a "remover of evil," promoting it as definitely "man-centered" and as a good thing for the body-politic.[31]

Criticism and Estimate of Mo Tzu

The writer of *The Chuang-tzu* criticized the Mohist School for following the ancient rules of frugality too strictly, especially in their opposition to all music and to all unnecessary funeral expenses. To quote:

"There was to be no singing in life, no mourning garments at death. Mo Tzu taught universal love and mutual benefit, and condemned fighting. His teaching excluded anger. . . . Such teaching is too barren. . . . It is contrary to human nature and would not be tolerated."[32]

In this regard, H. G. Creel is of the opinion that Mo Tzu's 'universal love' was purely an intellectual attitude, not an emotional thing at all; moreover, that his dogmatism was disliked by contemporary and later thinkers as violating 'the normal Chinese attitude' of maintaining sweet reasonableness and 'balance in all things.'[33] This may indicate one reason why the Mohist School failed to survive. Another may be found in Hsün Tzu's stricture of Mo Tzu: "Mo Tzu was blinded by utility and did not know the value of culture."[34]

Along with these criticisms, there is the modern estimate of Mo Tzu written by Liang Ch'i-ch'ao, who says: "No one denies that the ideals of the Motze School are lofty and powerful. But they have been found too difficult to be put into practice. . . . His (Mo Tzu's) view of life is partial. We cannot say that he neglected spiritual development in favor of the material, for his teachings clearly show that he cultivated the spiritual life. . . . But our most serious objection to Motze's system is that when one looks at life purely from the view of dollars and cents, one has truly missed the whole significance of life. . . . This is exactly where Motze's system is not worthy of a great Sage. It fails to appreciate the spiritual value of things."

Then, as though feeling that perhaps he had condemned Mo Tzu too harshly, Liang added these words by way of appreciation: "Nevertheless, no one can deny the fact that Motze attained spirituality in an extraordinary degree. To do this he suppressed his material life to the point of zero. For depth of sympathy, for vigor of altruism, and for the richness of the spirit of self-sacrifice, there is none like him, save Christ, in the whole world."[35]

Other Freethinkers

Yang Chu

Only brief notice can be taken here of the controversial figure, Yang Chu (c. 420–340 B.C.), a contemporary of Mencius, whom, with Mo Ti, the Confucianists classed as a dangerous 'free-thinker.' The unorthodoxy of his views is reflected in the remark made by Mencius that he must combat the ideas of Yang and Mo, because "the principle of Yang Tzu is 'Each one for himself.'"[36]

The reference in *The Han-fei-tzu* to a man who would not risk his neck for the world (supposedly referring to Yang Chu) carries the implication that Yang Chu cared only for his own personal safety, comfort, and pleasure; whereas, in *The Huai-*

nan-tzu we find the mildly approbative statement: "Completeness of living, preservation of what is genuine, and not allowing outside things to entangle one's person: these were what Yang Tzu established, and were condemned by Mencius."[37] While it is true that Yang Chu argued for the freedom of self-realization, it is probably also true that he was somewhat misrepresented by the writer of *The Lieh-tzu,* who painted him as a rank hedonist,[38] and thereby led many readers astray.

On Yang Chu's so-called 'hedonism,' Fung Yu-lan makes this favorable comment: "Such stress on the importance of life does not mean an uncontrolled giving in to the desires, however, for desires which are uncontrolled are injurious to life. . . . Hence the Sage who has a proper regard for life 'must first of all put his desires into proper harmony' . . . But the reason why life is to be prized is because through it we may enjoy sounds, colors, and tastes. . . . (Yet) we must already at an early age decide not to enjoy to excess. Such was Yang Chu's philosophy of abstemiousness, a philosophy developed by Lao Tzu and Chuang Tzu in more acceptable form." [39]

The Logicians

Chinese philosophy was given a sophistical slant by the so-called Logicians, Hui Shih (c. 380–305 B.C.) and a younger contemporary, Kung-sun Lung (c. 320–250 B.C.), who liked to make paradoxical statements about 'abstract universals' and 'concrete particulars.' Kung-sun Lung's chief contention seemed to be "that particular things in the universe are made up of an infinite number of 'universals' . . . which remain ever unchanging and distinct from one another, although the physical objects in which they are temporarily manifested and combined may change or disappear."[40] Of the works of the logicians, or dialecticians, the only one preserved is the fragmentary *Kung-sun Lung-tzu.* From its second chapter, E. R. Hughes has recorded the "Discussion on White Horses" and other paradoxical discussions in his *Chinese Philosophy in Classical Times.*[41] Yi-pao

Mei's recent translation of *The Kung-sun Lung-tzu* in the *Harvard Journal of Asiatic Studies* brings a measure of intelligibility to an otherwise abstruse work.[42]

The Logicians are also referred to as The School of Names (*Ming Chia*), because they sought to analyze the relation of the actuality, or thing, and its name.[43] Inasmuch as Chapter XXXIII of *The Chuang-tzu* contains quotations from the current sophistry of the School of Logicians, it may be assumed that their pungent, dialectical wit was common property and must have influenced Chuang Tzu and others of his time.

Chapter 5

The School of Legalism

"All words and actions not in accord with the law must be prohibited. . . . For one good man who can be trusted, there will be a thousand who must be 'bent' or 'stretched' in order to make them conform to the laws."

—Han Fei Tzu in *The Han-fei-tzu**

Bearing in mind the fact that the rise of ideas antedates their crystallization into formal schools of thought, the probable order of early, indigenous Chinese philosophic schools may be taken as the Pre-Sinistic, Taoist, Confucian, Mohist, Yin-Yang, and Legalist. Whereas most of these schools discussed the principles of government from the point of view of the people, the last named Legalist School argued from the vantage-point of the ruler and the ruling class. As the Legalists aided the movement toward centralization of power, they naturally incurred the enmity of feudal nobles and their advisers.[1]

In the Period of the Warring States (403-221 B.C.), when the trend away from feudalism placed more power in the hands of state rulers, government by customary morality (*li*) gave way to government by law (*fa*). At first, the personal relationship existing between over-lord and vassal was preserved as far as possible, but with the frequent shifting of masters this relationship became increasingly tenuous. Then was felt the need for codes, and the earliest codes were drafted as penal

* Fung Yu-lan paraphrase.

laws for criminal cases. As feudal control passed, the rulers wanted written legal principles to place in the hands of magistrates and advisers on court procedure. The first written law-code has been dated as early as 536 B.C.[2] and this may have served as a prototype for later codes.

Shang Yang—The Code-Maker of Wei

The best known of the earliest code-makers was Shang Yang (c. 400-338 B.C.), or Kung-sun Yang, known also as Wei Yang, because he served the King of Wei.[3] Believing that society could be governed best by means of a rigidly administered system of rewards and punishments, he drew up a code of laws to be enforced under dire threat of heavy penalties for violations. He may, therefore, rightly be called the father of the School of Legalism. His scheme was based on three simple principles: a penal law written in black and white; complete confidence in the justice of the code; and strict enforcement of the law. Whether or not Shang Yang was made warden of the state penitentiary and was killed by escaping prisoners is not definitely known, but tradition has it that the codifier of this early penal code suffered a violent death in the year 338 B.C.

Kuan Tzu, Han Fei Tzu, and the Principles of Legalism

During the century that followed, Shang Yang's ideas became further crystallized in the writings of Kuan Tzu and Han Fei Tzu, two outstanding exponents of the legalistic philosophy. Formerly, *The Kuan-tzu**—a speculative work of twenty-four sections—was attributed to Kuan Chung, or Kuan I-wu, who was born about 710 B.C. and died in c. 645. As a native of Ch'i and Duke Huan's Minister of State, he is said to have instituted

---

* Recently edited and published under the title: *Economic Dialogues in Ancient China: Selections from The Kuan-Tzu* by Lewis A. Maverick; (With the collaboration of T'an Po-fu and Wên Kung-wên).

salt and iron taxes, thereby strengthening the hand of government by increasing its revenue.[4] Later scholars, however, believe the work was probably put into its extant form late in the fourth century B.C. The section on "The Meaning of Laws" argues that written regulations will prevent craftiness on the part of officials and people alike.[5]

Han Fei Tzu (ca. 280-233 B.C.), a prince of the state of Han, who lived also in the state of Ch'in, was a strong advocate of the principles of the Legalists. In the biography of this philosopher in the *Shih Chi,** he is represented as one who "delighted in the study of punishments . . . laws, and methods of government" . . . (and who) constantly urged upon the King of Han the necessity of enforcing . . . (authority) so as to command 'obligatory respect' from his subjects.[6]

As royal adviser, Han Fei Tzu thoroughly believed in promulgating well-defined laws and having them obeyed without question. Furthermore, he urged that policies of statecraft be carefully enunciated for the guidance of all officials. As the *sine qua non* of all administration, he held to the principle of rewards for the observance and strict but fair penalties for the violation of laws.[7]

In general, the Legalists, using the Taoist concept of *Tao* as a principle of change, opposed entrenched custom and any appeal to history or tradition, if these hindered change.[8] To their mind, new times demanded new ways and old customs must die or be modified by changing conditions. "All words and actions not in accord with the law must be prohibited."[9] This doctrine found great favor with Ch'in Shih Huang Ti (221-207 B.C.)** and his prime minister, Li Ssu, who kept a close watch on the scholars, whose teachings were often con-

---

* The *Shih Chi or Historical Records* of Ssŭ-ma Ch'ien (ca. 100 B.C.), most of which has been translated into French by Edouard Chavannes.

** Actually, the House of Ch'in (roughly modern Kansu and Shensi) had ended the rule of the House of Chou in 256 B.C. and Ch'in Shih Huang Ti had come to power in 247 B.C. Hence the death of Han Fei Tzu in 233 B.C. is said to have occurred "in the fourteenth year of Ch'in Shih Huang." (Cf. Fung, *History,* I, p. 320.)

sidered subversive. Before long, in 213 B.C., this early "Strong Man of China" found it necessary to mete out death by immolation to hundreds of 'parasite scholars' and burn as many of their books as his henchmen could lay hands on. It was his way of interpreting the old principle of "absolute agreement of names and actualities."[10]

Legalistic Cynicism in Regard to Human Nature

As former pupils of Hsün Tzu, both Han Fei Tzu and Li Ssu followed his cynical bent in their estimate of the potential good in young men. In *The Han-fei-tzu,* the great leader of the Legalist School expressed his firm conviction that, as all men are by nature self-seeking, they can be governed only by a system of rewards and punishments. He argued that a government which trusts to people's goodness and tries to govern by reason alone, gets nowhere. For one good man who could be trusted, there would be a thousand who must be 'bent' or 'stretched' (like the wood used in making bows or wheel-rims) in order to make them conform to the laws.[11]

Another axiom of the Legalists stated that inferiors will always interpret kindliness in superiors as weakness. Strictness, therefore, is the secret of control. Non-activity (*wu wei*) can be exercised only by a puissant sage-ruler whose subjects know he will brook no recalcitrance on their part. Where the Taoists had taught that you could harmonize the *Tao* of Nature (in the ruler) with the *Tao* of Man (in the subject),[12] the Legalists, though much influenced by the Taoists, leaned away toward Hsün Tzu's dour skepticism.[13]

Yet, in strange contrast to his general approval of regimentation, Han Fei Tzu took issue with the Confucian theory of land-equalization on the ground that men should be given as much chance as possible for free competition.[14] Under this *laissez faire* theory, the farmers were expected to be more frugal and produce more if rulers did not take away their private initiative. In practice, this plan presumably worked more successfully in the case of those who had received fiefs for having supported a usurping ruler.

However far they may come from actual realization, ancient and modern ideals are not too widely divergent. The highest ideal of the Legalist School was that all persons, from king to peasant, should obey the law of the land.[15] Great as his defense of high ideals was, and great as his reputation was for good writing, Han Fei Tzu never seemed to enjoy the confidence of either the King of Han or the King of Ch'in enough to be given official status. Finally, through the machination of his arch-rival Li Ssu, he was thrown into prison and suffered death by poisoning.[16]

Chapter 6

Syntheses of Taoist and Confucian Thought

> "When one looks into the intention of Heaven, one finds it to be extremely benevolent."
>
> —Tung Chung-shu in the *Ch'un Ch'iu Fan Lu**

For several centuries, roughly from the second century B.C. down to the seventh century A.D., creative thought followed a number of divergent lines.[1] The old *Yin-Yang* ideas, especially, were further developed into various correspondence theories to show the harmony existing between the world of Nature and man himself. One of the more influential of these theories, coming from the Former Han period, was found in the writing known as *The Huai-nan-tzu*. Like the *Lü-Shih Ch'un Ch'iu,* it was a compilation and consequently suffers for lack of unity. It is said to have been composed by eight guests of Liu An, Prince of Huai-nan, who, having conspired unsuccessfully against him, were forced to commit suicide in the year 122 B.C.

Representing the same kind of cosmological inquiry as the *Appendices* to the *Book of Changes,* the *Huai-nan-tzu* contained twenty-one essays on the origin of the cosmos and how the True Man is to live in it. Reflecting the same Taoist principles as those in the *Tao Tê Ching,* it taught that because Heaven's four seasons and Earth's five elements find correspondence in man's four limbs and five viscera, the True Man will live "as if he had not yet separated from the Great Oneness."[2] Selecting eight of these essays, Evan Morgan, in his *Tao, the Great*

---

* Yao Shan-yu translation.

Luminant, has translated them under the titles: Cosmic Spirit, Beginning and Reality, Life and Soul, Natural Law, Response of Matter to the Cosmic Spirit, Influence of the Cosmic Spirit, Generalship and Prevention of Anarchy, and Endeavor and Duty. The writer of the seventh essay on "Generalship and Prevention of Anarchy" was bold enough to advocate the killing of kings who were tyrants and to declare that the king depends on the good will of his people for the security of his throne.[3]

Under Taoist influences such as these, Confucian orthodoxy became little more than a state-cult—the religion of Chinese officialdom; while Taoist philosophy degenerated into magic art in the Former Han period.[4] It remained for Tung Chung-shu to bring a semblance of order out of the prevailing chaos by giving an orderly application to the *Yin-Yang* philosophy.

Tung Chung-shu's Application of the Yin-Yang Philosophy

A Confucian scholar of no mean stature, Tung Chung-shu (ca. 179-104 B.C.) played an important role in the history of Chinese culture. As Han Wu Ti's prime minister, he memorialized the throne to suppress all 'unorthodox' schools and keep Confucianism. Tung not only helped found the Imperial University and the civil-service examination system, but also systemized and amplified the *Yin-Yang-and-Five-Elements* theory to interpret the Chinese *Classics.* Moreover, he pioneered a daring textual criticism of those classics which was later to bear much fruit.[5] Through the years, however, since his day, very little notice had been taken of Tung Chung-shu until a modern revival of the New Text School (from ca. 1800 to ca. 1927) brought forth renewed interest in him and his teachings.

Tung's major extant work, a commentary on the *Spring and Autumn Annals,* known as the *Ch'un Ch'iu Fan Lu* or "Luxuriant Dew of the Spring and Autumn Annals," makes clear that he regarded Confucius as a king appointed by Heaven to establish a new dynasty through the writing of the *Ch'un Ch'iu* (*Chronicles of Lu*). Showing throughout a strong Taoist leaning, Tung wrote at length on "The Cosmic Order," "Individual

Human Nature," "The State and the Sovereign," and "Social Ethics."

(1) *The Cosmic Order*

a) "The *Yüan* (or *Tao*) existed before Heaven and Earth. . . . Heaven and Earth are the roots of all beings and are the origin of our forefathers. . . .

b) "With the exception of the *Yüan,* the phenomenal world is built of opposites. . . . Everything has its correspondency. Hence there are beauty and ugliness . . . joy and anger, day and night. . . . The *Yin* is the correspondency of the *Yang.* A wife is the correspondency of a husband; a son, that of a father; and a minister, that of a ruler. . . .

c) "Heaven sends out the *Yang* to . . . control the work of the year . . . also the *Yin* to . . . assist the *Yang* at the proper time. . . . The *Yang* creates things; the *Yin* destroys them. Hence the *Yang* always occupies the active position and rules the time of flourishing. But the *Yin* always resides at the inactive position and rules at the end (of the year) . . . ."[6]

From this point, Tung went on to elaborate the functions of the Five Elements:—very briefly, wood gives birth to fire; fire produces earth (ashes); earth produces metal; metal yields water (as dew on a mirror); and water in turn produces wood (as trees). In another mode, wood conquers earth; earth, water; water, fire; fire, metal; and metal, in turn, conquers wood. Earth is the noblest element, because its function is to assist all the other elements. According to seasons, wood is associated with spring; fire and earth with summer; metal with autumn; and water with winter.

The rotation of Nature's opposing yet complementary forces of alternating growth and decay forms the cycle of the year. Where older diagrams (like that in the *Huai-nan-tzu*) depicted *Yin* and *Yang* moving in the same direction around a dial, Tung Chung-shu conceived of them moving in opposite directions. Their meeting in the north indicated the winter solstice (with *Yin* dominant), while their meeting in the south again (with *Yang* dominant) indicated the return of the summer solstice. In between, at the half-way points, would come the spring and autumn equinoxes when the *Yin* and *Yang* forces were in equilibrium. Thus, annually, at the time of the 'Great Cold' (about Jan. 21st), after all harvests were stored away, the work of Heaven and Earth would be completed and the great forces of Nature would begin anew their yearly cycle.[7]

(2) *Individual Human Nature*

Taking his cue from *The Huai-nan-tzu,* Tung Chung-shu elaborated the likeness of the human members to the various forms of Nature and their ways of working. For example:—

"Heaven uses the numbers of the entire year to finish the human body. Hence the 366 smaller joints (in a man's body) correspond to the number of days (in a year). The 12 bigger joints correspond to the number of months. The 5 organs (heart, liver, spleen, lungs, and kidneys) within the body correspond to the five elements. The four limbs on the body correspond to the four seasons.
"(Similarly, a man's) waking hours and sleeping time correspond to day and night. His severe and gentle dispositions correspond to winter and summer respectively. Sadness and happiness correspond to the *Yin* and the *Yang*. The cogitation of the mind corresponds to the rules and numbers (laws of the universe). The ethics of human conduct corresponds to Heaven and Earth."[8]

Since human beings are superior in intelligence to the lower animals, the ruler must show respect for them by providing an education that will develop their potential goodness. It was this concern for an adequate educational system that led Tung to promote a national university that would offer degrees and to sponsor civil-service examinations as prerequisites for obtaining government positions.

(3) *The State and the Sovereign*

Again elaborating on ideas found in *The Huai-nan-tzu,* Tung Chung-shu expatiated on the 'divine right of kings,' declaring:

" (The ruler is Heaven-appointed). . . . He should conform to the will of Heaven and obey its command. He should devote his attention to the people's enlightenment, to perfect their normal nature. He should set up correct laws, to regulate people's desires. If a ruler can attend to these three measures, the great fundamentals of the state will be accomplished. . . .

"The effect of the imperial emotions on national prosperity is incalculable:—Spring is (the time for) joy; summer is (for) happiness; autumn is (reserved for) anger; winter is (for) sadness. If a ruler manifests his emotions improperly, the era is one of chaos. . . . By acting in conformity with the principles of the movement of the *Yin* and the *Yang,* the ruler is able to conform to the ways of Heaven and give completeness to his virtuous reign." [9]

Likewise, the emperor should conform to the seasonal influences of the Five Elements. In the spring, he should "encourage farming, should not conscript forced labor more than three days per year. . . . In summer, the emperor should promote Confucian scholars, reward meritorious ministers and give alms to the poor. . . . In the last month of summer, the sovereign . . . should respectfully observe the marital relationship, and be kind to relatives. . . . In the autumn . . . the ruler should train his armies, repair the city wall, and plan any punitive expeditions that can be justified. . . . Finally, in winter . . . the sovereign must observe sacrifices, punish criminals, and forbid emigration." [10]

(4) *Social Ethics*

In like manner, social ethics will depend on the true functioning of the ruler. If the emperor would regulate himself and his court on the pattern of Nature, society would follow his example in every relationship. If the superior would practice love, uprightness, and wisdom, the inferiors' moral nature would be educated. When ruler, father, and husband obey the *yang* of Heaven, then minister (subject), son, and wife will of course obey the example of the *yin* of Earth by showing loyalty, filial piety, and chastity.[11]

Although Tung Chung-shu believed in the divine right of kings and accepted the class-system, at the same time he held the ruler rigidly responsible for maintaining some curb on the cupidity of his nobles. Inequalities in living standards could be lessened, he urged, if access to material resources could be equalized under governmental controls. Failure to do this would lead to arrogance and oppression on the part of the wealthy. If rulers would only imitate the virtues of the ancient sage-kings of Hsia, Shang, and Chou, whose faithfulness, respectfulness, and refinement were proverbial, they would themselves become models for future generations.[12]

In the ways outlined above, Tung Chung-shu meticulously worked out a systematic philosophy of history. He saw in the recurring changes of dynasty a "Cycle of New Beginnings," ordained by Heaven's decree, which must be acknowledged by each new incumbent of the dragon throne with appropriate sacrifices and ceremonial appointments. Only as each emperor announced his regard for and subserviency to the will of Heaven as expressed in the three cardinal virtues of faithfulness, respectfulness, and refinement, could he hope to gain the favor of Heaven and win the support of the people.[13]

It would be difficult to calculate how lasting the influence was of this attempt in the Former Han period to fuse *Yin-Yang,* Taoist, and Confucian principles into one universal system of thought that would comprehend and cement together all individual, social and political relationships. This unification of natural and social phenomena was a natural concomitant of the political unification taking place under Han Wu Ti and his successors. So great was the urge for systematization that critical thought turned to the texts of the sacred scriptures themselves—the fountain-head of accepted truth. Fung Yu-lan gives Tung Chung-shu the credit for inspiring the "New Text" School's critical investigation of the *Classics,* in order to systematize their astronomy, mathematics, medicine, and music according to currently accepted *Yin-Yang* theory.[14] Scholars of the time went to great lengths to produce new interpretations of the *Spring and Autumn* (*Annals*) or *Ch'un*

Ch'iu. Some went even so far as to describe Confucius' miraculous birth in a hollow mulberry tree, in order to raise him to the rank of a supernatural being. Other writers busied themselves adding their *Appendices* to the *Book of Changes* (*Yi Ching*) to bring it into line with current Confucian thought.[15]

In the Later Han period, however, a powerful reaction to the speculations of Tung Chung-shu took place, which brought Confucianism back to its senses; but before that, in the period immediately subsequent to that in which Tung flourished, there arose a most significant, though short-lived, socialistic movement spearheaded by a most unforgettable character.

The Socialism of Wang Mang

After a succession of child-emperors had brought the affairs of the Former (or Western) Han dynasty to a low ebb, Grand Duke Wang Mang, a former Minister of War and now (A.D. 5) the Imperial Tutor and Acting Emperor, quietly assumed the prerogatives of real emperor, changed the dynastic name from "Han" to "Hsin," and announced that it was "the will of Heaven."[16] All this was accomplished after close observation of magic portents and study of the prognostication literature then current.

In A.D. 9, Wang Mang issued an early decree which inaugurated three radical reforms: nationalization of land, abolition of slavery, and equal distribution of land. He based his innovations on the *Chou Li,* or "Ceremonies of the Chou Dynasty,"* (which Hu Shih is convinced was a forged product of the Han scholars in Wang Mang's régime, because it had never been mentioned by any earlier writers). This decree provided:—

> ". . . . that all land in the Empire shall be henceforth known as 'the Emperor's land' (and furthermore) . . . that all . . . slaves shall be called 'private retainers,' and that neither land nor retainers shall be bought or sold by the people.

---

* Translated into French by M. Biot in 1851.

"It is further decreed that any family having not more than eight adults and possessing over 800 *mou,* shall distribute the superfluous land among fellow-clansmen, neighbors, and fellow-citizens . . .

"Anyone who dares oppose the Land Policy . . . shall be exiled to the distant land of the barbarians. . . ."[17]

These reforms were even more drastic than those advocated by Tung Chung-shu a hundred years before. Three years later (A.D. 12), they had to be rescinded and another decree was issued that permitted landowners not only to sell land but also to own and sell slaves. Pursuing his reform policies, however, Wang Mang promulgated two other decrees, one in A.D. 10, the other in A.D. 17, aimed at establishing what he called "The Six Monopolies and Five Equalizations," as follows:—

"The Six State Controls (shall cover) salt, . . . wine, . . . iron, . . . mines and forests, , . . . money and coinage, . . . and banking and price controls, in order to protect the people and supply their needs."

"None of these six can be operated by the average citizen. . . . Therefore, he becomes the victim of economic exploitation and must accept whatever price the rich and the strong are pleased to dictate to him. The sages of ancient times realized all this evil and resolved to check it by means of governmental control."

". . . The Five Equalizations (to implement the control of banking) shall be:— (1) Determining the index number of all prices; (2) Buying of unsold goods from the market; (3) Stabilization of prices; (4) Loans without interest; (and) (5) Loans to be used as working capital."[18]

"How exceedingly modern these words sound in our ears!" writes Hu Shih. . . . "Whereas the land policy of Wang Mang may be described as communistic, his Six State Monopolies . . . may very well be characterized as state socialism. . . . These edicts certainly deserve to be ranked as the earliest conscious statement of the theory of state socialism in the history of the social and political thought of mankind."

"If the *Chou Li* was a product of the Han scholars in the Wang régime," continues Dr. Hu, "it only proves the indebtedness of later generations to the very advanced political and social ideas of Wang Mang's 'New Dynasty' . . ."

"The *Chou Li* has always been a source of inspiration for all political reformers in later ages. It was the basis of the policy of equalization of land attempted by the statesmen of North Wei during the 5th century. It was the political textbook for most of the reformers of the Sung Dynasty and especially for the great statesman, Wang An Shih (A.D. 1021-1086), who wrote a commentary on it and whose land policy and economic reforms were largely based on it."[19, 20]

The scheme failed, Hu Shih believes, because Wang Mang and his "Brain Trust" were too far ahead of their time, did not have enough trained personnel to manage it, and because those who were appointed to carry out its provisions were merchants and capitalists of Lo-yang and Shantung who cared more to make money than to look out for the welfare of the common people.

Wang Mang's power was overthrown when insurgents assassinated him in Chang-An in A.D. 23. "He was the first man to win the empire without an armed revolution. He did it by deliberate planning and by a life-long practice of studied virtue and covert cunning. For nineteen centuries his name has been a curse. He has been called 'Wang Mang the Usurper,' . . . and no historian, however liberal, has ever said a word in his defense, . . . yet he must be regarded as one of the greatest statesmen China has ever produced. In a brief period of thirty years, he left a lasting mark on almost every phase of Chinese civilization."[21] His interregnum gave place to the Later (or Eastern) Han dynasty, which held the throne from A.D. 25 to 220.

Reaction Against Tung Chung-shu and the Yin-Yang School

In the Later Han period, there came a revolt against all the bizarre interpretations that had been made under the influence of the Yin-Yang-and-Five-Elements philosophy. As the texts in current use were considered corrupt, scholars hunted for older versions of the *Classics*. Whereas the *"New Text"* School had favored the *Kung-yang Chuan* as the best commentary on the *Ch'un Ch'iu,* the "Old Text" School preferred the *Tso Chuan*. The "Old Text" School, or the "Old Learning" (*Ku Hsüeh*) has long been associated with the names of Liu Hsin (ca. 46 B.C.-A.D. 23), and, more notably, Yang Hsiung (53 B.C.-A.D. 18) and Wang Ch'ung (A.D. 27-ca. 100).[22] Fung Yu-lan believes the "Old Text" School was formed gradually by several scholars, whose versions of the *Classics* were not forged by one man (Liu Hsin) in the time of Wang Mang, as some, like Hu Shih, have claimed.[23]

In his *Great Mystery* (*T'ai Hsüan*), Yang Hsiung's reflections on the *Lao-tzu* and the *Book of Changes* are clearly colored by *Yin-Yang* ideology. In his other work, the *Model Sayings* (*Fa Yen*), however, he gave final allegiance to the true Confucianism of Confucius and Mencius and endeavored to reconcile the views of Mencius and Hsün Tzu. Like Hsün Tzu, however, he did not stress the *Ch'un Ch'iu* in his thinking, as had Tung Chung-shu and the "New Text" School of *Yin-Yang* theorists.[24] "His chief merit," concludes Fung "is that he, more systematically than most other members of the 'Old Text' School, restored Confucianism from its intermingling with the *Yin-Yang* beliefs," thereby opening the way for its amalgamation with philosophical Taoism in the Wei (A.D. 220-265) and Chin (Tsin) (A.D. 265-419) dynasties.[25]

The "famed skeptic and controversialist," Wang Ch'ung (or Wang Chung-jên), criticized current *Yin-Yang* ideas and went on to make what Warren H. Stuart calls "a pungent attack on superstition and uncriticial attitudes generally."[26] In his *Critical Essays* (*Lun Hêng*), Wang revived Taoist naturalism, with its stress on spontaneity, to combat the "neurological prognostications" of the "New Text" (or *Yin-Yang*) School. He took special exception to their theory that human actions could influence the operations of Heaven, on the ground that it violated the principle of spontaneity in the universe. Whereas other thinkers had usually idealized antiquity, Wang Ch'ung held that history is progressive and that consequently the present age was even better than the past. He argued, likewise, that any historical or scientific statement must be supported by such facts as, interpreted by the intellect, accord with actuality.[27]

Although, like Mencius and Hsün Tzu, Wang Ch'ung believed in the moral responsibility of the human race, he also felt certain that Destiny or Fate brings to men good or bad luck, irrespective of their good or bad qualities of character. Unable to free himself completely from *Yin-Yang* belief in omens, Wang even intimated that men were predestined to be lucky or unlucky and could be caught in the toils of a National Fate over which they had no control.[28] For him, life ends at death and man's soul reverts to the primal ethers from which it came.[29] W. T. Chan, however, urges us not to class Wang Ch'ung as an out-and-out materialist, believing that he "merely elaborated the Taoist doctrine that all things are 'self-transformations.'"[30]

Neo-Taoism in the Period of Disunity

Following Wang Ch'ung, in what has been called the "Period of Disunity" (ca. A.D. 220-620), there came a noticeable revival of Taoism called "Neo-Taoism" or "Mysterious Learning" (*Hsüan Hsüeh*). It took the form of a revolt against static Confucian morals, which amounted to an abandonment of current social conventions and found expression in a materialistic and mechanistic view of life.[31] This was doubtless due to the confusion and suffering caused by a series of invasions that put the Tatars in control of the north while Chinese rulers still held sway at Nanking in the south. At first (in the 3rd century, A.D.), men turned for comfort to Taoism; but later (in the 4th to 6th centuries), they sought help from Buddhism.[32]

Especially notable was the expression of materialism in *The*

Lieh-tzu, traditionally attributed to Lieh Yü-k'ou, a Taoist in the latter part of the Chou dynasty, but now by some considered to be from a later hand, reflecting as it does ideas of the Wei or Chin dynasties. Its main argument contended that changes in Nature and human life were equally mechanistic in their working. There was no freedom observable either in the cosmos or in human activity; nor was life to be thought of as in any way teleological.[33] As a natural corollary, it was argued since life is fleeting and futile, leading only to annihilation, "Let us hasten, therefore, to enjoy our life, for why should we worry about what comes after death!"[34]

In other words, for the writer of the *Lieh-tzu* only pleasure gives value to life. . . . The more the desires are satisfied, the more pleasurable life becomes. The desires which the famous "Yang Chu" chapter (VII) selects as worthy of satisfaction are the bodily pleasures, because these may most readily be gratified. "Each one for himself," as Master Yang said, "is the best policy."[35] By the same logic, immediate pleasures were regarded as highly preferable in order to escape long-term pain and suffering.

Yet life was not to be prolonged; neither was death to be feared. Even fame, power, and profit were not worth the trouble involved in attaining them. Avoid suffering at all costs!, urged Lieh Tzu. Do not sacrifice even a single hair to benefit the world or to gain the whole world. The disorders in the world might be solved if men would eliminate all struggles for power and personal profit.[36]

The urge for freedom of self-realization, however, could not be completely smothered by any kind of fatalistic reasoning. In his *Commentary on the Chuang-tzu,* Hsiang Hsiu (A.D. ca. 221-300) gave a new interpretation of non-activity. For him, it was not "folding one's hands and remaining silent." It was, rather, "embracing the *Tao,* cherishing simplicity, and giving free scope to the inevitable, then (finding that) the world will take care of itself." . . . The Perfect Man is one who is not only interested in the solitary, contemplative life, but also responds to the outside world. As a man of affairs, he may "respond to all things without becoming ensnared by things." Out of his non-activity, he may enter the sphere of activity to tranquilize the world.[37]

In practical agreement with Hsiang Hsiu was his contemporary, Kuo Hsiang (d. ca. A.D. 312), who likewise emphasized the Taoist principles of spontaneous self-transformation, interdependence of all things, the necessity for responding positively to universal flux, and agreement with what is natural. Since the universe is self-existent and all things spontaneously produce themselves, there is, Kuo Hsiang felt, no free will in human affairs; as all things are in flux, social institutions change with times and circumstances. Each man, therefore, must live his own life without regard to what others do or say. Imitation of others, consequently, is to be studiously avoided. By shifting early Taoism's stress on the solitary, contemplative life into a new philosophy of this world and the ordinary people in it, both Hsiang Hsiu and Kuo Hsiang brought neo-Taoism closer to the orthodox Confucian position.[38]

Another Neo-Taoist calling for mention here is Ko Hung (ca. A.D. 268-334), known also as "Pao-p'o Tzu," who made *Tao* the philosophical basis for alchemy's search for the elixir of longevity.[39] Deserving of more space than can be given to him here, is Wang Pi, an early Neo-Taoist, who interpreted Lao Tzu and Chuang Tzu in a way different from the *Huai-nan-tzu,* which was cosmological and positive of actualities. Wang Pi, however, preferred the ontological approach and made no positive assertions about actuality. More significant, perhaps, than any other idea from this period, was Wang Pi's concept of *Tao* (*Li*) as a "transcendental absolute," above all forms yet "uniting all things." This seed-thought will be found again in the thinking of Ch'eng Yi. The above-mentioned Neo-Taoists, and many others like them, kept the torch of true Taoism burning with their emphasis on naturalism and spontaneous transformation.[40]

PART II

THE INFILTRATION OF BUDDHIST PHILOSOPHY

Chapter 7

The Rise of Mahāyāna Buddhism in India

> "The sorrows of men come from their longings and desires. Fear comes from these sorrows. If freedom from desire is attained, what (cause for) grief and fear will remain?" . .
>
> —Gautama Buddha in the
> *Sūtra of Forty-two Sections**

> " (The merits obtained by) my practice of the unique vows . . . from which boundless and marvelous blessedness is produced, are all to be turned over to the beings who are deeply sunken (into the sea of pain and sorrow). Wishing them all to be delivered, I pray that they may soon attain to the country of the Buddha of Infinite Splendour."
>
> —Samantabhadra in the
> *Avataṃsaka Sūtra***

Historic Origins of Buddhism in India

Out of the life-experience and teachings of high-born Prince Siddhartha Gautama of the Śākya clan in the kingdom of Magadha, who lived from 560 or 550 to 477 B.C. sprang the religious philosophy we know as Buddhism. Turning away

* Chu Ch'an translation.
** Pi-cheng Lee translation.

from Hindu polytheism and palace pleasures, Gautama began searching for answers to the riddle of life's sufferings:—disease, old age, and death. He explored Brahminic philosophies, then tried the rigors of asceticism, but all to no avail. Finally, while resting and meditating in a grove of trees, he came to a clear realization that the solution lay in his own mind.

As Noss has well expressed it: "The stumbling block to his (Gautama's) own salvation, and the cause of all human misery, he reasoned, was *desire*—too intense desire—desire for the wrong things, arising out of the carnal will-to-live-and-have. The intensity of his own desire had defeated him. If he could get rid of that desire! If he could, he would know what peace was, the peace the Brahmins sought, the peace of high Nirvāṇa. As this insight with all its implications grew upon him, Gautama realized that *he was, now, without desire;* he felt no sensual yearnings, was purged of 'wrong states of mind.'"

"The Buddhist books say he then passed into an ecstasy having four phases, culminating in 'the state that, knowing neither satisfaction nor dissatisfaction, is the consummate purity of poised equanimity and mindfulness.' It seemed to him 'ignorance was destroyed, knowledge had arisen, darkness was destroyed, light had arisen,' as he sat there 'earnest, strenuous, resolute.' Also he was convinced that 'Rebirth is no more; I have lived the highest life; my task is done; and now for me there is no more of what I have been.' He thus experienced the earthly foretaste of Nirvāṇa. From now on he was the Buddha, the Enlightened One."[1]

From here on, Gautama's life was devoted to sharing his "Dharma" or Law of Salvation—a simple presentation of the gospel of inner cultivation of right spiritual attitudes, coupled with a self-imposed discipline whereby bodily desires would be channeled in the right directions. He omitted any appeal to the gods as currently conceived; definitely rejected philosophical speculations; and spurned all recourse to ancient scriptures, outmoded rituals, or priestly incantations. Convinced that the way of escape from pain and misery lay in the transformation of one's mind and that liberation could come only with a sloughing off of all vain clinging to the things of this life, Buddha set about sharing his discovery with any who would listen to him.

Reduced to its simplest form, the teaching of Buddha has been set forth traditionally in the "Four Noble Truths," leading into the "Eightfold Path" to perfect character or *arhatship,* which in turn gave assurance of entrance into Nirvāṇa at death. In the Four Noble Truths, Gautama taught that life is full of suffering; suffering is caused by passionate desires, lusts, cravings; only as these are obliterated, will suffering cease; such eradication of desire may be accomplished only by following the Eightfold Path of earnest endeavor.

Briefly, these eight steps are *right belief* in and acceptance of the "Four-fold Truth"; *right aspiration* for one's self and for others; *right speech* that harms no-one; *right conduct,* motivated by good-will toward all men; *right means of livelihood,* or earning one's living by honorable means; *right endeavor,* or effort to direct one's energies toward wise ends; *right mindfulness* in choosing topics for thought; and *right meditation,* or concentration to the point of complete absorption in mystic ecstasy.

The way to salvation, in other words, lies through self-abnegation, rigid discipline of mind and body, a consuming love for all living creatures, and the final achievement of that state of consciousness which marks an individual's full preparation for entering the Nirvāṇa of complete selflessness. In this state, the effects of the Law of Cause and Effect (*Karma*) are overcome; the Cycle of Rebirth is broken; and one may rest in the calm assurance of having attained a heavenly bliss that will stretch into all eternity.

Before long, the Buddha found himself surrounded by an increasing number of adherents—men like himself, willing to leave the comforts of home, don the robe of a monk and, with staff in one hand and begging bowl in the other, follow their leader as wandering mendicants. These were soon organized into the "Sangha," or Order of Monks (and later nuns also). With single-hearted purpose, this brotherhood of believers dedicated itself to a life of self-purification, in total loyalty to the Buddha, the Dharma, and the Sangha. It likewise committed itself to a life of poverty whose sole aim was the "evangelization" of India through their dissemination of the doctrine of the Middle Way between extreme asceticism and self-indulgence.

At first, the Order lived under ten simple rules: "Refrain from destroying life; do not take what is not given; abstain from unchastity; do not lie or deceive; abstain from intoxicants; eat moderately and not after noon; do not look on at dancing, singing, or dramatic spectacles; do not affect the use of garlands, scents, unguents, or ornaments; do not use high or broad beds; and do not accept gold or silver."[2] As time went on, many more rules were embodied in the Buddhist book of monastic discipline.

During the Buddha's lifetime, a certain unity prevailed in the Order and in the interpretations given to the Dharma. After his death, however, a need was felt for putting the sayings of Buddha into writing, or at least for getting them fixed in the oral tradition. Hence, about 477 B.C., some five hundred disciples gathered in a First Council at Rajagaha (Rājagṛha) and together "recited and chanted the precepts now found in the Tripiṭaka."

A century later, in the Second Council at Vesali (Vaiśālī), in ca. 383 or 377 B.C.,[3] it was found desirable to make changes to ease the burden of Buddhist discipline. By the time of King Aśoka, who came to power about 273 B.C., Buddhism was flourishing despite the fact that sectarian differences had arisen. Therefore, in a Third Council, at Pātaliputra (modern Patna), in 245 B.C., a serious effort was made to reform and reorganize the Order, after which the more ardent Buddhists embarked upon a program of expansion. Under Aśoka's royal patronage, missionaries were sent south to Ceylon and eastward to Burma, Siam (Thailand), and Cambodia, bearing the orthodox message of original Buddhism.

At this point, the history of Buddhism begins to take on new interest for the student of Chinese Buddhism, because, from the time of Aśoka down to the reign of King Kanishka and the Council of Kashmir in the first century A.D., a process of accretion, from both within and without, had resulted in such radical changes in doctrine and practice as to require a new alignment within the Buddhist fold. Already, in these three centuries, differences of emphasis and interpretation had found expression in two major schools: the southern Theravāda (conservative) and the northern Sarvāstivāda (liberal) Schools.

It was among the northern Sarvāstivādins, who originally called themselves the "Mahāsāṅghikās," or Great Community, that the "Mahāyāna" or Greater Vehicle of "reformed" Buddhism developed. The Theravāda, with its eighteen schools of thought, became known as the "Hīnayāna," or Lesser Vehicle of Buddhist thought. Underlying them all, however, were certain basic Hindu concepts, which were carried over and continued to influence Buddhist thought and practice.[4]

From earliest Vedic times down through the Brahmanic speculations found in the Upanishads, Indian metaphysical thought had concerned itself with the problem of the Primal Origin of Being. On the one hand, it was conceived esoterically as impersonal and supra-ethical, with which the Brahmin had a natural affinity through superior knowledge; on the other hand, it was conceived exoterically as Pure Being manifested in personal form in numberless deities related to this universe and to whom the masses might hope to establish a saving relation.

A second problem—of the reality of the phenomenal universe—assumed no great importance until Brahmanic thinkers became convinced of its unreality. To their way of thinking, since Universal Soul (Brahman-Átman) was the only reality, all else must be illusion, or "Maya." In this form of monistic philosophy, known as *Advaita*, ethics had no great importance;

the only need was to see through the delusion of believing in the material world.[5]

The question of how the individual soul came into being and how it could be re-absorbed into the Universal Soul was more or less side-stepped by the earlier thinkers of Brahmanic mysticism. Later, as the doctrine of reincarnation developed, it held that man's soul must gain some individuality through experience with the consequences of deeds done in this life. As the Brahmins, however, felt that they were only spectators in this human drama, they need have no worries about the material world or empirical issues. On the other hand, ordinary persons felt it necessary to obtain some liberation from the world of sense, if not in reabsorption into the Universal Soul (vouchsafed only to Brahmins), at least in some kalpa-long state of blissful existence as individual souls.[6]

As for the relation of soul to body, Brahmanic teaching held that the soul was untouched and unaffected by its bodily manifestation, thus ruling out the validity of ethics. Believers in the doctrine of reincarnation felt that soul must in some way share in and have its destiny influenced by actions done in the body; otherwise, there is no meaning to *Karma.* Both Hindu and Buddhist minds, therefore, were caught up in this basic conflict between theoretical "world-and-life-negation" and an insistent, practical "world-and-life-affirmation."

Along with their aloofness to this illusory world, the Brahmins paralogistically insisted on obedience to caste rules as "action of a higher order." Hence they found a real place for ethical considerations in their plan to work as priests for the first half of their life, anticipating complete world-renunciation during the second half. Yet, to be logical, how could actions aimed at fulfilling caste obligations stand in the face of an insistent demand for a self-submerging world-renunciation aimed at deliverance from reincarnation or mystic union with the Brahman?

Owing to a feeling, apparently, that "a foolish consistency is the hobgoblin of little minds," caste regulations as a practical means of attaining world-renunciation finally won the day over a theoretical world-and-life-negation (as may be seen in the *Bhagavad-Gītā*).

Influence of the Sāṃkhya Philosophy

Another, and very ancient, line of reasoning known as the Sāṃkhya,[7]—a system of dualism growing up parallel to Brahmanic monism—later had great influence in Buddhist and Jaina circles, as well as in the popular Hinduism reflected in the *Mahābhārata* and *Rāmāyana*. This philosophy taught that soul-substance and fine matter subsist eternally; that matter is composed of three strands or *guṇas*: one of light and goodness; one of endless activity; and one of darkness and delusion. Immaterial souls entering into connection with matter soon become conscious of their complete independence of matter (body). The world of humans, therefore, consists of countless soul-entities united to matter-entities which at death will fall apart. That which is reincarnated, however, is only the highest *guṇa* or imperishable strand of the former soul-matter union, for it is the carrier of *Karma,* which determines the direction—whether up or down—of its rebirth. After all immaterial souls are freed from their connection with matter, then will come the consummation of the age and redemption of the world. Both soul- and matter-entities will then have returned to their primal, original state of rest, and a new world-period will begin.[8]

Other Influences and Developments

Influencing the growing Mahāyāna Buddhism perhaps even more than Hindu philosophy in the period under discussion, was the increasing spread of *bhakti* religion in the form of self-devotion to a particular god, such as Vishnu or Śiva, or the avatars of Vishnu—Krishna and Rama—coupled with a certain emphasis on ethical service as an expression of devotional mysticism. In addition to the *bhakti* movement in southern and central India, there appeared in the north-west in the second and first centuries B.C. the influence of Greco-Bactrian culture, which undoubtedly played a part in the growth of theistic Buddhism, as well as in the development of Buddhist art and architecture at Gandhara.

After the overrunning of Afghanistan and the Pānjab (Punjab) by the Kushans (*Yüeh Chi,* or White Huns) in the first century A.D. and the establishment of their capital at Pesháwar (guarding the approach to the Khyber Pass), King Kanishka became the patron of Buddhism. Very soon, about A.D. 70, he is said to have called the Council of Kashmir at Jālandhara. Here, at this fourth Buddhist council, attended by some 500 *Arhats* (Arahants) led by the conservative, southern school of Theravādins and as many *Bodhisattvas* led by the liberal, northern school of Sarvāstivādins, an attempt was made to find a core of beliefs on which they could agree. As a result, the *Tripiṭaka* (Three Baskets of the Dharma) was re-affirmed and eight commentaries on it composed, which were placed in the hands of the great scholar, Aśvaghoṣa, to be put into good literary form.[9]

The Widening Rift Between Mahāyāna and Hīnayāna

From this time on, the rift between northern and southern Buddhists widened until the Sangha was split into what came to be known as the *Mahāyāna* (Greater Vehicle) and *Hīnayāna* (Lesser Vehicle), respectively. The Hīnayānists, though yielding to the pressure for deification of their earthly Teacher as *Gotama Buddha* (Chinese: *Śākyamuni Fo*), claimed they were remaining closer to the original teaching and discipline of the one Buddha, whom they were content to worship and whose doctrine they were committed to propagate. Ultimately, Hīnayāna Buddhism became the dominant religion of Ceylon and the "Southern Tier" of Asian countries to the east and southeast (Burma, Thailand, Cambodia, and the Island of Bali).

The Mahāyānists, on the other hand, in the following centuries, pushed out of India through Nepal and Kashmir into Tibet and Turkestan, and finally into China, Mongolia, Korea, and Japan, with a reformed Buddhism which, nevertheless, claimed to be based on the original teachings of Buddha. While still in northern India or Nepal, Mahāyāna Buddhist circles had evolved a pantheon of this order:—the Eternal Absolute, the Primal Creative Spirit of the Universe (corresponding to the Hindu Brahman-Átman) they called *Adibuddha*. From him or by his word there came into being the five Eternal Dhyāni-Buddhas of Contemplation (ruling five aeons and five universes), of which the fourth is *Amitābha,* Buddha of Immeasurable Light, under whose benign rule this present world exists. From each of these Dhyāni-Buddhas sprang by spontaneous generation five spiritual sons—the Mānushi-Buddhas, active in the creation of worlds and the beings who inhabit them. The fourth, associated with this earth, is *Gautama-Buddha* (to the Chinese: Śākyamuni, Lord of the Śākya Clan), who, having known the sufferings of men by experience and having attained the enlightenment of Buddhahood, is the better able to save all sentient beings.

Each Dhyāni-Buddha was provided with an active reflex or creative agent, Amitābha's being the Bodhisattva *Avalokiteśvara* (Avalokita), the "Lord Looking Down From Above," who represents the infinite mercy or compassion of the contemplative Amitābha reposing in his beautiful Paradise-of-the-Western-Quarter (of the Universe). Strangely enough, in Tibetan Buddhism, Avalokita came to receive greater veneration than Amitābha; while, on the other hand, in Chinese Buddhism, Amitābha became more popular than Śākyamuni or Gautama-Buddha. As we shall have occasion to notice, the Mahāyāna pantheon later was enlarged still more to include other Buddhas and Bodhisattvas functioning in countless "Buddha-fields," yet doing the will of the great *Tathāgata* (Śākyamuni Buddha), who in popular thought replaced Adibuddha as the primordial *Chen Ju,* or Universal "Thusness."

Thus, by a slow and subtle process of intellectual change, Mahāyāna Buddhists had set their Founder in a framework of Heavenly Buddhas and Bodhisattvas; had found escape from Brahmanic pessimism in an optimistic faith in many Buddhas; had gained a vastly expanded world-view and become possessed of a vastly increased store of sacred literature with which to propagate the faith. For them and their converts in East Asia, several roads to salvation (Chinese: *fa-men,* literally "law-gates") were now open: holiness through good works (*karman*); enlightenment through knowledge or wisdom (*jñāna*); enlightenment through meditation (*yoga*); and salvation or release through surrender and devotion (*bhakti*).[10]

The pivotal issue upon which Mahāyāna swung away from Hīnayāna Buddhism was the motive and method of the quest for salvation. Was it to be merely saving one's self by one's own effort or a saving of one's self and others by appeal to and trust in the power of Another, a savior-god, and oneself becoming a self-denying savior of men? The older *Arhat* (Chinese: *Lohan)* ideal of detachment or passionlessness, had changed to the *Bodhisattva* (Chinese: *P'u-t'i-sa-to,* abbreviated to "*P'u-sa*") ideal of kindness, compassion, forgiving love, and long-suffering service. Whether or not this change could in any way have been due to outside influences coming from contacts with Hellenistic mysteries or Iranian Mithraism and Zoroastrianism, is still a matter of conjecture. The suggestion has come from more than one source that, in the centuries immediately following the time of Kanishka (roughly from A.D. 100 to 500), certain elements from Manichaeism and Nestorianism could have crept into Mahāyāna Buddhism on its way through Central Asia. Herbert A. Giles, however, has expressed the opinion that Mahāyāna Buddhism was well on its way before the writings of Irenaeus and Tertullian became known toward the end of the second century A.D., thus ruling out Christian influence.[11]

The Crystallization of Mahāyānist Thought in India

Whatever the extraneous influences may have been, certain it is that in north and north-west India Mahāyāna Buddhism developed its own strong thinkers, of whom three may be mentioned whose writings later became extremely influential in the development of Chinese Buddhism. The first of these, *Aśvaghoṣa* (Chinese: *Ma-ming),* living at the end of the first and into the early part of the second century A.D., wrote a Life of Buddha in metrical form, known as the *Buddha Carita Kavya* (*Fu Pên Hsing Ching*), which was translated by Gobharana, one of the earliest Buddhist missionaries to China, and again by Dharmarakṣa about A.D. 414-421. Aśvaghoṣa is also credited with the authorship of the famous *Awakening of Faith in the Mahāyāna (Mahāyāna-śraddhotpādaśāstra,* or *Ch'i Hsin Lun*), translated into Chinese by Paramartha in A.D. 553. Mahāyānists generally revere Aśvaghoṣa as the first of their Indian patriarchs.[12] It was through him that the doctrines of '*ālaya*-consciousness' and 'Thusness' gained credence among Buddhist believers.[13]

Following Aśvaghoṣa as the second Buddhist patriarch, *Nāgārjuna* (*Lung-shu*) of South India, in the latter half of the second century, A.D., gave great impetus to Mahāyāna metaphysics by his scholarly commentaries:—one on the *Avataṃsaka Sūtra* and one on the *Prajñā-pāramitā Sūtra,* the latter known as the *Mahā-prajñā-pāramitā Sūtra* (Chinese: *Mo-Ko Pan-Jo Po-Lo-Mi-To Ching,* or in simpler form the *Ta Pan-Jo Ching*). As the reputed founder of the Mādhyamika (Middle Doctrine) School, Nāgārjuna created a revolution in Buddhist thought, for, as T. R. V. Murti has stated, it was on the Mādhyamika doctrine of *śūnyatā* (emptiness) that all subsequent Buddhist thought turned.[14] Moreover, the later Yogācāra-Vijñānavāda Idealism of Vasubandhu "explicitly accepts the *śūnyatā* of the Mādhyamika and gives it an idealistic turn."[15]

To follow Murti's appraisal, as given in his *The Central Philosophy of Buddhism,* we find him saying that metaphysically speaking, the Mādhyamika dialectic represented a change from pluralism to absolutism (or unity underlying all discrete entities). Epistemologically, it was shifting from empiricism and dogmatism to dialectical criticism. Ethically, it revealed a change from the ideal of self-salvation to the ideal of universal salvation for all beings or from the *arhat* to the *bodhisattva* ideal. Religiously, it represented a movement away from the original Hīnayānist reverence for a human teacher to the Mahāyānist devotion to a transcendent Being—the Buddha as the essence of all Being (in three Bodies).[16]

The Mādhyamika doctrine of *śūnyatā,* according to Murti, is neither nihilism nor positivism—but an absolutism which conceives of the Absolute as both transcendent and immanent. The Mādhyamika rejects the pretensions of any dogmatic metaphysics that wrongly understands the transcendent in empirical modes or extends to the unconditioned those categories of thought that are valid only within the realm of phenomena.[17]

Furthermore, the Mādhyamika thinks of the Absolute as Prajñā-Pāramitā or Ultimate Truth discerned only by intellectual intuition. Its emphasis is on the epistemological (attitude of knowing) rather than on the ontological (or approach to the thing known). Others criticize Mādhyamika as having a "no-doctrine" attitude which they interpret as a "no-reality" theory of appearance. But in fact, the Mādhyamika doesn't deny the real, only doctrines about the real. . . . "When the entire conceptual activity of Reason is dissolved by criticism, there is Prajñā-Pāramitā." Freedom comes with "insight into the nature of the real"; it is gained by "the dissolution of the conceptual function of the mind."[18]

And finally, Murti feels that the Mādhyamika discipline leads directly to the apprehension of *Tathāgata* as the personified embodiment of Prajñā-Pāramitā. Conversely, Prajñā-Pāramitā (Absolute) is the source or matrix from which many Tathāgatas (Buddhas) have sprung. Without transcendent Being, there can be no religious worship. Mādhyamika, therefore, is also a religion of the Triple Body of Buddha (Trikaya).[19]

As Sir Sarvepalli Radhakrishnan in his *India and China* has pointed out, what Nāgārjuna introduced into his Mādhyamika School of Mahāyānist thought was simply a large admixture of Hindu *Advaita Vedanta* philosophy.[20] Quoting Nāgārjuna's statement: "There is no production, no destruction, no annihilation, no persistence, no unity, no plurality, no coming in and no going forth," he goes on to interpret him as follows:

"This view points out that there can be no predication of existence or non-existence of what is beyond the world of phenomena. It also shows that things of the empirical world are self-discrepant and therefore not ultimately real. They have only a relative being. . . . Nāgārjuna says that the Buddha speaks of two kinds of truth, the one absolute . . . the other relative. . . . As the Advaita Vedanta argues, the world of experience is neither one with nor different from the world of reality. It is wrong to hold that the Mādhyamika system looks upon the world as utterly non-existent. Its very name indicates that it is the school of the middle way.[21] The world is neither fundamental being nor utter non-being. Objects have no absolute or independent being, only the Absolute has that kind of reality; nor are they absolutely non-existent. They exist by virtue of their relations."

"By a subtle and bold dialectical criticism of the categories of experience, Nāgārjuna attempts to prove that we do not attain any certainty of knowledge. Yet we have an interior vision of reality—luminous, unfathomable, of ineffable depth and infinite transparency. *The intuition of the essential nature, prajñā-pāramitā, the perfection of wisdom, is attainable.* The world of phenomena is different from it in one sense and one with it in another. In this position, which is that of Saṃkara . . . the Mādhyamika system is in agreement with the teaching of the Buddha. 'That things have being is one extreme; that things have no being is the other extreme. These extremes have been avoided by the Tathāgata and it is the middle doctrine that he teaches.'"

Despite his insistence that the Absolute alone is real, Nāgārjuna, along with other Mahāyānists, held that "theism along with many incarnations has validity in the world of ordinary experience or relative truth." He saw no inconsistency in advocating the worship of Amitābha, for instance, since in the Mahāyāna system the hope of rebirth in the Western Paradise replaces the Hīnayāna aspiration for Nirvāṇa.[22]

Nāgārjuna's "Mādhyamika Wing" (of Mahāyāna), with its dialectic theories of the Void and of non-conceptual knowledge, was later transplanted by Kumārajīva and continued for a time to grow on Chinese soil as the San-Lun Tsung, or Three Śāstras School (q.v.). We turn now to gain some understanding of Vasubandhu's "Yogācāra Wing," which was transplanted by Hsüan-tsang into China and continued to flourish as the Wei-Shih Tsung, or Mere Ideation School (q.v.).

The third great Mahāyānist writer was Vasubandhu *(Shih-ch'in)* of North India (ca. A.D. 280-360), whose older brother Asaṅga, had founded the Yogācāra School of Mahāyānist thought, known also as *Vijñānavāda.* At first, Vasubandhu (recognized as the 20th patriarch in the Buddhist Order) wrote the *Abhidharma-kośa-śāstra,* a general exposition of the essays in the *Abhidharma-Piṭaka,* as his contribution to Hīnayāna realism. Then, after aligning himself with his brother's point of view, he wrote as a contribution to Mahāyāna idealism the *Viṁśātikā,* or *Completion of the Doctrine of Mere Ideation* (*Ch'êng Wei-Shih Lun)* containing ideas culled from older sutras, more especially the *Laṅkāvatāra Sūtra.*[23] He is likewise credited with commentaries on the *Mahāyāna-saṁparigrapha* and the *Mādhyānta-Vibhaṅga-śāstra.*

In the Mādhyamika statement that the Absolute may be "transcendent to thought" but "thoroughly immanent in experience," the Yogācāra school detected a duality of subject and object which it rejected as unreal. For the Vijñānavādins, the "unreal phenomenal world takes on substance when identified with Pure Consciousness which is devoid of duality." Holding that the ultimate reality of all things is consciousness *(vijñāna)* only, they argued that *"dharmas* (elements of existence) were neither to be considered real (as Hīnayānists say) or void (as Mādhyamikas say) but as representations in consciousness only, or as functionings of the mind rather than independent entities."[24] While consciousness may exist apart from objects, objects exist only as products of consciousness.

Vasubandhu conceived of phenomena as "thought-relations" or "thought-events," and set forth his analysis of the mind and its functioning in this fashion: Consciousness (*vijñāna*) operates at four levels or moves through four stages, we might say. At the top of the ideation-pyramid, the (eighth) "ideation-store" consciousness (*ālaya-vijñāna*), like an "Unconscious Mind," deep and potential, is perpetually producing "appearances" or "external manifestations" which are being constantly "perfumed" by its stored "seeds," which are both "results of previous actions and potentialities of future actions." All the other stages of consciousness are simply developments of this basic "receptable-consciousness" which is the "receiver of all effects, the source of all causes." Here takes place the "first transformation" of all ideation. At the next level, the (seventh) "mind-consciousness" categorizes and makes decisions in a self-centered process of intellection that is deeply affected by evil self-interest. Here takes place the "second transformation"—an activity of the mind "by which the potential is actualized and experience is synthesized." At a third level or stage, the (sixth) "co-ordinating consciousness" is the sense-center which forms conceptions out of the data furnished by the five senses. Here takes place the "third transformation" (including introspection), whereby objects in the external world are discriminated and evaluated. And finally, the processes of ideation at their lowest level are wrought by the (five) sense-consciousnesses (sight, hearing, smelling, tasting, and touch). Here takes place a "fourth transformation" whereby the external object becomes a projection of consciousness in all its functional modes. As T. R. V. Murti puts it: "Not only is the object unreal; even the idea is unreal so far as it is dependent on the object for its determinate character."[25]

As W. T. Chan summarizes it: "Thus all *dharmas* and the self are used in a two-way traffic of understanding channeled from and returning to the *ālaya*-consciousness . . . so named because it stores the 'seeds' or effects of good and evil deeds which exist from time immemorial and become the energy to produce manifestations." . . . In other words, Perfect Wisdom is attained in four stages: the wisdom of action (in the first five consciousnesses); the wisdom of insight (in the sixth consciousness); the wisdom of equanimity (in the seventh consciousness); and the wisdom of magnificent mirror (in the eighth or *ālaya*-consciousness). Only thus may the *śrāvaka* attain the four-fold Wisdom of the Buddha, after he has passed through the ten stages of the *Pāramitās*.[26]

In his *Indian Philosophy,* Sir Sarvepalli Radhakrishnan notes briefly that the Vijñānavāda represents the idealistic views of the Yogācāra School, and goes on to state: "The school is called Yogācāra, since it declares that the absolute truth or *bodhi* manifested in the Buddhas is attainable only by those who practice *yoga*. . . . In other words, Yogācāra stresses the practical side of the philosophy, while Vijñānavāda brings out its speculative features."[27] In short, by formulating an idealism that reduced all reality to thought-relations, Vasubandhu overcame the duality implicit in Nāgārjuna's *śūnyatā*. For this reason, he may be said to have adopted the correct "Middle Way" (*Mādhyama*) between the two extremes of realism and nihilism, and made "the last comprehensive synthesis of Buddhist doctrines."[28]

Chapter 8

The Inner Development of Chinese Buddhism

"Subhuti, whoso perceives that all material characteristics are in fact no characteristics, perceives the Tathāgata."

—Buddha in the *Diamond Sūtra**

"A gleam of enlightenment is enough to make any living being the equal of Buddha."

—Hui Neng in the *Sūtra of Wei Lang***

The Transplanting of Buddhism into China

While the writers mentioned in the preceding chapter never made the long journey to China in the flesh, other ardent Mahāyānists who had caught their spirit endured the hardships of travel by land or sea to carry their philosophy of life to the peoples of the Far East. In the beginning, the Indian monks were intent on propagating Buddhism as a whole rather than any particular sect, but their teachings were largely determined by the sutras which they carried with them.

Although known in China considerably earlier, the transplantation of Buddhism to Chinese soil dates by tradition from the return of a group of Chinese emissaries from India to China in A.D. 67, accompanied by two Indian monks—Kāśyapa-mātaṅga (Shê Mo-teng) and Gobharana (Chu Fu-lan). These men brought to the court of Han Ming-ti (ruling A.D. 58-75) an

* A. F. Price translation.
** Wong Mou-lam translation.

image of the Buddha as a gift and many sacred sutras to be translated into Chinese. Among these, the only two of which scholars are reasonably sure were Aśvaghoṣa's *Life of the Buddha* and *The Sūtra of Forty-two Sections.*

It was, however, not until the fourth or fifth centuries A.D.* that Chinese Buddhism began to show the effect of those divisive differences of emphasis which, from the sixth to the tenth centuries were crystallized as definite sects with particular names. In the post-Han "Period of Disunity," more especially during the troubled Chin (Tsin) dynasty and after an incursion of Toba Tatars had forced a division into "North and South" in A.D. 420, court and people turned to Neo-Taoism and then to Buddhism for guidance and comfort. Both before and after the reunification of the country under the Sui dynasty (A.D. 589-618), Buddhism became a strong rival to Taoism and Confucianism.

Down into the early part of the Sung dynasty (*circa* A.D. 1000), Buddhism "absorbed the best energies of most philosophically minded Chinese, while the native philosophies suffered comparative eclipse."[1] Arthur F. Wright notes that Buddhism gained favor among the barbarian rulers from the steppes, who wanted some cultural framework for arbitrary rule and favored Buddhism as more acceptable because it was non-Chinese in ritual and ethic.[2] In this period arose eight major sects, or rather schools of Buddhist thought and practice, which had survival value. While the lines of demarcation are not always clearly marked, our effort in the succeeding discussions will be to discover the variations in the philosophies of the different sects, as far as possible in the general order of their emergence, and to indicate the strength of their position within the Buddhist fold.

As will be seen, two minor schools—Abhidharma-Kośa and Satyasiddhi—as well as one major school, the Vinaya, may be

---

* In 363 A.D., Shih Chi Lung, King of Chao, gave permission for Chinese to enter the Buddhist Order, thus opening the way for it to become self-governing and self-propagating. (Cf. Pratt: *Pilgrimage of Buddhism,* p. 276).

called strictly Hīnayāna; of the other seven major Mahāyāna schools, four stemmed more directly from their Indian prototypes (Mādhyamika, Meditation, Yogācāra, and Mystical), while three—the Pure Land, T'ien-T'ai, and Hua-Yen—grew up entirely on Chinese soil.[3] Yet it should be remembered that all of these schools drew their initial inspiration from Indian sutras translated into Chinese and in several cases were aided by Indian monks who had come as missionaries of the gospel of the Buddha.

Mahāyānists generally promulgated certain ideas brought from India to China; such as, the doctrine of the Void (*śūnyatā*), the illusoriness and impermanence of the self (*non-ātman*), cause and effect (*karma*), the causes of dependence (*nidānas*), the five aggregates (*skandhas*), Suchness or Thusness (*Bhūtatathatā*), the offer of universal salvation by faith, by vows, by abstinence, by gradual or sudden enlightenment (*bodhi*),* the attainment of transcendental wisdom (*prajñāpāramitā*), concentrated contemplation (*dhyāna*), all of which called for the coining of new Chinese terms to make adequate translations.[4] To these were added other great tenets; such as, belief in the universality of the Buddha-nature in human beings, belief in a continued existence in paradise, the transfer of merits by masses for the dead, the prohibition of meat-eating, and such ethical ideals as tolerance, striving for perfection, compassion for and service to others.[5]

Different schools stressed the particular ideas which appealed to them most, and we shall discuss them in the following order:—(1) the Pure Land School (*Ching-T'u Tsung*); (2) the Mādhyamika School (*San-Lun Tsung*); (3) the Meditation School (*Ch'an Tsung*)—(together with brief mention of certain minor sects which were ultimately absorbed either by the Ch'an or by some other school); (4) the Harmonizing

---

* Arthur F. Wright calls attention to Chu Tao-shêng (A.D. 365-434) as probably the earliest Buddhist to bring out the contrast between "gradualism" (gradual enlightenment) as similar to Confucian thought and "subitism" (sudden enlightenment) as similar to the Taoist point of view. (Cf. *Buddhism in Chinese History*, p. 47.)

School (*T'ien-T'ai Tsung*); (5) the Discipline School (Vinaya or *Lü Tsung*); (6) the Mere Ideation School (*Wei-Shih Tsung*); (7) the Wreath School (Avataṃsaka or *Hua-Yen Tsung*); (8) the Esoteric (Mystical) or True-Word School (Tantrayāna, or *Chen-Yen Tsung*). As we proceed, it will be well to bear in mind the fact that Buddhism is both philosophy and religion. As philosophy, it is "a matrix of systems rather than a unitary system of thought";[6] as a religion it offers an otherworldly world-view and universal salvation to all sentient beings.

1. *The Philosophy of the Pure Land School (Ching-T'u Tsung)*

The Founder and Favorite Sutras of the School

By the fourth century A.D., the teachings of the many different Buddhist scriptures, translated into Chinese, had permeated China sufficiently to familiarize the minds of Taoists and Confucianists alike with the varying roads to salvation which Buddhism offered. It remained for a Taoist monk of Shansi Province, named Hui Yüan (ca. 334-416), with the aid of Buddhayaśas (ca. 380) and Buddhabhadra (ca. 410), to promote the new religious philosophy of "salvation by faith" in the grace of Amitābha (*O-mi-t'o Fo*). Into Hui Yüan's hands had been placed certain scriptures which set forth very attractively the power of Amitābha to save all mortals to his glorious "Pure Land" in the Western Quarter of the Heavens.

As W. T. Chan has pointed out, the Chinese mind saw in the Pure Land offer of rebirth in the Western Paradise an extension of the age-old Taoist search for "everlasting life on earth" and the Confucian ideal of sageliness or perfection of character and therefore gave it hospitable reception as something not too foreign to their humanistic way of thought.[7]

Settling finally in the Lu-Feng Monastery in Hupeh, noted for ponds of white lotus blossoms, Hui Yüan attracted many pilgrims who gave to his school the name of "White Lotus Religion" (*Pai Lien Chiao*). Later, in the fourteenth century, when a secret political society adopted the same name, the White Lotus School, to avoid suspicion on the part of governmental authorities, changed its name to "Pure Land School" (*Ching T'u Tsung*).

Hui Yüan and his successors drew their inspiration largely from the *Greater Sukhāvatī-Vyūha Sūtra* (*Wu-Liang-Shou Ching*), with its vivid descriptions of the "Pure Land," as well as from the *Smaller Sukhāvatī-Vyūha Sūtra* often called the *Amitābha Sūtra* (*O-Mi-T'o Ching*)—a condensation teaching the infinite compassion of Amitābha and the way to reach his Land of Perfect Bliss. These sutras had been translated as early as A.D. 148-150, probably by the Parthian Prince Anshikao and his Indo-Scythian colleague Lokaraksha, both of whom were among the earlier missionaries to China.[8] Another of their translations became one of the favorite Pure Land sutras, namely the *Amitāyur-dhyāna Sūtra* (*Kuan Wu-Liang-Shou Ching*) or "Reflections on the Buddha of Immeasurable Longevity."[9] If the *Awakening of Faith* had been put into Chinese before this time, as would have been quite likely, the translation was lost. Not until A.D. 553, over a century after Kumārajīva, the greatest of the translators, did Paramartha's version of the *Mahāyānaśraddhotpāda-śāstra* appear as the *Ch'i Hsin Lun* (*Awakening of Faith*), which became standard for Buddhists down to the present day.

Chief Tenets of the Pure Land School

While it is true that the Pure Land School is the least philosophical of all Buddhist schools, yet certain tenets were basic in Hui Yüan's mind:—a concept of Buddha's infinity, a firm belief in the indestructibility of the human soul, a belief in *karma* or retribution, and a strong belief in the universality of the Buddha-nature in all creatures.[10]

Briefly, the Pure Land School teaches that a devotee may

hope to attain salvation by the simple act of faith in the saving power of Amitābha (*O-mi-t'o Fo*), Buddha-Lord of the Western Paradise (Pure Land). In this he will be aided by the ministrations of Amitābha's two angel-powers: the Bodhisattva Avalokita (*Kuan-yin*) (best known as the "Goddess of Mercy"), representing Amitābha's heart of infinite compassion, and Mahāsthāma (*Ta-shih-chih*), representing Amitābha's all-wise omnipotence, who has broken the power of the law of Cause and Effect (*Karma*).

At death, the faithful believer will be transported over the sea of death, bridging the dangers of hell, to be re-born within a lotus-bud in the Pure Land of Bliss. There, by continued instruction and growth, his spirit is prepared for eventual entry into the state of Buddhahood or Complete Enlightenment (Nirvāṇa). As the *Awakening of Faith* says:

"First consider those who . . . desire to get right faith, but are timid and weak. . . . Thus they fear they cannot attain to this perfect faith and they have a mind to renounce the search after it.

"These should know that *Ju-lai* (*Tathāgata-Buddha*) has most excellent means for strengthening their faith. By having the mind set only on the things of Buddha and being constantly with him far from all evil, one attains this end.

"As the sutra says, If a man sets his mind to think only of Amitābha Buddha, who is in the happiest realm of the West, and if his good deeds are in the right direction, and if he desires to be born in the happy paradise, he will then be born there, and as he is always in the presence of Buddha, he will never fall back."[11]

"We have here all the ingredients of a (Hindu) *bhakti* religion," comments Dr. Radhakrishnan. "Amitābha draws men to himself and sent his son Gautama to lead men to him. He is ever accessible through the holy spirit of Avalokiteśvara. Here is salvation by faith. If we contemplate the glorious figure of Amitābha in the last moments, we reach his heaven."

In fact, Radhakrishnan sees much in Mahāyāna Buddhism

that reveals its inner relation to Hinduism. "The Mahāyāna teaching is in consonance with the spirit of Indian religion in that it is large enough to include an endless variety of symbolic representations of the Absolute. . . . The Mahāyāna system with its Advaita metaphysics and theistic religion is akin to the teaching of the *Bhagavadgītā* in many of its principles and their detailed application."[12]

Where the Ch'an or Meditation School's 'enlightenment,' offering salvation by self-effort directed toward the liberation of the mind from all entangling alliances with the phenomenal world, held great appeal for the Confucian élite, the Pure Land School's 'salvation by faith alone' appealed to the imagination of the masses. Salvation by *bhakti* (devotion) was decidedly easier than by *karman* (good works), or by *jñāna* (wisdom by study of scriptures), or by wearisome *yoga* (meditation), or by any metaphysical speculations. While accepting orthodox Buddhist teaching as to the illusory character of this life and the need for surmounting its miseries, the Pure Land masters turned the minds of their adherents to those sutras that promised help from infinitely superior beings—the Bodhisattvas and the Buddhas—in reaching the Other Shore, instead of depending upon one's own meager resources.

In the *Essence of Wisdom Sūtra,* for example, a devotee could read of how

"The Bodhisattva Avalokiteśvara, while meditating deeply on the 'Perfect Wisdom', . . . perceived clearly that the five constituents of being are all *śūnya* (void or empty). . . . They neither come into existence nor pass out of existence. . . .

"Because there is no attainment in knowledge, the Bodhisattvas rely on the 'Perfect Wisdom,' by means of which . . . they do away entirely with . . . perverse, dreamy thoughts, and finally reach Nirvāṇa.

"So we know that the 'Perfect Wisdom,' by means of which one reaches the Other Shore, is a great divine formula . . . which can remove all kinds of suffering. . . . The formula is said thus:

'Ferry, ferry, ferry over to the Other Shore!
Ferry all beings over to the Other Shore!
Perfect Wisdom! Hail!' "[13]

By repeating this formula, the devotee could avail himself of the Perfect Wisdom of the Bodhisattva to reach the haven of Nirvāṇa's shore. He might even aspire to be a Bodhisattva himself, after reading in *The Mahavastu* the wonderful qualities of those who have set their feet on the Way to Buddhahood:

"They are Bodhisattvas who . . . have won the mastery over *karma,* and made their deeds renowned through their accumulation of merit. . . . They are endowed here in this world with the profound attributes of a Buddha. . . .

"They are gifted with insight . . . and skilled in teaching. . . . They are skilled in bringing solace to those in trouble. . . . They know how to win the affection of all creatures. . . . They win converts by . . . means of sympathetic appeal. . . ."[14]

Present-day Propagation of the Pure Land Faith

Four scriptures are used in temple rituals, in monastic meditations, and in the private devotions of lay men and women:—(a) The *Avataṃsaka Sūtra (Hua Yen Ching)* has been called "the greatest Buddhist Scripture" (literally, "the flower-embellished Scripture"). A recent devotee has translated from the thirty-ninth chapter "The (Sixty-two) Vows of Samantabhadra" (P'u Hsien), because they offer spiritual encouragement to all Buddhist aspirants.

These vows open with *adoration* to all "lion-hearted" Bodhisattvas who have become Buddhas and give special homage to Tathāgata Buddha. This is followed by *repentance* for past evil (sec. 8) and by a vow to enter the Path Toward Bodhi (sec. 14). Along this path there is much to be done; for example, its *activities* include preaching to all men (sec. 18), cultivation of the bodhi-heart by following the six pāramitās* (sec. 19), and freeing oneself from worldly cares (sec. 20). Gradually, the "Would-be Buddha" acquires such *attainments* as the power . . . to penetrate the universal . . . to show great compassion . . . the power . . . which subdues all maras, until he can exclaim: "I have cultivated merits and wisdom boundlessly and thereby gained an inexhaustible store of equanimity in meditation . . . and emancipation from bondage" (sec. 27). Finally, at the end of the Path, appears the *Vision of the Goal,* for nothing can now prevent his entrance into the peaceful and happy world of *Amitābha's Heaven.* Convinced that his "vows are eternal, unless the infinitude of the universe comes to an end," Samantabhadra turns and offers salvation to all who will recite his vows and follow in his footsteps.[15]

(b) The *Aparimitāyur Sūtra* is also thought to have great converting power because of the (forty-eight) "Vows of Dharmakara" contained therein. Their faith-sustaining appeal may be even stronger than the Vows of Samantabhadra, because it is written that Dharmakara by faith became the Buddha Amitābha, whereas there is no record of Samantabhadra's actually attaining Buddhahood. The tenor of these vows may be gathered from the following selected passages:—

(Sec. 18) "Provided I become a Buddha, if the beings of the ten quarters, after having heard my name and thus awakened their faith and aspiration of rebirth in that country of mine, are not destined to be born there . . . then may I not attain enlightenment.

(Sec. 1, 2) (Sec. 16) ". . . there should be no evil (hell, animal or hungry-ghost state) in that country of mine; even its name (should be) unknown. . . . If in that Buddha-country of mine the beings who are born there should pass away into the three evil realms, then may I not attain enlightenment.

---

* (Note by translator P. C. Lee) :—"*Pāramitās* are the six stages of study by Bodhisattvas, or Gates of Enlightenment: (1) Charity or almsgiving, (2) Observance of Precepts, (3) Patient resignation, (4) Skillful means of study, (5) Meditation in equanimity, and (6) from which Wisdom follows."

(Sec. 32) "If . . . there should not be (a heaven full of) magnificent palaces (and all sensuous enjoyments, such as) lakes . . . streams . . . trees . . . jewels . . . (and) perfumes . . . (whereby the Bodhisattvas shall) have their minds directed to Bodhi, then may I not attain enlightenment."[16]

(c) As a third source of inspiration for devotees of the Pure Land School, the *Amitāyur Dhyāna Sūtra* consists of sixteen meditations on the Buddha Amitāyur (another name for Amitābha, or *O-mi-t'o*) and on his two active reflexes the Bodhisattvas Avalokiteśvara (*Kuan-yin*) and Mahāsthāma (*Ta-shih-chih*). There are also meditations on the glorious excellencies of the Pure Land (Sukhāvati, or *Hsi T'ien*—the Western Paradise). In the *Fourteenth Meditation,* Buddha thus addresses Ananda and Vaidehī (Queen of Magadha) :—

"The highest existence of the Superior Grade (in *Hsi T'ien*) is attainable . . . by those who possess the compassionate heart, refrain from taking life . . . recite the sutras of Mahāyāna . . . practice the 'Six-fold Thought'—of the Buddha . . . the Dharma . . . the Sangha . . . the Precepts . . . Almsgiving . . . (and) Nirvāṇa—and direct such meritorious thoughts toward the desire of re-birth in that (Buddha) country. . . ."

"In the twinkling of an eye (the devotee) will perceive himself . . . born in that country and will see the glorious figures of the Buddha and Bodhisattvas . . . and hear voices preaching the wondrous law which will enlighten him with the endurance of Nirvāṇic life."

For those whose merit is not so great, there is reserved a medium existence of the Superior Grade; while for the many whose stock of merit is rather low, there is held open a lowest existence of the Superior Grade. Yet even they will be borne to the Pure Land within the bud of a golden-lotus flower, which will unfold slowly so that in three weeks they will be able to see and hear clearly the Buddha and the preaching of the Law.

Since compassion is infinite, and the results of *karma* must be computed on an endlessly graduated scale, there is described, in the *Fifteenth Meditation,* an Intermediate Grade with its highest, medium, and lowest stages of existence, where the Path to Bodhi is considerably longer. And, finally, for those deluded and stupid humans who, headed for hell because of their evil deeds and unrepentant hearts, may chance to lift a prayer to Amitābha, there is a loophole into an Inferior Grade of existence on three levels, as minutely described in the *Sixteenth Meditation.* Thus, Heaven's gate is open to all who are earnestly repentant, until at last they are permitted to join the great assemblage of Arhats and Bodhisattvas who are enjoying the blessings of Amitābha's Heaven.[17]

(d) Since rebirth in the Pure Land of Amitābha after death is the goal of most good Buddhists' aspiration, to have a detailed description of that beautiful World of Peace and Happiness in the *Greater Sukhāvatī-Vyūha Sūtra* (*Wu-Liang-Shou Ching*) is a comforting climax to any devotee's devotional reading in the Pure Land Scriptures. Its attractions are suggested in the following three passages:—The Buddha addressed Elder Śāriputra thus:

"Passing over ten million Buddha-lands from here, there is in the West a world named Sukhāvatī (City of Supreme Happiness), where a Buddha known as Amitābha now preaches the Dharma . . .

"This Sukhāvatī is surrounded with seven lines of ornamental railings, seven curtains of netted tapestries, and seven rows of precious trees arranged in order, all adorned with four kinds of gems. Therefore, it is named Sukhāvatī. . . .

"Again, O Śāriputra . . . there are lakes (lined with golden sand and precious stones) . . . (with) lotus flowers . . . fair and fragrant . . . celestial music . . . mandarava-flowers . . . wondrous birds . . . singing . . . to proclaim the five roots of virtue . . . the five powers . . . the seven-fold path of Bodhi . . . and the eight-fold path of holiness. . . ."[18]

A Final Pure Land Apologetic

In a long introduction to the *Aparimitāyur Sūtra* (*Fu-Shuo Wu-Liang-Shou Ching*), the late Pi-cheng Lee, a modern translator, begins her apology for the Pure Land doctrine with this apostrophe:—

"*OM!* Adoration to the Buddha Amitābha,* whose Dharmakāya (Body of Law) is omnipresent in all universes. *OM!* Adoration to all the Bodhisattvas and Pure Beings of the Ocean-wide Assembly of Sukhāvatī. *OM!* Adoration to all the Buddhas and Saints of Past, Present, and Future, and of the Ten Quarters of the Chiliocosmos."

Then, continuing, Miss Lee says that since there is no possibility of reforming this present world, in which suffering and misery and bodily putrefactions prevail and men live as in a prison-cell of illusory self-content, it is far better to live in the hope of being reborn in the Pure Land of Amitābha's Paradise. This easiest and shortest, shining way to salvation is available only to those with the eye of faith and it has been followed successfully by countless Chinese Buddhists. The requirements are simple:

First, one must learn to control himself by practising the five abstinences; *viz.,* Abstain from (1) taking life (of man or animal); (2) stealing; (3) sex indulgence; (4) lying; and (5) intoxicants or narcotics.

Second, one must hold the six sense-organs free from all sensations (of sight, hearing, smell, taste, touch, or thought) so as to achieve serenity unsullied by worldly thoughts.

Third, one must daily recite the Holy Name of the Lord Amitābha, or meditate fixedly on Him, as long as possible, without distraction or thought of merit.

---

* (Translator's Note:) In Sanskrit, '*Amita*' means infinite, and '*abha*' means splendour.

Fourth, one must repent of all sinful deeds committed in the past and refrain from evil-doing thereafter.

Fifth, one must direct his mind to the great goal of salvation for all sentient beings (animal as well as human), wishing to deliver not only himself but all others also. This is the doctrine of Mahāyāna.

Her apology is concluded with the verses so well known in Buddhist circles, the four great vows of Mahāyāna novices:—

The Four Vows of Novices

"I take my solemn oath that I will save
All sentient beings that know life's cruel pain
And, by the Dharma teaching, for them pave
A road by which the Buddhahood to gain.

"I take my solemn oath that I will break
The power of evil passions and desire
And, through the grace of Buddha, undertake
To quench for now and ever sorrow's fire.

"I take my solemn oath that I will aspire
To learn the countless systems of the Law,
And, having learned each one, to go still higher
Till ignorance has fled forevermore.

"I take my solemn oath that I will strive
Among the Bodhisattvas to enroll,
Nor shall I ever rest till I contrive
To reach the Tathāgata's highest Goal." [19]

The reader will have noted the strong appeal of this form of Mahāyāna Buddhism—as a religion for the common people, with a graphic presentation of Buddhas and Bodhisattva-Saviors and a promised "Land of Bliss" for their worshippers.

For the literati, however, Buddhism offered a discussion of philosophical principles such as the unreality of the phenomenal world and the doctrine of the Void, which we find at the core of the Mādhyamika philosophy.

2. *The Philosophy of the Mādhyamika School (San-Lun Tsung)*

Since Kumārajīva (Chiu-mo-lo-shih) (A.D. ca. 343–ca. 416) was brought a captive first (A.D. 384) from Kucha on the borders of Tibet to Kansu and later to Ch'ang-An (modern Sian) early in A.D. 402, his intensive translation work may have begun in the Kingdom of Liang (modern Kansu) as early as A.D. 384 and extended (in Ch'ang-An) to as late as 416. Both Hīnayāna and Mahāyāna texts were put into Chinese in rapid succession. Two of Nāgārjuna's (*Lung Shu*) writings—the *Prāṇyamūlaśāstraṭīkā (Chung Kuan Lun)* or *Middle Doctrine Treatise* and the *Dvādaśanikāyaśāstra (Shih-êrh Mên Lun)* or *Twelve Gates Treatise*—as well as the *Śata Śāstra* (*Pai Lun*) by Āryadeva (*T'i P'o*) and Vasubandhu (*Shih Ch'in*) were made the basis of a Chinese version of the Mādhyamika School[20] of thought, that came to be known as the San-Lun Tsung or "Three Shastras Sect" under the leadership of Kumārajīva's disciple, Chia Hsiang.[21] In the T'ang dynasty, it flourished under the direction of the monk Chi-tsang (A.D. 549-623).

One great problem shared by Taoists and Buddhists alike was the antithesis between the Absolute (*Chen Ju*) and the temporal; between permanence and change; between Nirvāṇa and the cycle of life and death. In Chinese terms, it was the antithesis between *wu* (non-being) and *yu* (being) ; between *ching* (quiescence) and *tung* (movement) ; or between *wu-wei* (non-activity) and *yu-wei* (activity) .

The Mādhyamika School's answer stemmed from a belief that the nature of Ultimate Reality is something which cannot be described. Call it 'infinite' and you immediately limit it by the very definition, because you imply that *it is something* and not something else. This is just what the negativistic San-Lun Tsung wished to avoid. The school's teaching has been summarized briefly by John Blofeld as follows:

1. "It is better to describe the world as void than to say it exists.
2. "There is neither void nor existence, yet
3. "There is nothing which can be described as non-void or non-existence.
4. " (On the other hand, the converse is true that) There is nothing which can be described as not being non-void or not being non-existence."[22]

This 'Doctrine of the Void' (*śūnyavāda*) will be found also reflected in the *Diamond Sūtra* (*Vajracchedika*) and in the rest of the "Perfection of Wisdom" *(Prajñāpāramitā)* series, whose authors defend the claim that everything is relative to an Absolute (Void) which cannot be defined.[23]

The infiltration of Mādhyamika philosophy into the Chinese mind is best illustrated by the writings of Seng Chao and Tao-sheng in the early fifth century; by Seng-yu in the early sixth century; and by Chi-tsang in the early seventh century. Among the pupils who came under Kumārajīva's own instruction were two Taoists named Seng Chao (A.D. 383–414) and (Chu) Tao-sheng (A.D. 365–434), who may have helped him with his extensive translations. It was but natural that they should become imbued with Buddhist doctrines and that these ideas should crop up in their own later writings. Their essays, as well as the essays of Seng-yu (A.D. 445–518), and an essay by a later systematizer (An) Chi-tsang (A.D. 549-623) – all give in great detail this *"fa-hsing* idealism," as it has been called.[24]

Seng Chao's writings, in particular, represent an interesting combination of Buddhist and Neo-Taoist thought. In his *Chao Lun,* translated by Walter Liebenthal as *The Book of Chao,*[25] are found, for example, three passages of special interest: one on "The Immutability of Things,"* another on "The Emptiness of the Unreal," and a third on "Prajñā is not Knowledge."

In regard to the immutability of things, he maintains that although things and events, when viewed in succession, give an illusion of movement (like the images on a moving-picture film), yet by themselves they are fixed in their own time-period and their effects (*karma*) likewise remain immutably fixed. . . . "The true aspect of things (*dharmas*) is that they are neither in movement nor in quiescence." In his translator's note, Dr. Bodde adds by way of clarification, "Thus what Seng Chao calls 'immutability' (*pu-ch'ien*) is a mystical concept that transcends both quiescence (*ching*) and movement (*tung*) as ordinarily conceived."[27] This is to follow the Middle Path.

In regard to the unreality of things, Seng Chao wrote:**

"If you wish to speak of their non-being, their manifestations have forms. These phenomenal forms do not constitute non-being, yet, not having absolute reality, they also do not constitute real being. This, then, elucidates the theory of the emptiness of the unreal. . . . (Thus being and non-being do not involve an antithesis. . . . By saying that there is neither being nor non-being, we follow the Middle Path)."[28]

When Seng Chao wrote that Prajñā is not knowledge,*** he meant that 'sage-wisdom' (like that of the Bodhisattva) is not the same as ordinary 'knowledge.' Being 'concerned with absolute truth' and believing that all things are actually 'non-existent,' he conceived of *Prajñā* as a form of knowledge that is unconditioned by 'phenomenal qualities.'[29]

Beneath the heavy veneer of Buddhist terminology, one can detect certain basic Taoist ideas from the *Lao-tzu* and the *Chuang-tzu* that had become ingrained in Seng Chao's thinking.[30]

Chu Tao-sheng, a native of northern Kiangsu Province, was a contemporary of Seng Chao and, as a pupil of Kumārajīva, likewise became an ardent Buddhist. Indirectly, through other

* Chapter 1 in the *Chao Lun,* entitled "Wu Pu-ch'ien Lun."[26]

** In Chapter 2, "The Emptiness of the Unreal" (*Pu-chen K'ung Lun*).

*** In Chapter 3, "On Prajña Not Being Knowledge" (*Pan-jo Wu-chih Lun*).

writers like an early contemporary and possible teacher, Hui Yüan (A.D. 334-416)—founder of the Pure Land School*—we learn of Tao-sheng's belief that

> "The retributions of punishment or blessing depend upon what are stimulated by one's own (mental) activities. . . . (If no mental activation is involved, the cycle of transmigration is transcended and, therefore) "our acts no longer entail any retribution."[31]

This position set Tao-sheng off from his contemporaries as an independent thinker. Moreover, his early acceptance of the theory of 'instantaneous enlightenment' was significant enough to call for mention by a contemporary, Hsieh Ling-yün (A.D. 385–433) in his *Discussion of Essentials* (*Pien Tsung Lun*).[32] In itself, this rejection of the doctrine of "gradual enlightenment through book-learning to free the mind from ignorance" cast a long shadow down through the history of Buddhist thought, adumbrating as it did the position taken three centuries later by the Sixth Patriarch, Hui Neng.

In the minds of modern critics like W. T. Chan, Tao-sheng exerted a profound influence in another significant way. While rejecting Hui Yüan's teaching on the indestructibility of the human soul, his conviction that the Buddha-nature is the true nature of all men, pervading even the spirits of despised outcastes (*icchantikas*), led him to preach a doctrine of universal salvation which Confucianists could accept because it was based on the infinite potentiality of human nature. In other words, Tao-sheng is believed to have provided the theoretical basis for the development of the Ch'an School's philosophy.[33]

At the beginning of the sixth century, and also of the seventh, we find debates on "The Immortality of the Soul" in the writings of Seng-yu (A.D. 445-518) and Tao-hsüan (A.D. 596-667), who strongly opposed the Buddhist teaching of the reincarnation of the human soul, carrying its *karma* over with

* In his treatise "On the Explanation of Retribution" (*Ming Pao-ying Lun*).

it into a new bodily form.* The Taoists argued that soul perishes with body, so why worry! And àpropos of this controversy, Seng-yu, in his *Collected Essays on Buddhism* (*Hung-Min Chi*), included one by Fan Chen (A.D. 450–515) entitled "Essay on the Extinction of Soul" (*Shen Mieh Lun*) to support his own contention.[34]

The old problem of the antithesis between the Absolute and the temporal cropped up again in the writings of the philosopher (An) Chi-tsang, living into the early seventh century. In his *Essay on the Double Truth* (*Êrh-Ti Chang*),[35] Chi-tsang refers to this 'Double Truth' as being on three levels:[36]

Absolute Truth	*Relative Truth*
1. Affirmation of Non-Being.	1. Affirmation of Being.
2. Denial of both Being and Non-Being.	2. Affirmation of either Being or Non-Being.
3. Neither affirmation nor denial of both Being and Non-Being.	3. Either affirmation or denial of both Being and Non-Being.

From these statements he argued that since Absolute Truth merges into Relative Truth at different levels, only the denial of both would constitute the Middle Path, or Highest Truth. Ultimately, Chi-tsang was caught on the horns of the dilemma of the apparent necessity either of discarding or of preserving the 'Double Truth.' Feeling that he could do neither, he clung to the conviction that in the end there is no illusion in accepting the emptiness of the Real along with the illusoriness of the Relative or Mundane. As Fung Yu-lan concludes, "this nihilistic approach to Reality, this emphasis on emptiness (*śūnyatā*) is a persistent reminder of certain sayings of Lao Tzu and Chuang Tzu."[38]

---

* In a translator's footnote, Derk Bodde points out that "this is a distortion of the Buddhist teaching, which affirms not that soul endures but that the *karma* of one existence is carried over into and influences the succeeding existence." (As, in billiards or croquet, one ball striking another imparts both direction and force of movement to it.)[37]

Echoing Nāgārjuna, the Mādhyamika School in China maintained that reality is to be understood as "the total absence of specific character." To express its meaning, one must follow the "Middle Path of Eightfold Negation"—(no production or extinction, no permanence or annihilation, no unity or diversity, no coming or departure). While every thing or event may be conceived as having temporary reality, in the last analysis it has no ultimate or unconditioned reality, like that of the Absolute.[39] * Pratt concludes that the Mādhyamika philosophy is only trying to say that truth, though possible and real, cannot be put into any form of words; that "words are things" (i.e., they "are not the realities to which they refer.") [39a] We are told that Chi-tsang's radical development of the 'Middle Doctrine' teachings caused his school to be known as "The New San Lun School";[40] yet it ultimately (after the eighth century) became a sub-division of the Meditation (Ch'an) School.[41]

3. *The Philosophy of the Meditation School (Ch'an Tsung)*

With the coming of Bodhidharma (*P'u-t'i-ta-mo,* or *Ta-Mo*) of the Dhyāni (Meditation) School in India, we find the center of gravity of Northern (Mahāyāna) Buddhism shifting to China. After him, counted as the twenty-eighth of the Indian Patriarchs, Buddhism either moved out of India completely or was gradually re-absorbed by Hinduism. Arriving at Canton by sea perhaps as early as A.D. 475 (rather than 520, as has been held by some authorities), Ta Mo became the first patriarch of the transplanted Dhyāni, or Ch'an, School in China.[42]

Moving northward at the invitation of Emperor Ta T'ung of the Liang dynasty, Ta Mo spent some time in Nanking, then pushed farther north to Loyang (in modern Honan).

---

* As will be seen later, the T'ien-T'ai and Hua-Yen Schools synthesized all these opposing views.

There, by tradition, he spent nine years facing a wall in the Shao Lin Monastery to exemplify his doctrine of the supreme value of deep contemplation. Scorning the worship of images and disregarding the study of scriptures, he taught by precept and example that the best way to achieve the Buddhist goal of escape from life's chains was simply to concentrate on the Buddha-nature within one's own heart and mind. Our inner, real nature is the 'Essence of Wisdom,' which is identical with the Ultimate Reality underlying all phenomena. To apprehend this in a sudden awakening of the mind constitutes 'Enlightenment.' There comes a mystical inflowing of intuitive perception of the supreme meaning of Nirvāṇa as the life of non-attachment to earthly things or bodily desires.[43] The general effect of this teaching was an abandoning of the usual Buddhist concern for dogmas, book-knowledge, organization and ritual by focusing on introspection of the mind as all-sufficient for salvation through self-realization.[44]

Before his death in A.D. 536, Ta Mo passed on to his disciple, Hui K'o, his robe and begging-bowl as symbols of appointment to the high office of Second Patriarch. Hui K'o, a converted Taoist, carried on the leadership of the sect and was succeeded in turn by four other patriarchs, the sixth (and last) being Hui Neng (A.D. 638–713). During this period, the Buddhists had to face strong opposition by both Taoists and Confucianists on social and political, as well as on philosophical, grounds. In the reign of Liang Wu Ti (A.D. 502–550), an ardent Buddhist, a certain Hsün Chi made himself obnoxious by his violent asseverations that Buddhism was subversive and undermining the already weakened power of the state.[45] Nevertheless, Buddhism continued to grow and flourish because it offered many advantages that other systems did not offer, especially to minds troubled by the political and social chaos of the period.

Despite its emphasis on the adequacy of well-focused contemplation, Ch'an Buddhism, in the long course of its influential history, has made great use of the study of primary and secondary scriptures. For example, as primary scriptures (supposedly produced in India and made available to Chinese in translation), the Meditation School uses, as fundamental reading for newly ordained monks, the *Sūtra of Forty-two Sections,* together with the *Sūtra of the Doctrine Bequeathed by the Buddha,* and the *Sūtra of the Eight Awakenings of the Great Ones.* In addition to these, in common use are the famous *Diamond Sūtra (Vajracchedika Mahāprajñāpāramitā Sūtra,* or *Chin Kang Ching*—The Jewel of Transcendental Wisdom),[46] the *Heart Sūtra (Smaller Prajñāpāramitā Hridaya Sūtra)*, containing the essence of Ch'an doctrine, and the *Sūraṅgama Sūtra (Leng-yen Ching),* used at the morning mass to cleanse the heart for the day.[47] As secondary scriptures, emanating from Chinese sources, may be mentioned the *Sūtra of Wei Lang* (*Hui Neng*)—of great importance in modern Buddhism—together with two commentaries on it: Hsi Yün's *Huang Po Doctrine of Universal Mind* and Hui Hai's *The Path to Sudden Enlightenment.*

As Ch'an Buddhism may be considered the core of Chinese Buddhist philosophy, we shall examine briefly four of the primary Indian sources and the three secondary Chinese sources mentioned above.

A. *Primary Indian Sources*

1. The *Sūtra of Forty-two Sections** (*Szŭ-shih-êrh Chang Ching*) introduces the Buddha as teaching disciples in the Royal Park near Benares, and saying, in effect:—

Those who leave family, become monks, and observe the 250 precepts will be known as *'Śramaṇas,'* who break away from the phenomenal world and abide in perfect quietude of mind. (Sec. 2). (*The Duty of a Śramaṇa*) The *Śramaṇa* clings to nothing within or without—"is not shackled with dogmas, nor is he enmeshed by *karma.* [Pondering nothing . . . practising nothing, and manifesting nothing, without passing through all the successive stages (of dis-

---

* Translated from Sanskrit into Chinese jointly by Kāśyapa-Mātaṅga and Gobharana from Central India at Loyang in the Later Han dynasty. Translated into English for the Buddhist Society of London by Chu Ch'an in 1947. Here greatly condensed.

cipline), he (nevertheless) reaches the loftiest of all]. This is what is meant by 'The Way.' " * (Sec. 3).

(*Above all, the Way is Inexpressible*) "The Way which can be expressed in words stops short; there is nothing which can be grasped. Those who can come up to this, progress; while the stupid regress." (Sec. 19).**

(*A Closing Admonition*) . . . If the Way is followed in the mind, of what use are actions? (Sec. 40).***

(*Some 'Acceptance Vows' of a Śramaṇa*)

". . . I look upon the state of kings . . . as upon . . . dust; . . . upon . . . gold and jewels as upon rubble; . . . upon . . . finest silk as upon . . . rags . . .

". . . I look upon the Supreme Vehicle as upon a dream of abundant wealth. . . .****

". . . I look upon the impartial attitude (of a Buddha) as upon Ultimate Reality." . . . (Sec. 42). *****

2. *The Doctrine Bequeathed by the Buddha****** gives final admonitions before his entrance into Nirvāṇa:—

"O monks," he said, "after my passing you should pay the

* (Translator's note) :—Some think the part in square brackets was added later by Ch'an monks.

** (Translator's note) :—This passage, whether original or not, expresses the essence of Ch'an, the highest development of Buddhism. In this higher sphere, nothing exists (in the sense that all the attributes of individual existence are illusions pertaining to the phenomenal world), yet everything exists (in the sense that the ultimate reality possesses within itself the power to produce every kind of phenomenon without any limitations of space and time).

*** (Translator's note) :—Prof. T'ang Yung-t'ung takes this sentence for a Ch'an substitution.

**** (Translator's note):—*Supreme Vehicle*—Mahāyāna, whose followers aim to enlighten all sentient beings.

***** (Translator's note) :—*Impartial attitude*—in the sense of being unmoved by desire for or aversion to anything whatsoever.

****** (Translator's note):—Translated from Sanskrit into Chinese by the Indian monk, Kumārajīva (d. ca. A.D. 416 or 418), in the reign of Emperor Yao of the Later Ch'in dynasty. . . . This sutra, as translated into English by Chu Ch'an in 1947, has been incorporated in the same binding with the *Sūtra of Forty-two Sections* (as pp. 24-34).

greatest respect . . . to the 250 precepts. . . . You should know that they are your chief guide. . . . Maintain especially these ten precepts in all purity":—

*Ten Commandments for the Buddhist Order**

(1) Thou shalt not engage in buying or selling.
(2) Thou shalt set aside property and all that it entails.
(3) Avoid seeking wealth by working the land; (especially) —
(4) Do not clear ground of bushes or trees, break new soil, or dig the earth.
(5) Thou shalt not engage in mixing drugs, practicing divination or sorcery, or fortune-telling (by astrology).
(6) Thou shalt live alone in chastity and simplicity. . . .
(7) Thou shalt neither cater to the rich nor contemn the poor.
(8) Seek enlightenment with minds properly under control.
(9) Perform no magical wonders to startle people.
(10) Be content with gifts of clothing, food, bedding, and medicine, but do not hoard anything.

(Then, as though to impress his disciples with the fact that great merit resides in obedience to rules, the Buddha continued with further admonitions and regulations for the monastic life) :—

*Ten Further Admonishments Preached by the Buddha***

(1) Fear indulgence (of mind and body) more than . . . robbers. . . .
(2) Cultivate the abstemious life. . . . Regulate sleep. Be conscientious!
(3) Beware of hatred! . . . Cultivate forbearance!
(4) Avoid arrogance! Forswear contemptuousness!
(5) Diminish all desires for selfish profit!
(6) Let contentment reign, even when forced to sleep on the ground.

* Slightly rearranged and condensed.
** As paraphrased in condensed form.

(7) Live in seclusion and thus avoid suffering and please the gods.*
(8) Strive against laziness by an alert quest for knowledge.
(9) Concentrate your mind to attain knowledge,** which is like a raft, a light, and an axe (that cuts down affliction), yet avoid useless discussions.
(10) Diligently observe the teachings and resolve all doubts about the Four Noble Truths.***

3. *The Sūtra of the Eight Awakenings of the Great Ones*****

The disciples of the Buddha earnestly recite this sutra constantly day and night, for it teaches:—

(1) (*The Unreality and Evil of this Life*) :—

"The world is impermanent and . . . the four elements (which constitute the body: earth, moisture, heat, and vapor) are a source of pain and (are in reality) void. The five aggregates (form, sensation, conception, discrimination, and cognition)***** do not constitute the real self. . . . The mind is the source of evil and the body the lair of wickedness. By such perception comes gradual freedom from (the circle of) birth and death." ******

---

* (Tr. note) :—The Buddha did not deny the existence of the gods, who had formed an important part of his early background, but he was slightly contemptuous of them, regarding them as part of the unreal world of phenomena and subject to death and rebirth. . . .

** (Tr. note) :—Here, it would seem, both kinds of knowledge are meant (i.e., for the Mahāyānist, intuitive knowledge—the fruit of concentration; for the Hīnayānist, knowledge acquired from study).

*** (Tr. note) :—The Four Noble Truths form the basis of the Buddha's teaching. They are: (*a*) *dukkha,* the doctrine that sorrow is inseparable from sentient existence; (*b*) *samudaya,* that the accumulation of sorrow is caused by desire or the passions; (*c*) *nirodha,* that the extinction of sorrow is possible; (*d*) *marga,* the doctrine of the Way leading to its extinction. This Way is the Noble Eight-fold Path (*Aṣṭa-mārga*).[48]

**** As paraphrased and condensed. This sutra was translated from Sanskrit into Chinese by An Shih Kao in the Later Han dynasty (A.D. 25-250). It is incorporated in the same binding with *The Sūtra of Forty-two Sections,* as translated into English by Chu Ch'an in 1947, on pp. 34-37.

***** (Tr. note) :—The aggregates are also called the five *'skandhas,'* which cause the illusion of the phenomenal world.

****** (Tr. note) :—The freedom which implies entrance into Nirvāṇa.

(2) (*Elimination of Desire Brings Release*) :—

"When desires are diminished . . . the mind and body exist independently* of the chain of cause and effect (and free from all illusion)."

(3) (*The Pursuit of Knowledge Leads to Tranquillity*):—

"A Bodhisattva . . . ** tranquilly accepting his lot . . . keeps to the Way, indulging in no activities other than the pursuit of knowledge. . . ."

(4) (*Strive Against Lazy Backsliding*) :—

"Laziness and neglect lead to backsliding. It is necessary to strive diligently . . . to destroy the afflictions (of desire, hatred, and ignorance)."

(5) (*Pondering the Way Gives Power to Convert All Beings*)

(6) (*The True Disciple—or Bodhisattva—Gives Lavishly to All Alike*)

(7) (*Let the Laity Leave Home and Desire Behind, Practice Purity of Life, and Show Compassion Toward All Beings*)

(8) (*Become a World-Savior; Help Others to Enlightenment*) :—

". . . Cultivate the Mahāyāna heart and be equally ready to rescue all beings. Be willing to suffer numberless afflictions on their behalf and lead them all to find joy at the last."***

---

* (Tr. note) :—The Chinese *tzu tsai* (Sanskrit *iśvara*) can mean 'lord,' in the sense of 'lord of oneself' . . . (or) 'master of one's own destiny' (i.e., no longer in the bonds of illusion).

** (Tr. note) :—"This title can be used in a complimentary sense, as here, to denote one who has formed the firm intention to become a Bodhisattva and who is working toward that goal. . ."

*** (Tr. note) :—"It is this, above all, which (to my mind) marks the superiority of Mahāyāna to all (other) religions. . . . As far as I know, it is only the Mahāyāna follower who undertakes to work throughout eternity, regardless of the cost, for the sake of all sentient beings."

(4) *The Diamond Sūtra* (*Chin Kang Ching*)

A fourth basic, primary Indian sutra, familiar to all good Ch'an Buddhists, is the *Vajracchedika* (or Diamond Cutter) section of the *Mahāprajñāpāramitā Sūtra (Perfection of Transcendental Wisdom)*, more commonly referred to as *The Diamond Sūtra* (*Chin Kang Ching*) or *Jewel of Transcendental Wisdom.*[49] It rings the changes on standard Buddhist doctrines, which, like a rhythmic refrain, fall from the lips of Tathāgata Buddha:—

At an assembly of 1250 friars of the Order of Buddhist Monks (the Sangha), convoked by the Buddha at Anāthapiṇdada's Park near Śravāsti, he replied thus to Subhūti (Sec. 1):*

(A) (*There is no Individuality*): "No real Bodhisattva cherishes the idea of separate individuality." (Sec. 3).

"Subhūti . . . whoso perceives that all material characteristics are in fact no characteristics, perceives the Tathāgata." (Sec. 5).

"Because Subhūti abides nowhere: therefore, he is called 'Joyful-Abider-in-Peace, Dweller-in-Seclusion-in-the-Forest.' " (Sec. 9).**

(B) (*There is no Cosmic Reality*): (The integral principle of the Great Way is that nothing is self-existent!) To which Subhūti replied: ". . . If reality could be predicated of a world, it would be a self-existent cosmos. (But the Tathāgata teaches that 'cosmos' is merely a figure of speech)." (Sec. 30).*** [50]

(C) (*Perfect Peace Lies in Non-Attachment*): "Furthermore, Subhūti . . . a Bodhisattva . . . should practice charity . . . with

* The ensuing dialogue has been rearranged according to the relation of ideas.

** (Tr. note):—"Claiming spiritual superiority is separative and tends to enhance the illusory personality . . . 'Abider-in-Peace' means not subject to any of the agencies which condition phenomenal existence. 'Dweller-in-Seclusion-in-the-Forest' means ascetic hermitage and also dwelling aloof and immune from distraction and temptation in the dark forest tangle of human perplexities and desires."

*** (Tr. note):—"The riddle of existence cannot be elucidated by objective reasoning. . . . Any fixed proposition which may be asserted as to the real nature of the universe can be refuted by dialectic."

a mind detached from any formal notions." (Sec. 4). . . .* "The mind should be kept independent of any thoughts which arise within it." (Sec. 14). . . . "Bodhisattvas who achieve merit should not be fettered with desire for rewards." (Sec. 28). . . .** "(Even my teaching will have to be given up by men of merit and faith in 'no qualities'). . . . (If) the Buddha-teaching must be relinquished: how much more so misteaching!" (Sec. 6-b).***

(D) (*Truth is Inexpressible and Wisdom Unattainable*): (Subhūti): "As I understand Buddha's meaning, there is no formulation of truth called 'Consummation of Incomparable Enlightenment . . .' because truth is uncontainable and inexpressible. It neither *is* nor is it *not*." (Sec. 7). (Buddha): ". . . The basis of Tathāgata's attainment (of enlightenment) . . . is wholly *beyond;* it is neither real nor unreal . . . therefore, it is called 'Realm of Formulations.'"**** (Sec. 17). . . . (Subhūti): ". . . World-Honoured One, in the attainment of the Consummation of Incomparable Enlightenment did Buddha make no acquisition whatsoever?" (Buddha replied): "Just so, Subhūti . . . I acquired not even the least thing; wherefore it is called 'Consummation of Incomparable Enlightenment.' " (Sec. 22).

(E) More specifically,

---

* (Tr. note):—". . . The idea of reality implies the idea of unreality and *vice-versa,* . . . but by objective comparison they are contradictory. So worldly knowledge is dichotomizing, . . . but Tathāgata-knowledge is formless, . . . and free from all dualism."

** (Tr. note):—"Cf. the Hindu *Bhagavad-Gitā,* Bk. II, 46, 47:—"Thy right is to the work, but never to the fruits; let not the fruit of thy work be thy motive, nor take refuge in abstinence from works. Standing in union with the Soul, carry out thy work, putting away attachment, O conqueror of wealth; equal in success and failure, for equalness is called union with the Soul." (51)

*** (Tr. note):—"The last sentence is quoted from the *Majjhima Nikaya* 1-134. So long as the mind is attached even to Buddha's teaching as a basis, it will cherish the idea of 'I' and 'Other'."

**** (Tr. note):—For an account of Gautama Buddha's prediction concerning Subhūti and others, see the *Lotus Sūtra,* chaps. 6, 8, and 9. In the 8th century, C.E., the 33rd Mahāyāna patriarch, the Venerable Hui Neng (Wei Lang) related in his autobiography that he first contacted Buddhism through hearing a street-recital of this Discourse, and later became thoroughly enlightened during a sermon upon section 10 (quoting Wong Mou-lam's translation of the *Sūtra of Wei Lang,* chap. 8). On 'wholly beyond'; 'neither real nor unreal':—The Norm, or the Mean, is entirely outside the scope of dualistic opposites and correlatives.

(*Enlightenment is Attained in Freedom from Self*) :—(Buddha): "Furthermore, Subhūti, This (enlightenment) . . . is straightly attained by freedom from separate personal selfhood and by cultivating all kinds of goodness. (Yet) . . . the Tathāgata declares that there is no 'goodness'; such is merely a name." (Sec. 23)*

(F) It is asserted positively that

(*Nirvāṇa Does not Mean Extinction*):—(Buddha): "Subhūti, if . . . anyone in whom dawns the Consummation of Incomparable Enlightenment declares that all manifest standards are ended and extinguished, do not countenance such thoughts. . . ." (Sec. 27).

(G) And finally,

(*The Value of Reciting This Discourse is Incalculable*) :—(Buddha answered): ". . . If anyone receives and retains even four lines of this Discourse and . . . explains them to others . . . (his) merit . . . will be greater (than that of) . . . anyone who gave away countless gifts of alms . . . (or) a good man or a good woman (who) sacrifices as many lives as the sand-grains of the Ganges." (Sec. 13 and Sec. 8).**

Conclusion: "When Buddha had finished this Discourse, the Venerable Subhūti, together with the bhikshus, bhilshunis, lay brothers and sisters, and the whole realm of gods, men, and titans, were filled with joy by His teaching, and taking it seriously to heart, they went their ways."***

---

* (Tr. note) :—To assert the *being* of Good would imply the *being* of Evil.

** (Tr. note) :—If *Vajracchedika Prajñā-Pāramitā Sūtra* is taken in the sense of "Cutter of the Diamond," we might consider the title as "The Discourse on the Penetration of the Impenetrable." "*Prajñā*" means wisdom of the highest and clearest kind. . . . "*Pāramitā*" is derived from *parama*: superlative, best, Alpha. It is often translated as 'Gone over to the Other Shore,' explained by: Having crossed the troublous flood of mortal existences and reached the haven of Nirvāṇa; but this interpretation must be considered symbolical.

*** (Tr. note) :—To awaken (in every person) the thought of enlightenment is to begin to penetrate the mists and veils of mutually interdependent created things in our search for union with That which is beyond all names, connotations, characteristics, qualities, appearances, and concepts.

B. *Secondary Chinese Sources*

Thus far we have been looking at the main sources of Ch'an Buddhist thought as found in the sutras originating in the Indian Mahāyānist mind—in other words the direct teachings of the Buddha to his disciples as recorded in the original Sanskrit and later translated into Chinese. We now come to examine the three above-mentioned scriptures which, probably more than any others, reveal how the Buddha's teachings filtered through the Chinese mind, and how it reacted to them.

1. *The Sūtra of Wei Lang (Hui Neng)* [52]

The standard classic for modern Ch'an (or Zen) Buddhists, *The Sūtra of Wei Lang* (or *Hui Neng*)*—the Sixth (and last) of the Chinese Buddhist Patriarchs (A.D. 638–713)—is the only sacred Chinese Buddhist writing to be honored with the rank of *Ching* or *Sūtra*. As leader of the Southern Branch of the Ch'an School, Hui Neng reputedly taught "sudden enlightenment" for at least two years (676-678) at the Nanhua Monastery at Chükiang (Kukong) in Kwangtung Province.[53] By analyzing and rearranging the order of Hui Neng's thought, we arrive at a natural sequence of ideas, as presented below.

A. *Description of the Goal—Enlightenment of the Mind*

At the very outset, Hui Neng began his discourse on the "Great Wisdom to Reach the Opposite Shore" with comments on the *Mahā-Prajñāpāramitā Sūtra* in this wise:

(1) (*The Mind Contains the Essence of Wisdom*):—"With our infinite capacity of Mind, we can realize that the Voidness of the

---

* This sutra was translated into English by Wong Mou-lam and edited (1944, 1947) by Christmas Humphreys for the Buddhist Society of London.

Universe is not vacuity but filled with . . . heavenly bodies, mountains, rivers, good and bad men, *deva*-planes, hells, oceans, etc. . . . Yet we are neither attracted to nor repelled by the goodness or badness of (these things or) other people. . . . This voidness of mind is not blankness, however, for . . . the mind . . . pervades the whole Dharmadhātu (Sphere of the Law, Universe) . . . . When our mind works without hindrance and is at liberty to 'come' or to 'go,' then it is in a state of wisdom (*prajñā*) . . . . All wisdom comes from the Essence of Mind and not from an exterior source. . . . This is called the Self-Use of the True Nature. . . . This is what is meant by realizing one's own Essence of Mind for the attainment of Buddhahood."[54]

(2) *Purity of Mind Makes a Paradise in the Heart*) :—In a question-and-answer period, the Patriarch explained that merit is not gained by doing good deeds. Only by preserving purity of mind and an attitude of equality will felicity be gained. The pure in mind are near to the Western Paradise . . . (for) . . . by clearing away the eight errors one . . . arrives at the Paradise Within the Heart or Mind. . . . Invoking Amitābha will not avail, for . . . "one whose heart is impure cannot be born in his Western Paradise. . . ." Furthermore, Hui Neng continued:

"Those who wish to train themselves (spiritually) may do so at home. It is quite unnecessary for them to stay in monasteries. . . . Only let your mind . . . function freely . . . let it abide nowhere. . . . Then you will be in peace of mind (*samādhi*) all the time, and may be called *a man of super-eminent mind*."[55]

(3) (*Straightforwardness is the Key to Peace of Mind*) :—In unequivocal terms the Patriarch enunciates this principle or masterkey to tranquillity of mind (*samādhi*) :

"Make it a rule to be straightforward on all occasions. . . . Don't let your mind be crooked and practice straightforwardness with your lips only. . . . When . . . our outward appearance and our inner feelings harmonize with each other, it is a case of the equilibrium of tranquillity and wisdom. . . . Those under delusion . . .

don't realize that straightforwardness is the holy place, the Pure Land. . . ." [56]

(4) (*The Essence of Meditation is the Achievement of Imperturbability*) :—"Those who train themselves for imperturbability, should . . . ignore the faults of others. . . . To meditate (therefore) means to realize inwardly the imperturbability of the Essence of Mind. To be free from attachment to all outer objects is true meditation; to attain inner peace is *samādhi*." [57]

B. *The Way to the Goal of Enlightenment*

(1) (*The Way of the Five Incenses*) :—Purification of mind comes first through freedom from taint of jealousy, anger, avarice, or hatred (*śīla*). This will bring one to the state of an imperturbable mind (*samādhi*). Being free from impediments, one then becomes full of wisdom (*prajñā*), which enables one to be respectful toward superiors . . . and sympathetic with the poor. . . . After that, one feels a sense of *liberation*. . . . Finally . . . the mind explores Buddhist principles . . . and attains *knowledge* of its true nature. "This Five-fold Incense fumigates us from within; we should not look for it from without." [58]

(2) *The Way of True Repentance*):—The source of sin . . . can be cast out in the twinkling of an eye by sudden repentance and turning to righteousness as a 'Treader of the Path' of Mahāyāna doctrine. . . . By taking refuge in the three-fold Body-of-Buddha within the 'Essence of our Mind,' we become crystal clear, free from all evil, and transformed unto righteousness, thus attaining enlightenment by our own efforts. . . .[59]

(3) (*Three Correct Ways of Thinking*) :—Hui Neng here warns his disciples that it is a great mistake to cease from all exertion of mind. They should take, he says, three principles as guides to their thinking: (a) "If we do not let our minds attach to anything, we shall gain emancipation. . . . Even in time of quarrels . . . we should treat our intimates and our enemies alike and never think of retaliation." (b) "We should also free our minds from absorption in external objects, so that the Dharma will be pure. . . ."

and (c) ". . . By avoiding the mistakes of delusion, we fix our minds on the true nature of Tathatā (Suchness) . . . and our own true nature may be self-manifested all the time. This is what is known as 'idealessness.'"[60]

(4) (*The Way of Spontaneous Realization*) :—Advising everyone to study and recite the *Diamond Sūtra,* Hui Neng urged the possibility of becoming Buddha by spontaneous realization of one's true nature by introspection of the mind. . . . "He who . . . attaches no importance to rituals and whose mind functions always under right views . . . is said to know his Essence of Mind. . . ."* ". . . . *A gleam of enlightenment is enough to make any living being the equal of Buddha.*" In his "Formless Stanza," which he urged all to memorize, Hui Neng concludes with these lines:

> "Kalpa after kalpa, a man may be under delusion,
> But once enlightened, it takes him only a moment
> to attain Buddhahood."[61]

On the question of 'sudden' *versus* 'gradual' enlightenment, the Sixth Patriarch, with a note of finality, then gives the following pronouncement:

"He who realizes the Essence of Mind may dispense with such doctrines as Bodhi, Nirvāṇa, and 'Knowledge of Emancipation. . . .' Since it is with our own efforts that we realize the Essence of Mind, and since the realization and the practice of the Law are both done instantaneously and not gradually . . . the formulation of any system of Law is unnecessary. As all Dharmas are intrinsically Nirvāṇic, how can there be gradation in them?"[62]

C. *Description of the Goal of Nirvāṇa*

In reply to a question from one Chi Tao as to the meaning of Nirvāṇa in a certain passage in the *Mahā-Parinirvāṇa Sūtra,* the Patriarch enunciated the first of two criteria:

---

* Chang Chen-chi points up Ch'an Buddhism's agreement with the Yogācāra School's recognition of the self-witnessing or self-awareness portion of consciousness as the pure form which is "intrinsically non-dualistic and functions without any external stimulus." This is Zen's "seeing one's own Mind-Essence." (64)

"At any one moment, Nirvāṇa . . . is the manifestation of *Perfect Rest and Cessation of Changes* . . . which has neither enjoyer nor non-enjoyer. . . . (As my stanza reads) :–

"The Supreme Mahā-Parinirvāṇa
Is perfect, permanent, calm, and illuminating–
(neither) . . . death, (nor) annihilation. . .
Only those of super-eminent mind can understand
what Nirvāṇa is . . ." [63]

In other words,

"He who is above affirmative and negative rides permanently in the White Bullock Cart (the Vehicle of Buddha (i.e., he already possesses Enlightenment-knowledge, or *Bodhi*).

" (In Enlightenment), the states of deluded consciousness (*vijñānas*) are dissolved into wisdom (*prajñā*) and one can then abide forever in peace of mind (*samādhi*). This is (called) a 'sudden transmutation.'

" . . . To understand thoroughly all Dharmas . . . to be above Dharmalakṣaṇa (things and phenomenon), and to be in possession of nothing, is the Supreme Vehicle . . . of Thusness." [65]

The second criterion was enunciated when thirteen-year-old Ko Shin Wui came from the Gradual School (at the Yuk Chuen Monastery of Shih Shan) in North China to tender homage to the Sixth Patriarch. When the boy was asked, "What is the fundamental principle?" he replied simply: *"Non-attachment is the fundamental principle."* The Patriarch then tested him further and brought the matter to a conclusion by stating that nirvanic knowledge of the Essence of Mind can be obtained only intuitively (i.e., neither by study of books nor by questioning others to get verbal authority, but only by showing neither attachment nor indifference to Nirvāṇa) . . .[66]

Years later, Ko Shin Wui, after himself becoming a Dhyāna-Master (known as Ho Chak), wrote *An Explicit Treatise on Dhyāna Teaching*, in which he said:

"After the Parinirvāṇa of the Exalted One, the twenty-eight patriarchs of India all transmitted the 'Mind of Non-attachment' to their successors. What is referred to as 'Non-attachment' is the real state of things (i.e., *Nirvāṇa*). . . . In such a state, truth and falsehood merge into one. Call it 'Unity,' it is of many kinds. Call it 'Duplicity,' it is non-dualistic."[67]

At the end of the sutra, the editor concludes by remarking: "From the above, it will be seen that this sentence—'Non-attachment is the fundamental principle'—is the keynote of the Dhyāna teaching (of the Meditation School)."[68] *

* * *

While, in the main, preferring to follow the impact of Buddhist philosophy on the Chinese mind, we may do well at this point to digress enough to learn how the Dhyāna or Ch'an (Zen) teaching of Hui Neng has been interpreted by a noted, contemporary Japanese Buddhist scholar, Dr. Daisetz Teitaro Suzuki of Otani University in Kyoto, in his *The Zen Doctrine of No Mind* (or *The Significance of the Sūtra of Hui Neng or Wei Lang*).[69]

In his introduction to Hui Neng (Wei Lang in the southern dialect; Yeno in Japanese), Dr. Suzuki refers to *The Platform Sermons of the Sixth Patriarch* (*Lu-tso T'an-ching*) as having created a sensation among eighth century Buddhists for two reasons: In them Hui Neng appealed to the masses by his rejection of Shen-hsiu's** conceptualism*** as a wrong in-

---

* (Tr. note):—An editorial comment by Mr. Dih Ping-tsze. (Author's note): H. G. Creel reminds us how similar Ch'an Buddhism is to early Taoism, and that despite the fact that it "discards many of the trappings of the Mahāyāna," (nevertheless) "much of what is left is remarkably like early Indian Buddhism."[70]

** Shen-hsiu (A.D. 605-706) was abbot of the northern "Gradual School" of Ch'an Buddhism, located in the Wutang Mts. (modern Hupei), which disappeared before very long. (71) Hu Shih believes to be a pure fabrication Shen Hui's contention in 734 that Hung-jên (d. 674) had given his robe to Hui Neng. Nevertheless, it was Shen Hui's espousal of the Southern School's teaching that caused a revolution in the North; and, in fact, after his death (760), he was given the title of "Seventh Patriarch" not only by a council of Ch'an Masters but also by an imperial decree. (72)

*** Chang Chen-chi makes clear the Zen objection to intellection and its "clinging pattern" in his art. "The Nature of Ch'an (Zen) Buddhism." (73)

terpretation of Supreme Wisdom (*Prajñā*); he also warned against the danger of misrepresenting Meditation (*Dhyāna*) as the 'tranquilizing drug' of a passive quietism.* Dr. Suzuki then gives his interpretation of Hui Neng's idea of the relation of Wisdom to Meditation, as well as his conception of the Unconscious.

Hui Neng's Idea of Wisdom (*Prajñā*) *through Meditation* (*Dhyāna*)

"The motive of the compiler of the *T'an-ching* was evidently to expound. . . . Hui Neng's idea of Wisdom and to distinguish it from its original understanding.

"Hui Neng's conception of Meditation . . . was not the art of tranquilizing the mind. . . . One-sided meditation is sure to tend toward quietism and death. . . . Meditation has nothing to do with mere sitting cross-legged in contemplation, as is generally supposed by outsiders . . . it is rather acting, moving, performing deeds, seeing, hearing, thinking, remembering. . . .

"Hui Neng . . . lays stress on the significance of the inner eye, which . . . sees into the mysteries of Self-nature—the spark of the ultimate constituent of all things. . . .

"When True Wisdom functions, one finds oneself, all of a sudden . . . facing the emptiness of all things (*śūnyatā*). . . . (In this way), the unattainable is attained and the eternally serene is perceived. . . .

"According to this school, the movement from ignorance to enlightenment is abrupt and not gradual. . . . This is 'Seeing into one's Self-nature.' . . . Once this viewpoint of wisdom is gained, all the essential irrationalities found in religion become intelligible." [74]

---

* For practical purposes, the English equivalents of these technical Buddhist terms may be taken as: *Dhyāna* meaning "deep contemplation" or "inner communion with the Self"; *Prajñā* meaning "intuitive wisdom," inner awakening," "spiritual illumination," or "enlightened ecstasy."

Hui Neng's Understanding of the Unconscious

(The discussion is presented under six points) :—

(1) (*Two Planes of Living*) —"There are two planes of living: the one is the plane of consciousness (*yu-hsin*); the other is that of unconsciousness (*wu-hsin*). Activities belonging to the first plane . . . are governed by the laws of *karma,* while those of the second plane are . . . characterized by purposelessness and therefore meritlessness. . . ."

"So long as there are conscious strivings to accomplish a task, the very consciousness works against it, and no task is accomplished. . . . Only when . . . you give yourself up . . . (then) . . . your unconscious mind is still intensely at the work and, before you realize it, you find the work accomplished. 'Man's extremity is God's opportunity.' This is really what is meant by 'to accomplish the task by no-mind.'"[75]

(2) (*"No-Mind," or the Unconscious, is Principle and Goal*) — "According to Hui Neng, the concept of the Unconscious is the foundation of Zen Buddhism. . . . As Hui Neng said: 'I establish no-thought-ness (*wu-nien*) as the principle (of my teaching).' Seeing all things and yet to keep your mind free from stain and attachment, this is no-thought-ness.

"Suchness means the Absolute, something which . . . cannot be grasped by means of form . . . This . . . unattainable is Emptiness, or Void (which) . . . is not in the realm of names and forms. . . . (It) is thus . . . beyond grasping . . . (yet) . . . is always with us and . . . conditions all our life. . . ." *

"Wisdom . . . lays its hands on Emptiness . . . or Self-nature . . . (but) this grasping . . . is accomplished by non-discrimination—an act arising from self-nature itself, which is the Unconscious."[76]

(3) (*The Unconscious has a Metaphysical Connotation*) "Hui Neng's Unconscious is thus fundamentally different from the psychologist's Unconscious. It has a metaphysical connotation. . . .

---

* Here is a clear indication of the influence of the Mādhyamika teaching on Ch'an Buddhism. (78)

For, according to Zen philosophy, we are all endowed with the Buddha-nature, from which Wisdom issues, illumining all our activities, mental and physical. . . .

"To see the Unconscious is to be conscious and yet to be unconscious of self-nature, because . . . (it) is not to be determined by the logical category of being and non-being (and, therefore, cannot be brought into the realm of empirical psychology) . . . . The Unconscious is thus the ultimate reality, the true form, the most exquisite body of Tathāgatahood. It is certainly . . . not a mere conceptual postulate, but a living experience in its deepest sense." [77]

(4) (*Knowing the Unconscious is a Deep Personal Experience*) "One must really have an experience," Suzuki continues, "in order to get into the spirit of the (*Zen*) master, and then the understanding will follow by itself. . . .

"So long as . . . there is no 'seeing into self-nature,' we return literally to a static quietness of inorganic matter. Hui Neng was very much against this conception of *Dhyāna;* hence his philosophy of *Prajñā* and the motto of Zen Buddhism: 'the seeing into self-nature is becoming the Buddha. . . .' In other words, 'seeing' involves dynamic participation in the creative nature of Being. Therefore, it is not mere quietism.

"We must remember that Hui Neng never advocated the doctrine of mere nothingness, or mere doing-nothing-ness . . .

"Both in Tê-shan and Huang-po (Hsi Yün) Zen is taught to be something in direct contact with our daily life. . . . In truth, Buddhism is based on personal experience as much as Christianity. This is especially the case with Zen Buddhism, which stands firmly on experience as the basic principle of its teaching." * [77a]

(5) (*Experience of the Unconscious Has a Passive Aspect*) (In seeking to understand our own self-nature), "We are back again at the relationship of Meditation (*Dhyāna*) to Wisdom (*Prajñā*) . . . . Those who emphasize Wisdom, like Hui Neng and his school, tend to identify Meditation with Wisdom, and insist on an abrupt, instantaneous awakening in the Unconscious (where meditation and wisdom become identical) . . . . The awakening

---

* Chang Chen-chi makes the same observation; viz., that "Zen consists in . . . personal experience, not in philosophical speculation." (79)

is never to be taken for . . . an accomplishment as the result of . . . striving. As there is no attainment in the awakening of Wisdom in the Unconscious, there is no abiding in it either. This is the point most emphatically asserted in all the *Prajñā-pāramitā Sūtras.* No attainment, and therefore no clinging. . . . This very Mind which has no abiding place anywhere is the Buddha-mind itself . . . The doctrine of the Unconscious . . . is . . . that of absolute passivity . . . It may also be represented as the teaching of humility. . . ."[80]

(6) (*Knowing the Unconscious Also Has an Active Aspect*) (Finally), "The conception of the Unconscious leads to many wrong interpretations when it is taken as pointing to the existence of an entity to be designated 'the Unconscious.' Zen masters do not assume such an entity behind our empirical consciousness. . . . (Nevertheless), Buddhist philosophy makes use of two concepts—'Body' and 'Use'—in explaining reality. The two are inseparable, where there is any functioning there must be a Body behind it, and where there is a Body its Use will inevitably be recognized. . . . (In conclusion): "The intellectual seeing into (one's) self-nature, so deeply cultivated by the Indian mind, now exhibits what may be called the practical demonstration phase of Chinese Zen. In terms of Chinese Buddhist philosophy, we can state that the (dynamic) 'Use' of Wisdom is now more in evidence than the (static) 'Body' of Wisdom. . . . (In other words), 'Seeing into one's self-nature' involves dynamic participation in the creative nature of Being."[81]

On the above, Dr. Suzuki makes this concluding remark: "As far as the 'seeing into one's inner being,' known as 'self-nature,' is concerned the matter is more or less on the epistemological plane, and does not seem to affect our practical life from the ethical point of view. But when Wisdom is considered not from the point of view of *seeing* but from the point of view of *acting,* it goes directly into the very heart of life."

"Ma-tsu and Shih-tou, both disciples of disciples of Hui Neng, may be regarded as the originators of the 'Dynamic School' of Zen, great agents of 'Use' . . . (That) dynamic demonstrations (like striking or kicking your interlocutor, dancing or clapping hands, overturning a table, or making cryptic remarks) constitute the essential characteristic of the later development of Zen thought, is one of the most remarkable incidents in the history of religious culture in the Far East."[82]

On the question of "cryptic remarks" (*kung-an,* or *koan*), which he calls "abrupt judgments given by Ch'an masters," Carsun Chang contends that Ch'anists (along with Confucianists and Taoists) believed that one must have an intellectual foundation for intuition of truth; that a directive purpose combined with an intense love of a great cause formed the only true synthesis of reason and intuition.[83]

* * *

We come now to the second of the typically Chinese expressions of the Ch'an (Dhyāna or Zen) philosophy; namely, Hsi Yün's *Huang Po Doctrine of Universal Mind* (*Huang Po Ch'uan Fa Yao*),* as recorded eight years after his death (ca. A.D. 850) by his devoted disciple, P'ei Hsiu. Hsi Yün is said to have been the fourth in the line of succession from Hui Neng and lived on Huang Po Mountain in Kiangsi Province.

In his note of introduction, the translator tells us this scripture "is one of the most important of the numerous Chinese works expounding the doctrine of the Dhyāna (Ch'an) Sect and forms an almost complete exposition of the main tenets of that sect." It is presented here in very condensed form.

2. *Hsi Yün's Huang Po Doctrine of Universal Mind***

(1) (*There is but one Reality—formless Mind-Source*):
". . . .The Master (Hsi Yün) said to me: '. . . Bodhidharma . . . only spoke of universal mind and transmitted this single *dharma*. . . . *Prajñā* is wisdom, but wisdom, too, is this formless mind-source. . . . You must avoid (all) dualist notions and all liking and disliking . . .

---

* Translated by Chu Ch'an in 1947 and published by The Buddhist Society of London.

** As condensed or paraphrased and rearranged.

then you will be able to mount the chariot of the Buddhas.' (Sec. 16). . . . This mind, which has always existed, is unborn* and indestructible. . . . It does not cling to the categories of things which exist or do not exist. . . ." (Sec. 1). . . . Mind-Source, or Buddha-reality, finds expression in Voidness, in the Principle of Manifestation, and in its outworking in all phenomena. (Sec. 24).

(2) (*Bodhi is Supreme Realization of Oneness with Universal Mind*) (Sec. 3):

". . . (This) may come slowly or quickly. . . . Moreover, whether you accomplish your aim in a single flash of thought or by going through the Ten Stages of a Bodhisattva's Progress,** the achievement will be the same, for this state admits of no degrees, but the latter method leads to kalpas of unnecessary suffering and toil." (Sec. 6). ". . . Many people are unwilling to empty their minds for fear that they may plunge into the void, not knowing that their real mind is actually void. The foolish man eschews phenomena but not mentation, while the wise man eschews mentation but not phenomena." *** (Sec. 21). ". . . As to the merits . . . which come from performing the six *pāramitās* . . .**** you should not try to supplement that perfection by such meaningless practices. . . . Only awake to universal mind and realize that there is nothing whatsoever to be attained. (Sec. 2). . . . To experience Pure Mind is to exist independently of everything mundane." (Sec. 9).

---

* 'Unborn' is a word selected to imply a state . . . above the normal categories of logic or thought.

** (Tr. note) :—To Hsi Yün's way of thinking, a man is either enlightened or he is not; partial enlightenment is something quite impossible. . . . Merit is merit . . . but has nothing whatever to do with (the sudden leap into) Enlightenment.

*** (Tr. note) :—. . . "If reality is perceived to be 'void' in its absolute aspect, it follows that its relative aspect is also void, but the voidness of phenomena (its relative aspect) can neither be perceived nor understood except in relation to the 'voidness' of the Absolute. That is why 'the wise man eschews mentation but not phenomena'."

**** (Tr. note:) —"The six *pāramitās* are *dana* (charity), *śila* (keeping the precepts), *kṣānti* (patience under insult), *virya* (zeal and progress), *dhyāna* (meditation), and *prajñā* (wisdom). . . . The point made here is that . . . charitable acts . . . should be absolutely disinterested. . . . Since we and the Buddhas are nothing but universal mind, . . there is no such thing as 'becoming a Buddha'; we have but to realize intuitively what we already are."

(3) (*Inherent in Men are all Buddha-qualities Personified in the Bodhisattvas:* e.g., Manjusri (*Wên Shu*), Samantabhadra (*P'u Hsien*), Avalokita (*Kuan-yin*), Mahāsthāma (*Ta-shih-chih*), and Vimalakirti (*Wei-mo-chieh*) (Sec. 5.). . . . ". . . Fathoming one's Buddha-nature is by instantaneous intuition." (Sec. 8) . . . .* Bodhi is attained merely by effortless realization of the Buddha within. . . . "For fear that people would not believe this . . . (Buddha) drew upon what is seen with the five sorts of vision and spoken with the five sorts of speech." (Sec. 10) .**

(4) (*Logical Thought Can Never Comprehend the Absolute*) :— (This is the purport of a long dialogue between student and Master in Section 27) . . . . Tacit understanding of Dharma rules out all so-called 'realizing' and 'grasping' by mentation. (Sec. 17) . . . . The sage no longer seeks to gain knowledge or to teach doctrine, for "there is no doctrine that can be taught." (Sec. 33). . . . "When body and mind achieve spontaneity, the Way is reached and universal mind can be understood." (Sec. 29) .***

(5) (*Errors Will Cease When Distinctions Are no Longer Made*) (Sec. 32) —". . . To perform good actions**** or bad, equally implies attachment to form. . . . Differentiation arises from wrong thinking . . . and . . . thus . . . all kinds of *karma* are created."

---

* (Tr. note):—"This (Section 8) is intended to illustrate the fact that the achievement of the Gradual School, which seeks Enlightenment by endless *kalpas* (aeons) of self-perfecting practices, is no other than the achievement of the Sudden School, members of which reach the same full Enlightenment by a single flash of intuition."

** (Tr. note):—"Many Mahāyāna sects . . . explain the teachings upon which rival sects are based by stating that those teachings are but relative truths propounded by the Buddha for the benefit of disciples who are not capable of comprehending the highest truths. . . . Indeed, one of the . . . tenets of the T'ien-T'ai (Sect) is that apparent contradictions in the teaching of the various sutras can all be resolved if the latter are regarded as having been preached at different times and to different audiences. Altogether five periods and eight methods of teaching are distinguished by this Sect." (84)

*** (Tr. note):—This passage has a strangely Taoist flavour.

**** (Tr. note) :—"It is fully explained in many books of the Dhyāna Sect that good actions should be performed, but only for their own sake, not with a view to obtaining a reward (which would imply attachment). . . . As Sir Charles Eliot correctly remarked: '. . . Zen (Ch'an) Buddhism could never have influenced Chinese philosophy, including Confucian philosophy, if it had not contained an ethical element.' "

(Sec. 7). . . .* There is no distinction between 'common' and 'holy.' (Sec. 31). . . . When no distinctions are made, one can escape the law of cause and effect. (Sec. 30).

(6) (*The Illusion of Objectivity Obscures the Nature of the Real Dharma*) (Sec. 15). . . . True Dharma means relinquishment of all seeking after truth and all clinging to *objects.* (Sec. 13). . . . (He who is free from entanglements) "will indeed be one who leaves the world without the faintest tendency towards rebirth. . . . This is the fundamental principle." (Sec. 18). ("In other words, only those who are quite unmoved by all appearances and who have given up the idea that they possess anything individual which may be called an ego can hope to reach Enlightenment and avoid rebirth."). . . . Even enlightened ones are, through sensory perceptions, bound to the objective world, which they know is unreal. (Sec. 25). (This means that) "those who have already reached the point where they have a theoretical conception of the universe as being constituted of universal mind, nevertheless, are still dependent on their senses and, owing to their inability to conceive the inconceivable, visualize the Absolute as something pure and bright (i.e., in terms which are still somewhat concrete)."

(7) (*Dispassionate Wisdom Thinks of All Objects of Cognition with Neither Attachment Nor Revulsion*)
. . . (Question): "What is meant by 'worldly truth?' "
(Answer): ". . . Fundamentally, everything is pure. . . . (Those who study the Dhyāna doctrine should) do as I do, letting go of each thought as though it were void . . . or else just making the slight response suitable to the occasion. . . .** Not to see that all

---

* (Tr. note):—"Distinction or differentiation is held to be the chief cause of continued operation of *Karma,* and *Karma* is thought to come to an end once distinctions are eliminated."

** (Tr. note):—"This is a very important remark. So many people . . . (suppose) that Dhyāna practice aims at making the mind a complete blank . . . (whereas) the (real) aim . . . is to eliminate from mental processes all feelings . . . which arise from the belief that things have independent or permanent entities of their own. . . . According to the Dhyāna Buddhists . . . it is possible to react to the circumstances of daily life in a way . . . to deal with them satisfactorily while remaining . . . fundamentally unaffected by them. . . ."

the stages along the Way are impermanent is (to remain in) the sphere of phenomena which arise and pass away." (Sec. 34).*

(8) (*The Dharma Must Be Transmitted Mystically from Mind to Mind*)—"Since the time when the Tathāgata entrusted Kāśyapa with the Dharma until now, the mystical transmission has been from mind to mind, yet those minds were identical with each other. A transmission of 'void' cannot be made through words and any transmission in concrete terms cannot be that of the (true) Dharma." (Sec. 23).
. . . (Question): "Hui Neng could not read the sutras.** How is it that he was made Patriarch? Elder Shen Hsiu was leader and instructor to 500 men. . . . Why was the robe not given to him?"
. . . (Answer): "Because the latter had not eliminated mentation and so transcended phenomena . . ." (Sec. 36)

(9) (*Those Who Fail to Intuit the Dharma of Their Own Minds Are Called 'Icchantikas.' If You Fail in Sudden, then Seek Gradual Enlightenment.*)
. . . "Icchantikas are those whose faith is not complete . . . who do not believe that they (already) possess the potentiality of Buddhahood . . ." (Sec. 20, par. 1)
. . . "Those who do not reach Enlightenment from their own minds, . . . attain to it only stage by stage*** and neglect their real minds. If they could arrive at a tacit understanding of real mind, there would be no need for them to seek any Dharma, for that mind *is* the Dharma." (Sec. 20, par. 2) . . . "If you will . . . at all times , . . . concentrate on eliminating mentation, . . . you will inevitably discover the truth. . . . If you are to understand this,

* (Author's note) :—D. T. Suzuki quotes this passage in his *The Zen Doctrine of No-Mind* to illustrate the idea of absolute obedience (to the True Mind).[85]

** (Tr. note):—"The entire illiteracy of the Sixth Patriarch (Hui Neng, or Wei Lang) is, beyond all doubt, a fiction. It is probable, however, that his book-knowledge was of a low order compared with that of most great monks of his time."

*** (Tr. note):—"This suggests a form of 'relative' Enlightenment which seems to contradict the usual Dhyāna teaching that one is enlightened either fully or not at all."

you must make the most strenuous efforts.* . . . (Yet) none of them compare to perceiving the reality that is (pure) mind." (Sec. 35) . . . (As the stanza reads):

> "Its strength once spent, the arrow falls to earth.
> The life you make may not fulfill your hopes.
> How far below that transcendental way
> Whereby one leap can gain Nirvāṇa's shore?" (Sec. 34b)**

Having examined *The Sūtra of Wei Lang* (Hui Neng) and Hsi Yün's *Huang Po Doctrine of Universal Mind,* we are ready to take a close look at the third of the important Chinese writings that reveal the Ch'an Masters' reactions to the Indian Dhyāna teaching of the Buddha, as they re-interpreted it to their disciples in successive generations.

3. Hui Hai's *The Path To Sudden Attainment* (*Tun-wu Ju Tao Yao-mên Lun*)***

The author, Hui Hai, a Ch'an Master living during the T'ang dynasty (A.D. 620–907), in the direct line of 'apostolic succession' from Hui Neng and Hsi Yün, begins his teachings with the following prefatory remarks:

"I prostrate myself with hands raised in salutation to all the Buddhas of the Universe and to all the Company of Great Bodhisattvas. In

* (Tr. note):—"Buddhists of all sects believe that it is a rare and difficult thing to be born a human being . . . (and it is only from the human state that Enlightenment and Nirvāṇa can be reached, humans being superior to gods in this respect). . . . Hence they feel the urgency of attempting to cover in this life as much of the path to Enlightenment as possible, fearing that such an opportunity may not come again for many *kalpas* (aeons)."

** (Tr. note):—"The verse is a quotation from a poem attributed to the monk Yung Chia (d. 713), entitled 'The Song of Enlightenment' (*Ch'êng Tao Ko*). This has been translated in full by Dr. Walter Liebenthal and published in the *Journal of Oriental Studies of the Catholic University of Peiping.*"[86]

*** Translated for The Buddhist Society of London in 1948 by John Blofeld (87), who calls it "A Treatise of the Ch'an School of Chinese Buddhism." The 60 sections are here very much abbreviated and combined.

undertaking the composition of this treatise, I fear that I shall not achieve the necessary degree of holiness, and wish to express my profound regrets; but if I can attain to such holiness, I will bestow it on all sentient beings in the hope that, in time to come, they will all become Buddhas."

Then, in sixty sections, he reaffirms the basic Ch'an doctrines that we have met in the preceding sutras, using the question-answer method. These may be summarized briefly under eight topical propositions, as follows:—

(1) Deliverance (from *Karma*) is through Sudden Apprehension and not to be attained by the study of innumerable sutras. (Sections 1 and 15)

(2) Assurance of Buddhahood comes, paradoxically, by means of neither acting nor abstaining from action (i.e., in fixed, contemplative abstraction, meditating on your own true nature.). (Sections 3, 17, 25, 48, 60)

(3) To perceive without consciously perceiving is deliverance (or Nirvāṇa): e.g., not allowing thoughts to arise of opposites (like sorrow-joy; birth-destruction; hatred-love, etc.); not to practice the ten evils (killing, stealing, adultery, frivolous babble, lascivious talk, a deceitful tongue, wicked speech, covetousness, anger, and perverted views); and not even to let the mind think of forms of existence (good or evil)—that constitutes the indestructibility of goodness. (Sections 8, 14, 35, 36, 49)

(4) The non-abiding mind (like Buddha's) relinquishes all delusions, speaks without distinctions, abides nowhere, and, (like the sun) shines with unfeeling light.* (Sections 4, 24, 19, 20, 21, 30, 16, and 50)

---

* (Tr. note:)—(Sec. 30) "This is intended to demonstrate that Mahāyāna Buddhism does not admit the doctrine of complete annihilation. All ordinary feelings depending on distinctions between this and that must be eradicated. On the other hand, it would be wrong to infer that nothing is left. There remains something which, relatively speaking, can be described as void but which, since it is not identical with complete annihilation, is simultaneously described as non-void."

(5) *The Law of Perfect Wisdom is Inexpressible*: (therefore we say) 'The Absolute is both Void and Non-Void.' (Question) : "According to the *Vajracchedika Sūtra,* the Law cannot be expressed in words. What does this mean?" (Answer) : "The nature of perfect wisdom (*prajñā*) is utterly pure. . . . In the voidness and stillness of this perfect wisdom, of the forms of activity, . . . there is none which is not comprehended (or none which is not incomprehensible). That is . . . (why) (the Law) is called inexpressible." . . . (Sec. 26) "This, then, is a discourse on the intangibility of the Absolute . . ." Sec. 51)
— (Postscript) : " (Therefore), do not seek after the empty name (of an Enlightened One), speaking of the Absolute with a mind like an ape; that is to disregard the (proper) concordance between words and actions and is called self-deception. . . . Do not seek a lifetime of empty name and happiness, without knowing that you will suffer punishment for endless *kalpas.* (Do not deceive yourselves!) Strive with all your might! Sentient beings must save themselves! The Buddhas cannot save them! . . . Do not rely on the strength of the Buddhas! . . ." *

(6) Uttermost stillness of mind, or non-reception, is the 'Superior Vehicle' of the apprehension of the Buddha. (Sections 28, 29, 37—quoting the *Precepts of the Bodhisattvas;* and 53—quoting the *Vimalakīrti Nirdeśa Sūtra.*)

(7) Escaping from inconsistencies and extremes is the Middle Way. —"When words and actions are opposed, that is speaking with comprehension without in fact comprehending. . . . When words and actions do not differ, that is comprehending in fact as well as in speech." (Sec. 39)**

(8) Status in rebirth will follow one's *karma*:—
(Question) : "In the next rebirth, will the many students of different schools of thought all be together?"

---

* (Tr. note):—"This may imply a criticism of such sects as the Pure Land Sect" (which depends on Buddha O-Mi-T'o's saving power).

** (Tr. note):—"This is a very important point. Mere intellectual comprehension, as simplified in the phrase 'speaking with comprehension,' is deemed to be of little or no value. The truth is something to be *experienced,* not merely understood in theory."

(Answer): " (Yes), if they have reached the same stage of illumination; but (as) their *karma* is not the same, they will be in the same stage but will not be together. The Sūtra says: 'While following the current, one's real nature remains unchanged.'" (Sec. 52)
— (Postscript)—" (Therefore), . . . keep careful watch on your own actions and do not bring up the faults of others. . . . (As) the *Book of Verses for Repetition* says: 'Forbearance is the first step. It is first necessary to eliminate the ego. When anything takes place, there must be no reaction. That indeed is to (break the chain of *karma* and) possess the body of Enlightenment.'"

* * *

Although true holiness seemed reserved for those who took monastic vows, nevertheless, many Buddhist laymen and laywomen have found refuge in the practice of Ch'an meditation within their own homes. As Sir Sarvepalli Radhakrishnan has noted:

"Mahāyāna Buddhism called men not only to the paradise of the buddhas but also to an ordered and sane life on earth, with the objective of making all men happy. Life in the world should be inspired by the spirit of religion. Even as the ideal of the *arhat* was replaced by that of the *bodhisattva,* the hermit ideal was replaced by that of the householder. The desire was to live in the world, while yet being not of the world. The tradition of the holy monk persisted, but the godly layman is also exalted.

"The figure of Vimalakīrti, as described in the Sanskrit work, *Vimalakīrti Nirdeśa Sūtra** (*Wei-Mo-Chieh So-Shuo Ching*), points out how we can mingle among men, live in houses, be a friend of the publicans and sinners and yet be saintly. Vimalakīrti (for example) resided at Vaiśālī, but

* (Tr. note):—"The Sanskrit original is lost, but the Chinese version has been rendered into English by Professor Idumi in the *Eastern Buddhist,* III, (1938-39). The Chinese version by Upasunya (A.D. 502-557) is probably the one referred to; namely, the *Ta Ch'êng Ting Wang Ching.*"

"Though he was but a simple layman, yet
observing the pure monastic discipline; . . .

though possessing a wife and children,
always exercising pure virtues; . . .

manifesting to all the error of passion,
when in the house of debauchery;

persuading all to seek the higher things,
when at the shop of the wine-dealer;

preaching the Law when among wealthy people;
teaching the Kṣatriyas patience;

removing arrogance when among Brahmins;
teaching justice to the great ministers;

teaching loyalty and filial piety to the princes;
teaching honesty to the ladies of the court; . . ." [88]

* * *

In concluding this investigation of the philosophy of the Ch'an or Meditation School, we take note of five of its tenets gathered by Fung Yu-lan from the writings of (Lu) Hui Neng, whose teachings finally gained credence in the sect. They are in effect:

(1) *The Highest Truth* (*Principle*) *is Inexpressible*: because it . . . is actually 'beyond the realm of causations and the conscious mind.'

(2) *Spiritual Attainment Cannot be Cultivated*: It is better to avoid cultivation of enlightenment, to avoid creating evil *karma,* by having no deliberate mind or purpose in whatever one does. . . . By losing all sense of attachment to things in the daily routine of life, . . . one may enter into actual oneness with non-being or 'silent identification' (with the Highest Truth). This abrupt identification is 'instantaneous enlightenment.' . . .

(3) *In the Last Resort Nothing is Gained*: Enlightenment doesn't change anything, because the daily life of the enlightened sage is the same as that of the ordinary man. Therefore, obtaining is not obtaining and nothing is gained.

(4) *There is Nothing Much in Buddhist Teaching*: Once the veil of paradox is pierced, there is nothing fantastic or secret. . . . The cosmological and psychological theories of original Buddhism are regarded by the Ch'anists as arguments which are . . . useless furniture . . . only fit to be thrown away. . . . A pupil of Huang Po (Hsi Yūn) later went to study under another teacher and after achieving enlightenment remarked: "At bottom, there is nothing very much in Huang Po's Buddhism."

(5) *In Carrying Water and Chopping Wood: Therein Lies the Wonderful Tao*: To pass from delusion to enlightenment means to leave one's mortal humanity behind and enter sagehood. Once this has happened, however, the life of a sage is no different from that of ordinary men, for the ordinary mind is the Tao and the sage's mind is the ordinary mind. . . .
. . . "(Yet) spirit-like understanding and divine functioning lie in carrying water and chopping wood—when performed by the sage. . . . In other words, one must be 'amid the phenomenal yet devoid of the phenomenal,'—to be so identified with non-being that 'what the man does is no different from what he did before; it is only that the man himself is not the same as he was.'"[89]

At this point, Fung Yu-lan raised the question of why fathers and kings, as well as water-carriers and wood-choppers couldn't "synthesize the sublime with the common." If so, why then must men abandon their social obligations to become Ch'anist monks? He believed that the Neo-Confucianists of the Sung (A.D. 960–1279) and the Ming (A.D. 1368–1644) periods found the answers to this problem of how to cultivate the mysterious *Tao*.[90]

Certain Short-lived Minor Sects

Early in the Buddhist period in China, certain minor sects sprang up, apparently on the basis of the popularity of one particular sutra, as interpreted and promoted by one individual or small group. The Ch'êng-Shih Sect (Satyasiddhi* or Śūnyatā School of Hīnayāna), for example, was based on the *Satyasiddhi-śāstra,* written by Harivarman of Central India about A.D. 250 to 350 and translated into Chinese by Kumārajīva in A.D. 411. It was called "Ch'êng Shih" (Completion of Truth), because it purported "to 'complete' the Buddhist doctrine by showing that both the ego and the eighty-four *dharmas* recognized by the school are void and non-existent."[91] Flourishing for several centuries, the sect later merged with the San Lun (Three Shastras) or Mādhyamika School, and both were ultimately absorbed by the Ch'an School.[92]

Another early minor Hīnayāna sect, the Chü-Shê (Abhidharmakośa School of Realism) based its teaching on the *Abhidharma-kośa Śāstra* (The Store of the Higher Law) (*Chü Shê Lun*) of Vasubandhu, an exposition of the *Abhidharma Piṭaka* which had probably been brought to China by Hsüan-tsang and translated by him fairly early (i.e., ca. A.D. 651–654), according to Radhakrishnan.[93] The school held a belief in the unreality of the self coupled with a belief in the real entity of all *dharmas.* The latter, it held to be of two kinds: created (sense-objects, mind and its functionings, etc.), which are taken as elements of positive becoming; non-created (like 'space' and 'extinction'), which are considered elements of negative becoming. As W. T. Chan sums it up, "All *dharmas* have their effective causes and conditions of existence, although they co-exist but momentarily in the actual world due to the constant fluctuations in the dynamic operation of the various causes and conditions."[94]

This (Chü-Shê) sect flourished from the sixth to the ninth century, but was also absorbed by the stronger Ch'an School.[95]

A third sect, that became quite influential, was the Lin-Chi school founded by I-hsüan (d. 866) in Western Hopei after the "Great Persecution" of A.D. 845. Its motto of "Recognize Yourself" revealed a complete disregard of all Bodhisattvas

* Sanskrit: "Completion of Truth."

and Buddhas, rather stressing man's control of his own destiny. This emphasis on freedom of intellectual life attracted Confucian scholars and made the sect dominant in Ch'an circles from the ninth through the eleventh century.[96]

4. *The Philosophy of the T'ien-T'ai School* (*T'ien-T'ai Tsung* or *Fa-Hua Tsung*)

About the middle of the sixth century, certain Ch'an monks, disturbed by the growth of sectarian divisions within the Buddhist Order, began to associate themselves together as a Harmonizing School under the leadership of Hui Wen (ca. 550), their first patriarch. Hui Ssu became their second leader and Chih K'ai (or Chih I) the third patriarch, who lived A.D. 538–597. He is recognized as the real founder of the T'ien-T'ai School ("Tendai" in Japan), so named from the range of mountains (T'ien T'ai Shan) in eastern Chekiang, south of Ningpo, where Chih K'ai finally settled and attracted many followers.

Chih K'ai felt that all sects and all sutras had a place in the Buddhist system and could be harmonized. Those who wished to worship images of particular Buddhas and Bodhisattvas, those who wished to study the scriptures, those who wished to devote themselves to meditation, and those who desired to ponder the deep things of metaphysical speculation—all could find refuge and welcome in the sequestered monastic life at T'ien-T'ai Shan.

His favorite sutras were the *Lotus Scripture of the Mysterious Law* (*Miao-Fa Lien-Hua Ching* or simply *Fa-Hua Ching*), a translation of the Sanskrit *Saddharma-puṇḍarīka Sūtra,** made originally by Dharmarakṣa about A.D. 310,[97] together with its supplement, the *Shastra of Great Wisdom* (*Mahāprajñāpāramitā Śāstra,* or *Ta Chih-Tu Lun*). More than

---

* *Vide* H. Kern's translation in Vol. 21 of the *Sacred Books of the East* (Oxford, Clarendon Press, 1909); also W. E. Soothill's selected translation—*The Lotus of the Wonderful Law* (Oxford, Clarendon Press, 1930).

any other Buddhist Scripture, the "Lotus Gospel" carries those teachings of the Mahāyāna that make Buddhism "The Religion of Infinite Compassion." Neither a philosophical essay nor a theological treatise, the *Lotus* presents in dramatic form the 'One Great Vehicle' whereby all men may attain salvation by becoming Bodhisattvas and ultimately Buddhas.[98] It has been pointed out that the (unknown) writer of the *Lotus Scripture* was more interested in the popular side of the Bodhisattva doctrine than in the new metaphysical speculations then current in the growing Mahāyāna movement in India. "Though it mentions (in Chapter 14) . . . the doctrine of the Void, it (*The Lotus Sūtra of the True Law*) is devoted (more specifically) to expounding the new doctrine of the nature of a Buddha."[99] In later chapters (23 to 28), its author deals at length with various Buddhas and Bodhisattvas as objects of devotion, especially Avalokiteśvara (*Kuan-yin*).[100] *

In the above-mentioned sutra and shastra, Chih K'ai found comfort in such teachings as "the identity of the Absolute and the phenomenal; the eternity of the Buddha; the existence of an infinite number of Bodhisattva-saviors; and the latent power of everyone to become a Buddha."[101] But it was the transcendental passages in the sutra that fascinated Chih K'ai most, for he is said to have produced two expositions of the *Lotus Gospel* itself and by it was also reputedly inspired to write his own essay on *Mahāyāna Method of Cessation and Contemplation (Ta-Ch'êng Chih-Kuan Fa-Mên).* These writings were recorded by a disciple named Kuan Ting and are held in much esteem by members of the T'ien-T'ai School as their own "Three Great Books" (*San Ta Pu*).[102]

The philosophy contained in these supposed writings of Chih K'ai have been briefly stated as follows: It centers around the principle of "The Perfectly Harmonious Threefold Truth," which W. T. Chan explains as (1) "All things are Void because they are dependent on causes and, therefore, have no

---

* For the best recent description of "The Lotus Sūtra," see W. T. Chan's detailed paper of that title read at the Conference On Oriental Classics in General Education at Columbia University, Sept. 12-13, 1958.

self-nature. (2) But they do enjoy temporary existence.[103] (3) Being both void and temporary is the nature of *dharmas* (things), and such is the 'Mean.'

"These three realms of truth (Void, Temporariness, and the Mean) are so . . . inter-related that they . . . (not only are) . . . 'immanent in a single instant of consciousness . . .' (but also, in turn), involve all possible realms of existence. Their totality is . . . Absolute Reality, Ultimate Void, Thusness, or Nirvāṇa. Since everything involves everything else, it follows that 'Buddha-nature is everywhere over the world,' and every being can be saved . . . (This teaching) completely rejects the *icchantika* (devoid of Buddha-nature) theory . . . but strongly insists on the doctrine of 'salvation of all. . . .' "[104]

Here Dr. Chan would interject a reminder to note how the T'ien-T'ai interpretation of the phenomenal world as very real, as "none other than the Middle Path," is in sharp contrast to the Indian Buddhist conception of the external world as *maya* or illusion. To say that all truths merge into the one truth that "All is One and One is All," paved the way for the Meditation School's emphasis on seeing into one's own Buddha-nature and represented "a fundamental transformation of Indian philosophy," which re-interpreted Nirvāṇa in terms of "permanence, bliss, ego, and purity," rather than in terms of Hīnayānist "non-ego."[105] "The T'ien-T'ai School," concludes Dr. Chan, "has developed a special formula of meditation called 'calmness and insight' (*chih-kuan*).* Calmness, literally 'at rest,' connotes putting the wrong mind at rest by realizing that *dharmas* are neither produced nor annihilated, and means the intuition of both the Void and the Temporariness of Reality."[107]

In more elaborated form, the T'ien-T'ai philosophy has been stated by Fung Yu-lan in six propositions,[108] which may be condensed and briefly set forth as follows:

---

* This formula is based on the underlying philosophy outlined in the *Ta-Ch'êng Chih-Kuan Fa-Men* (*The Mahāyāna Law-Gate of Calmness and Insight*), translated above (by Fung Yu-lan) as "The Mahāyāna Method of Cessation and Contemplation." According to Dr. Fung, its real authorship is uncertain. (106)

(1) *The Universe as Absolute Mind*:—"The universe in its entirety is regarded by the T'ien-T'ai School as consisting of a single absolute mind, known as the *Bhūtatathatā* or the *Tathāgata-garbha* (Genuine Thusness or Storehouse of the Thus-come, or *Chen Ju*)."

This 'Genuine Thusness' as undifferentiated substance potentially contains or is able to create both the impure natures of all sentient beings of this world and the pure natures of all the other-worldly Buddhas. Therefore, in its creative capacity *Chen Ju* is infinitely differentiated.

(Here we have a dualistic theory of ultimate reality aimed at explaining the presence of good and evil in the world. This paradoxical nature of the universe is further elaborated in the next proposition.)

(2) *The 'Three Characters' of Absolute Mind*:—The Absolute Mind, being potentially pure and impure, manifests itself as the eighth (or *ālaya*) consciousness, which functions in and through the other seven forms of consciousness. In the process, however, Pure Mind becomes polluted or 'perfumed' by the impure seeds of evil and *karma* appears. (Hence Genuine Mind may be viewed in its pure aspect of non-pollution or in its impure aspect of pollution.) This evidences the *'dual character of ultimate reality.'*

But, as Mind becomes manifested in 'the realm of things,' it takes on, in its polluted aspect, the *'character of dependency,'* or interdependence between it and things.

And things, in turn, have a way of assuming an erroneously real aspect, which is called the *'character of discrimination'* (in its polluted aspect).*

(3) *Universal and Non-Universal Consciousness in Individuals*:—Individual differences in perception and enjoyment of external phenomena are due to the varying degrees of *karma* in each person. A certain basic, or common denominator of, *karma* will produce a common or universal consciousness (perception); whereas particu-

---

* At this point, Fung Yu-lan calls attention to slight differences in the T'ien-T'ai and Mere-Ideation Schools' use of terms: e.g., T'ien-T'ai's 'character of ultimate reality' (by its dual nature) is less 'empty' than Mere-Ideation's idea of 'complete emptiness.' The 'character of dependency' is the same for the two schools, and T'ien-T'ai's 'character of discrimination' is the equivalent of Mere-Ideation's term 'character of sole imagination.' (109)

larized manifestations (or retributions) will appear to each person because of his special stock of merit or peculiar *karma.*

(4) *The Integration of All Things in the Mind:*—Apparent spatial differences become non-existent when integrated in a single mind's totality. Likewise, seemingly different periods of time become telescoped into one instant within the mind. Where the pantheist regards both phenomena and mind as having separate reality, the Buddhist holds all things to be the product of mind—with no reality of their own.

(5) *The Way of Calmness and Insight:*—Bringing to an end deluded thinking is a negative *cessation* (resulting in 'calmness'); whereas positive *contemplation* (producing 'insight') concludes that all objects of thought are illusory.

One may, therefore, come to the threshold of Nirvāṇa (by cessation), but refuse to enter into eternal bliss and return to save (by continued contemplation) this world's creatures from delusion.

(6) *Enlightenment the Goal of the Unenlightened:*—"Since sentient beings with impure nature lack enlightenment (*bodhi*), they live in ignorance and impurity which in turn gives rise to impure *karma.* Hence they can only be described as living in a dream and deserving of compassion. On the other hand, the distinction between Buddhas and ordinary beings is simply one of enlightenment as against unenlightenment."

It is needful, therefore, to strive for that rarefied state of the Buddha-mind that enables one to live in, but not be contaminated by, this evil world. Believing that "through the pure *karma* that arises from the pure nature, men can gain this enlightenment," we press on toward the goal of achieving the supreme wisdom (*jñāna*) of Buddhahood.[110]

A corollary of this last proposition; namely, that "if all things are manifestations of Genuine Mind in its totality, then even inanimate things possess a Buddha-nature," was defended by the Ninth Patriarch of T'ien-T'ai (Chi Chan-jan, A.D. 711–782). This goes a step farther than Tao-sheng's and Hsi Yün's contention that the Buddha-nature is possessed even by *icchantikas* who have not yet learned to believe in their own 'pure mind' as an earnest of their eternal inheritance.[111]

* * *

5. *The Philosophy of the Discipline* (*Vinaya*) *School* (*Lü Tsung*)

Following the emphasis of its founder, Tao Hsüan (A.D. 595–667), this small but influential Hīnayāna school laid great stress on monastic discipline, using as its basic scripture the *Sūtra of Brahma's Net* (*Fan Wang Ching*). This manual of laws and regulations, taken evidently from the *Vinaya-Piṭaka* and said to have been translated by Kumārajīva in A.D. 406, gives the rules for organization and a code of conduct for the daily life of monks and nuns. It contains also many later additions which make it very different from the *Brahma's Net* in the Pali Canon.

Although most of the Chinese Buddhist temples and monasteries, with the exception of the Esoteric (*Chen Yen*) School, follow very much the same regulations as the Discipline or Law School, nevertheless the latter to a late date has maintained at its center on Pao Hua Shan, near Nanking in Kiangsu Province, a wide reputation for high requirements for ordination, for scriptural knowledge, for austerity of life, and for the fulfillment of pilgrimage vows.[112]

6. *The Philosophy of the Mere-Ideation School* (*Wei-Shih Tsung* or *Fa-Hsiang Tsung*)

Of the ten years (A.D. 633–643) which the famous Chinese Buddhist pilgrim, Hsüan-tsang, spent in India, five are said to have been devoted to the study of *Vijñānavāda* (Chinese: *Wei-shih*) in the Buddhist University of Nālanda (near modern Patna), under the tutelage of Śīlabhadra, who had been trained in the Pure Consciousness (Yogācāra) School of Asaṅga and Vasubandhu (A.D. 4th century) at Peshawar in Gandhāra.* On his return to China, Hsüan-tsang (A.D. 596–664) became the first patriarch of the Wei-Shih or Fa-Hsiang (Dharma-Character) School—the Chinese offshoot of the Yogācāra School, which is now known as the Mere-Ideation School. The most important of the many earlier translations which Hsüan-tsang found ready to use was that of the *Viṁśātikā* of Vasubandhu or *Treatise On Achieving Pure Consciousness* (*Ch'êng Wei-Shih Lun*) or *Completion of the Doctrine of Mere Ideation,*** to which were added some interpolations of his own. He also found useful the *Trimsikā* or *Treatise in Thirty Stanzas on Mere Ideation (Wei-Shih San-Shih Lun)****, which had been translated in A.D. 557 to 569. He himself, in 661, translated its shorter counterpart, *The Treatise in Twenty Stanzas On Representation Only* (*Wei-Shih Êrh-Shih Lun*),**** also by Vasubandhu. These three treatises are expositions of the theory of "Consciousness Only," which, in turn, is said to have been based on the much older *Laṅkāvatāra Sūtra.*

In Hsüan-tsang's version of Vasubandhu's *Treatise in Twenty*

---

* According to E. J. Thomas: *History of Buddhist Thought* (pp. 236-238), the teaching of this school was a restatement of ideas current in the time of Aśvaghoṣa and reflected in the *Awakening of Faith.* The word 'Yogācāra' means "practice of yoga" (mysticism, with some tantric admixture). For a general estimate of the Vijñānavāda (Yogācāra) School, see P. T. Raju: *Idealistic Thought of India,* pp. 273-276. Pratt refers to it as the Dharmalakshana Sect (Hosso in Japan) 113

** (Tr. note) :—In Sanskrit, the full name is *Viṁśātikā-Vijñāptimātratā-siddhi-śāstra,* translated into Chinese in A.D. 508 to 535, and into French by Louis de la Vallee Poussin (Paris, 2 vols. 1928-29) . (114)

*** Translated into French by S. Levi in 1932.

**** The *Wei-Shih Êrh-Shih Lun,* translated into Chinese as early as A.D. 430 and 443, has been re-translated into English by Dr. Clarence H. Hamilton and published as a monograph of the American Oriental Society (New Haven, Series XIII, 1938) . See P. T. Raju; *Idealistic Thought of India* (pp. 259-266) for a discussion of ideas in this treatise.

(*Note*):—For Hsüan-tsang's account of his travels to and from India, see Thomas Watters' translation: *On Yuan Chwang's Travels in India* (London, 2 vols., 1904-5).—A parody on this, presumed to date from the Yüan dynasty, known as the *Hsi Yu Chi* or *The Journey to the West* (a Chinese "Pilgrim's Progress"), has been very popular in the modern Chinese theater. (115)

Stanzas on Representation Only* according to Clarence H. Hamilton, "we have some of his (Vasubandhu's) reasonings to prove that no world of extra-mental entities exists beyond the realm of consciousness. This idealism he believed was Buddha's inner intention, though not expressed in the earlier dogma." Vasubandhu's main argument in Stanzas X to XVI (from Hamilton's translation) is presented here in précis form:—

"When a questioner asked if there was not an outer realm of reality existing as object of our sense consciousness, Vasubandhu replied in effect: 'No, because the atom is not proved' . . . Because, if atoms join other atoms (each on six sides), the aggregate must still be like one atom. If atoms don't combine and still are thought to have spatial divisions, there is error and the reality of the single atom is (still) in doubt."

(On the other hand), "If we deny spatial divisions, we are in error, . . . because we cannot explain 'mutual occultation or 'obstruction' of one part (of an atom) by another, or of one atom by another. And what is true of atoms must also be true of 'aggregates' of atoms: i.e., they can have neither shadow nor occultation; nor can they have external sense-quality of color, of unity, or of multiplicity."

(Furthermore), "if we assume the unity of all things, there can be no perceptible . . . differences in the many, . . . and, since we have argued that there is no real single atom, we must agree that only representations in the mind can exist and we cannot prove existence outside of consciousness. . . .

(In other words), "what we call 'immediate awareness' is only unreal dreaming. Even to argue that awareness is of 'some previously experienced object', . . . (this) is also false reasoning; (for) memory takes hold only of a 'representation,' not of an external reality. Just as we aren't aware of unreality while dreaming, so we have to wait in our waking life for that time of 'true awakening' when our purified understanding will become aware that all objects are unreal."[117]

---

* Radhakrishnan suggests "Ideation" as a preferable translation (of vijñaptimātratā or wei-shih), because "Representation" suggests but does not deny external reality. (116)

In great detail, then, the Mere-Ideation School aimed to show that man's belief in his own existence, as well as in the reality of external objects, is entirely illusory. Both the world and the ego are "mere ideation"—"mental representations dependent upon the evolutions of consciousness." Yet, as Fung Yu-lan has pointed out, "while denying the real existence of external things as such, the Mere Ideation School affirms the existence of consciousness, thus taking the middle path and avoiding the doctrine of 'emptiness' on one hand and 'being' on the other."[118]

This pure idealism may be summed up in the dictum: "The only reality is consciousness or ideation," or "nothing is real but consciousness." As Blofeld has succinctly put it, the "seeds" of thought produced by dependence on the six senses (sight, hearing, smell, taste, touch, and thought) are planted (through the seventh consciousness) in the eighth, or *ālaya*-consciousness; and "these seeds determine the various transmigrations through which all individuals must pass." *

The Completion of the Doctrine of Mere Ideation (*Ch'êng Wei-Shih Lun*) explains the Eight Forms of Consciousness briefly as follows:—

(1) *The First Six 'Perceptive Forms of Consciousness,'* which apprehended the (seemingly external) objects, follow the functions of the five senses . . . plus a sixth faculty or sense-center which . . . coordinates the ideas derived from the senses (i.e., a thought-consciousness) . . . The five sense-modalities function only when their conditioning factors permit. . . . Therefore, their operations are crude and unstable and intermittently manifesting.[119]

———

* Blofeld points out, however, that this (subjective) idealism is somewhat more realistic than the Mādhyamika (*fa-hsing*) idealism, yet "the term realism (*fa-hsiang*, or *dharmalakṣana*) applied to this system is somewhat misleading, unless understood in the sense of something which is a less pure form of idealism than that propounded by the Hua-Yen, T'ien-T'ai, and Esoteric Sects; because, in fact, all Mahāyāna doctrines are idealistic to a greater or lesser degree." (121)

(2) *The Seventh* (*or Manas*) *Consciousness* (Intellection or Discrimination) always thinks in a way to link the self perpetually with the four *kleśas,* or sources of affliction; namely, delusion as to the self, wrong clinging to belief in the principle of an ego, self-conceit, and greedy attachment to selfish interest. These pollute (or 'perfume') both the innermost mind (*ālaya-consciousness*) and the other six forms of consciousness, thus binding sentient beings to the cycle of transmigration.[120]

(3) *The Eighth Consciousness* (*Ālaya-Vijñāna*), called the "Storehouse Consciousness" (*tsang shih*), is the final, evolving consciousness, which produces "universal seeds" of external mountains, rivers, etc., as well as the bodily or physical basis for the sense-faculties of other people (which in their totality constitute the body of the person concerned).

This maturing consciousness, (as 'perfumed' by the other seven consciousnessess) also evolves "non-universal seeds" of its own sense-faculties and their bodily basis. [Another way of classifying "seeds of thought" is to call some "tainted" and some "untainted." The tainted are causes of all the impure objects which belong to the phenomenal world; the untainted seeds are causes of all the pure *dharmas* which belong to the transcendental world.][122]

In all this discussion, as Fung points out, no explanation is made of how the seeds of one person's consciousness can coincide exactly with those evolved in another person's consciousness. Moreover, the description of the *ālaya*-consciousness "seems to make of consciousness something like a 'universal consciousness' greater than that of the individuual human consciousness, in which the latter is caught up and swept along as it were in an irresistible flood of uncertain existence."[123] *

---

* (Tr. note):—(There seem to be four divisions of impure consciousness): "These four functional *divisions* of consciousness should not be confused with the eight different *kinds* of consciousness. . . .** The process is one in which there are: (1) the manifestations by consciousness of seemingly objective objects and phenomena, which are (2) perceived by a seemingly subjective consciousness. The resulting sensed images are (3) checked upon by the self-corroborating division, resulting in the accumulation of organized knowledge. (4) A second corroborating division further checks this knowledge to insure its correctness." (124)

** (Author's note):—The term '*divisions* of consciousness' used here may be

Pratt's understanding is slightly different, when he says: "The real inner self which is the creator of my world is the *ālaya-vijñāna*. There is no universal *ālaya-vijñāna* but a multiplicity of individual ones. . . . All our potentialities . . . are within it. It is eternal and its action is endless and continuous. . . . The world which it creates—the world of our perception—is in constant flux, changing with unimaginable rapidity. . . . Phenomenal personality changes at the same rate. . . . But underneath all this flux is the eternal *ālaya-vijñāna*." [123a]

Undoubtedly, Hsüan-tsang promoted the *Completion of the Doctrine of Mere Ideation* (*Ch'êng Wei-Shih Lun*) because in it he found a clear enunciation of two fundamental doctrines:—

(1) *The Character of Ultimate Reality* (*Chen Ju* or Genuine Thusness): . . . If one can grasp this view of the *'Bhūtatathatā'* or *'Dharmadhātu'* (Nature of Absolute Reality) as 'the underlying, unifying reality which is the ground or cause of all *dharmas* or things,' one will be treading the Way to (Pure) Enlightenment or Nirvāṇa, which brings the transformation of consciousness into wisdom.

(2) *The Transformation of Consciousness into Wisdom*: By accepting the concept of 'Mere Ideation,' the novitiate gradually cultivates . . . that superior knowledge of reality which obliterates . . . delusions and worldly knowledge (false belief in a seeming reality of objects). Moving into the stage of 'unimpeded understanding,' the Truth-seeker . . . (finds that) undiscriminating wisdom which . . . accepts no . . . sophistry about (the seeming) appearance (of the external world). (At that moment) he experiences *Chen Ju* or *Chüan Yi* (revulsion of the base), or complete emancipation of the *ālaya*-consciousness (by the) removing of taint from all its stored "seeds." Thus, the eight kinds of consciousness are transformed into *Jñāna* or true wisdom, which manifests the aspects of Buddha which mark the end of the 'Truth of the Right Path.' [125]

---

compared to *'functions* of consciousness'; while *'kinds'* of consciousness,' as used here, corresponds to the *'elements* of consciousness' as used by Wendell Cruze in his discussion of consciousness in his *General Psychology* (N. Y., Prentice-Hall, 1951), p. 22, paragraph 2.

Thus, under the influence of Vasubandhu, Hsüan-tsang struck the keynotes of Chinese Buddhist philosophy, which, down through the centuries, have, like an atomic chain-reaction, affected the minds of Buddhist thinkers, including many of the present generation like T'ai Hsü Fa-Shih. There were those, however, who took issue with Hsüan-tsang and his "Wei-Shih"doctrines, as will become clear in the next section.

* * *

7. *The Philosophy of the Avataṃsaka ("Wreath") School (Hua-Yen Tsung)*

Within the ranks of the Buddhist fold, came a decidedly adverse reaction from one of Hsüan-tsang's own pupils, one (K'ang) Fa-tsang (A.D. 643–712), who left him to propagate the teachings of two other monks (Tu-shun, 557–640, and Chih-yen, 601-668) based on the *Hua-Yen Ching,* or *Avataṃsaka Sūtra,** together with his own commentaries on it—the *Hua-Yen Yi-hai Pai-men* and the *Hua-Yen Huan-yüan Kuan.*[126] This school became known as the Hua-Yen or Wreath School (Kegon Sect in Japan).

Fa-tsang's reaction was stirred up by Hsüan-tsang's stress on differing potentialities in different persons for achieving Buddhahood; his doctrine of gradual enlightenment; and his stout adherence to the doctrine of the unreality or non-existence of

---

* Its full name in Sanskrit being *Buddhāvataṃsaka-Mahāvaipulya Sūtra,* or "The Expanded Sutra of the Adornments of Buddha"; it is said to have been the first discourse of Buddha only two weeks after his Enlightenment, preached to Bodhisattvas because it was beyond the comprehension of mortals, to whom he then preached a simpler doctrine. Nāgārjuna is the reputed discoverer of the sutra and is, therefore, acclaimed as the first Indian patriarch of this school.

Sir S. Radhakrishnan believes the *Hua-Yen Ching* was translated into Chinese as early as 150 A.D., and Nāgārjuna's commentary on it was translated by Kumarajiva in ca. A.D. 400. The sutra appears in a modern, condensed form as *"The Theology of the Hua-Yen Ching"* (*Hua-Yen Hsüan-T'an*). (128) Dr. M. Winternitz's *History of Indian Literature* is quoted as stating that one translation of this sutra was made in A.D. 418 by Buddhabhadra together with other monks. (129)

the phenomenal world. Harking back to Seng Chao's loophole in the "Emptiness of the Unreal," Fa-tsang felt impelled to preach the doctrines of the *Hua-Yen Ching,* which allegedly come from the lips of Lochana Buddha. This sutra, one of the most important in Chinese Buddhism, is referred to by Reichelt as a very large scripture that "gives in a detailed way the whole development of thought from primitive Buddhism up to the complete program of Mahāyāna, opening up as it were a previously closed world full of religious mysticism." [127]

It suggests three periods for Buddha's teachings: the *first,* when the Hua-Yen doctrine was preached; the *second,* the preaching of Hīnayāna doctrines; and the *third,* when Mahāyāna doctrines were preached. Or, by another arrangement, the teachings of Buddha are given a logical sequence as the Hīnayāna, the Mahāyāna idealistic, the Mahāyāna realistic, the 'Sudden Enlightenment' (or Dhyāna), and the highly metaphysical Hua-Yen doctrine.

This last has been summarized by Blofeld, to show how a devotee might move through four ascending stages of concious understanding, in which he would, *first,* believe in the objective existence of phenomena of form and appearance, of sensation and mind; he would come, *second,* to believe all these to be transitory and void; *third,* he would come to reconcile the concepts of absolute and relative existence; and, *fourth,* he would arrive at an understanding of the essential unity of phenomena which seem to be differentiated, but he would realize there were no real distinctions between them.[130]

The principles enunciated by Fa-tsang are best found in his sophistical *Essay on the Golden Lion* (*Chin Shih-Tzu Chang*), in which he sought to save the world of appearance by showing the interdependence and harmony of all things by reason of universal causation.[131] In the year 704, while attempting to explain the *Hua-Yen Ching* to Empress Wu (ruling A.D. 684-705), he used the figure of a golden lion as symbolic of the ideas he was propounding:*

* Here re-stated in paraphrased and condensed form.

(1) If we assume the gold metal to represent the "realm of principle" (noumenon, or primary cause) and the lion-form to represent the "realm of things" (phenomenon, or secondary cause), we arrive at the theory of the combination of primary and secondary causes or that *all things come by causation.* (Sec. 1)

(2) Yet, as the lion-form is merely appearance, and the gold alone is 'real,' we arrive at the principle of the "emptiness of matter," which is neither a "state of being' nor an annulment of being. (Sec. 2)

(3) Furthermore, while we become aware that all objects (like the lion) seem to have qualities such as 'generalness' (in the whole) and 'speciality' (in the parts), 'similarity' (when products of the same cause) or 'diversity' (when produced by different causes or when each remains distinct); . . . yet, at the same time, we come to realize that *matter is really qualityless,* for these 'qualities' are merely products of mind and have no inherent nature of their own. (Secs. 8, 4)

(4) "Since mind . . . is dependent on (phenomenal) causation, and since matter . . . is dependent on mind," . . . (therefore), the manifestations which they combine to generate are both illusory and indeterminate. This leads us to the principle of 'non-generation' or (at least) 'non-real generation.' (Sec. 5)

(5) On the other hand, we must deduce (among other things) two resolved mysteries: namely,

(a) There is 'mutual compatibility' between the gold (noumenon, the one) and the lion (phenomenon, the many) which enables each to manifest itself without interference from the other. (Sec. 7, parts 3 and 6)

(b) There is 'relying on phenomenal things' to arrive at truth and there is also 'relying on the noumenal' to reveal truth. "By combining the two approaches, one reaches the highest (*ālaya*) consciousness." (Sec. 7, parts 5 and 8)

(6) Finally, we come to the inevitable conclusion that when 'all illusions have no reality,' when the qualities of both 'gold' and 'lion' become extinguished, then ignorance vanishes and we enter a

'new state of being' in which we dwell neither in the cycle of life and death nor in Nirvāṇa that implies complete extinction. When both concepts (of 'emptiness' and 'being') are discarded, the pure mind rests in that state of 'non-attachment' which Mahāyānists call 'intantaneous enlightenment.' . . . "This is the perfect teaching of the One Vehicle, or Highest Buddhist Truth." (Secs. 9, 10, and 6) [132]

As Fung Yu-lan has intimated, Fa-tsang's philosophy "is a system of objective idealism" in which "a permanently immutable 'mind,' which is universal . . . in its scope . . . is the basis for all phenomenal manifestations." Yet, there is sufficient realism, he thinks, in Fa-tsang's system to permit the objective world "to survive even when separated from a subject." It becomes clear, then, in Fung's view, that the 'character of ultimate reality' as described by Fa-tsang differs from that of Hsüan-tsang, the 'emptiness' of the Void being "less uncompromisingly 'empty'" for the former than it is for the latter. Moreover, Fa-tsang accepts 'phenomenon' "as necessary to the scheme of the universe." In these respects, Fung concludes, the general trend of Chinese thought has followed Fa-tsang rather than Hsüan-tsang.[133]

8. *The Philosophy of the True Word (Esoteric) School (Chen-Yen Tsung* or *Mi-Tsung) (Mantrayāna* or *Tantrayāna)*

This school has had an interesting, though somewhat complicated history. Originally developed in India and exceptionally strong in Bengal in the early part of the eighth century, A.D., the Mantrayāna (Tantric or Mystical) School's esoteric teachings were brought to China first (A.D. 716) by Subhākarasiṃha *(Shan Wu Wei)* (A.D. 637-735), who translated the basic scripture of the school—the *Mahāvairocana Sūtra (Ta Jih Ching)*. Shortly afterward, in 719 or 720, came two other monks, Vajrabodhi *(Chin Kang Chih)* (A.D. 663-723), who translated the *Vajraśekhara Sūtra,* and Amoghavajra

(*Pu K'ung*) (A.D. 705-774), a pupil of Vajrabodhi, who later translated the *Tattvasañgraha Sūtra.*[134]

In the first-named sutra, Vairocana (*P'i-lu-chê-na*), the Sun God, represents the Buddha's Law Body (Dharmakāya, or Ultimate Reality), while Lochana (*Lu-shê-na*) represents his Compensation Body (Sambhogakāya or Body of Bliss)—(i.e., ultimate reality expressed in the transitory, phenomenal universe)—and Gautama Buddha is his Transformation Body (Nirmānakāya or personification of the essence of reality). From Blofeld's summary of the underlying philosophy of the sutra, it appears that all existences take form through the working of Vairocana's mind (*vajradhātu,* aspect of wisdom) on the mystical matrix or basic substance of reality (known as *garbhadhātu,* aspect of principle).

Every aspect of form or consciousness is visualized in the Four Circles (*mandalas*):—the general or basic *Matrix* (*Character*) *Mandala,* the *Law Mandala* of ideas and forms (*Name*), the *Teacher* (*Function*) *Mandala,* and the *Mandala of Concentration* (Form). Here 'function' is taken as meaning "that animating force which, proceeding from the essence of reality, relates it to phenomena (despite the belief that reality and phenomena are essentially the same)." Each of these Circles or Mandalas in any or all levels of existence involves all of them in all levels of existence. In terms of elements, the nature of the universe is said to consist of the Six Great Elements of earth, water, fire, air, space, and consciousness, all of which are mutually dependent and interpenetrating. None can exist without the others.

Continuing the cosmology of the *Mahāvairocana Sūtra,* the activity of the universe consists of the Three Mysteries: of Thought, Speech, and Action. All phenomena are the thought, speech, and action of the Great Sun Buddha (Vairocana). Esoteric practice is based on these three secrets, which are imparted by teachers to devotees who seek personal identification with a particular Buddha or Bodhisattva in order to secure their own enlightenment. "They comprise *mudrās* or symbols, made by placing the hands and fingers in certain (intertwined) positions; *dhāraṇīs* or secret formulae (true words) to be repeated in a certain tone of voice;* and *yoga*-concentration or the visualization of the form of one or more of the (Buddhas or) Bodhisattvas." [135]

"This three-fold ritual is considered the only effectual means of communion with the Buddha (or Bodhisattva). It is from the second mystery that the School derives its names: True Word (*Chen Yen*) and Mantra (Secret, *Mi Tsung*) (Japanese: *Shingon*). Concentration leads to identification with the Buddha, resulting in the ecstatic state of 'Buddha-in-me' and 'I-in-Buddha.' As this may take place in the present life, one can 'become the Great Sun Buddha right in this body.' Because of these mystical tendencies, the School has always regarded itself as *esoteric* and others as *exoteric*." [136]

Among other phases of a complicated ritual, comes the *kuanting* or baptismal ceremony (a sprinkling with holy water) before the devotee is admitted to the presence of a (Buddha or) Bodhisattva, who will bestow mental and magical powers on the suppliant. All this seems a far cry from the metaphysical subtleties of Mahāyāna Buddhism, and yet, underneath the tantric (*yoga*) practices, the devotee is constantly reminded that the Buddha or Bodhisattva with whom he seeks to be identified is to be found in (and has no existence apart from) *his own mind*.[137]

Because the spread of the esoteric Mantrayāna (Vairocana School into China coincided in time with the active propagation of Nestorianism in the same northwest area around Sian, Reichelt is of the opinion that Amoghavajra's stress on 'masses for the dead' must have received impetus from his observation of the great hold which Nestorian 'prayers for the dead' had on the Chinese people.

---

* Probably the most famous of these secret formulae is that addressed to the Bodhisattva Avalokiteśvara: "*OM MANI-PADME HUM,*" usually associated with Tibetan practice. It is found in Chapter 21 (*'Dhāraṇī'* or 'Spells') in the *Lotus Sūtra,* and is usually translated: "She who has a jewel in the lotus" or "The jewel is in the lotus,"—the jewel being Avalokiteśvara. This *dhāraṇi* also carries a veiled phallic reference, giving religious significance to the facts of sex.

Strangely enough, both of these foreign forms of religion disappeared about the same time (9th century). Of this historic enigma, Reichelt remarks: . . . "It is perhaps no mere chance that the apparent disappearance of the 'Great Sun Religion' (Esoteric Mantrayāna) and the 'Shining Religion' (Ching Chiao or Nestorianism) took place at about the same time. The Vairocana School was merged with the other Buddhist schools, and for many years now it has been difficult to find any traces of its special forms and expressions. Indeed, one must hunt long even in the best monastery libraries before one finds the old *Ta Jih Ching* (*Great Sun Scripture*)."[138]

The disappearance of the old Vairocana School did not, however, mark the total eclipse of tantric Buddhism in China, for from two directions it reappeared and continues to be active down to the present day.*

Padmasaṃbhava, contemporary and classmate of Vajrabodhi and Amoghavajra in the Mantrayāna School in Bengal, was invited by King Khri-Srong to Tibet and sojourned there from A.D. 747 to 802. Through his labors, esoteric Buddhism was planted there and, with a strong admixture of native exorcism (Bön or Pön), ultimately dominated the whole of Tibetan religion. Later it was carried through Eastern Turkestan (Sinkiang and Tsinghai) into Mongolia where it became the religion of the Mongol founders of the Yüan dynasty and flourished greatly, especially from the time of Kubilai Khan (A.D. 1216-1294). It is, therefore, known as the 'Western' or "Tibetan Esoteric Sect" (*Tsang Mi Tsung*). The Mantrayāna which Kobo Daishi took to Japan in A.D. 806 and which, as the Shingon Sect, is rated second in strength and influence in modern Japanese Buddhism, has been re-introduced into China, especially in Kwangtung and Shanghai, where it is known as the "Eastern Esoteric Sect," with followers also among the Buddhist laymen of Hong Kong.[140]

Cultivated for political reasons by successive dynasties in

---

* W. T. Chan states that "only certain of its rituals are practised in Lamaism" today. (139)

Peking and recognized by both the Republican (Nationalist) and the People's Government of recent times, "Lamaism," as the Western (Tibetan) Esoteric Sect is popularly called, is still the religion of thousands of Chinese in the North and Northwest. In its philosophical form, it has found credence among those intellectuals influenced by the Pantchen (or "Tashi"–) Lama, refugee titular head of the "Yellow Hat" (Reformed) Tibetan Buddhists, based formerly at the Tashi-Llumpo Monastery. He was regarded as the earthly reincarnation of Amitābha in contradistinction to the Dalai Lama at Lhasa, who was revered, at least formerly, as the reincarnation of Avalokiteśvara. Unfortunately, he is now a refugee in India.

In the larger centers, like Peiping, Tientsin, Nanking, and Shanghai, will be found devotees of this Western Branch of the Esoteric Sect, who will be seeking the mystical 'secret of reason' through *mudrās* and *dhāraṇis* primarily, but also through poring over the sacred books and through deep, intuitive meditation. If the old *Great Sun Scripture* is unavailable or outmoded, they will at least have access to a modern version of the *Vairocana Sūtra*, the *P'iluchena Ch'êng Fu Ching*, as well as to the *Diamond Apex Sūtra* (*Chin-Kang-Ting Ching*).[141]

By intensive contemplation, esoteric devotees will seek to be identified with the Buddhas Vairocana or Amitābha, or with the Bodhisattva Avalokita, or with the great Bodhisat-Savior, Kshitigarbha (*Ti Ts'ang Wang*). In the words of Sir Charles Eliot, "Buddhas are the visible expression of Dharma (Fa, or Law). Hence (they) are identified with it, and the whole process of cosmic evolution is regarded as the manifestation of Buddhahood."[142] To find the Dharmakāya immanent in his own soul, is the hope of every mystic in the Esoteric School, for only thus will his ultimate objective—peace and safety in the future life—be assured.

In conclusion, while Buddhism made great changes in Chinese philosophic thought, it in turn was modified to a noticeable degree as it became part of the Chinese mind. The Chinese humanized Buddhism by making it less other-worldly and more practical in its piety, and, more especially, by harmonizing conflicting viewpoints.[143] While, in a way, it may be correct to look upon the Ch'an, T'ien-T'ai, and Hua-Yen Schools as "purely Chinese" schools, yet the inner content of the ideas they stressed are traceable to Indian sources. Certain it is that the Chinese re-shaped most of the ideas besides adding many of their own to build a more elaborate Pure Land School, for example, and to revolutionize the Ch'an concept of meditation into "No-Mind."[144] Despite every attempt of later Neo-Confucianists to eradicate Buddhist influence, Buddhism left an indelible mark on all subsequent Chinese philosophy.

PART III

CONFUCIAN AND TAOIST REACTIONS TO BUDDHIST THOUGHT: CONFUCIANISM REASSERTS ITSELF

Chapter 9

Early Neo-Confucians

(Of the T'ang and Sung Dynasties)

"If one follows the straightforward Way, giving free play to sincerity, one will then come to comprehend all things."
—Shao Yung in the *Kuan Wu P'ien**

"There is nothing more primary than rectifying the mind and making the thoughts sincere."
—Ch'eng Yi, commenting on the *Ta Hsüeh**

The impact of Buddhist philosophy on the Chinese mind was felt down through the centuries from the Later Han (ca. A.D. 200) into the late Sung dynasty (ca. A.D. 1250)—the "nay-saying" philosophy of India locking horns with the "yea-saying" philosophy of China in a veritable life-and-death struggle that well-nigh proved the death of both.

The present chapter deals with the period of strongest Buddhist influence, stretching from the middle T'ang (roughly A.D. 750) into the late Sung (about A.D. 1250), when both Taoists and Confucianists rose to defend their indigenous *Sinism* against the subtle infiltration of an alien, and other-worldly, philosophy. More specifically, in the T'ang dynasty (toward

* Derk Bodde translation.

the latter half), at the peak of Buddhism's popularity, the *Tao Hsüeh Chia,* or "School of the Study of the Tao," also had a revival and grew into Neo-Confucianism, with certain Buddhist and Taoist ideas permeating Confucian thought.[1]

Confucian Reactions Against Buddhism and Taoism

In this transitional period, a strong Buddhist influence is to be noted on two Confucian scholars, Han Yü (A.D. 768-824) and his pupil, Li Ao (d. 844). While Han Yü showed some tolerance for Buddhists and their ideas, he felt that neither they nor the Taoists could claim any monopoly on the *Tao,* which Confucians had known since the days of Yao and Shun. In his *Inquiry into Tao,* he gave his defense of Confucianism against Taoism and Buddhism, maintaining that the true meaning of *Tao* and *Tê* could be found by studying the Confucian *Classics.* His chief objections to the Taoists and the Buddhists were that both were anti-social and overly speculative. The strength of his crusading for Confucian orthodoxy is commented upon by Wing-tsit Chan, W. Theodore de Bary, and Carsun Chang in their appraisals of Neo-Confucianism.[2] For the excellence of his literary style, Han Yü still stands high in the estimate of Chinese scholars.

In his *Essays on Returning to Human Nature* (*Fu-Shing Shu*), Li Ao re-interpreted the *Doctrine of the Mean* (*Chung Yung*) in the light of Buddhist teachings by saying that one may arrive at 'utter sincerity' or the 'silently immovable mind' by developing the basic nature from within. Reflecting the *Prajñā-pāramitā's* attainment of wisdom, he went on to say that a sage is first "awakened," then "enlightened," and then can look at the world "with a sense of detachment."[3] Under the influence of Taoist ideas of 'quiescent contemplation,' he re-interpreted the *Great Learning*'s dictum: "the extension of knowledge lies in the investigation of things" by adding that it must be accomplished without effort and without losing the quality of imperturbability. Furthermore, Li Ao gave to his teachings a truly Confucian objective of "harmony in the larger relationship of life" by urging that a scholar could best develop sagehood not merely within himself but in relation to others and to the universe.[4] We may, therefore, safely include Li Ao among the forerunners of Neo-Confucianism.

As a result of the anti-Buddhist agitation of men like Han Yü, Li Ao, and others, the T'ang Emperor Wu Tsung was persuaded to issue a proscription against alien religions. In the "Great Persecution" of A.D. 845, a wave of iconoclasm destroyed images and temples and swept thousands of Buddhist monks and nuns out of razed monasteries back into productive economic life.[5] Nevertheless, Buddhism continued to be a potent influence in succeeding centuries.

It becomes clear also, that, in a time when Taoist doctrines of the *Yin-Yang* School (which had come into Confucianism as early as the second century B.C. and been reflected in Tung Chung-shu), were still potent in Confucian circles, there was considerable borrowing of ideas back and forth between the two schools. While the Taoists were reinterpreting the *Lao-tzu* and the *Book of Changes* (*Yi Ching*) in the light of Confucian texts, their chief aim was to acquire a power over Nature that would enable them to mix an "elixir of immortality." But the Confucians criticized them severely for stressing the magical element beyond the realm of verifiable human experience.

By the year A.D. 1000, these competing schools had reached such a stage in the development of their ideas that they needed only men who could begin to put it all into one great system of Neo-Confucianism.[6] Such thinkers were Chou Tun-yi, Shao Yung, and Chang Tsai.

Influence of the YI CHING *on Chou Tun-yi and Shao Yung:—*

Feeling that the Buddhist world-view should be matched with an indigenous world-view based on a Chinese source, Chou Tun-yi, known as "The Master of Lien-hsi" (A.D. 1017–

1073),* turned to the *Book of Changes* (*Yi Ching*) and gave it a Confucian interpretation.** From his mountain retreat near Kuling, Chou Tun-yi also produced a work on *Comprehensive Unity (T'ung Shu),* in which he discussed the various aspects of human life. For him sagehood is based on *jên* (love) and *i* (righteousness), which derive from the essence of *Ch'ien* (*Yang*), the creative power of the serene *Tao* or Ultimate Reason. The sage, therefore, possesses the attributes of "primordiality," "perseverance," and "potentiality of success," and all this can be proved by the hexagrams in the *Book of Changes.*[7]

For these writings, which had such a profound influence on the thinkers of his time, Carsun Chang has called Chou Tun-yi "the peerless founder of Sung philosophy," simply because "the effect of Buddhist metaphysics was to drive (him and other) Chinese Confucians into thinking in universal terms." But their Supreme Ultimate was real, not void; their human nature was not illusory; and their mind became stimulated by the Ch'an stress on the mind. Being imbued with both the metaphysical Principle of the Supreme Ultimate and the material Essence of the Five Elements, man is, in the opinion of Chou Tun-yi, the highest of all creatures. His nature, in its original state of non-activity, is fundamentally sincere; when stirred into activity, however, its manifested conduct may be either good or evil (or both). His progress toward sageliness, then, will be marked by a slow return to original sincerity, through elimination of desire and straightforward conduct into complete impartiality or universality of spirit, which is the goal of life. In this way, Chou Tun-yi initiated the use of *li* (immaterial principle) and *ch'i* (material

---

* As prefect of Nan K'ang, Kiangsi, he built a retreat on Lu Shan, near Kuling, which he called the "Lien-Hsi Studio." (*Note*):—The name of Chou Tun-yi appears also as Chou Lien-hsi or Chow Lien-hsi; also as Chou Mao-shu and Chou Tun-shih.

** For this reason, among others, A. C. Graham thinks Chou Tun-yi was "merely a Confucian-Taoist syncretist" and that his influence was felt "only after the death of the Ch'engs," this despite Chou's radically new interpretation of the "Supreme Ultimate." (8)

essence), which later, as elaborated by the Ch'eng Brothers and Chu Hsi, became standard Confucian concepts.[9]

The place of Chou Tun-yi as the real founder of the Neo-Confucian Movement is stated in no uncertain terms by Wing-tsit Chan, who says: ". . . Most students agree (with Chu Hsi) that Master Chou was the one who laid the foundation of Neo-Confucianism and determined its direction. He provided the cosmology and ethics for later Confucians. His doctrine of the Supreme Ultimate as One, and *Yin* and *Yang* and the Five Agents as Many, his emphasis on stillness, his equal stress on the Mean, correctness, benevolence, and righteousness, his general rational tone, and his singling out the concepts of principle, decree, and nature from the *Book of Changes* were all seeds for later development in the Ch'engs and others. The equal stress on the *Mean,* correctness, benevolence, and righteousness, for example, paved the way for the Ch'eng Brothers' doctrine of 'composure to straighten one's internal life and righteousness to square one's external life. . . .' "[10]

Greatly influenced, apparently, by a Taoist named Ch'en T'uan (d. 989), Shao Yung (or Shao Yao-fu, A.D. 1011–1077) attempted to write his own philosophy of human life out of the cosmology in the *Book of Changes* (Appendix V). In elaborating the evolution of natural phenomena, he made use of the symbolism of the Five Elements and the Eight Trigrams (*Pa Kua*), multiplied into the Sixty-four Hexagrams, to represent the annual cycle of the seasons in their recurrent functioning under *Yin* (Earth) and *Yang* (Heaven). Shao Yung then described man as the product of the creative activity of the Supreme Ultimate (*Li* or *Tao*), working through the *Yin* and the *Yang;* but, unlike other creatures, man has an almost unlimited capacity for mental, moral, and spiritual perfectibility. He pursued this thought at some length in his *Treatise on the Observation of Things (Kuan-Wu P'ien,* a section of his larger *Huang-Chi Ching Shih* or *Cosmological Chronology.*)[11]

As a frame of reference, Shao Yung took a passage in the *Book of Changes* (*Appendix V*) which reads: "They plumbed

Principle to its depths and completely penetrated the nature, thereby reaching to (an understanding of) Destiny."[12] . . . "These three kinds of knowledge are the real knowledge of the world, and even the sage cannot go beyond them."[13] . . . Shao Yung then proceeded to give an exposition of the 'sageliness' of the sage who can comprehend the Absolute, can penetrate the innermost nature of man, and has reached an empirical understanding of Destiny—all through his own powers of observation, perception, and discrimination. But he has a word of warning for the sage who wishes to cultivate his best self:—

. . . "If one follows the straightforward Way, giving free play to sincerity, one will then come to comprehend all things. . . But if one uses a knowledge which calculates (the personal profit of a course of action), . . . this results in a forcible twisting of (the Way of) Heaven and Earth, . . . Is it not distressing?"[14]

A strong Buddhist influence may be seen in Shao Yung's "Table of Cosmic Chronology," where he not only gives a date for the creation of the world (67,017 B.C.) but also predicts its end in A.D. 62,583.[15] In this prediction is revealed the Buddhist theory of four world-periods (formation, existence, destruction, and non-existence) which, through Shao Yung, came to exert a pronounced influence on all Neo-Confucian cosmologies.

It is worthy of note that, for Shao Yung, the laws of growth and decay applied not only to the world of Nature but also to the realm of government, as for example when he says:

"He who (in his government) employs the principle of non-activity, is a *Sovereign;* who employs kindliness and good faith is an *Emperor*; who employs justice and correctness is a *King*; who employs scheming and force is a *Tyrant* . . . (Government) below that of a tyrant is one of *Barbarians,* and that below the barbarians is one of beasts."[16]

Here he implies that tyrannical and barbaric governments bear within themselves the seeds of their own destruction. Though little appreciated in his own time, the breadth of Shao Yung's mental horizon made considerable impression on Chu Hsi.[17]

Chang Tsai's Reaction Against Buddhism—

Continuing in the Neo-Confucian tradition, Chang Tsai* (A.D. 1020–1077), principal of his own "School of Philosophers" at Kuangchung, Shensi, in his *Correct Discipline for Beginners* (*Cheng Mêng*), commented on the *Great Harmony* (*T'ai Ho*) or *Supreme Ultimate* (*Tao*), calling it "Ether" (*Ch'i*) or "Great Ethereal" (*T'ai Hsü*). Though imperceptible, it is not non-existent but has two embodiments: spirituality (*shen*) and transforming force (*hua*), which produce all things by expansion and contraction of the all-pervading Ether.[18] Here Chang Tsai was declaring the oneness of *Tao* and *Ether* by insisting on the primordial character of *Ch'i* or Ether.[19]

In observing the orderly sequence of natural processes, he discovered four universal truths: (1) "All things good and evil are equally products of the Great Ethereal (i.e., Principle is one but its manifestations are many); (2) Among created things, there is no one exactly like another; (3) No one thing can exist in absolute isolation from other things; and (4) Evolution is a continuous cycle of creation and dissolution."[20] In other words, by making the Great Ethereal the principle of all change [as unconsolidated, it is *Tao;* as consolidated upward, it is *Yang* (motion); as consolidated downward, it is *Yin* (rest)], Chang Tsai saw it manifested in all Being or phenomena. Therefore, all apparent dichotomy is resolved in the all-inclusive unity of the "Great Harmony." In this way, he sought to combat the Buddhist concept of the emptiness of all Being (the Void). Moreover, by making the great virtues of *jên, i, li,* and *chih* independent of the physical nature, he gave them a cosmic significance and force.[21]

Two sections of the 17th chapter of the above-mentioned

---

* Literary name—Chang Heng-ch'ü, because he was born in Heng-ch'ü, in Shansi Province.

Cheng Mêng* were published separately as the *Eastern* and the *Western Inscription.* The latter, used as a primer for beginners, emphasized the importance of the practice of *jên* in relation to parents and "all men without discrimination." Such a statement not only re-echoes Mo Ti's universal love but also reflects the Buddhist ideal of the Bodhisattva as exemplified in the figure of the saintly Vimalakīrti.[22]

In this same popular *Western Inscription* (*Hsi Ming*), Chang Tsai, though conscious of a modicum of ether-endowed evil in his personality, yet expressed his firm conviction of being *en rapport* with the universe and with his fellow-men, saying:

". . . I, therefore, am the substance that lies within the confines of Heaven and Earth, and my nature is that of (the two Commanders) —Heaven and Earth. (All) people are my blood-brothers and (all) creatures are my companions (equals) . . ."[23]

This clear enunciation of the essential nature as good and the physical nature as variably good or bad but susceptible of improvement by spiritual cultivation was praised by Chu Hsi. And, undoubtedly Chang Tsai's solution of the problem of evil by making it due to the varying endowment of ether was, in Carsun Chang's opinion, a great help to the thinking of the Ch'engs and Chu Hsi.[24] According to Fung Yu-lan, however, certain later Confucianists considered Chang Tsai's attitude of *chien ai* (love for the whole universe as well as for all men) too much like the undiscriminating universal love of Mo Ti and, therefore, unorthodox.[25] On the other hand, they quite approved of his use of *liang chih* (good knowledge) as originating in Mencius and made capital of by Wang Yang-ming as "intuitive knowledge."[26]

Although notable in his own right, Chang Tsai gained even more renown as the mentor of two famous, eleventh-century Neo-Confucianists, his nephews Ch'eng Hao and Ch'eng Yi, who by their diverging views set the direction of philosophic thought for years to come.[27] At the same time, as W. Theodore

---

* Which Carsun Chang renders into English as *Corrections of Youthful Folly.*

de Bary feels, a good deal of credit should be given to Hu Yüan, the "Master of Anting" (A.D. 993–1059), for influencing the Ch'eng Brothers while they were pupils in his preparatory school.[28]

As provincial commissioner of justice under Wang An-shih and later employed in the Ministry of Ceremonies, Chang Tsai twice incurred the court's displeasure and was forced to resign.[29] After his death, many of his pupils left Kuangchung and enrolled in the Ch'engs' school at Loyang (in Honan); it may be assumed, therefore, that this joining of forces formed the "ancestor" of all later Neo-Confucian thought.[30] Yet the disciples of the Ch'engs claimed that Chang Tsai's school had borrowed from the Ch'engs and this view had the effect of raising Chou Tun-yi over Chang Tsai in the minds of later twelfth-century thinkers like Li T'ung who became Chu Hsi's teacher.[31]

The Influence of the Ch'eng Brothers

Ch'eng Hao (A.D. 1032–1085) :–

Ch'eng Hao,* the older of the two brothers (also known as the "Master of Ming-Tao"), held several government posts but seems not to have given much thought to politics. In fact, both he and Chang Tsai lost their official position because of their quiet resistance to the radical reforms of Wang An-shih, who had become Minister of State under Emperor Shen Tsung.[32] As Ch'eng Hao's interest lay, rather, in philosophy, he is looked upon as the forerunner of the Neo-Confucian Idealistic School, later known as the "Lu-Wang School" or *Hsin-Hsüeh Chia*—School of the Study of Mind. His main ideas, found in *The Literary Remains of the Two Ch'engs* (*Êrh Ch'eng Yi-Shu*), center around 'Heavenly Principle' and 'Spiritual Cultivation.'

---

* Styled Po-ch'un.

Ch'eng Hao looked upon Heavenly Principle as a natural principle (*tao-li*) or force "without any sign of artificiality." He "did not explicitly refer to it as independently subsisting apart from actual things; he seemed to think of it rather as immanent, not as transcendent."[33] In fact he apparently made little distinction between physical and metaphysical.

As for human nature and its cultivation, Ch'eng Hao believed that man is endowed at birth with Ether, which is both good and bad, since for every *yang* there must be a corresponding *yin*. Evil, however, is not inherently so . . . it is only a going too far or not going far enough. Humans need only to see that they do not deviate from the golden mean and thus fall into evil ways. Spontaneous acts are deemed good (as Principle); acts motivated by calculating selfish desires are judged evil (as un-principled). Since his original harmony with the universe has become dimmed by self-centered desires, man needs to return to a renewed union of spirit with the Heavenly Principle in the universe.[34] Both Ch'engs felt the force of Chang Tsai's emphasis on the unity of man with Heaven-and-Earth, Ch'eng Hao taking it as a rich, vital experience of a creative power operating not only within the universe but also in the moral life of man himself.[35]

By diligent cultivation of intuitive knowledge and intuitive ability, which are never destroyed, this restoration of harmony can be definitely achieved. But as long as man is "mentally calculating, he can't take intuition as his natural guide." These beliefs were elaborated in a letter to his uncle,* Chang Tsai, discussing the "Composure of the Nature" (*Ting-Hsing Shu*), in which Ch'eng Hao said in part:

"Rather than deny the external and affirm the internal, it is far better to forget that there is either external (allurement) or internal (emotion). Forgetting both, one reaches a limpid state in which one is disturbed by nothing. This state of non-disturbance results in composure; composure results in enlightenment; and

---

* Or father's cousin, according to some sources.

being enlightened, how can one's reactions to things be regarded as encumbrances imposed by them." . . .[36]

Emotionless impartiality thus becomes, for Ch'eng Hao, the goal of scholarly living, reflecting an unadmitted yet strong Buddhistic and mystical trend in his thinking. It is said that he practiced so well his philosophy of composure that he gained a wide reputation for imperturbability under all provocations.[37]

Ch'eng Yi (A.D. 1033–1107) :—

Only slightly younger than his brother, Ch'eng Yi* (also referred to as the "Master of Yi-Ch'uan") became just as ardent a Confucianist under the tutelage of Chou Tun-yi, Hu Yüan, and his uncle, Chang Tsai. During the extreme reforms of Wang An-shih (in power A.D. 1055–1085), the Ch'engs were highly critical of his methods. Ch'eng Yi was tutor to the young Emperor Chê-Tsung for a year (1086–1087) but retired to private teaching when the reformers returned to power. In 1097 he was exiled to Fuchow in Szechuan for three years and later (in 1103) was forced to disband his school or again go into exile.[38]

Ch'eng Yi's independent thinking made him the forerunner of the Neo-Confucian Rationalistic School, later called the "Ch'eng-Chu School" or *Li-Hsüeh Chia*—School of the Study of Principle. Probably his most significant work was his *Commentary on the Book of Changes.*[39] Like his brother, he also had much to say about 'Heavenly Principle,' 'Human Nature,' and 'Spiritual Cultivation'—ideas for the most part recorded by his disciples.

For him, Heavenly Principle subsists eternally and unchanging, apart from things. The myriad phenomena are all contained within Heavenly Principle, whether activated or not. Each individual thing has its own individual Principle,

---

* Styled Cheng-shu.

complete in itself. All Principles are contained within our mind, enabling it to react in harmony with them, either in quiescence or in movement. Yet Heavenly Principle is independent of all human manipulation, because it is transcendent.

In Ch'eng Yi's mind there was a sharp line of demarcation between the world of *Li* (Principle, *Tao,* idea, form) and the world of *Ch'i* (Ether, matter, phenomena)—i.e., between the physical and the metaphysical, in a way strikingly similar to Plato's thought. On the other hand, Carsun Chang insists that Ch'eng Yi did not regard *Li* (*Tao*) as completely separated from *Ch'i,* yet calls him "more of an intellectualist than Ch'eng Hao" (much as Hegel was, in his opinion, "more of an intellectualist than Kant").[40]

When discussing the origin of species, Ch'eng Yi argued that the first members of each species in the world of things were produced by the evolutions of Ether in a kind of spontaneous generation. When the bodies of material things (including the human) approach the stage of dissolution, their Ether is dissipated and not used over again (as intimated in the Buddhist concept of reincarnation).[41] This idea of a universe growing by continuously new generation is recognized as the most significant contribution made by Ch'eng Yi to Neo-Confucian philosophy.[42]

Like his brother, Ch'eng Yi held human nature to be unvaryingly good (as Principle). Its capacity (*ts'ai*), however, is variable (as endowment of Ether): if it is clear, it makes men worthy; if turbid, it makes people stupid. As every form of life has its cycle of waxing and waning, Ch'eng Yi (like Shao Yung) interpreted goodness as positive growth and evil as negative decay, rather than in any definite moral sense. The quality of a man's virtue (*jên*) is innately part of his nature, whereas the expression, for example, of the emotion of love (*ai*) is part of his capacity.[43]

In discussing spiritual cultivation, Ch'eng Yi stressed not only the development of inner composure through complete impartiality, but also an exhaustive study of the principles in things over a long period of time and over a wide range of examples. Whether or not he borrowed this two-fold approach from Ch'an Buddhism's *dhyāna* (meditation) and *prajñā* (wisdom) is an open question.[44] At any rate, he was fond of saying: "A true knowledge of Principle means a true perception of right and wrong." In other words, an undeviating adherence to Principle gives a unity of mind which is manifested in utter sincerity or integrity. Convinced of the essential unity of knowledge and conduct, he would say: "There is no man who has (true) knowledge, yet cannot carry it out." Here is the seed-thought that later captured the imagination of Wang Yang-ming.[45]

In a nutshell, Ch'eng Yi's philosophy affirmed four things: creative evolution is a process of continuous generation of new forms; the Principle of a single thing is the Principle of all things; understand that Principle and you understand the Principle of the self; thus one develops composure in one's own nature and attains to *jên,* or Heavenly Decree *(ming)*. His criticism of those in high places caused him to be placed on their blacklist and ultimately he found himself exiled for his "philosophy of integrity" too freely expounded in his lectures and essays.[46]

On many points, the two brothers, Ch'eng Hao and Ch'eng Yi, were in complete agreement. Without defining it very clearly, both supplanted 'Supreme Ultimate' with 'Heavenly Principle' *(t'ien-li)* and spoke of it as a substantiated Reality over against the Buddhists' 'Great Void.' As universal, it is opposed to Ether. As particular in each object, it is complete for each object.[47] Following Mencius, both recognized human nature as originally good. Where, however, Ch'eng Hao held that man could discover Principle within his own unchanging nature, Ch'eng Yi taught that since one's nature was blurred by its admixture of Ether, one must turn to the external world of people and events to discover true Principle.[48] On the other hand, we must say that both brothers recognized in *jên* a term signifying complete unity with the universe and, therefore, it becomes for them the fundamental ground of ethics, the life-giving force in human personality.[49]

Both brothers saw moral and social implications in their understanding of the cosmos. For them, ethics was based in metaphysics, and they reasoned, therefore (as de Bary reminds us) that ethical conduct, including government, needed revising to fit the pattern of true manhood. Reforms must be applied to agrarian policies (including implementation of the old well-field system of land utilization), to the maintenance of a standing army, and to the system of education to make it universal and compulsory:—all in order to equalize the economic burdens of the people.[50]

To sum up, the Ch'eng Brothers, in their expounding of the Buddhist-Taoist concept of the One and the Many, stripped it of mystical and illusory content in order to preserve man's unity with the universe and with human society. But, as we have seen, Ch'eng Hao's speculation became monistic, whereas Ch'eng Yi's followed a dualistic trend, declaring that Principle (perceived by mind) is quite other than Ether (perceived by the senses).[51] In a word, as Wing-tsit Chan has pointed out, they were the first Neo-Confucians to make *Li* (Principle) "the sole basis of a whole philosophical system." So great was their influence that the entire Neo-Confucian Movement has been called the 'Philosophy of Li' (*Li Hsüeh*).[52]

When it came to stressing the extension of knowledge by the investigation of things, an inner content in Ch'eng Yi's thought different from that of Ch'eng Hao has been detected. Where Ch'eng Hao tended to limit reality to the noumenal sphere (that which is "above shapes"), Ch'eng Yi rather accepted the objective reality of the phenomenal world (that which is "within shapes"). In other words, with these two brothers the stream of Chinese philosophic thought begins definitely to divide into two channels: from Ch'eng Hao stems the line of thought developed later by Lu Hsiang-shan and Wang Yang-ming and called the Lu-Wang School, or Mind School; from Ch'eng Yi and his followers (Yang Shih and Li T'ung) stems the line of thought which was elaborated by Chu Hsi and called the Ch'eng-Chu School, or Reason School.

It was the latter school that dominated the shaping of Confucian thought in succeeding generations.[53]

The Reforms of Wang An-shih:—

As the affairs of the Ch'eng Brothers were greatly affected by their bold criticism of court politicians, some notice should be taken especially of the drastic reform measures promulgated by Premier Wang An-shih. In a manner reminiscent of the Han dynasty usurper, Wang Mang, he used his power to again institute state socialism, primarily through a monopoly of commerce, governmental price-ceilings, equalization of taxes, military conscription, and a system of forced labor for the state.[54]

After the death of the Emperor Shen Tsung, and upon the recommendation of Ch'eng Hao, the Empress-Regent appointed the historian, Ssŭ-ma Kuang, as her Prime Minister and he reversed the policies of Wang An-shih for a brief time. He did not live long enough, however, to gain much success other than to complete his own famous *History of China.*[55]

Wang An-shih is to be remembered, however, not only as a powerful statesman, but also as a vigorous writer of essays on true methods of education and on the application of classical learning to the practical affairs of government. In an essay "On Seeking to Apply One's Principles to the Affairs of State," he praised Confucius as truly a "Superior Man" *(chün-tzu)*—one who was willing to advise kings and dukes even though he knew that, as a rule, they would not follow his advice.[56] We turn now to another admirer of Confucius, Chu Hsi, the greatest of the Sung Neo-Confucianists, who ranked the Great Sage with Yao and Shun—a model ruler whose example the kings and emperors of his own day would do well to imitate.

Chapter 10

The Neo-Confucianism of Chu Hsi
(Late Sung Dynasty)

"A true heart is the citadel for the learner."

"People fly through the days and never stop to collect their minds."

—Chu Hsi "On Human Nature" *

The philosopher Chu Hsi, better known among Chinese as Chu Tzu (Japanese: Shushi), was born in Fukien in A.D. 1130 and died in 1200 at the age of seventy. He early showed a leaning toward Buddhism but in his more mature years, after a close study of the writings of Ch'eng Yi, became an ardent protagonist of Confucianism. His lectures at Pai Lu Tung (White Deer Grotto), in the foothills of the Lu-Shan Range near Kuling, Kiangsi, brought fame to the old Confucian University there, as well as to himself.

It is upon his great commentaries on the *Four Books* (the New Testament of Confucianism) that Chu Hsi's fame chiefly rests, although his revision of Ssŭ-ma Kuang's *History of China* was a notable achievement. While not so creative a thinker as Ch'eng Yi, Chu Hsi has long been associated in the minds of Chinese intellectuals as the systematizer of the Ch'eng-Chu School of Rationalism.[1] Called also "The Great Synthesizer,"**

* J. Percy Bruce translation.

** A sobriquet conferred by Carsun Chang, who points out (*Op. Cit.*, p. 253) Chu Hsi's two-fold principle of organization: (as) "the unity of reason and the manifoldness of the phenomenal world."

Chu Tzu gave to Confucianism a new philosophical foundation and set a fashion in Neo-Confucian interpretation that became standard for eight centuries.

From his studies of *The Collected Writings of Chu Hsi* (*Chu Wên-Kung Wên-Chi*) and *Classified Conversations of Chu Hsi* (*Chu-Tzu Yü-Lei*), Fung Yu-lan has made an extensive résumé of Chu Hsi's philosophy. He has described his metaphysical system as "primarily based upon the cosmogony expounded by Chou Tun-yi in his *Diagram of the Supreme Ultimate Explained.* With this it combines Shao Yung's numerological theories; Chang Tsai's theory of the Ether or *ch'i;* and the distinction established by the two Ch'engs between 'what is above shapes' and 'what is within shapes,' as well as between Principle *(li)* and the Ether *(ch'i),* and between the Way (*Tao*) and 'instrument' or 'instruments' (another *ch'i*). . . . Thus Chu's philosophy may be said to be a summation of the Neo-Confucian School before his time."[2]

Chu Hsi's main ideas may be presented best under the following topics: (1) On Principle or the Supreme Ultimate; (2) On the Ether and Cosmogony; (3) On Human Nature; (4) On Spiritual Cultivation and Love as the Fulfilling of Law; (5) On Political Philosophy, and (6) On the Weakness of Buddhism.

(1) *On Principle or the Supreme Ultimate*

In the beginning, there subsisted only a multiple Principle or Supreme Ultimate, which is eternally 'above shapes,' transcending time and space. (To quote in effect) :—

> It is not 'empty,' as the Buddhist would claim. It is full of the many normative Principles governing the *yin* and the *yang* and the Five Elements that go to make up the multitudinous entities in the universe. Principle subsists eternally before things exist; therefore, it transcends both existence and non-existence, both movement and quiescence. . .[3]

While the Principles determining the movement and quiescence of Ether in objects and events cause change, they themselves do not undergo change. When active, Ether produces *yang;* when stilled, it produces *yin.* Though each object contains the Principles of all things, this is not tantamount to saying that Principles and things are identical, any more than the reflection of the moon in 10,000 streams makes the moon equivalent to water. In other words, Principle in relation to matter is both immanent and transcendent—the incorporeal *Tao* manifesting itself in corporeal things.[4]

Feeling that Confucius had not gone far enough in his interpretation of ultimate reality, Chu Tzu declared:—

"Whenever you consider principles you must apprehend clearly the fountain-head. . . . Confucius in his teaching enunciated principles on any and every subject as they were presented to him, but did not point out One Supreme Principle. But if you take things which are all about us and generalize concerning them, you will perceive a general law. . . .

"If now we apprehend the Supreme Ultimate clearly, we shall certainly be able to recognize the numerous laws . . . of the universe as all proceeding from it. . . .Inherent in every single thing is its 'rule of existence.'[5]

"Whether high or low, fine or coarse, root or fruit, there is but one Law in the universe—alike the Law of the Supreme Ultimate and the Two Modes (of *Yin* and *Yang*) ."[6]

At this point, Carsun Chang would urge that Chu Hsi was neither monist nor dualist but both; that, believing in a 'bifurcation of nature,' he held nonetheless to the unity of Reason (Supreme Ultimate) despite the variety of its phenomenal manifestations.[7]

(2) *On the Ether and Cosmogony*

Chu Hsi persistently maintained that the Ether (*ch'i*) does the creating in the world of shapes, whereas "Principle lacks volition or plan, and has no creative power."[8] As Ether condenses and thus creates, it uses the individuating principles of *li*. Their relation is like that of the architect's blueprint to the builder's materials. Materials take shape according to plan. Plan may (invisibly) inhere in house but is not a material part of it. On the other hand, house visibly represents or reveals plan.[9]

Here Fung points out that where Chou Tun-yi and the Taoists thought of *Tao* (Li, Non-Being, or *wu*) as producing Being, or *yu*, out of which are produced the ten thousand things—Chu Hsi argued that *Tao* (Principle) doesn't 'produce' anything; it only "contains the Principles governing movement or quiescence through which the Ether is respectively activated or stilled, in this way generating *yang* or *yin* matter."[10] In other words, Principle works through Ether as its particularizing agency, thereby differentiating the One into the Many. As these (*li* and *ch'i*) are mutually dependent, all things in the cosmos and human life are mutually interdependent and harmoniously comprehended in the human mind.[11] And here W. T. Chan would add that Chu Hsi's philosophy may rightly be termed "organismic," viewing reality as a process issuing in "relatedness"; and feels that Needham's translations of *li* as "principle of organization" and *ch'i* as "matter-energy" are extremely apt, thus interpreting the Neo-Confucian as a truly scientific concept of a very real, organic universe.[12] *

Chu Hsi's cosmogony, which follows Chou Tun-yi rather closely, may be briefly stated: As the *Yin* and the *Yang* grew out of Ether (*ch'i*), they became differentiated into Five Elements (water, fire, wood, metal, and earth)—the basic materials out of which all objects were created, each exhibiting its own peculiar pattern (*li*). This creative process he described as primarily a rotary grinding of inchoate Ether's elements

---

* Needham thinks that Leibniz got his inspiration for "monads" and their harmonious relationships from Chu Hsi, as translated by the Jesuits, that the philosophy of organicism stemmed directly from Neo-Confucian correlativism. (13)

until enough sedimentation could take place in water to consolidate Earth (*Yin*) at the center, while from (*the purer*) fire the firmament (Heaven or *Yang*) could take shape with its sun, moon, and myriad stars on a continuously revolving perimeter.[14]

The creation of man, according to Chu Tzu, took place in this wise:—

"Evolutions of the Ether occurred when, in the beginning, individual human beings were spontaneously produced without having any progenitors. Propagation in the (same) image (genetic generation) occurred when, there being these individual human beings, propagation thereafter took place from one to another without end."[15]

For Chu Tzu, then, all creation was an evolutionary process from simple to more complex life, through a continuous succession of life, decay, death, and re-creation.* The span of man's life being uncertain (according to his etherial endowment), he must never calculate gain or loss, but should always accept Divine Law and do the right at whatever cost.[16]

In regard to 'Heaven's Decree,' while Chu Tzu generally interpreted Heaven as impersonal, yet at times he seemed to lean somewhat toward a personalized conception:

"Man is true and great," he said, "whence we may know that the feelings of Heaven-and-Earth are true and great. But the truth and greatness of Heaven-and-Earth are absolute; there is never anything false, there is never anything small in them . . ."[17]

While commenting on the *Yi Ching* ('Fu Diagram'), Chu Tzu spoke of certain passages that seemed to indicate "a person, as it were, ruling in it all. The Mind is his agent, and the feelings are his purpose."[18] Later on, he wrote: "But still this Ruler is none other than Law. . . . In the whole universe,

---

* *Note*:—The idea of 'a succession of universes' is distinctly a Buddhist concept, which became applied to humans in their doctrine of 're-incarnation.'

there is nothing higher than Law, hence the term Ruler."[19] Pointing to a sentence in the *Shu Ching,* he found the very word 'confer' conveying the idea of 'One who exercises authority.' When asked, "Is it simply that the Supreme Ultimate is the *pivot* on which all transformations turn, and, therefore, that the universe is what it is by a process of self-evolution?" Chu Tzu replied, "This is the same question as the one already answered (about the Ruler)."[20]

(3) *On Human Nature*

On this subject, Chu Tzu had much to say. His major premise is very concisely stated:

". . . All men's capacity to speak, move, think, and act is entirely (a product of) the Ether; and yet within this (Ether) Principle inheres."

In other words, as Fung Yu-lan interprets it, "The Principle that is thus contained within the Ether to form an individual human being is then known as 'the nature,' or *hsing."*[21]

Man's physical and mental endowments are determined by the ever-present relation in him of pure Principle and impure Ether. His goodness and evil will vary by the measure in which the purity of Principle can dissolve the turbidness of Ether. The sage reflects the higher, and the dullard a lower, distillation of endowment. Men and animals, therefore, have different capacities, even as medicinal herbs (like rhubarb and aconite) have particular uses according to the nature (*hsing*) implanted in them.[22]

Man's mind (intellectual faculty or consciousness) reveals the interaction of Principle and Ether, though it remains in the sphere of the physical. Principle manifests itself in consciousness much as light manifests itself while burning the oil in the lamp. "We of the Confucian cult," Chu Hsi was wont to say, "regard the nature (*hsing*) as real. Buddhists regard it as unreal." He was careful to insist, however, on the discreteness of the nature and the mind, or intellectual faculty.[23]

The nature in man, as Chu Tzu conceived it, has many facets, especially *love* (associated with the element wood); *righteousness* (associated with metal); *propriety* (associated with fire); *wisdom* (with water); and *sincerity* (with earth)—which he called the 'Five Constants'. These he took to be the real expression in man of Eternal Principle, making man's nature originally and universally good.[24]

The mind of man, on the other hand, after being acted upon by external influences, begins to lose the poise of ethical purity, although we can never say that we have two natures: one good, one evil. Man has received the choicest excellence of the Five Elements; therefore, just as fire has its good side (when it cooks) and its evil side (when it burns—yet couldn't cook if it didn't burn), so man's mind, when acted upon by the external world, becomes active and gives rise to emotions like love, joy, pleasure, and also to harmful feelings such as anger, hate, and desire. (To quote):—

"If the endowment (of the Five Constants) is great in one direction, it is at the expense of some corresponding defect in another direction; as when tender-hearted men are lacking in the judicial faculty, while men in whom the judicial faculty is prominent tend to be tyrannical; for the more love is developed, the more is righteousness obscured, and the more righteousness is developed, the more love is obscured." (25)

Emotions or feelings, for Chu Hsi, are the impulsive reactions of mind to desirable or undesirable external stimuli. They may be controlled by that reasoning power of the mind known as 'capacity' (*ts'ai*). Mind includes the nature as its substance and feelings as its operation, though at all times mind is the controller. "Mind is the unifying agent between the nature and the feelings."[26] The nature is wholly good, but feelings may be perverted.

Man's goal, therefore, is a steadfast mind, actuated by high altruism. As W. T. Chan has pointed out, Chu Hsi, by insisting on "self-evident premises and moral preparation for knowledge," as well as on the necessity of having "a fine degree of receptivity to obtain *rapport* with the realities of the objective world," proved himself both empiricist and rationalist.[27] We must learn, he urged, to respond with broadness of mind to the right impulses, avoiding self-concentration and the calculating mind. Men should beware of the self-concentration of the Buddhists, which is selfishness, he declared more than once.[28]

In discussing the conative in relation to the cognitive faculty, Chu Tzu argued that where feelings are the ability to act, motive is the consideration how to act. These both issue from mind, for, as he phrased it:

"The mind is the ruler of the entire person. The motives are the emanation of the mind. Feelings are the movements of the mind. The will is the direction of the mind, and is stronger than feeling or motive".... (29)

... (Again, in effect):
Motive lies in the background; will is assertive and altruistic; yet motive is the basis of the backward and forward workings of the will, which is the mind in its doing and calculating aspect. (30)

4. *On Spiritual Cultivation and Ethics*

Since motivation (conation) is a mental process (cognition) leading to action, it behooves man to give attention to the cultivation of proper thinking. Basic training of the virtuous mind becomes the central Confucian (and Neo-Confucian) concern, in the elucidation of which theme Chu Hsi wrote:

"The nature of men and other creatures is essentially the same. . . . Beasts have some things in common with man but no moral principle. . . .
"Man, however, is born endowed with the '*Mean,*' the attribute of

Heaven-and-Earth . . . (so that he can perfect the Four Virtues)." (31) (*)

"Now, for the nature to attain the *Mean* is as natural as for water to be cold and fire hot; but the *Mean* is disturbed because men becloud it by habits engendered by the material element (in the ethereal endowment)." (32)

Crediting the Ch'eng Brothers with clarifying the point that evil in man is due to the ethereal element rather than to his nature which is originally good, Chu Tzu stoutly insisted that "all evil is good originally, but it has lapsed."[33] Hence,

"The object of the sages was to teach men to reverse the evil, attain to the *Mean,* and rest therein." (Quoting the *Shu Ching* and the *Shih Ching* in support of this belief in the moral improvability of every man, who already possesses this indwelling 'spark of the divine'). (34)

For Chu Tzu, then, the problem of education was two-fold: psychical and ethical, to insure the ascendancy of dependable moral principle over unstable ethereal endowment expressed in selfish desires. Hence the stress, first of all, on the exhaustive investigation of principles in order to preserve the mind. Effort must be concentrated on expanding the mind, until "complete understanding . . . of all the multitude of things . . . will open before one . . . and every exercise of the mind will be marked by complete enlightenment."[35]

Here Fung Yu-lan's translator, Derk Bodde, has called attention to the fact that for Chu Tzu the 'investigation of things' was not a search for pure knowledge (in the modern, scientific spirit), but was merely the 'means to a moral end—namely, self-cultivation and clarification of the mind.'[36] It was precisely here—on the value of investigation—that later the Lu-Wang School took issue so strongly with the Ch'eng-Chu School.

---

* At this point, Carsun Chang (*Op. Cit.,* p. 266) reminds us how closely Chu Hsi's thought runs to that of Aristotle. The "Four Virtues" referred to here are: Love, Righteousness, Reverence, and Wisdom.

Pursuing the thought of 'expanding the mind' still further, Chu Tzu was wont to say: "Learning originates in thought; it is by thought that intelligence is evoked (and perspicacity achieved)."[37] Then, continuing, he would add (in effect): Evil thoughts must be excluded and not allowed to be actualized in action. Desire may be repressed by thought, but we are not to be immersed in No-Thought, as the Buddhists sometimes are. We should think on what we ought to think and not violate moral principles. We should be serious, earnest, and whole-hearted, and problems will unravel themselves. When a pupil asked, Does not the secret of it all lie in seriousness? Chu Tzu replied:

"Seriousness is not a separate thing, it is constantly to stir up the mind. People fly (*) through the days and never stop to collect their minds." (38)

As will be seen readily, the (psychical) pursuit of knowledge was, for Chu Tzu (in true Confucian manner), inextricably bound up with the (ethical) attainment of virtuous character. "By education, the nature . . . may be made to follow *Virtue*," he said; "without such education, the nature . . . remains (in the grip of) an ethereal endowment. . . ."[30] From here on, Chu Tzu became avowedly the moral philosopher. (To quote):

"Take, for instance, the feeling of solicitude: if from this you trace backwards you will arrive at love (*jên*), which is inherent in the mind; but Love is the Principle of Origin, one of the Divine Attributes . . . the positive and active mode of the Supreme Ultimate. Thus, by tracing backwards stage by stage we arrive at the fountain head"—[the *Tao* (which) finds substance and operation in Love (*jên*)]. (40)

(Or again):

"To serve one's parents is the virtue of filial piety: . . . as cherished in the heart, it is called 'Virtue'; as seen in action, it is called

---

* Literally, "swoop down like a hawk."

'Conduct'." (41) . . . "The virtue of the ear is alertness, the virtue of the eye is clearness, the virtue of the mind is love (*jên*) . . . . But the ability to practice righteousness is by the operation of love . . . (which is) buoyant like the richness of new wine." (42)

Chu Hsi gave to *jên,* or love, as the fulfilling of the law, a warmth of interpretation not hitherto attained in Confucian thought, unless it be found in Mo Ti's enthusiasm for its universal application. (To quote) :—

"It is after we have received this vital impulse (*jên,* love) and are thereby in possession of life, that we have *reverence* (or propriety), *wisdom, righteousness,* and *sincerity.* From the point of view of greatness, love is greatest. . . . The reason why love is called the virtue of the mind is that it is the source of affection. (It gives the unselfish outlook); it enables a man to look upon others as one with himself." . . . (43)

(The philosopher said further) : Although Love appears to have the quality of strength and directness, it really is a mild and gentle thing; (in its operation there is moral insight, courtesy, and judgment), these three, before the deed of Love is complete," . . . (44) . . . "That is, when by his efforts he had attained to Love, there was spontaneous joy, altogether independent of poverty, or wealth, or high estate, or low estate, so that they could not affect it." (45) . . . "It vitalizes the mind so that it can know humility, conscientiousness, right and wrong." (46)

Chu Hsi distinguished love from altruism by saying that where altruism is the (negative) lack of selfishness, love is more positive, like water that pours down the stream if the dam is removed. By removing the dam of selfishness, one becomes unselfishly altruistic, thereby giving love a free course.[47]

Sincerity (for Chu Hsi) expresses the reality of the other four virtues: love, righteousness, propriety, and wisdom . . . (which give substantive existence to the nature which) . . . "Heaven has implanted . . . in man. . . . This Heaven-implanted nature is best expressed in the word *ch'êng,* meaning absolute truth or sincerity based on Divine Law. It includes also seriousness or apprehension, lest self-deception creep in to spoil its (ingenuousness or) guilelessness."[48]

"A true heart," declared Chu Tzu "—this is the citadel for the learner. . . ." In other words, as J. Percy Bruce interprets, "the learner must have a 'true heart' as the citadel of his personality if he is to be successful. . . ." (Chu Hsi) :—"If one only states the half and is not willing to state the whole, it is disingenuousness. To say a thing is when it is and is not when it is not, is Truth" . . . "Ingenuousness is truth in the heart." . . . "Ingenuousness or seriousness (truth) may be compared to sincerity . . . as branch is related to root. . . . Love, righteousness, ceremony, and music . . . are cultivated . . . in order to manifest the *Tao*." . . . (And, finally), "To be sincere, empty of self, courteous and calm is the foundation of the practice of love. . . . To love others as we love ourselves, is to perfect love."[49]

5. *On Political Philosophy or Ideal Government*

Pointing back to the Golden Age of the six sage-kings (Yao, Shun, Three Kings of the Primitive Dynasties, with the Duke of Chou) and the one 'worthy' (Confucius), Chu Hsi ever maintained their supremacy as model rulers and contended that kings and emperors of his own day needed only to follow their example. As the 'mind of the body' is ever at variance with the 'mind of the spirit,' this struggle is ever reflected in a ruler's wrong or right conduct in government. If he can maintain an even balance (the *Mean*), like the Platonic and the truly Confucian sage-king, then the Heavenly Principle within him will never be dissipated by his human desires.[50]

6. *On the Weakness of Buddhism*

Chu Hsi strongly opposed the Buddhist stress on 'pure consciousness' divorced from any transcendent *li* (taken as ethical), their doctrine of the 'emptiness of the Void,' and consequent teaching on 'the illusoriness of human nature and life.'[51] He felt that they had completely disregarded the Five Relationships and had flouted marriage as the foundation of society by their formation of an unnatural society of celibate monks and nuns.[52]

It was his firm conviction of the inherent goodness of human nature based on *li* that led Chu Hsi to attack the Buddhist conception of mind as 'pure consciousness only.' Where, for the Buddhists, mind as "innermost consciousness" had "nothing to do with the external world," for the Neo-Confucianists the mind had not only a transcendental or essential level (endowed with Principle) by which men instinctively recognized love, duty, and wisdom; but also a natural physical level (endowed with Ether) whereby they could distinguish right from wrong. In this way, Chu Hsi and his followers preserved moral values in a mind that was not mere emptiness, as some Buddhists said; that was not free from the necessity for discriminating right and wrong; and that could be *trusted* to see the evidences of truth correctly.[53]

* * *

There is no doubt, as Fung Yu-lan has suggested, that Chu Hsi's philosophy comes closer to neo-realism than to idealism. "Like his predecessors, he paid scant attention to the purely logical in his philosophic thinking. What he calls 'Principle,' therefore, which might otherwise be a wholly logical concept, has for him ethical qualities as well. As these two aspects become fused, the Principle of a thing, to his mind, not only makes that thing what it is but at the same time makes it what it ought (morally) to be, thereby showing that his interest was more largely ethical than logical."[54]

In conclusion, we may say that Chu Hsi strengthened Confucian rationalism by his emphasis on the dual nature both of the universe and of man, by his vigorous defense of the objective reality of Pure Principle and of the unsullied character of the real nature of the inner man, as well as by his optimistic campaigning for improved education and decent government.

Chapter 11

Later Neo-Confucians
(Of the Sung and Ming Dynasties)

> "There is a universal mind in which all sages participate, be they from East, South, West, or North, Past or Future."
>
> —Lu Hsiang-shan: *Conversations**

> "The superior man does not seek the approbation of others, for if he has confidence in himself, that is enough."
>
> —Wang Yang-ming: *Letter to Shu Kuo-yung**

> "Heaven, Earth, and all things are within the manifestations, use, and activities of my intuitive faculty."
>
> —Wang Yang-ming: *Yang-ming Chi-Yao***

Strongly divergent from Ch'eng Yi's and Chu Hsi's Reason School (*Li Hsüeh*) was the so-called Mind School (*Hsin Hsüeh*) established by Lu Hsiang-shan (A.D. 1139-1193) in the Sung dynasty and elaborated by Wang Yang-ming (A.D. 1472-1529) in the Ming dynasty. Both men, undoubtedly influenced by Ch'eng Hao, took mind as identical with the universe and

* Siu-chi Huang's paraphrase.
** Frederick G. Henke's translation.

as the expression of the Moral Law, their intuitionism later being referred to as the Mind School of Lu-Wang Idealism in Chinese philosophy.

Taking as their point of departure Confucius' 'rectification of mind' and Mencius' 'preservation of mind,' they were also undoubtedly influenced by Ch'an Buddhism's stress on 'tranquil repose.' [1] David S. Nivison notes that the Ch'an Buddhist philosophy had presented the ideal of a completely satisfying experience of perfect enlightenment that takes place in the mind. In Neo-Confucian thought, this resolved itself into the discovery of a mystical consciousness of ultimate reality within one's self.[2] To this we may add that, whereas the Ch'an Masters leaned strongly to belief in a sudden, ecstatic illumination of the mind, the Confucian Idealists viewed inner enlightenment more as a slow process whereby one achieves utter unselfishness or 'empty impartiality.' [3]

Lu Hsiang-shan: Founder of the Lu-Wang School of Idealism:—

Born in Kiangsi in 1139, Lu Hsiang-shan (whose personal name was Chiu-yüan) was educated privately under his father and other tutors. In 1172, he successfully passed the third degree of *Chin Shih, magna cum laude,* and entered the *Kuo Hsüeh* or Imperial Academy, then located in Hangchow, Chekiang, the then capital of the Southern Sung dynasty. Later he became widely known as a lecturer at Elephant Mountain in Kiangsi Province and hence took the name of "Hsiang-shan."

While serving as a magistrate at Ching-Men in Hupeh Province, Lu made many improvements in the administration of his office, was well-liked and frequently gave lectures on civic responsibility. Although he successively held several government posts, he was apparently more interested in teaching than in the work of a magistrate. His death occurred in 1192 or 1193.

Writing on "The Cultivation of the Superior Man," in his *Complete Works of Lu Hsiang-shan* (*Hsiang-shan Hsien-Sheng Ch'üan-Chi*), Lu insisted that the purpose of study was to rid the mind of all those things by which it is blinded, thus enabling it to return to its originally pure condition. Every man, he urged, is responsible for his own beclouded condition of mind and must strive to attain clearness of vision, avoid material desires and self-assertive dogmatism. Re-affirming Ch'eng Hao's reliance on Principle, he urged men to eschew selfish, cunning calculation and thus attain the goal of 'empty impartiality.'[4]

Lu criticized the Buddhists for being unable to reach this goal of impartiality, because they aimed only at escaping from this sorrowful world; whereas the Confucians considered life in the world well worth the struggle to attain impartiality.[5] While admitting that evil in man is inescapable and reprehensible, Lu combatted any theory of 'original sin.' Only by his yielding to physical desires has man allowed evil to creep in. The whole purpose of Confucian training is, therefore, to help men develop their inborn capacity for reflective knowledge.[6] More specifically, as Lu Hsiang-shan insisted,

"there must be no utilitarian aim in true education. . . . All who wish to learn must first understand the difference between righteousness and profit. . . . The purpose of learning is solely to learn to be men without ulterior motive. . . ." (7)

This accords with the opening words of the *Chung Yung*:— "What Heaven confers is called 'nature'; accordance with this nature is called *'tao'*; the cultivation of *tao* is called 'education'."[8] In his theory of education, Lu Hsiang-shan, under Buddhist influence, leaped the dualistic gap left by Chu Hsi and equated the 'Mind of Man' with Principle (*Tao, Li*); whereas Chu Hsi had felt that the 'earthy' human mind, belonging as it did to the lower sphere of 'shapes' (*ch'i*), could only by careful cultivation be transformed into the 'Mind of the Spirit' (*tao hsin*).[9]

Feeling that Chu Hsi's system was too complicated, Lu developed his philosophy on the basis of a universal Law, present in and apprehended by the mind, as the 'moral criterion of human conduct.' (To quote) :—

"Since the Law is universal, the world of sense is real, but can best be understood in the mind. A man exists by reason of his thinking capacity; therefore, the universe and my mind are one. There is a universal mind in which all sages participate, be they from East, South, West, or North, Past or Future. . . .
"If I can develop my mind completely, I, therefore, become identified with Heaven. To acquire learning consists of nothing more than to apprehend this." (10)

In other words, Lu refused to consider as important any acquisition of factual knowledge by external 'investigation,' for the mind *is Li* (*Tao*) and not on two levels as Chu Hsi had claimed.[11]

In 1175 a meeting took place between Chu Hsi and his younger contemporary, Lu Hsiang-shan, but in their discussion they could come to no agreement. Six years later, they met again at Nan-K'ang (perhaps with a boat-ride on P'o-yang Lake), and by request Lu lectured to Chu's students at White Deer Grotto. In 1187 was begun their long correspondence on the "Diagram of the Supreme Ultimate."[12] But as long as Lu clung to a monistic, and Chu to a dualistic view of the nature of reality, their debates could never lead to any harmonizing synthesis.[13]

As Siu-chi Huang has pointed out, "Lu liked to use the term 'original mind' (*pên hsin*) to avoid the dualistic tendency in the Ch'eng-Chu School and, often referring to Mencius,[14] explained it in this wise:
"The feeling of commiseration is the basis of human-heartedness. The feeling of shame and dislike is the basis of righteousness. The feeling of modesty and complaisance is the basis of propriety. The feeling of right and wrong is the basis of wisdom. All these are the Original Mind." (15)

Of the four virtues—human-heartedness (*jên*), righteousness or justice (*i*), propriety or decorum (*li*), and wisdom (*chih*)—Lu was inclined to stress righteousness, where Chu would have stressed human-heartedness.[16]

Among later thinkers, four definitely followed Lu Hsiang-shan's example. His monistic idealism was carried on by his disciple Yang Chien (A.D. 1140-ca. 1225), and was passed on to Ch'en Hsien-chang (A.D. 1428-1500) and Chan Jo-shui (A.D. 1466-1560), both of whom felt attracted to Lu's conception of Principle as "ceaselessly operating and permeating all things at all times and all places."[17] More especially, however, in Wang Yang-ming (A.D. 1472-1529) is Lu's influence clearly seen, although Wang was also undoubtedly influenced by his older contemporaries, Ch'en and Chan.[18]

Because of its dearth of philosophical thinkers, the Yüan or Mongol dynasty (A.D. 1280-1368), whose chief interest of a literary nature lay in the development of the drama, is passed over without comment in order to review in some detail the philosophy of Wang Yang-ming, the greatest philosopher of the Ming period (A.D. 1368-1644).

* * *

Wang Yang-ming—Great Protagonist of Lu-Wang Idealism:— The writings of Wang Shou-jên, better known in China as "The Master of Yang-Ming," or Wang Yang-ming,* have had much influence in modern Oriental thinking, especially in the early decades of the twentieth century, after Chinese students had discovered in what high esteem he was held by the Japanese, who knew him as "Oyomei." Born in Yü-yao, in the province of Chekiang, in A.D. 1472 and living until 1529, this Emerson among Chinese philosophers filled his fifty-seven years with fruitful studies in religion and philosophy, became a poet of no mean quality, a master of military affairs, and served as magistrate in three different provinces. A more comprehensive thinker than Lu Hsiang-shan, Wang Yang-ming is acknowledged by all as the leader of the Mind School in the Ming period.

It is recorded that while he was living in Peking Wang's health broke and he was long troubled with a hacking cough.

---

* Also referred to as (Wang) Wên-ch'eng by Huang Tsung-hsi (A.D. 1610-1695) in his biographical sketches of Ming dynasty Confucianists (*Ming-Ju Hsüeh-An*). (19)

Nevertheless, he accepted an invitation to speak at the rededication of the repaired Tzu Yang College at Pai Lu Tung* in Kiangsi Province. In this connection he wrote a preface to a collection of essays to honor the memory and teachings of Chu Hsi, whose name had long been associated with that famous institution. Wang also wrote a preface to the *Complete Works of Lu Hsiang-shan*** to acknowledge his indebtedness to his favorite philosopher-mentor.[20] Like Lu (who, while influenced by Buddhism, disclaimed being a Buddhist), Wang avoided the otherworldliness of the Ch'an Buddhists and stressed the moral cultivation of the self in this life.

Siu-chi Huang has selected three basic ideas which, *prima facie,* Wang inherited from Lu Hsiang-shan: (1) the unity of mind and law (principle); (2) the development of intuitive knowledge without cognition and without outside corrupting influences; (3) the unity of knowledge and action, because intuitive knowledge grows by understanding and discipline of self and by applying this knowledge to the practical concerns of everyday life.[22] The discussion of these and other of Wang Yang-ming's ideas falls naturally under the following topics: (1) The Intuitive Faculty and the Investigation of Principles; (2) The Unity of Knowledge and Action and the Unity of Activity and quiescence; (3) On Good and Evil, or The Nature of Moral Man; (4) A Criticism of Mo Tzu's 'Universal Love'; (5) On Being A Good Ruler; (6) On Religious Attitudes; (7) On Teaching and the Learning Process.

(1) *The Intuitive Faculty and the Investigation of Principles*

In his treatise on *Questions on the Great Learning* (*Ta Hsüeh Wên*), Wang Yang-ming reaffirmed older Confucian convictions by saying:—

---

* The same "White Deer Grotto" that is mentioned above (pp. 198, 214).

** A version of this work was published in A.D. 1561 by one Wang Tung-mu, High Commissioner of the Treasury in Kiangsi, who commented on Wang Shou-jên's appreciation of Lu Hsiang-shan. (21)

. . . "To manifest the 'illustrious virtue' is to establish one's state of unity with Heaven, Earth, and all things. . . . When the highest good is manifested, right is right and wrong is wrong . . . which is also what I call 'intuitive knowledge'." (23)

"If now we concentrate our thoughts upon extending the intuitive knowledge, so as to sweep away all the barriers (caused by selfish desire), the original state will then again be restored, and we will again become part of the profundity of Heaven" . . . (24)

Wang felt that his intuitive knowledge was like the sun; its location could not be pointed out if obscured by clouds of desire.[25] Moreover, it needs no strengthening, he urged, "for it is able to foresee deceptions; it is perfect; without cogitations, it knows and is free from . . . hypocrisy."[26]

Nevertheless, Wang recognized that the mind must go forth; that in his eager pursuit of knowledge the sage would even forget his food (as is indicated in the *Analects* VII, 18, 2), for learning is increased by earnest application to the affairs of life.[27] Neither does nourishing the mind include asceticism. Because Buddhists abnegate all things, seeking metempsychosis and Nirvāṇa, they cannot govern the Empire.[28] Furthermore, extending one's intuitive knowledge, does not mean "to stupefy oneself with shadows and echoes and suspend oneself in empty unreality (as the Buddhists do in their meditations on 'emptiness')." . . . "(No), it is necessary to accept the reality of (external) affairs. Hence the 'extension of knowledge' necessarily consists in the 'investigation of things'."[29]

This, however, is not a concession to the Ch'eng-Chu way of thinking, for, as his thought continues in his *Yang-Ming Chi-Yao* (*Important Selections from Wang Yang-ming*), Wang states clearly that "intuitive knowledge of good . . . is not attained through external investigations , . . since 'nothing exists apart from the mind', . . (and) . . . it is not necessary to add one whit from without."[30] (To quote) :—

". . . I mean by this (investigation of things) an extension of our mind's *intuitive knowledge* to affairs and things, then each such affair and thing will thereby partake of this Principle. . . . In this way, mind and Principle are made one." (31)

In brief, where Chu Hsi had held that only the nature, not the mind, is to be equated with Principle, Wang Yang-ming thoroughly believed there could be no Principle outside of or apart from the mind. Where Chu maintained that our mind contains within itself not only the Supreme Ultimate (Principle) but also all the various Principles of things, Wang insisted that Heaven, Earth, and all things are actually present within our minds. He reported on one occasion that he and a friend each had tried to investigate the principles of the bamboo and had failed. He, therefore, concluded that investigation can be done only with reference to one's own mind.[32]

Wang Yang-ming's theory of reality, then, is a sort of "consubstantiationism" of internal and external reality—a Chinese version of Berkeley's *esse est percipi*.[33] It is a philosophy of pure idealism with which Chu Hsi could never agree, and this divergence represents the fundamental distinction between their two schools. On the other hand, Huang I-fang thinks Chu and Wang were very close in spirit and method; they simply stressed the outer and the inner aspects of one indivisible whole.[34]

(2) *The Unity of Knowledge and Action* *and* *The Unity of Activity and Quiescence*

A recurrent note in Wang Yang-ming's philosophy was the oneness of knowing and doing. (To quote) :—

"There is no such thing as knowledge which cannot be carried into practice, for such knowledge is really no knowledge at all. . . . Intuitive knowledge is the beginning (or guide) of conduct; conduct is the completion of (or work carried out by) knowledge." (35)

Wang was sure that if his mind judged something to be wrong, he wouldn't dare consider it right, even though Confucius himself had taken it to be right. It was this emphasis upon independent judgment, as well as his insistence on the mutuality of knowing and doing, that held great appeal for Japanese *samurai* and Chinese men of action alike. Later on, it could be seen working in the minds of Sun Yat-sen and Chiang K'ai-shek, likewise men of affairs and men of destiny, seeking to prove for themselves the worth of this phase of Wang Yang-ming's pragmatic intuitionism.

In an article entitled "The Problem of 'Knowledge' and 'Action' in Chinese Thought Since Wang Yang-ming," David S. Nivison has noted that Wang and other Ming philosophers were trying to synthesize age-old dualism found in earlier Chinese thought—of 'principle and practice,' 'words and deeds,' 'thought and behavior.' He goes on to state that, whereas Chu Hsi had held that natural knowledge needed further acquisition of facts (from the external world) to complete its knowledge of principle, Wang Yang-ming believed thoroughly that the mind held within itself sufficient, innate, moral knowledge, which could express itself in moral action if only the mind could be rid of its muddy confusion. This quieting of the mind might take some time but would eventually lead to self-realization in the ecstasy of true sincerity (or the union of knowledge and action).[36]

Moving from the ethical back to the epistemological, Wang Yang-ming repeatedly reminded his pupils that we can perform action externally, the while preserving a state of non-action within our own minds. This combined achievement he summed up as the unity of movement or activity (*tung*) and quiescence (*ching*):—

". . . In his state of quiescence, (the superior man) remains ever perceptive . . . always ready to respond (to whatever may arise). In his state of activity, he remains ever composed, . . . always ready to retire. . . . Hence, once . . . (he) . . . conforms to Principle, then, despite all (his) . . . responses to . . . the manifold vicissitudes of life, (he) still remains always quiescent." (37)

". . . Gently and harmoniously, . . . he penetrates everywhere in his movements. His acts and demeanor . . . always accord with propriety. . . ." (38)

(3) *On Good and Evil—or The Nature of Moral Man*

As with most of China's philosophers, the task of achieving good character was ever uppermost in Wang Yang-ming's mind. Here, "the problem of moral evil arises out of Wang's belief that everything under Heaven is found in the mind and can be taken as a single thing (i.e., as a-moral)."[39] In Wang's own words:

"The highest good is the mind's original substance. Whatever goes beyond this original substance is evil . . . Joy, anger, grief, fear, love, hate, and desire are . . . all equally inherent in the human mind . . . (as) functions of the intuitive knowledge, and cannot be divided into good and evil. . . ." (It is much like the flowers and weeds in a garden, Wang said):—"Wishing to have flowers to look at, you then consider them good and the weeds evil. But should you wish to use the weeds (as medicinal herbs), you would . . . consider them good. Thus, . . . good and evil spring from the likes and dislikes of your own mind. . . ." (40)

At the same time, Wang recognized that the problem of maintaining good growth in the garden of the mind was not a simple one. Innate goodness, or clarity, could be preserved only at the price of eternal vigilance, as he has declared in the following passage:

". . . We need a mind earnest in doing good. When the (earnest) mind sees virtue, it will advance toward it, and when it has erred, it will reform. (That) . . . is called devotion . . . to the task. . . . He who merely seeks better circumstances, or speaks of results, fosters . . . the defect of forcing the growth and of going to external things. It should not be identified with pursuing the task." (41)

In other words, Wang would declare that considering doing good is the same as begetting equilibrium in the mind, but selfishness, as a root of evil, must be eradicated.[42] Everyone must drive out passion and obey natural law (not to gain a Buddhistic tranquility, but to establish the mind on firm principles) . . . (Not) tranquility, but action unmoved by passion will be the state of the highest good.[43]

In similar strain, Wang Yang-ming argued that a man is not a mere machine. The mind must rule the senses; confusion comes from lust of one kind or another; such as sex, fame, gain, and these, if not swept out daily, will cause 'an intermittent fever' in the mind. Where feelings are stirred, the mind becomes disorderly and unmannerly. The pure heart guards against passion and subdues it when it appears. The intuitive faculty clears itself of feculence and obscuration and gives accurate information on matters of truth, as a clear mirror gives a faithful reflection. In the last analysis, morality is a matter of keeping the mind clean and personal objectives high. To each generation of students, Wang's admonitions followed a similar pattern:

"If you devote yourself to the intuitive faculty, why should evil thoughts come?" . . . (And in effect):—When the purpose is fixed, everything is unified. . . . Seek an equilibrium of passions and vicissitudes in your living. . . . Avoid salacious thoughts, (for) passion causes distraction! . . . Mastering the mind means to master moral principles. . . . One must fix his determination to keep Heaven-given principles. (44)

Furthermore, he declared:

". . . Rid yourself of your vulgar, plebeian ideas and return to your former purpose." (i.e., avoid coveting merit and gain!) (45)

In a letter to Shu Kuo-yung, he wrote:

"The superior man does not seek the confidence of others, for, if he has confidence in himself, that is enough. He does not seek notoriety or popularity: if he knows himself, that is enough. . . ."[46]

Putting it into a nutshell, Carsun Chang intimates that both Lu Hsiang-shan and Wang Yang-ming "fused the upper level (*hsing,* or stored reason) and the lower level (*hsin*) of awareness and consciousness as the expression of reason through mental processes." [47]

(4) *A Criticism of Mo Tzu's Universal Love*

Wang Yang-ming criticized Mo Tzu's teaching on 'universal love' (*chien ai*) as being too undiscriminating when compared to the Confucian concept of *jên.* By long tradition, he said, Confucians have held it to be entirely natural for a parent to love his child or a son to love his father first of all. Partiality is 'a natural principle within our intuitive knowledge' and is, therefore, to be sanctioned as part of the 'natural Mean.'

"But Mo Tzu's universal love has no gradations," Wang complained. "It regards the father and son, elder and younger brother, of one's own family in the same light as it does a passerby. . . . How then can this be called *jên*?" (48)

In another passage, however, Wang Yang-ming's thought ran very close to Mo Tzu's 'universal love,' when he wrote that the mind of a sage sees a brother or a child in anyone who has blood and life. (To quote) :—

"There is no one whom he (the sage) does not wish to see perfectly at peace and whom he does not wish to nourish." (49)

(5) *On Being A Good Ruler*

From his own wide experience, Wang Yang-ming knew how difficult it was to be a good magistrate, and sought to pass on to young men under his instruction those gems of wisdom which he had extracted from that experience. In commenting on the *Doctrine of the Mean,** where Confucius is giving advice to Yen on good government, Wang remarked:

---

* *Chung Yung,* Ch. 20, par. 4, 8, and 12.

"Where character is sincere, then he (the ruler) is really able to govern the country." (50)

And again, in his first instructions for the practical life of a local magistrate, Wang spoke of human-heartedness (*jên*) as an inward, spiritual love for all mankind, on the part of both ruler and people. While interpreting the words of Confucius in the *Great Learning:* 'To cultivate one's self so as to give peace to the people,' as implying that no ruler could give peace to his people unless he loved them, he added:

"The highest excellence consists in nothing else than a mind completely dominated by heaven-given principles—especially the honoring of one's parents." [51]

In another connection, Wang exclaimed that

"Heaven, Earth, and sages are all one! But even a sage (-magistrate) should never strive for exalted position, to appear like T'ai Shan and be looked up to by others." (52)

After being ridiculed by some villagers because, as a magistrate, he was too 'ardent,' and by others for being too 'cautiously decided,' Wang wrote to his friend, Chou Tao-tung:

"Each one should discuss his own mistakes and not those of the philosophers Chu and Lu. . . . Formerly, people were in the habit of saying: 'He who attacks my shortcomings is my teacher'." (53)

Being himself a modest man, Wang Yang-ming felt that too many rulers had "drifted into the false condition of ruling by might and did not know themselves." [54] He ever applied to himself his own teaching:

". . . The sage-magistrate carries out a program of work with fixed mind. . . . He must be open-minded and without favoritism, for then he is manifesting the original nature of the mind. Know this and you know the state of equilibrium (in judging cases)." (55)

(6) *On Religious Attitudes*

To a young man inquiring about the correct attitude to take toward the genii or immortals, Wang Yang-ming replied:

"Immortality is perhaps an accomplishment of Heaven and not the result of any strenuous effort on man's part."

Skeptical of Taoist claims to immortality as an extension of the present life, yet not rejecting the idea completely, he went on to add:

"If you wish to hear about immortality, you must live in the mountain forest (like a Taoist hermit) for thirty years. . . . At present, you are still far from the path of immortality." (56)

Although certain parts of his writings reflect the Buddhist influence, Wang is reported by a disciple, Ts'ü Ai, as strenuously rejecting the Buddhist idea of Nirvāṇa or the contemplation of it. He preferred to re-emphasize the age-old Confucian stress on the original, Heaven-sent principles of *jên* (human-heartedness, benevolence) and *i* (righteousness or justice) in the natural disposition of mankind.[57]

Tolerant of the time-honored religious customs of his compatriots, Wang is known to have approved, on at least one occasion, of their resorting to divination in order to ascertain the will of Heaven in a time of crisis. But he once remarked that a good man need have no fear of evil spirits; he need fear only that the mind be depraved by salaciousness, covetousness, anger, or fear. Many men, he observed, fail to attain any equilibrium in time of sorrow; for the most part, the people of his generation appeared unable to achieve this true harmony.[58]

(7) *On Teaching and the Learning Process*

While disagreeing with Chu Hsi on many points, Wang Yang-ming nevertheless held him in wholesome respect as a teacher, saying:

"The sage ('Hui-an', or Chu Hsi) established his teachings (Confucianism) in order that one might silently treasure knowledge of the intelligence of the mind, and be dignified and peaceful, and further, that one might consider these as the root of investigating principles." (59)

". . . The difficulty of the task rests wholly in investigating things for the purpose of developing the intuitive faculty to the utmost." . . . (60)

Wang evidently thought his own teaching about the intuitive faculty the most important of all, yet the most difficult to teach and for students to receive with understanding. For this reason, he urged his disciples to aim persistently at becoming sages and to pay strict attention in no 'dazed and vague fashion.' Realizing that some were quicker and some slower in their mental processes, he advised them to remember this when they, in turn, should go out to become teachers. (To quote) :—

"Following my words, you should adapt yourselves to the individual when offering instruction, and then there will be no defects." . . .(61)

In his correspondence with Wang Shih-t'ang, Wang Yang-ming gave expression to some of his most mature philosophic reflections on the whole subject of helping men along the road to wisdom. Among other things, he wrote:

(A thing is identical with the functioning of its purpose.) Nature and feeling are included in mind, (which) the philosopher Ch'eng says . . . is a unity. Its structure is perfectly tranquil, and in functioning it responds immediately when it is stimulated. . . ." (62)

In other words, structure and functioning are complementary. The student, therefore, should try to understand the structure of mind by its functioning. (Continuing the quotation) :—

"You, my brother, should apply further energy at the point where there is stirring. . . . If there is harmony in the stirrings of the feelings, there is equilibrium in tranquillity". (63)

And to Huang Tsung-hsien he wrote in similar vein:—

"In our devotion to study, we should expend the energy of our mind and marrow in penetrating into the essentials, for then it will be trustworthy and clear." (64)

And again:—

"The aim of scholarly study should be definite. . . . Avoid prejudice in study! Allow none of the affairs of life to interrupt the task! . . . The difficulty of the task interrupts neither activity nor tranquillity. . . . Even in times of exuberant growth, you can still have a discriminating and, therefore, a calm, peaceful mind." (65)

Along with definiteness, calmness, and persistence, Wang Yang-ming had constantly to remind his students of two other factors in the learning process: *first,* there are no short-cuts to knowledge; neither can one rest upon former efforts. *Second,* the true scholar maintains a humble attitude at all times. He saw love of fame as a common defect in students, which reduced their devotion to truth. We find Wang often referring to this:

"Humility is the foundation of all virtue; pride is the chief of all vices.". . . (66)
"If you bring your study to bear upon yourself, you will realize that you are in many respects imperfect. How will you find time to reprove others? . . . Whenever anybody needs to be reproved or criticized, you should expel the selfish desire to be the big man. . . . Only by descending (being humble) is one truly great." (67) "Mutually strive to be humble; for then you will derive benefit from your friendship.". . . (68)

Whether at the teacher's or the magistrate's desk, Wang Yang-ming liked to mull over in his mind certain great seed-thoughts growing out of his own 'investigation of things,' which had practical bearing on his profession of scholar-magistrate. We find him expressing these axioms in epigrams like the following:—

—"One's (innate) virtuous nature is best honored by maintaining constant inquiry and study.". . . (69)
—"Truth is by nature inexhaustible. The more inquiry is made . . . the more its minutiae will be apparent." . . . (70)
—"A sage does not need to know the details of everything. If he needs to learn, he can make inquiry!". . . (71)
—"Our knowledge does not depend on remembering everything which we see or hear!". . . (72)
—"Reading is for understanding, not remembering, and for understanding your own deepest self through what is read.". . . (73)
—"It is better to preserve virtue than life. If principles are violated, of what use is it to preserve life." (74)

When an under-official excused himself to his chief (Wang) on the ground that he was 'too busy with official duties to devote time to learning,' the latter counseled him:—

"I have never taught you to detach yourself to learn in a speculative way. Since you have your official duties to perform, verily true learning lies in your official duties. . . . One lives centuries in one day of vital experience.". . . . (75)

Fortunately, Wang Yang-ming recognized the need of both officials and scholars to take time off for recreation, for "the mind is by nature joyous, even though (it may be) eclipsed for a while by a period of grief and weeping." (To quote) :—

"Let relaxation and enjoyment be found in the polite arts, (which means that) . . . singing songs, reading books, playing on stringed instruments, practising archery, and the like, regulate the mind and give it skill." . . . (To Wang's mind . . . "Ancient music has a vital relation to public morals.". . .) (76)

And again:

"From the method that Confucius used to teach benevolence and filial piety . . . we can learn the true meaning of teaching. . . ." (77) . . ."To give instruction according to individual differences is (true) education. Each man (student) ought to develop his particular abilities, but there is only one goal, namely the Good." (78)

Conclusion:—In reviewing the "Sung and Ming Philosophers On Character Culture," Leonard Tomkinson has suggested certain propositions on which there was general agreement among Neo-Confucians, even though belonging to different schools of thought. They agreed, for example, that individual character-influence was a prime factor in perfecting the social order; that the example of a perfect ruler could cause his people to delight in righteousness. All agreed, therefore, on the cultivation of good personal character as the *sine qua non* of any system of education; furthermore, that this end would be accomplished best by achieving *sincerity* in each individual.[79]

The Lu-Wang idealists regarded concentration (*ching*) as a prime means of attaining sincerity, and agreed that absolute control should be given to the original nature, regarded partly as 'intuitive knowledge' and partly as 'conscience.' In a favorite expression *"Liang Chih, Liang Neng"* (lit. "good knowledge, good ability"), Wang Yang-ming defended his thesis that (intuitive) knowledge could enable a man to distinguish right from wrong and always succeed in doing the right. It was undoubtedly this defense of rugged individualism that prepared the awakening of Japan in the nineteenth century and the awakening of China in the twentieth century.[80]

Chapter 12

The Return To Empirical Realism
(In the Ch'ing Dynasty)

> "*Li* is the internal structure or system in things, and this it is the business of the mind to discover, unclouded by its own prejudices and undeceived by the prejudices of others." *
>
> —Tai Chen on "Reality" *

Introduction:—

For the student of philosophic trends in this period, the reactions of the men of the Empirical School in the Ch'ing (or Manchu) dynasty (A.D. 1644-1911) are probably the most important. As both Fung Yu-lan and Wing-tsit Chan have pointed out, the Neo-Confucianists of the Ch'ing period reacted strongly against the idealistic scholasticism of Ch'eng-Chu rationalism and Lu-Wang mind-philosophy as too speculative. Ch'ing scholars felt that the Sung-Ming Neo-Confucians (*Sung Hsüeh*) had been too much influenced by Buddhist and Taoist ideas. They wanted objective thinking that was more closely related to life. Hence, the cry arose: "Back to the early Confucianism of the Han period!"

The *literati* felt it imperative to go back to the classical commentaries of the Former Han dynasty as being older than Buddhism and religious Taoism and, therefore, nearer to the

---

* Fang Chao-ying translation.

mind of Confucius and Mencius. Delving feverishly into the musty volumes of ancient Han Learning (*Han Hsüeh*), they hailed it as the only orthodox, unalloyed Confucianism. There was thus brought about in China a Confucian Renaissance, similar to the Renaissance in Europe, which W. T. Chan has characterized as "a re-examination of classical philosophies, (an) emancipation from scholasticism, the rediscovery of society and the individual, the rise of independent and critical thinking, and the development of the scientific method," [1]—in short, the return to empirical realism.

In an article written some years ago, entitled "Ch'ing Dynasty Criticism of Sung Politico-Philosophy," [2] Mansfield Freeman pointed out, first of all, how the T'ang philosophers "had hopelessly mixed the doctrines of Confucius with Buddhist and Taoist thought," and then how the Sung critical thinkers had sought to give a truer interpretation of the Confucian Classics. He described how, under the leadership of Ssŭ-ma Kuang, the heterodox thinkers: the Ch'eng Brothers, Chou Tun-yi, Yang Kuei-shan, Chang Tsai, and Chu Hsi, had lost out to Wang Anshih's party in the struggle for political favor at court. At this point, De Bary would insist that Wang An-shih, despite his debt to the Legalists, was nevertheless honestly striving to put into practice reforms based on the Confucian tradition as incorporated in the *Institutes of Chou* (*Chou Li*), for which he wrote his own *New Interpretation of the Institutes of Chou* (*Chou Kuan Hsin-I*).[3]

As Freeman goes on to explain, the loss of political prestige had naturally driven the Sung thinkers into an introspective seclusion. Becoming imbued with Buddhist and Taoist speculative thought, they developed a Neo-Confucianism that was very different from the simple ethical teachings of Confucius and Mencius. They felt a need for some religious content in their philosophy of life, as the Buddhists and Taoists were winning the masses by "throwing back the gates of the spiritual world and giving to the earnest seeker visions of the realms beyond." [4] "They were driven, therefore, to find in the *Classics* a new meaning that would support their new emphasis on the metaphysical aspect of life, for which they claimed to have the stamp of Confucius' own approval. Only thus could they hope to establish themselves as the true followers of the Great Sage."[5]

Freeman then went on to describe how the Sung philosophers "had felt it necessary (not only) to attack openly Buddhism and Taoism . . . (but also) . . . to repudiate their debt to Han and T'ang scholars in order to gain acceptance for their own views as being in the true succession of Yao and Shun and Chou thought. . . . (Although) they gradually convinced the court that their theories were correct, . . . (it was) not until the Ming dynasty (that) they were recognized and re-instated as 'orthodox' and their writings put into all libraries as the *Hsing Li Ta Ch'üan*."[6] Thus it came about that, after a hundred years, the ideas of the Sung philosophers, who had been dubbed the *Yüan Yu T'ang* (Origin Protecting Society) by their rivals and been persecuted by the court, were finally accepted and ruled Chinese thought until the time of the Ch'ing dynasty.

Yet when Ming statesmanship failed and the dynasty faced collapse in the emergency caused by an internal revolt under Li Tzu-ch'eng and a threatened invasion by the ever-watchful Manchus, Ming scholars began to question the validity of the old methods of education under Sung rationalism and idealism, which had not been realistic enough to provide decisive thinking and patriotic, victorious action.

After the establishment of the foreign Manchu or Ch'ing dynasty in 1644, certain scholars, who had survived the change of régime, believed that only by returning to the 'simon-pure' teachings of its founders, as best interpreted in the Han commentaries, could Confucianism regain prestige, make the country strong, and save it from the clutches of a foreign power.[7]

Early Representatives of the Revolt Against Sung-Ming Philosophy:—

In the first half-century of life under the Manchus, a group of scholars arose, largely in the reign of K'ang Hsi (A.D. 1662-1722), whose thought became articulate along three related lines. They directed criticism against the *Sung Hsüeh,* which they held responsible for the Ming debacle; under the sting of defeat, they who had been born under the Mings expressed their loyalty to Chinese ideals by reaffirming Confucian standards of good government; and they began researches into their ancient heritage which fostered The New Learning (*Hsin Hsüeh*). Their work included the criticism and classification of old texts, studies in philosophy and semantics, the writing of new commentaries, and the publication of new works in history, geography, astronomy, and mathematics.[8]

Among those strongly motivated by a nationalistic spirit, may be mentioned Ku Yen-wu (A.D. 1613-1682), Wang Fu-chih (A.D. 1619-1693), and Huang Tsung-hsi (A.D. 1610-1695). A native of Kiangsu Province, Ku Yen-wu (known also as Ku T'ing-lin) vowed never to accept any post under the hated foreign despots and devoted much of his influence to stirring up a counter-revolution. Deploring both introspective meditation and doctrinaire (Sung) philosophy alike, he preached simple dependability of character and efficiency in work as more important than speculative theories about the universe and man's relation to it.[9] He himself devoted much time to making local observations on the geography, customs, and economic conditions of his day. He called men back to the practical teachings of the Great Sage as applied to actual life-conditions, especially emphasizing a sense of honor as the prime requisite of a good citizen: "When the scholars and officials lack honor," he said, "the nation is dishonored."[10] His stress on the values of classical (i.e., philological) scholarship has led one recent critic to consider Ku Yen-wu even more typical of Ch'ing dynasty thought than Yen Yüan.[11]

Another patriot who wouldn't work under the Manchus was Wang Fu-chih (also known as Wang Ch'uan-shan), a native of Hengyang in Hunan Province. As was true of Ku Yen-wu, a strong vein of nationalism may be found running through the works of Wang Fu-chih, who declared that the state existed for the people, not for the rulers. It must, however have centralized authority without alien rule. A nation must be strong to defend itself, may legitimately assimilate its neighbors, but only by civilizing them, not by conquering them by force.[12] First published by Teng Hsien-ho in Changsha in 1840-1842, Wang's writings were apparently destroyed in the T'aiping Rebellion, but were reprinted in Nanking about 1865 by Tseng Kuo-fan under the title of *The Collected Works of Wang Ch'uan-shan* (*Wang Ch'uan-shan I Shu*).[13]

More outspokenly democratic than his nationally-minded contemporaries, was Huang Tsung-hsi (A.D. 1610-1695),* whom Andrew Tod Roy describes as "an idealist of the Wang Yang-ming School," whose *History of Sung and Yüan Thinkers* (*Sung-Yüan Hsüeh-An*) and *Lives and Works of Ming Scholars* (*Ming-Ju Hsüeh-An*) (1676) have been "generally regarded as the first great history of Chinese philosophy."[15] Huang is even more famous for his *Treatise On Political Science* (*Ming-I Tai-Fang Lu*), written in 1662 and published in 1673.[16] "According to Lin Mou-sheng," says Roy, "it is 'probably the most systematic political treatise in the Chinese language' and undoubtedly influenced Liang Ch'i-ch'ao and other young revolutionaries at the end of the Ch'ing dynasty (first decade of the 20th century."[17] In this treatise we find expressed such modern-sounding ideas as (in brief) :—

—A ruler must have regard for the interests of the people. . . . Education should be conducted in an atmosphere of intellectual freedom, without government attempts to control thought. . . .
—Land should be more equally distributed. . . . Production by farmers and artisans and distribution of products by merchants should be encouraged (by government) . . .
—Military officers should be under the civil officers of a state. . . . Precious metals should be used as backing for paper currency. . . . (18)

Three less notable figures in this transitional period; namely, Chang Li-hsiang (A.D. 1611–1674), Fei Mi (A.D. 1625–1701),

---

* A native of Yü-yao, Chekiang. Known also as Huang T'ai-ch'ung, but perhaps best known as Huang Li-chou. (14)

and Hu Wei (A.D. 1633–1714), made contributions to the Empirical School of their time which are by no means negligible. Chang Li-hsiang, of Chekiang, a bitter opponent of Wang Yang-ming's philosophy, harked back to Chu Hsi's dictum: "the investigation of the principles in things is essential to true knowledge and a life of human-heartedness (*jên*)." His collected works were printed in 1871. Two essays (1652 and 1665) contain memoranda on pedagogical principles gleaned from long years of teaching. Another treatise, on agricultural methods, grew out of his efforts to till his own fields and prune his mulberry trees.[19]

Son of a scholar-philosopher in Szechuan, Fei Mi likewise undermined the Sung philosophy, saying that it had stressed contemplation and speculation instead of tending to the pressing needs of the world. (To quote):

"What can be applied to all four classes of society is the correct doctrine. Holding to one's own idea is a partial truth. What is seen in our daily life is the real thing. The preaching about 'human nature' and 'Heaven's decree' is empty teaching." (20)

"Man's Way is concrete and can be seen. Therefore, it can regulate the human relations and establish the ceremonies and rites. For this reason the sages paid attention to it." (21)

(And again):

"Activity must have a benefit to the work. In private life there must be benefit to the home. In public life there must be benefit to the nation." (22)

In other words, "only as philosophy betters living conditions, is it worthwhile. Scholars should study and teach and practise only what is useful. Only as orderly, stable government is the fruit of scholarly thought, can that thought be called useful. A pragmatic, utilitarian point of view, to be sure—but called for in those times of chaos and unscrupulousness."[23]

Hu Wei, a late contemporary of Chang Li-hsiang and also from Chekiang, while acting as private tutor in the Feng family, produced (1697) a compilation of works on geography which was rated as the best book of the time on that particular subject. The author himself referred to it humorously as 'a pointing at the earth with an awl,' to indicate 'a modest approach to a vast subject.'

His second work, a *Clarification of the Diagrams in the Changes* (*Yi Ching*) (1706), has been designated by Liang Ch'i-ch'ao as "the most valuable contribution of Hu Wei to Chinese scholarship." By differentiating the diagrams and their names from the actual text of the *Book of Changes,* Hu Wei "was able to deal a severe blow to the cosmology of Sung Neo-Confucianism and thus place the study of the *Changes* on a sound historical basis."[24]

Although the philosophers of this period represented a revolt against Sung orthodoxy, they had, if possible, to keep the favor of the Manchu court; for the emperor K'ang Hsi was cracking down on free-thinkers, ruling that only the Ch'eng-Chu School was to be considered orthodox, while the Lu-Wang idealists were to be eradicated. This naturally slowed down the progress of creative thinking.[25] Nevertheless, two great thinkers emerged in the late seventeenth and the middle of the eighteenth century—Yen Yüan during the reign of K'ang Hsi and Tai Chen in the time of his immediate successors, Yung Cheng (A.D. 1723–1736) and Ch'ien Lung (A.D. 1736–1796)—who persisted in their efforts to bring court and people back to a realization of the simple essentials of true Confucian teaching.

Two Great Leaders of Ch'ing Dynasty Empirical Realism

Yen Yüan (or Yen Hsi-chai)—Down-to-Earth Pragmatist:—

"Yen Hsi-chai (A.D. 1635–1704), greatest of the (17th century) leaders in the early Ch'ing revolt against the *Sung Hsüeh* philosophy, is highly respected by modern Chinese scholars," wrote Mansfield Freeman, "if chiefly because of his critical appraisal of his predecessors and as forming with Li Shu-ku (Li Kung) an important school of criticism. . . ."[26]

"Hsi-chai and his disciple, Li Shu-ku, tried to bring philosophy 'down to earth' and make it simple and applicable to everyday life, instead of talking over the heads of people. If it hadn't been for Li's calling the world's attention to Yen Hsi-chai's four short essays, they might never have been noticed."[27] The topics of these essays were *"Ideal Government"* (*Ts'un-chih Pien*) (ca. 1659); *"On Human Nature"* (*Ts'un-Hsing Pien*) (1669); *"Education (Before Confucius)"* (*Ts'un-Hsüeh Pien*) (1669); and *Ts'un-Jên Pien* (1682), a denunciation of Buddhism. From these writings, as well as from his lectures, Yen's philosophy became well known as that of one who believed that men who tested their theories in purposive action could become the arbiters of their own destiny.

Son of a poor but industrious farmer in the village of Liu Ts'un in Chihli Province (modern Hopei), half way between Tientsin and Peking, Yen Yüan early developed a passion for reading when not occupied with farm chores. Under various tutors he studied the *Classics* and also Taoist and Buddhist literature. Well-read at the age of thirty, he still felt dissatisfied, especially with the Sung philosophers, whom he dutifully followed up to the age of thirty-eight. After the death of his foster-grandfather in 1673, Yen Yüan turned away from the Sung and Ming interpretations of family mourning rituals, because he found discrepancies in the then accepted texts, and, more especially, because he found them colored by Buddhist concepts.[28]

Sensing that they had missed the point of fundamental Confucian teaching, he probed more deeply into the meaning of the *Classics*. To his mind, *Sung Hsüeh* "had failed to achieve the desired results in education: namely, the true cultivation of the individual, the regulation of the family, the right governing of the state, and the tranquillity of the empire, because there had been too much theory and not enough practice:—too much book-stuff and that purely for personal advancement in politics and business, and also because there had been too much imitation of the past."[29]

"The evil resulting from this useless chatter," he said, "is worse than the burning of the books or burying of the scholars." *

Yen opposed the extensive reading of books for acquiring knowledge, claiming that the really great among the ancients did not have many books to read.** There was too much commentary on old books, he thought, and not enough original, creative thinking going on. He felt, moreover, that Confucianism had lost converts to Buddhism because, no matter how superior Confucianism might be in the realm of ethics and government, when it competed with Buddhism it got bogged down in "endless and fruitless discussions of philosophical subtleties that benefit nobody." He constantly urged that work alone is the panacea for the world's ills. Practice and experiment rather than much reading and writing make for real learning and broad culture. Why waste time on reading, writing, and endless controversies! Only doing the thing, only practice without clever distinctions will avail any good for the people.[30]

The *Classics,* Yen Yüan argued, were to be used not for idle contemplation of theories but as guides for action. "From a practical point of view," commented Freeman, "Hsi-chai maintains that too much reading is bad for a man's health," (To quote) :—

"Today of all the men in the world who sit in their libraries, there is not one who is not weak and delicate, the laughing-stock of military men and farmers." (31)

Or again (in Warren H. Stuart's translation) :—

"To sit persistently all day in the study, causes men's minds to wilt and droop, causes the muscles and bones all to be tired and flabby; so that now in the empire there are no scholars who are not weak.

---

* Referring to Ch'in Shih Huang Ti's attempt to get rid of Confucian influences (in 213 B.C.).

** The invention of printing in the 9th century had stimulated the writing of many books by scholars who wanted to see their names in print.

. . . Further, after a long time in such ease-loving and empty-talk study, one comes to be irked with active affairs; when an affair comes up, one is all at sea. . . . Therefore, to muddle talent and bring to nought the nation's affairs is (the effect of) the Sung Learning.

"Furthermore, for developing the body there is nothing better than exercise; . . . The ideal man by careful demeanor becomes daily stronger. . . . Man's mind is an active thing. Kept active on affairs, it has something to lean on and does not move in vain; therefore, we scholars constantly actively *do* in order to discipline our minds. . . . Awaken the body and the mind, arouse them both together! . . . If the body has nothing to do, *find* something for it to do; if the mind has no principle to think about, *find* a principle for it to think about. . . . A body active is a body strong; a family active is a family strong; a nation active is a nation strong; an empire active is an empire strong!" (32)

In retrospect, Yen Yüan's harshest criticism was levelled at the Sung and Ming scholars for their failure to improve the government. In Freeman's paraphrase: "Even Chu had failed to change the life of the world. People still went on in their old ways. *Nothing happened!* So the pragmatic Yen Yüan turned away from them in disgust, saying that all theories must stand the acid test of results produced. . . . Talented people, by using their talents in the service of country, prove the value of their practical training."[33] Yen kept reminding himself and others that

"Confucius taught men to practice work. When they could see the principle in their work, then they had discerned it above and below. From here the teachings of Confucius and Chu Tzu divide." (34)

"Where Chu Hsi had given his students a counsel of perfection, of waiting 'until the Way is complete, the thoughts sincere, and the heart correct,' Yen felt that this *lack of derringdo* was fatal to any progress in knowledge or accomplishment in character. . . . Scholars . . . must *do* what the *Analects* say (in Yen's paraphrase):—

"Be in advance of them (the people)! Show them how to work! (For) if we scholars do not labor strenuously, WHO WILL?" (35)

Instead of preaching and letting the common people do the practising, scholars should 'learn by doing': in other words, by experimenting on pupils with the Six Liberal Arts: namely, the Ceremonies, Music, Reading (i.e., of history and poetry), Driving, Archery, and Mathematics,* Yen believed the aims of education could be achieved. Unfortunately, as he discovered, the simple practice of the Six Arts also failed to transform the society of his time.[36] For this reason, Yen Yüan set himself the task of carefully reviewing his own basic philosophy in order to arrive at a realistic defense of the goodness of human nature.

In his *Essay on the Preservation of the Nature* (*Ts'un Hsing Pien*), Yen clarified his position. In reconstructing the older Diagram of the Supreme Ultimate, he substituted Four Powers for the old Five Elements and made the Way of Heaven (with Shang-Ti, Upper Ruler, at its center**) operate first through Ether's *Yin* and *Yang* and then through the four dynamic Powers: of origination (*yüan*), diffusion (*hêng*), invigoration (*li*), and stability (*chêng*) to create all things. In this way he amalgamated the two realms of Principle (noumenon) and Ether (phenomenon) into a single creative continuum. Human nature, therefore, for Yen Yüan, also became an integral part of the 'potentiality of Heaven.'[38]

Elaborating on this concept, Yen declared that it is wrong to conceive, with Chu Hsi, of a dual nature: one (moral) the source of goodness, the other (physical) the source of evil. What is called 'evil' is simply the result of wrong reactions to circumstances or wrong choices made under the in-

---

* In addition to mathematics, Yen expanded the technical side of his curriculum to include such physical sciences as astronomy and mechanics, as well as military strategy and tactics. (37)

** On this point, Fung Yu-lan's comment is: "Nothing further is said about 'God' or Shang-Ti in the following text, and this concept would, therefore, seem to be superfluous in Yen Yüan's cosmology." (Cf. Fung: *History*, II, p. 638).

fluence of enticements of various kinds rather than being due to any *a priori fate*. For example, as the eye itself and its power of vision are not to be differentiated, so the nature of man (including both moral and physical) is of one piece.[39] "By their choices, men decide their fate," said Yen. "I believe that work and activity are near to benevolence (*jên*)."[40]

When Yen Yüan spoke of the physical element as 'conforming to Heaven's correct pattern' (only through self-exertion, to avoid enticements), he was, in Fung Yu-lan's opinion, actually in no way, or scarcely, different from the Rationalists who held that evil originates in the physical element (ethereal endowment) in man.[41] Between them, concludes Fung, "the major difference . . . is that for these men (Yen Yüan and others) Principle does not transcend the Ether, nor does the nature transcend the physical element. . . . As Li Kung has put it: 'Apart from affairs and things, how can there be anything called Principle?' . . . Where for the (Sung) Rationalists, Principle is 'transcendent to affairs,' in the later Ch'ing philosophers' minds Principle is 'immanent in these affairs.' Tai Chen takes a similar view."[42]

Under Emperor Ch'ien Lung (A.D. 1736-1796), thought-control was exercised by various scholar-cliques, notably the Soochow Party (*Wu P'ai*), led by Hui Tung (A.D. 1697-1758), and the Anhui Party (*Huan P'ai*), led by Tai Chen, whose work we shall now consider.[43]

Tai Chen—Greatest of the Ch'ing Empiricists—

The best representative of the Empirical School in the Ch'ing dynasty was Tai Chen (A.D. 1724-1777), a native of Huichow in Anhui Province and better known to many as Tai Tung-yüan. His early training included the usual study of the *Classics,* followed by reading of the Sung (Ch'eng-Chu) rationalists and then of the immediately preceding Yen Yüan-Li Kung pragmatists. Though several times unsuccessful in the imperial civil-service examinations, his diligence as a student was unexcelled. Taking up residence in Peking, Tai Chen became highly respected as a philosopher-teacher and "attempted a synthesis of philosophy which his predecessors had been unable to make."[44] Critics like Fung Yu-lan, Herrlee Glessner Creel, Fang Chao-ying, and Wing-tsit Chan all agree in saying that Tai Chen "became, in fact, the greatest of the few philosophic thinkers whom China produced in the Ch'ing period."[45] *

As a scholar of wide interests, Tai Chen, we are told, was interested not only in collecting old works on mathematics, but also in studying phonology and annotating a *Dictionary of Dialects* (*Fang-Yen*), as well as assisting in the editing of two local histories. From 1769 to 1772, he was busy with philosophical studies, as published in his *Hsü-Yen*. In 1773, he was called from the principalship of a preparatory school in Chinhua (Kinhwa), Chekiang, to become an editor of the famous 'Five-Foot-Shelf' of *Classics,* known as the *SSU K'U CH'ÜAN SHU*—a collection of literature undertaken by many well-qualified scholars at the behest of the emperor. To this work Tai continued to give part time until the end of his life.

In 1776, a year before his death, Tai Chen published a small volume entitled *A Treatise on the Nature of Goodness* (*Yüan Shan*), which, together with his *Hsü-Yen* and *General Survey of the Meaning of Mencius* (*Mêng-tzu Tzu-Yi Shu-Chêng*) and *Discussions of Human Nature in Appendix I of the Book of Changes,* contains most of his philosophical views. These may be found in *The Collected Writings of Tai Chen* (*Tai Tung-yüan Chi*), here used as a basis for a fresh appraisal of Tai Chen's thinking. The gist of his thought may be summarized under three dominant themes: "A Materialistic View of Reality"; "Human Nature and Desire"; and "A Concept of Law Versus Private Opinion."[46]

---

* Hu Shih's monograph: *Tai Tung-yüan Ti Chê Hsüeh* (*The Philosophy of Tai Tung-yüan*), as yet untranslated, should be consulted by the serious researcher.

(1) *A Materialistic View of Reality*

It is fair to say that Tai Chen took a clearly materialistic view of Reality (*Tao, Li,* Principle), that its meaning could only be found in its activity, eternally evolving the myriad forms of life through the interaction of *Yin* and *Yang* in the Five Elements.[47] Like Yen Yüan, he held Principle and Ether to be one and the same thing; that reality is one and indivisible. "Only in the extent of transformation that might take place in the operative action in things, could Principle be in any sense distinguished from its operation in Ether (as Vital Force."[48] "For him the universe was dynamic, not static."[49] (To quote):

"*Li* (Principle) is the internal structure or system in things, and this it is the business of the mind to discover, unclouded by its own prejudices and undeceived by the prejudices of others."...
"All the products of *Tao* have a structural form designated as *li* (reason or principle)—(a kind of fiber or texture in things like the grain in wood."...

"*Li* can be understood by the mind only as it observes basic facts; it is not revealed by meditation, neither does it come by enlightenment...." (50)

In complete agreement with Yen Yüan's approval of an analytic approach to all scientific investigations, Tai Chen wrote:—

"When things are considered in a penetrating manner, without losing sight of the slightest circumstance, then there will be no doubt on the part of the individual and, when this principle is applied to the government, the world, and the state, there will be nothing to regret."... (51)

(And again):—

"The law of affairs and things lies in dissecting and analyzing down to the minutest detail, then the (general) law can be discovered," ... (52)

Criticizing the dualism of both the Buddhists and the Rationalists, Tai Chen defended the 'immanence' over against the 'transcendence' of Principle in relation to Ether, which meant that he made 'things' as events in daily life the ground of empiricism rather than the speculative idealism of his predecessors. As a corollary, he felt that where feeling is expressed in moderation, following the Golden Mean, it could be harmonized with Principle. In this way, as W. T. Chan reminds us, the Empirical School in the person of Tai Chen continued to bring philosophy down to earth, "from the speculative to the empirical, from the universal to the particular," marking a return "from the abstract metaphysics of Chu Hsi and Wang Yang-ming to the socio-political interest of Confucius and Mencius."[53]

(2) *Human Nature and Desire*

Whereas the Rationalists held 'the nature' (of man, animal, thing, or event) to be an allotment of Principle (*Tao*) variably proportioned in individuals according to their 'capacity' yet never concreted, Tai Chen believed 'the nature' became concrete as its potentiality became actualized. Therefore, 'the transcendent' could manifest itself concretely only by becoming immanent in the 'world of shapes.' "Conceived of in this way, the nature is something concrete, and as such differs from the nature as conceived by the Rationalistic School."[54]

In other words, as Fung Yu-lan restates Tai Chen's position, "Human nature, for him consists simply of man's blood, breath, and mental faculty; . . . it is what the Neo-Confucian Rationalists would call 'the physical nature.' This physical nature does not itself actually contain the multitudinous Principles of all things. Nevertheless, it can, because of its faculty of knowledge, come to comprehend them. This explains why man, starting from what is purely natural to him, can elevate himself to what is morally necessary."[55]

In the aesthetic and moral sphere, as Tai Chen saw it,

Principle can never become completely actualized in human nature. Ordinary human beings will differ in their capacity to observe, comprehend, and cooperate with the constant norms of Principle. The sage, however, can elevate his natural bent to the nth degree simply by consciously seeking to conform his desires to 'what is morally necessary.'[56]

Since, for Tai Chen, goodness is achieved by maintaining a proper balance—the Golden Mean—between self-interest and altruism, so evil enters in whenever that balance is upset by deviating from a moral necessity equally applied to all alike. By developing a sense of righteousness and courtesy, man has progressed above animals. (To quote):—

"The desires of the nature are its spontaneous expressions while the virtue of the nature refers to those things which ought to be done. Those things which ought to be done simply complete what is spontaneous in the nature. This is called the complete fulfillment of the spontaneous." (57)

Instead of trying to explain the origin of evil by dividing human nature into two parts and finding the 'physical' to blame for evil, Tai Chen accepted it as arising from certain defects in knowledge, desires, or feelings, notably selfishness and delusion. Since, in his mind, knowledge is equated with morality, its deluding gives rise to evil. Basic desires, like food and sex, become evil only when they go to excess. "Desire refers to a thing, whereas Reason refers to its principle."[58] "The best way to get rid of selfishness," he declared, "is to strengthen altruism. . . . The way to strengthen altruism is to measure other men's desires in terms of one's own. . . . The best way to disperse delusion is to study."[59]

Desires and feelings are not to be suppressed but harmonized with Principle. The true Confucianist, according to Tai Chen, will "stress the release of repressions by activity over against the elimination of desires by contemplation."[60] H. G. Creel has commented on the modernity of Tai Chen's contention "that men's desires should not be repressed but socialized."[61] Like a modern psychologist, Tai would argue:

"When the mind attains to Heavenly Virtue, maintaining the proper restraint and correctness, the desires will not degenerate into license. . . . Yü controlled the floods by guiding the water through channels. The Confucian gentleman controls his desires by guiding them into the path of righteousness." (62)

"Virtue is, therefore, not the absence of desires, but their orderly fulfillment and expression. . . . The attempt to lessen or repress them results . . . in hypocrisy, injustice, and innumerable other social ills." (63)

(3) *A Concept of Law (Principle) Versus Private Opinion*

The effect on society of the 'orderly fulfillment of desires and expression of feelings,' Tai Chen recognized as a problem of great ethical import. The moralist had to devise a test for guiding the individual that was not too subjective. Tai insisted that only by taking the feelings and opinions of a sufficiently large number of persons could agreement on Principle be reached. (To quote):

"Only what minds generally agree upon can be called Principle and called righteousness. What does not meet general agreement, but is merely a single man's opinion, is neither Principle nor righteousness. General agreement exists when every individual maintains that a thing is so, and throughout the world all generations say it is something unchangeable. . . . (When a feeling neither goes too far nor falls short, it is then called Principle.)" (64)

"The highest morality consists of nothing more than insuring that the desires of all men reach fulfillment, and their feelings reach expression." (65)

Tai denied the infallibility of rulers or scholars who claimed prestige and power based on superior knowledge of Heavenly Law, or Principle. Who is to be the judge, he asked—the superior or the inferior man? By old tradition, the man in a lower rank may never judge the man in a higher rank, or he will be stigmatized as a rebel or even a criminal. Yet in either case, the danger is

"When one thinks of the Law (Principle) as concrete, received from Heaven and lodged in the mind, he will consider his own personal opinion to be the Law." (66)

As both Creel and Freeman have pointed out, the idea of a cosmic Principle *(Li,* or Law) that could be taken as supporting the wishes and decisions of an emperor or his advising scholars and from which there could be no appeal, was a concept entirely repugnant to Tai Chen. "This concept of Law," comments Freeman, "is apt to lead to fanatical bigotry and intolerance in government and religion. But Tai Chen felt that men should be left free to think, express feeling, and follow desires—not inhibited by too rigid law whose letter kills the spirits of men. . . . Tai held that law is a characteristic of things and not a quality or endowment of the mind. As the senses distinguish tastes, sounds, and color, so the mind distinguishes law and righteousness."[67] (To quote) :—

"While every man has a share of *li* to ennoble him, private interpretations of *li* are to be taken conservatively, lest it be bent to private ends by those who are powerful and unscrupulous." (68)

* * *

Concluding Estimate of Tai Chen:—

In all his philosophizing, Tai Chen kept his feet solidly on the ground, insisting on the validity of unified thinking and spontaneous feeling, all the while steering carefully between the scholasticism of the Ch'eng-Chu School and the mysticism of the Lu-Wang School. And yet he would agree with all scholars from Hsün Tzu down that the aim of the pursuit of learning was to dispel delusion and establish the virtuous nature. Moreover, as Fung Yu-lan has observed, "when the Yen-Li-Tai group (of pragmatic empiricists) oppose the Neo-Confucians, it is more the Rationalists (although they cannot fully substantiate or develop their differences) than the Idealists whom they criticize, very largely because they themselves lean more toward the views of the Idealistic School."[69] The leaning, however, was limited to the adoption of a monistic over against a dualistic conception of reality.

Tai Chen has been a controversial figure among Chinese scholars ever since he was accused of plagiarism in connection with the revision he made of an older work on China's waterways (*Shui-Ching Chu*). While assisting in the compilation of the Imperial Manuscript Library (*Ssŭ-K'u Ch'üan-Shu*), Tai contributed his revision of the work mentioned, which later was attacked as plagiarizing a parallel account by a certain Chao I-ch'ing. After carefully examining all the manuscripts and going over the whole century-long controversy, Hu Shih, in a note dated May 31, 1944, exonerated Tai Chen and in a concluding paragraph made this significant statement:

"In a sense, the long history of the posthumous persecution of Tai Chen was foreshadowed more than a century and a half ago in his own writings. He explicitly warned us that when *li* (reason) is not viewed objectively as the internal structure and texture in things, . . . there is always the danger of a self-righteous man condemning innocent persons to death in the name of *li,* which, unhappily is too often nothing more than his own unexamined opinion."

" 'Sympathy', said Tai Chen, 'is sometimes expressed for men who are murdered in the name of Law. But who will sympathize with those men who are murdered in the name of *Li*!' "

"It was the destiny of the philosopher who uttered these prophetic words to be himself condemned to a moral death—almost without redress and without sympathy for a hundred years—by a long line of righteous men who honestly believed that by stressing their private conceptions of *li* they were championing the cause of justice (*kung li*)." (70)

The popularity of atheism in the minds of China's young intellectuals in the 1920's and 1930's has been attributed somewhat to the influence of Tai Chen's writings, for he openly criticized Buddhism as foreign and unrealistic and Christianity as tainted with Western imperialism.[71] Certain it is that his stout defense of the Way of Man in contradistinction to the Way of Heaven held great appeal for later generations of Chinese thinkers as well as his own. In Fang Chao-ying's opinion, it was not until the twentieth century that Tai Chen's "nearness to Western thought became apparent" and "his really important place in the history of philosophy was appreciated."[72]

The Historical Criticism School

For the most part, Chinese scholars of the Ch'ing dynasty were to be found in four fairly well-defined groups: those favoring the Ch'eng-Chu School of Neo-Confucian rationalism; those who leaned more toward the Lu-Wang School of subjective idealism; those who called for a return to empiricism in what may be termed the Empirical (or Harmonizing) School and the scholars of the Historical Criticism School, who, when not acting as magistrates, were encouraged by the Ch'ing emperors to undertake what Gung-hsing Wang calls "scholars' work-projects,"[73] to occupy their time and energies. These lines, however, cannot be too strictly drawn, for we are told that the Lu-Wang School had either given up its concentration on meditation and introspection or been driven underground by the machinations of its political persecutors, and that even the adherents of the Ch'eng-Chu School, failing of success in their hypothesis and verification, had "turned from the study of 'things' in the outer world to 'things' recorded in the literary heritage of the nation."[74]

By the middle of the eighteenth century, a re-alignment of scholars had taken place, the *Han Hsüeh* allying themselves with the Modern Text (*Chin Wên*) interpreters, while the *Sung Hsüeh* naturally continued to hold with the Ancient Text (*Ku Wên*) interpretations. Controversy raged over the text of the *Book of History* (*Shu Ching*), for example, the

Modern Text School insisting that the hitherto accepted ancient text was a forgery and that "dependence should be placed on the *Ch'un Ch'iu Commentary* of Kung-yang Kao," dating from the beginning of the Han dynasty.[75]

Leaders of this Modern Text School, known also as the Historical Criticism School, like Chuang Ts'un-yü (A.D. 1719-1788), Liu Fêng-lu (1776-1829), and Kung Tzu-chên (1792-1841) "moved toward adaptation of ancient thought to present conditions and so led the way to the reform movement of the later Ch'ing dynasty."[76] In the opinion of one recent critic, Kung Tzu-chên's bold criticism of Ch'ing decadence undoubtedly influenced men like K'ang Yu-wei and Liang Ch'i-ch'ao. Such boldness is remarkable, coming as it did not so very long after the severe inquisitions instituted by the emperor, Ch'ien Lung (A.D. 1736–1796).

On the whole, scholars felt safer if they confined their activity to historical and textual criticism. Without going into the intricacies of the literary problems facing the Historical Criticism School, we shall mention here a few of the scholars who were active in scholars' work-projects at the very end of the Ch'ing period, reaching into the first decade of the twentieth century.

About 1862, a Soochow scholar, Yü Yueh by name, wrote his own *Commentary on Various Classics* and *Comments on Various Philosophers,* each containing thirty-five chapters. His two pupils, Sun I-jang (A.D. 1848-1908) and Chang Ping-lin (1868-1936), were men of wide interests. In 1905, Sun I-jang published a *Commentary on the Chou Li,* said by many to be the hardest *Classic* to explain. He also edited the *Complete Works of Mo Tzu* and assembled all the extant commentaries on him (1907).

Chang Ping-lin, living first at Yü-hang, just west of Hangchow, became famous for his researches into the morphology of characters on ancient inscriptions. After the first revolution (1911-12), in which he had taken an active part, Chang settled in Soochow, there to manage his own private school for income while he studied the *Tso Chuan* intensively, and the writings of the Dharma-Character Sect of Buddhism (*Fa-Hsiang Tsung*). At the time of his death in 1936, so great had his reputation as a scholar become, that he was given the exceptional honor of a state funeral.

Editing the *Classics* occupied much of the Ch'ing scholars' time. Wang Hsien-ch'ien (1842-1917), for example, busied himself with editing the works of Chuang Tzu and of Hsün Tzu, while, his cousin, Wang Hsien-shen (d. 1931), edited the works of Han Fei Tzu. Each scholar paid great attention to the etymology of words, to semantics, and to textual criticism in an effort to clarify the texts and interpret correctly the meaning of the various philosophers for the sake of those who should come after them.[77]

The Movement For Reform

K'ang Yu-wei—Research Scholar and Reformer

The leader of the Reform Party in the latter days of the empire and, according to some, the most powerful thinker in modern China, was K'ang Yu-wei. Born near Canton in 1858, he early proved himself a master of books and ideas. In rapid succession he produced essays, showing a wide range of historical reading on the restoration of the Emperor Mutsuhito in Japan, the decay of Turkey, the life of Peter the Great, and constitutional changes in the government of England. These *fin de siècle* writings brought him to the attention of the government and he was made secretary of the Tsung-li Yamen. The following year, 1898, he became chief adviser to the young Emperor Kuang Hsü, whom he influenced to issue the famous twenty-seven reform edicts which startled the old Empress Dowager, Tzu Hsi, into making her equally famous *coup d'etat*. K'ang barely escaped with his life, along with one of his students, Liang Ch'i-ch'ao, who was destined to become one of China's most prolific and illustrious essayists.

After residing abroad in the United States and Japan for a number of years, K'ang Yu-wei returned to China in the early days of the Republic, only to take part in the abortive, counter-revolutionary, monarchical movements of 1913 and 1917. K'ang thoroughly believed that a constitutional monarchy like that of Great Britain's was the solution to China's political problem, provided it remained true to the ancient Confucian ideal of seeking ever the public weal rather than private gain.[78] To the end of his days in 1927, K'ang Yu-wei never became reconciled to the republican régime, but, from his seclusion, wrote articles like "Three Essays on the Republic," in which he freely criticized the policies of Sun Yat-sen and his National People's Party (*Kuo-Min-Tang*).

As an indefatigable research scholar, K'ang Yu-wei published many papers, most original among them being "An Inquiry into the Spurious Classics" and "An Inquiry Concerning How Confucius Formulated New Ideas in the Name of Authority." Feeling that Tai Chen and others had over-stressed the Han classical tradition, K'ang revived the controversy over genuine and forged texts, aligning himself with the Modern Text School's versions. These, he was convinced, came from the Chou dynasty and were genuine products of the hand of Confucius himself; but the later Han versions, styled "Old Text," he claimed were forged by Liu Hsin for political purposes in the period of the usurper, Wang Mang. The fact that these were the texts used not only by the Sung Neo-Confucianists but also by the Yen-Li-Tai group, to K'ang's mind rendered all their interpretations invalid or at least suspect.[79]

Of the influence of his study of the Confucian source-books, including the *Kung-yang Chuan* (as elaborated by Ho Hsin's commentary—A.D. 129-182), K'ang Yu-wei writes as follows:—

"In this way I came to understand the transformations of the *Yin* and *Yang* (as portrayed) in the *Changes,* and the meaning of the 'Three Ages' in the *Spring and Autumn Annals*. . . . The course of humanity always progresses according to a fixed sequence. . . . When Confucius prepared the *Spring and Autumn Annals,* he extended it to embrace the Three Ages. . . . Confucius himself was born in the Age of Disorder.

"But at the present time, communications extend throughout the great earth, and Europe and America, through their vast changes, are evolving toward the Age of Approaching Peace. There will be a day when everything throughout the earth . . . will be like one. . . . With this uniformity will come (the Age of) Universal Peace. Confucius understood all this beforehand." (80)

By dilating upon the Confucian theory of the Three Ages, K'ang Yu-wei evidently "wished to bring the new knowledge and conditions of his day within the scope of traditional Chinese thought. In other words, he was trying to pour new wine into old wineskins. At the same time, he obviously hoped to establish a basis for his own political reforms."[81] In substantiation of this opinion, Fung Yu-lan quotes K'ang's *Commentary on the Doctrine of the Mean* (*Chung-Yung Chu*), where he says:

"The (spirit of the) regulations of Confucius is that they must be employed according to the proper period. If, in the Age of Dark Disorder, . . . one were to practise the institutions of Universal Peace, this would certainly result in great harm. But if, in the Age of Approaching Peace, one were to continue to cling to (the institutions of the Age of) Disorder, this too would result in great harm. The present time, for example, is the Age of Approaching Peace. It is, therefore, necessary to promulgate the doctrine of self-rule and independence, and the actualities of parliamentary and constitutional rule. For if the laws are not reformed, great disorder will result." (82)

K'ang Yu-wei's chief claim to fame may ultimately rest upon his *Book of the Great Unity* (*Ta T'ung Shu*) (also rendered *The Great Commonwealth*), in which he expressed the utopian vision of an early establishment of the "Age of Universal Concord." Written by K'ang at the age of twenty-seven (1884-5), while he was living as a mountain recluse on Hsi Chao Shan (but not published until 1901-2), this remarkable work reflected ideas gathered from his extensive reading of Confucius, Mencius, Chuang Tzu, Mo Ti, and Lu-Wang as well as Buddhist idealism, to which were added new ideas on internationalism and world-peace picked up from Europe and America.[83]

K'ang's panacea for the world's ills lay in a formula for achieving a communal type of life by discarding sex and family distinctions (advocating holding wives in common), abolishing all class and racial inequalities, removing distinctions of property-ownership, socializing production, and disregarding all national boundaries and barriers. "This Way of the Great Unity," he declared, "is the acme of fairness, justice, love, and good government. . . ."[84] "Thus will mankind achieve the Age of Universal Peace and Realm of Highest Happiness,"[85] echoing a recorded saying of Confucius in the *Chung Yung* two milleniums ago: "When our true central self and harmony are realized, the universe becomes a cosmos."[86] In another recalling of the Golden Age, Confucius is reputed to have repeated this conception of a perfect society: "When the Great Way prevailed, the world became a common state. . . . This was the Period of the Great Commonwealth."[87]

By making Confucian social and political ideals prime requisites in the practices of the modern "Well-To-Do-State" (as it had been called), K'ang Yu-wei laid the foundations of the world commonwealth which he so optimistically envisioned. At this point, however, Ch'ien Mu, in "A Critical Study on the Philosophy of K'ang Yu-wei," has suggested the inadequacy of K'ang's formula. Confucianism, Buddhism, and Christianity, he argues, all speak of 'selflessness' as the final answer to the world's problems. Even if you succeed in getting rid of the distinctions of nation, race, and sex, the problem of what to do with the *self* still remains. Religion says: Deny the Self!, but K'ang Yu-wei did not reach the same conclusion.[88]

K'ang, however, did sense the inadequacy of his visionary program, for in concluding his *Book of the Great Unity,* he wrote:

"After the Great Unity, there will first come the study of the (Taoist arts of the) immortals. . . . Lesser wisdom will devote itself to the immortals, and higher wisdom to Buddhism. The study of Buddhism, however, will itself be followed by that of 'roaming in Heaven'."[89]

In other words, one need not feel frustrated by the limitations of human institutions—even in the age of the *Ta T'ung*, sublime though it may be—for above and beyond it lies 'the limitless realm of Heaven itself.' Of this, K'ang wrote confidently in his *Commentary on the Doctrine of the Mean*:

"For above (these human institutions) there still exists Heaven, the origin of all origins, timeless, spaceless, without color, without smell, without sound, without substance. And there is *a separate realm* created by Heaven, unimaginable in thought and indescribable in words. Here roam the divine sages, whose desire it is to give to all living creatures the possibility to be, like them, transformed in the Heaven of Heavens. This is (the aim of) the highest Way of Confucius." (90)

"The whole work," writes Fung's translator, Derk Bodde, "is remarkable as a mixture of Chinese and Western Utopian thinking. It (the *Book of the Great Unity*) combines idealism, radicalism, and keen prophetic insight, with a curiously naïve confidence in technological progress as the key to human happiness, which in this respect makes it quite un-Chinese and typical of Western nineteenth century optimism."[91]

T'an Ssu-t'ung—Martyr for the Revolution

Rated a more precise thinker than K'ang Yu-wei, T'an Ssu-t'ung (1865-1898) explained the diversity of phenomena by the infinite number of combinations of chemical elements in the varied forms of matter. As their proportions fluctuate (by continual decay and renewal), they keep the phenomenal world in constant flux and this is taken as a logical basis for anticipating changes in the political structure.

Conversant with Western literature (including the New Testament), as well as with the *Classics* of his own Chinese culture (Confucian, Taoist, and Buddhist), T'an combined elements from practically all sources in his *Jên Hsüeh* or *Science of Love* (about 1896-8). The influence of Western science is seen in his interpretation of *jên* as in all things the unifying factor, like electricity in space ('ether') and in the human brain.[92] Close to Mo Tzu when he said "There being love, there must be pervasiveness,"[93] it remained for T'an Ssu-t'ung to interpret *jên* more metaphysically than did Confucius. Like Chu Hsi, Wang Yang-ming, and K'ang Yu-wei, he gave it the meaning of a universal spirit that unites all races of men, classes, and sexes in an all-pervading harmony in which all inequalities are eliminated.[94]

In his studies in Taoism, Buddhism, Confucianism, and Christianity, T'an came to feel deeply that their teachings all focused in their hope for man's attaining the perfect life. While he agreed with K'ang Yu-wei that in the day of the Great Unity, "when all men would be sublimely perfect," there would be no further need for religion,[95] he nevertheless realized that *in the present emergency* there was need for men to suffer as the great religious leaders of the past had suffered to attain their ends.[96]

Seeking to provide the only freedom in which society could grow, T'an Ssu-t'ung committed himself to the revolutionary party, saying:

". . . In seeking to return to love and to strengthen mental energy, the first thing would be to break the restrictive nets and the false teaching about monarchical rule. Unfortunately, those acting as monarchs are not Chinese. Therefore, reform must wait for revolution, must wait till monarchical control is broken, and then the false learning will decline . . . and the teaching about the constant obligations of morality cannot stand. . . . Then men will get equality so that they can use their mental energy to return to love or true manhood. Only then can we struggle for survival in the world and rid ourselves of evil fate." (97)

On the day before his arrest in Peking in 1898, when T'an was urged to flee (as K'ang and Liang had done), he is reported to have said: "In no country does reform succeed without the shedding of blood. Today China hears of no one shedding his blood for reform. Let Ssu-t'ung start it. I will not go."[98] The next day (September 28), T'an Ssu-t'ung, at the age of thirty-three, met death at the execution-block with calmness and fortitude, as befitted a martyr in the cause of human freedom.

Ku Hung-ming—"Last of the Great Confucians"

After K'ang Yu-wei and T'an Ssu-t'ung in the political thinker group came Ku Hung-ming, the last of the great Confucians who upheld the old tradition of high scholarship devoted to the interests of good government. Born in 1856, he was given a classical education and sent to Edinburgh University, where he graduated with the degree of Master of Arts. For seventeen years, he served as private secretary to Viceroy Chang Chih-tung, at the same time developing his own literary tastes.

For the sake of helping foreigners understand what was going on at the back of the Chinese mind, Ku early began to translate the *Classics* into English, beginning with the *Lun Yü* (*Analects*), which he rendered as *The Discourses and Sayings of Confucius*.[99] In his translation work, he often made allusions to English and European literature, including some quotations from Goethe. After the outbreak of World War I, Ku's *The Spirit of the Chinese People*,[100] published in Peking in 1915, included an essay on "The War and the Way Out." Five years later (1920), appeared his translation of the *Doctrine of the Mean* (*Chung Yung*) under the title of *The Conduct of Life*.[101]

Made naturally conservative by his long political and literary career, Ku Hung-ming, like K'ang Yu-wei, found it impossible to fall in line with the political and subsequent literary revolution that swept like a 'Hangchow Bore' against the old current of Confucian culture. Like many others of the old school, he felt a deep concern lest China lose her ancient cultural heritage, yet, with all his misgivings, he stoutly maintained that the classical culture was indestructible. This faith was firmly expressed in *The Conduct of Life,* where he said:

"Most people now believe that the old order in China is passing away, and they hail the coming era of the new learning and of the civilization of progress into this country. I for one do not believe that the old order of things in China can pass away. The reason is because I feel that the old order of things—the Chinese civilization and Chinese social order—is a moral civilization and a true social order and cannot, therefore, in the nature of things, pass away." (102)

Back in 1906, when the old order had begun to crumble, Ku Hung-ming had been in entire agreement with his equally conservative contemporary, Chang Chih-tung, who had "persuaded the court to establish Confucianism as the state cult and place Confucian rites on the same level with the sacrifices to Heaven and Earth."[103] In a day when the old civil service examinations had been abolished, he had been forced to admit that Western science might be studied if it was sufficiently diffused with the classical Chinese learning. Abhorring the idea of a republican parliament, and praising the inherent nobility of the Manchus as enlightened rulers, both Ku and Chang had urged all schools and scholars to hold firmly by their classical heritage. In the last analysis, as Andrew Tod Roy has stated it, "Ku had nothing but distaste for everything Western and saw beauty only in the Confucian past."[104]

Chang T'ai-yen—A Voice Crying in the Wilderness

More revolutionary in his thinking than Ku Hung-ming, was Chang T'ai-yen (1868-1936), a Confucian philosopher from Yü-hang, Chekiang, who had been strongly influenced by the democratic writings of Huang Tsung-hsi.[105] In his desire to further the political revolution, however, he encouraged people to study the Taoist naturalism of Lao Tzu and Chuang Tzu rather than the Confucians and to seek the fundamentals of knowledge rather than the non-essentials. At the same time, he expressed a fear that too much new knowledge might bring social catastrophe and the increase of crime.

While opposing traditional Chinese ideas, Chang was pessimistic about the new scientific civilization. He sought to revise, and thereby to revive, Taoist mysticism with a touch of Buddhist philosophy, and explained the indulgent Taoist love of freedom by frequent references to Western anarchism and hedonism. Strong individualist that he was, in his later years Chang T'ai-yen still showed deep interest in political changes, but gradually retired to his first love—the Taoist apostles of free-thought. Finally his interest turned to the same problem as that which was then absorbing the attention of Ou-Yang Ching-wu (1871-1943), namely the harmonizing of Buddhist philosophy with Confucianism as interpreted by the Lu-Wang School of idealists.[106] In this connection, Benjamin Schwartz finds Chang T'ai-yen's essay on evolution fascinating because of his treatment of the subject in terms of the Mere-Ideation (Vijñānavādin) School of Buddhist philosophy.[107]

Liang Ch'i-ch'ao—Reconstructionist for the New Day

Sensitive to the needs of the new day, Liang Ch'i-ch'ao (1873-1929), pupil of K'ang Yu-wei and survivor of the abortive reform-movement of 1898, took the position that all retrogressive elements in the old Confucian teachings must be discarded. For three decades he produced a great mass of writings, mostly on reconstruction in philosophy—political and moral. His book, *A History of Chinese Political Thought,*[108] gives a modern's estimate of the great thinkers of the early Tsin period and their contribution to present-day republican life. Opposed to Hsün Tzu and the Ch'eng-Chu School, Liang favored Mencius and leaned strongly toward the Lu-Wang mode of thought, arguing in an able manner for greater freedom from the controls of customary conventions.[109]

W. T. Chan sees signs of Neo-Mohism in Liang's essays (1921), in which he called attention to Mo Tzu's ideas on public economy and social welfare, and the benefits of peaceful production as opposed to warfare.[110] In similar vein, J. R. Levenson brings out Liang's opposition both to extreme materialism and extreme idealism; as well as his natural leaning toward "certain mystical phrases of Confucius and Lao Tzu" (rather than toward) "the pragmatism of the modern West."[111] "Liang felt that there were three (characteristic) views that formed the essential basis of Chinese morality and society." Having said that, Andrew Tod Roy gives the gist of these essential factors as follows:

> (1) The first (*pao ên*) could be called the "showing of gratitude" (in ceremonies and sacrifices) . . . to those who had benefited the people (whether it be the forces of nature, sages, or emperors) . . . The significance of '*pao ên*,' the expression of gratitude for grace received, lay in the fact that it was the cause of the firmly cemented union of present and past society. . . . It found expression in loyalty to family, clan, former sages, nation, and monarch. . . . This sense of solidarity, born of gratitude, had great power and was the reason for China's deeply rooted national character.
>
> (2) The second essential (*ming fên*) was the "knowing of one's duty" (i.e., for his own rank). . . . Those who were contented with their lot in the social order and acted according to duty were called good people. . . . They prospered as each person looked carefully to see where his duty lay, and then did his best at his particular post.
>
> (3) The third essential (*lü hou*) or "concern for the future" was not an 'otherworldliness,' but a concern for the continuing social organism and its welfare. . . . Out of a desire to prolong family life, self-respecting heads of families would do nothing that would cause worries for the future of their families.

These principles, according to Liang Ch'i-ch'ao, could be practised by the common folk as well as by the sages, and thus preserve the continuing solidarity of Chinese society.[112]

Conclusion:—

"Throughout the Ch'ing dynasty, the scholars . . . had been quietly preparing an ideological basis for social change. They had found in neglected aspects of Confucianism a concern for social justice, a justification of revolution, a theory of natural and social evolution, a sanction for adaptation to changing conditions and times, a theory of inductive reasoning and examination of facts to replace a blind following of precedent, a golden age when rulers voluntarily abdicated and thought more of the common welfare than of their personal and family interest, and many another useful tool for opening closed minds and societies. Yet these appeared only as twigs or branches, not as the trunk of a social and political system that could bear the weight of the new republican era. Therefore," concludes Dr. Roy, "in its crisis, China turned to the West for help."[113]

For the next two decades, the mind of young China was steeped in Western thought and practice. Students went abroad in increasing numbers to the United States, Great Britain, and the Continent. With them, they brought back a host of new ideas from professors' lectures and from books read,—ideas ranging from philosophy (pragmatism, neo-realism, idealism, materialism, and vitalism) to the natural and social sciences (stressing economics and engineering, and including physical education), as well as religion, music, and modern art.[114]

Returned students soon found themselves teaching in the new government or private schools and colleges (including over a dozen Western-church-sponsored institutions of higher learning) that were springing up all over the land. As writers, they expressed themselves in magazine articles or published their ideas in book form. At first, imported foreign modes of thought held sway, often expressed in foreign language patterns, but gradually, as the novelty wore off, Chinese minds began turning back to their own cultural thought and speech-patterns, until in the 1930's and 1940's they were able to make a truer reappraisal of their classical heritage than could ever have been made without the wider contacts with the West.

PART IV

RECONSTRUCTION IN CONTEMPORARY PHILOSOPHY

Chapter 13

Contemporary Philosophy Under the Republic

> "If philosophy can enable men to become sage-men (the reaching to the height of what it means to be a man), then this is the usefulness of philosophy's uselessness."
>
> —Fung Yu-lan in the *Hsin Yüan Tao**

Although it is difficult to bring contemporary life into focus for an adequate estimate of its personalities and values, yet certain lines of interest in the philosophical thinking of modern Chinese may be discerned, which conservatively follow or radically diverge from the hitherto-accepted Confucian point of view. In general, we shall discover two main trends: a horizontal comparison and harmonizing of Eastern and Western philosophies and a vertical harmonizing of the ancient, classical philosophy with modern thought, moving along a six-lane highway of major interests. In other words, modern Chinese are interested in a philosophy of life which has to do primarily with the political, economic, and social; they are also vitally concerned with the educational, religious and aesthetic, together with the more purely philosophical (including moral) aspects of daily living.

In this chapter, we shall follow the march of thought through three chief phases of modern and contemporary philosophy under the Republic, roughly from 1910 to 1950. *First,* the

---

* Ernest R. Hughes translation.

philosophical foundations of the Republic; *Second,* the influence of Western philosophies on the inquisitive younger generation of thinkers in the ensuing period of wide-ranging freedom of thought; *Third,* revaluations of China's own classical heritage, leading into positive and constructive re-statements of that heritage in modern terminology.

(I) *Philosophical Foundations of the Republic*

As the philosophers of the early Ch'ing dynasty had endeavored to discover why their traditional Confucian philosophy had failed to prevent the taking over of the empire by hated foreign rulers, so the philosophers of the first two decades of the twentieth century wrestled with a similar problem:—the failure of their philosophical heritage to prevent another major political cataclysm—a purely internal revolution, to be sure, yet one sparked by the invasion of foreign ideologies: political, social, religious, educational, and philosophical.

Again came the insistent inquiry: "Can Confucianism save China?" During the first revolution of 1911-12 and after the Republic had become a *fait accompli,* the Chinese philosophic mind grappled with this persistent yet most baffling problem: "What is to be our fundamental philosophy of life? In the republican era, we must have something basic to live by! Can it be that our Confucian heritage is entirely useless for our new society and for our new democratic form of government?" The conservatives and the radicals each had their say, while political leaders tried to steer between the two.

Advocates of Confucianism

In opposition to K'ang Yu-wei's support of a constitutional monarchy, Wang Ching-dao in 1912 published a small book entitled *Confucius and Modern China,* in which he gave his version of Confucius' idea of the state and its relation to constitutional government. If China is to enter upon a republican form of government, he maintained that any man in public office should still live up to the Confucian ideal of a good ruler who holds power only with the approval of the people. Where, in the days of the empire, national controls had been superimposed upon a village democracy, now, in a duly constituted republic, Wang saw the old gap between federal authority and local autonomy disappearing. Almost pathetic, however, was his appeal to his compatriots to retain their faith in the teachings of the Great Sage during the present period of painful transition. (To quote):

"During centuries," he wrote, "Confucianism sank down to a dead formalism. Posterity set up Confucius as a most holy man, but failed to realize what he really desired. The past we cannot recall, but the future is still in our power. Let us, therefore, study Confucius with more sympathetic appreciation and learn from him. . . . Now is the time for us Chinese with one accord to build a new house on our good old foundations." (1)

The same support of the new government coupled with the same desire to preserve the old Confucian cultural standards was manifested by Chen Huang-chang, a pupil of K'ang Yu-wei and youthful editor of *The Chinese Reformer*. As a scholar with the degree of *Chin-Shih* from the old civil-service examination, he went abroad to complete his studies at the University of Chicago and Columbia University. His doctoral dissertation in 1911 reflected his zeal for Confucianism, as is shown in the following typical sentences:

"As soon as the Chinese shall have established a constitutional government and secured perfect freedom of thought, Confucianism must enter on a new life."

Again, he urged that

"China must accept all the good things from the outside world and retain the good things of her own."

And, finally, he confidently asserted that

"the school of Confucius will be able to modernize China." (2)

Returning to his native land in the midst of the throes of revolution, Chen Huang-chang joined the efforts of K'ang Yu-wei and other Confucian scholars to stem the tide and preserve Confucianism from complete disintegration.

Believing that Confucianism was fully adaptable to changing conditions, Chen set about establishing a National Confucian Society and a Confucian University. In 1911 and again in 1913, he threw himself wholeheartedly into the attempts to gain for Confucianism the status of State Religion, but failed each time. This failure was due to Muslim and Christian opposition as well as to opposition from such recognized leaders of Confucian thought as Liang Ch'i-ch'ao himself. Chen then founded his own Confucian Church and invited others to continue with him the worship of the Great Sage. He felt that the views of Confucius on religion and social welfare had been understressed by Chu Hsi, whom he called the Martin Luther of Confucianism. To his mind, Confucianism was truly a religion, saner than Taoism or Buddhism, broader and more practical than Christianity.[3]

The Revolutionary Principles of Sun Yat-sen

Confucian ideals as such were not particularly promoted by that great "Apostle of the Revolution"—Sun Yat-sen (b. 1864), a baptized Christian, who, after his death on March 12, 1925, became the canonized patron of the National People's Party (*Kuo-Min-Tang*) and ultimately of the whole of republican China. His political philosophy, early inspired by reading K'ang Yu-wei's *Book of the Great Unity,* is well known to all those who have followed the course of China's modern development.

For their revolutionary campaign propaganda, both the

'Founder' and (later) the 'Generalissimo' of the new Republic (*Chung Hua Min Kuo*) seized upon the theories of the Lu-Wang School. Stressing, as it did, a self-consciousness which fitted the new emphasis on nationalism or racial self-consciousness and the new demand for judgments based on the present 'conscience,' the Lu-Wang School had established a fitting psychological foundation for both revolutions: that of 1911-12 and that of 1926-28.

Following Wang Yang-ming's dictum: "To do is easy, to know is difficult," Sun Yat-sen likewise held that ability to know calls for a corresponding ability to do. All modern progress was, in his opinion, an expression of the basic unity of knowledge and action. At the same time, he believed that men could do without first knowing. Applying it to the political scene, he argued that the revolution must first be *done*; then they could talk about knowing or learning to do it better.

"We must have the adventurous spirit to do things," he would say. "We must have faith that a revolution can be accomplished. We must have a scientific hypothesis and then work it out. We must have people who can go ahead with their idea and not wait to be told what to do or how to do it. Otherwise, we'll never get anything done at all." (4)

Despite the fact that he found knowing and doing equally difficult, Dr. Sun felt he must give his followers the psychological attitude that "doing is easy," otherwise they would never attempt the revolution. Where Wang Yang-ming had stressed the moralistic side of doing, Sun Yat-sen stressed the thrill of constructive action. Stressing conduct as a testing ground, Sun sought effective cooperation through a division of labor according to the dictates of conscience. While it was important for individuals to achieve a successful combination of knowing and doing, he also felt it necessary for groups of people to prove the unity of thought and action by cooperation in the reformation of society and in the reconstruction of business and government.[5] In 1918, Sun Yat-sen wrote a book *On Psycho-*

logical Reconstruction, in which he stressed the greater importance and difficulty of *knowing* well before attempting to *act.*[6] This apparent *volte-face* can be explained only by the slough of despond into which the actions of Yuan Shih-k'ai and his ilk had thrown him. Where was democracy in China heading, if the highest officials seemed to respect only the out-moded principles of autocracy? With characteristic vigor, the "Father of his country" began patiently to teach his people what he thought they had already learned.

In a course of political lectures, delivered in Canton in 1924, Dr. Sun defined "The Three Principles of the People." He showed how the new Republic-of-China government must seek to realize national sovereignty as a government 'of the people'; must implement democratic processes as a government 'by the people'; and must foster the raising of economic standards as a government 'for the people.' These were the three foundation principles upon which the Republic of China was established.

It must be added, however, that in support of the first principle, Dr. Sun did refer to the age-old Confucian virtues, stressed in the *Great Learning,* as a sound basis for a strong national life. In discussing the second principle of democratic procedures, he mentioned Confucius and Mencius as exemplary supporters of the people's welfare. And another reference to Confucius was made while he was discussing the third principle of the people's livelihood. But these passing references to the Great Sage, it should be noted, can hardly be interpreted as an attempt to sponsor a revival of Confucianism.[7] They were made not so much to defend an outmoded system as to use time-honored teachings to support the policies of the new republican government. Further details on the political philosophy of Sun Yat-sen may be found in *China's Response to the West,* a volume edited by Ssu-yü Teng and John K. Fairbank.[8] *

---

* Consult also Paul M. A. Linebarger: *The Political Doctrines of Sun Yat-sen;* or Donald G. Tewksbury: *Source Book on Far-Eastern Political Ideologies, Modern Period, China-Japan;* or Lyon Sharman: *Sun Yat-sen: His Life and Its Meaning.*

Other Revolutionary Theorists

Among the scores of political theorists in the early days of the Republic, may be mentioned two or three who made bold to differ from the leaders of the Kuomintang, both as to basic philosophy and in the choice of candidates for political leadership. For example, Chang Ping-lin (1867-?), who had joined Dr. Sun's *T'ung Mên Hui* in Japan, later (after 1911) organized his own Progressive Party (*Chin Pu Tang*) as a rival to the Kuomintang. Fearing that in the confusion of the times an ochlocracy or rule of the mob might become the order of the day, Chang based his bid for power on a platform more Buddhistic than Confucian, the chief plank of which was that Buddhist universalism could be successfully combined with nationalistic democracy.[9]

A strong influence from abroad at this time, already represented by Soviet advisers close to Sun Yat-sen, was Marxist-Leninist Materialism—the power behind Russia's own revolution (of 1917) and economic reconstruction. Its prominent Chinese advocate, Chen Tu-hsiu (1879-1942), for a time dean of Peking National University and as early as 1916 an outspoken anti-Confucianist, had early fallen under the influence of Haeckel's monism of substance and Jules Poincaré's *Science d'Hypothèse*. After 1919, he rapidly developed a passion for the dialectic materialism of Marx and economic determinism of the Russian Bolsheviks. More clearly was this seen after Chen had become editor of *La Jeunesse Nouvelle* or *The New Youth* magazine (*Hsin Ch'ing Nien*), in which he freely expressed his leftist and strongly anti-Confucian views.[10]

In 1921-27, Chen Tu-hsiu was active in directing the Communist Party in close association with Li Ta-chao,[11] and, in the years following the "September 18th Incident" of 1931, dialectic materialism became even more popular with forward-looking youth. Books on materialism were brought from Japan, translated into Chinese, and avidly read by thousands of youth who believed they were being progressive, like youth in other countries.[12]

While Liang Ch'i-ch'ao was advocating a popular nationalism devoted to the people's welfare, provided it did not develop into a 'people's imperialism' like that of Russia, a Chengtu lawyer by the name of Wu Yü (1874-1949), who had studied in Japan and leaned strongly to Taoist and Legalistic attitudes, argued (along with Chen Tu-hsiu) that Confucianism, being feudalistic, could not be adapted to modern democratic society. Writing in *La Jeunesse* an article entitled "Taoism and Legalism Equally Oppose the Old Moral Teaching," Wu Yü criticized the "Old Guard" (Confucian) scholars who had refused outright to support the new republican government. Calling them 'dung beetles,' who rooted around in the past and among a limited selection of old writings, he said they were not sufficiently aware of the fact that historically Taoism, Legalism, and Mohism had each in turn opposed the so-called 'old morality.'[13] *

Chiang K'ai-shek's Philosophy of Action

Sun Yat-sen's chosen 'Generalissimo,' Chiang K'ai-shek (1886-), carried out the 'Will' of his great 'Leader' (*Tsung-Li*), out of admiration for his character and acceptance of his basic philosophy. Although not a classical philosopher in his own right, Chiang, like his famous predecessor, necessarily held a philosophy whose keynote was 'action': to carry out the 'Will' of Sun Chung-shan, or Sun Wên (posthumous names for Sun Yat-sen), keeping it in harmony with Wang Yang-ming. Dr. Sun had differed from Wang by saying that conscience is primary but does not come from knowledge. To this Chiang added that we must carry out Sun Wên's theories according to our present conscience, without fearing the difficult or neglecting that which is easier. In fact, he encouraged all to attempt both with an eager zest that is born of a good conscience.

---

* The (as yet untranslated) *Essays of Wu Yü (Wu Yü Wên-Lu)* appeared in 1921, published in Shanghai by the Ya-tung Book Co.

In his theory of revolution, Chiang K'ai-shek (likewise a baptized Christian) asserted that by acting in accord with conscience one could know and strengthen his conviction of the truth of doctrine; in other words, for him action comes from conscience. For Chiang, however, action held a two-fold meaning: (a) action includes knowing; when a man studies science, he really learns theory by eager doing of his experiments. (b) Yet action is different from mere 'motion.' He contended that, whereas 'motion' (*tung*) is only passive, incidental, and temporary, 'action' (*hsing*) is active, certain, and permanent. Motion is impulsive, having in it both good and evil, but action is rational, having in it only good.

The chief difference between Chiang K'ai-shek and Wang Yang-ming, according to Professor Ho Lin of the Department of Philosophy in National Peking University, lies in the fact that where Wang found the kernel of the combination of knowing and doing in conscience, Chiang held it to be in action itself, which he called the reality of the combination of movement (*tung*) and quiescence (*ching*). To work is action and to rest is also action. To develop outwardly is action and to grow inwardly is also action. The relation between Truth and Love is expressed in doing, truth being the original force and love revealing the purpose of action. Truth and Love, therefore, are the 'body' or kernel of action, and action is the 'use' of truth and love. These three:—Truth, Love, and Action—make the eternal, interacting triad of life's reality.[14]

Finally, Chiang declared that man's nature is to love action. Where generally accepted opinion held that man hates labor and loves indolence, he averred the opposite to be true: that human nature is good; that man's nature is to be active; and, therefore, all action is good. He added the corollary that since to love means to serve humanity, the duty of the revolutionist is to love the people. With love, the spirit of action is easy. We not only prove it by eager doing, but show by love that knowing is easy.

Moving on from Sun Yat-sen's affirmation that knowing becomes doing, Chiang Chêng completed the cycle by declaring that not doing is proof of not knowing. Conversely, moving on from Sun's theory that we learn by doing, Chiang amplified it by saying that without action we come to know nothing. Inaction is proof of and leads to ignorance. Only the knowing that comes from doing has practical use, is actual knowing.[15] This philosophy received two notable testings, the first when Chiang nipped in the bud Communism's early bid for power in China by driving Eugene Chen and his Russian adviser, Borodin, out of Hankow in 1928 to complete the Nationalist Revolution. The second testing came when the Generalissimo and Madame Chiang launched the New Life Movement (*Hsin Sheng Huo Yün Tung*) in Nanchang in 1933-34, reviving the noble Confucian virtues of *Li* (decorum), *I* (uprightness), *Lien* (scrupulous honesty), and *Ch'ih* (modest self-appraisal). While this movement swept the country in a wave of popularity, it could not be interpreted as a general call for the revival of Confucianism as a state cult.[16] In his *China's Destiny* (*Chung-Kuo Chih Ming-Yün*), published in 1943, Chiang K'ai-shek's philosophy of action as the fulfillment of knowledge, dramatized in the New Life Movement and tested in the bitterness of warfare, found clear expression as a self-imposed discipline for society and government,[17] despite the fact that Robert Payne calls it "wildly unrealistic."[18]

Known to his closest friends as Chiang Chêng (Chiang the Upright, or Man of Integrity) and believing that spirit is important to strategy, Chiang K'ai-shek "became a good general because he fought with 'spirit' against greater economic equipment." When he decided to cross swords with the Japanese, Chiang well knew that he must fight Japanese *Bushido* as well as their armament. But he was convinced, also, that the spirit of the Chinese was on a higher level and must be so maintained, as the 'spirit of benevolent righteousness' (*jên i chih tao*). In this he has been likened to Fichte, who reputedly believed that if his people could recover what he termed 'the old morality,' they could overcome all their enemies. The Germans, he claimed, had a life-force and vitality of language greater than either the French or the English, all because of their stronger racial-spirit. So Chiang felt that China, too, must and could recover her ancient, indomitable 'spirit-that-breeds power.'[19]

(II) *The Influence of Western Philosophy on Republican China*

Introductory:—

Leaving the political angle of contemporary Chinese philosophy and moving on to the second phase of its development, we approach the overall influence of Western philosophers on the younger Chinese thinkers, so many of whom had gone abroad for study in the early republican period of wide-ranging freedom of thought. As Ho Lin has suggested, "Gradually China became aware that much of the West's power came from scientific knowledge. Then we Chinese learned the necessity of studying Western thought, working first on the utilitarian side, with the avowed purpose of testing it experimentally ourselves. We got interested in Nietzsche's *Philosophy of the Superman* (as translated by Li Shih-ts'en in 1928), in Marxist dialectic materialism, in Anglo-Saxon neo-realism, in the Vienna School, and other 'isms.' But we should have approached it from the theoretical side—from Socrates to Aristotle and from Kant to Hegel—if we were to get the best results from our study of Western philosophy."[20]

From an early uncritical stage, Chinese scholarship moved into a period of original research, translation, and harmonizing criticism, which helped to root Western philosophy in Chinese soil. Pioneering in this movement, Yen Fu (1853-1921) introduced, through translating, Huxley's *Evolution and Ethics,* as well as Spencer's *Study of Sociology,* in the year 1896.[21] Another pioneer was Chang I, who, after studying in England and America, where he wrote a doctoral dissertation on "The Theory of Hegel's Ethics," returned to China in 1923 and taught philosophy at "Pei Ta" (National Peking University). By his discussions of Kant and Hegel, he did much to standardize Chinese philosophy. From 1927, when Chang Tung-sun,

Chü Chüih-ming, and Wang Tzu-t'ung published their *Criticism of Philosophy,* a more general knowledge of Western philosophy was disseminated.

From 1927 to 1937, the professional philosophers found voice in the *Philosophical Critique* (*Chê-Hsüeh P'ing-Lun*), a magazine of their own sponsorship. By 1935, the Chinese Philosophical Society had been organized and not only encouraged translation work but stimulated original Chinese creative philosophizing, some of which found publication as articles in the *Philosophical Critique.*[22]

A Variety of Early Interests: including Science, Pragmatism, Neo-Realism, and Logic:—

Among the earlier translators of Western writers may be mentioned Ma Chün-wu, whose translations of Darwin's *Origin of Species* and *The Descent of Man* put him in the front rank of the so-called "apostles of transformism."[23] Wang Kuo-wei gave two years to the study and translation of the pessimistic voluntarism of Schopenhauer in his *Essays of Ching-An* (1905).[24] Nyi Chi-tao translated Sir John Herschel (England's noted astronomer-philosopher), Adam Smith, John Stuart Mill, and others; and Liang Ch'i-ch'ao's *The Development of Western Thought* introduced Hobbes, Descartes, Locke, Kant, and others to Chinese readers.

The work of these men paved the way for the Renaissance Movement led by returned students from abroad, who introduced William James's pragmatism and John Dewey's new educational outlook. In 1919-20, John Dewey and Bertrand Russell accepted invitations to lecture on pragmatism and neo-realism to scores of students in Peking and Shanghai. Chang Shen-fu promoted Russell's objectivism in his lectures at National Peking University and otherwise interpreted his ideas through magazine articles (ca. 1922). Hu Shih, also then a young professor of philosophy at "Pei Ta," showed the influence of Dewey in his writings on "Pragmatism" and other articles that sparked the Renaissance Movement in which he and others stressed new ideals in education, social reconstruction, and political reform:—a movement which became "the most influential philosophic influence in the modern period."[25] The publication in Chinese of the neo-realist William Montague's *The Ways of Knowing* influenced Fung Yu-lan and other young scholars, who wrote voluminously in succeeding months and years.[26]

By his translation of Henri Bergson's *Matière et Mémoire* and *L'évolution Créatrice,* along with five of Plato's *Dialogues,* Chang Tung-sun (1886-), gave added impetus to Chinese researches into Western philosophy. As a Shanghai newspaper editor with a strong interest in philosophic ideas, he then published in succession *A Philosophy of Morality* (a study of Western ethics) and *A Collection of New Philosophy,* in which he discussed Western trends in pragmatism, neo-realism, critical realism, the theory of creative evolution, and the new idealism. Later, under the influence of Kant's *Critique of Pure Reason,* Chang published his own reflective essays, including "The Pluralistic Theory of Knowledge Re-Stated," in which he rejected Kant's 'bifurcation of reality' but found reality synthesized in cognition based on experience. When dialectic materialism became a subject for discussion after 1932, Chang took an active interest in arguing against it from the 'pure knowledge' point of view.[27] Later, as we shall see, he became an active Marxist.

The early translation of Western logicians like Mill and Jenks, brought special appeal to certain minds like that of Chen Ta-ch'i, who, by 1917, had written his own *Elements of Logic.* Another who gave special attention to logic was Chin Yüeh-lin, who, after long years abroad, returned to teach at Tsinghua University. If Father Brière is correct, Chin tried to supplement the traditional lack of logical method in Chinese philosophy by writing his own book on *Logic* (*Lo Chi*) in 1935, which critics felt "was over-abstruse, though profoundly analytical."[28] Still another for whom logic held a fascination was Chang Shih-dao, the thesis of whose *Essentials of Logic* (in 1943) was that China had never lacked a logical method. He did not, however, attempt to unite the classical writers into a logical system.[29]

In a significant paper read in January, 1937,* while discussing "The Future Development of Chinese Philosophy," Shen Yiu-ting observed that Chinese thinkers were turning from intuitive perception to practical analysis, and, by adding a certain mathematical genius to their practical slant, were also evolving ideals which transcended the practical. Venturing a forecast of the modern period, he predicted philosophy would become activist, logical, and more idealistic, with art, music, and religion receiving their share of the new emphasis in the life of the nation.[30]

The Influence of Western Idealism:—

Quite early in the republican period, the influence of Western idealists was felt by Chinese thinkers like Hsieh Yu-wei, who studied more specifically the writings of F. H. Bradley and Josiah Royce. Certain of these he translated with his own introductions and annotations. In his *Outline of Ethics,* he followed his Western mentors in opposing utilitarianism and stressing the freedom of self-realization. Self-determination, he urged, calls for "respecting the inner, judicial law of my authentic self, the following of one's true nature, as taught in the *Chung Yung.*" He likewise appended his own estimates of Aristotle, Royce and Eduard Spranger.** In *A Criticism of Modern Philosophy* , he discussed various Chinese and Western philosophers, giving his criticism of Dewey, Hume, and the Vienna School of Logical Empiricists. About this time, Ssu Yu-tsung published his *Introduction to Metaphysics,* which was largely an exposition of Hegelian ideas.[31] The influence of Hegel is also seen on Chang Chen-ju, who, after studying in

* Before the Third Annual Meeting of the Chinese Philosophical Association in Nanking.

** Referring to Eduard Spranger: *Lebensformen—Geisteswissenschaftliche Psychologie und Ethik der Persönlichkeit.* Verlag von Max Niemeyer, Halle (3rd edition), 1922.

the United States, England, and Germany, taught Hegel and Kant at "Pei Ta" University. Likewise, Shih Yu-ching established himself as a subjective idealist by writing an introduction to Hegel in *Mind* (*Shuo Hsin*), adding a strong admixture of Bradley and Bosanquet's neo-Hegelianism.[32]

Another thinker of this period to be inspired by Western idealism was Ch'en K'ang, who spent ten years in Germany, learned to read Plato in the original Greek and translated his *Parmenides* with analytical notes and commentary. In comparing Plato and Aristotle, he felt that the latter had supplemented rather than contradicted the former, and supported this viewpoint by writing on "The Problem of Distinction in the Philosophy of Aristotle."[33] More of an objective idealist was Fu T'ung-hsien, a St. John's University professor, who discussed Locke, Berkeley, Feuerbach and others in his *The Problem of Knowledge* (*Chih-Shih Lun-Kang*), published in 1933. His later works include *Philosophy and Life* (*Chê-Hsüeh Yü Jên-Shêng*) (1947), and *Outline of Aesthetics* (*Mei-Hsüeh Kang-Yao*) (1948), in which he developed idealism in aesthetics and ethics, stressing conscience and moral judgment in social behavior.[34]

Two other writers call for brief mention here as giving stimulus to Chinese interest in idealism. In *The Road of Human Life.* T'ang Chün-i expressed his belief that all life is sacred and full of moral and spiritual ideals. The Law of things is in the Mind and is eternal. What we call 'Absolute Truth' is something whose essence lies in relative truths, their interrelatedness and interdependence. While we hold that there is no change in Eternal Law, yet, in our eyes, appearances are constantly new.[35]

Starting with an interest in Kantian idealism, Mou Chung-shan moved toward neo-realism, using some of Whitehead's ideas in his explanations of the *Yi Ching's* cosmology. During World War II, his *Models of Logic* came off the press, but, at war's end, his MS on *Understanding the World of Nature and Ideas* (*Li-Chieh, Li-Hsing, Yü Li-Nien*) remained still unpublished.[36]

Perhaps the most persistent of the idealists of the modern period has been Professor Ho Lin of the Department of Philosophy in National Peking University. After studying Hegel in Germany, he wrote commentaries on Wang Yang-ming and Sun Yat-sen, to show how close they were in their interpretation of knowledge and action. In 1941, he brought out his *Tang-Tai Chung-Kuo Chê-Hsüeh* (*Contemporary Chinese Philosophy*), and in the same year, as President of the Philosophical Society, appointed a committee to encourage such translations as Ch'en K'ang's *Parmenides of Plato*; Hsieh Yu-wei's *Royce's Philosophy of Loyalty;* T'ang Yüeh's translation of William James's *Principles of Psychology;* as well as his own translation of Spinoza's *Treatise on the Improvement of the Understanding.*[37]

In his *Brief Exposition of Idealism* (1942), Ho Lin attempted to synthesize Confucian idealism with that of Plato, Kant, Fichte, and Hegel. Then in 1947, his *Culture and Life* appeared, in which he taught that, while a study of theoretical concepts was important, still better was it to expose youth to the biographies of great men from whom they might absorb wisdom and virtue.[38]

The Influence of Vitalism and the Vienna School of Logical Empiricism

Another strong influence from abroad was the *Vitalism* that arose as a reaction against materialism and mechanistic science. Chinese disciples of Eucken, Bergson, and Driesch likewise upheld 'life' against 'mechanical law.' Among the earliest of these was Chang Chün-mai, who, after completing studies in Japan and Germany, was instrumental in bringing Driesch to lecture in China. He advocated a moral philosophy of life over against scientific positivism. According to Brière, Chang stirred up considerable controversy by arguing against men of science that life with its free will, creative intelligence, and personal unity, was a truer interpretation of ultimate reality than any scientific laws of cause and effect. In his contention that science could describe but not interpret life, and, therefore, that philosophy could solve problems which science could never solve, Chang was challenged by Hu Shih, but found supporters in Chang Tung-sun and Liang Ch'i-ch'ao.

Later he became active in the political field; set up a Political Institute at Woosung (near Shanghai); and still later, at Tali in Yunnan, promoted an Institute of National Culture where he advocated the realization of socialism through a democratic process.[39] In more recent years, under the alternate name of "Carsun" Chang, he has lectured in India and has published articles in *Philosophy East and West* (Honolulu), in *Orientalia* (University of Hamburg), and one on "Confucianism and Communist China" in *Ost Europa* (Germany). Last year his lectures on "A Comparative Study of Eastern and Western Philosophy" at Monterey Peninsula College in California were well received.

A like stress on vitalism is found in Fang Tung-mei, who admitted to having fallen, in his younger years, under the influence of Nietzsche's concept of power. As he grew older, he described the active life as characterized by overtones that could be created only by the triumph of reason over tragedy—a tone-quality that could be expressed only in the terminology of music and poetry. He will be remembered for his paper on "The Three Wisdoms in Philosophy," * in which he compared the Chinese, Greek, and Indian philosophies, pointing out the good points of each in an appreciative appraisal. During World War II, from his hermitage near Chungking, he wrote prolifically on the necessity of preserving a balance of passion and reason in life, if true civilization is not to fade and die out.[40]

In similar vein, came the influence on Chinese thought of the Vienna School of Logical Empiricism established by Moritz Schlick, who was allegedly executed by the Nazis about 1936, but whose ideas lived on in his associate, R. Carnap, and his students. Of the several Chinese who studied under him, Hung

* Read before the Chinese Philosophical Association at its Third Annual Meeting held in Nanking, January, 1937.

Ch'ien became his most zealous interpreter. In *The Philosophy of the Vienna School* (*Wei-Yeh-Na Hsüeh-P'ai Chê-Hsüeh*), he called attention to Schlick's division of truth into two parts: —a formal, subjective truth based on analytic definition or hypothesis, and an empirical, objective truth based on practical knowledge (like that derived from the natural sciences). Hung Ch'ien held, with Schlick, that metaphysics is "only a means to the enrichment of experience, that life is all-important. Only as a man follows the disinterested free-play of the will is he at his best. Culture lies in the recreative moods of the human spirit."[41] If the heart's natural gift of innate goodness be followed, whatever you choose to do will have a good result.[42]

Hung Ch'ien, therefore, criticized Fung Yu-lan's *New Wisdom* (*Hsin Chih Yen*) in 1946, as failing to reach the depths of the heart as traditional Chinese metaphysics rich in poetry has. Although Fung had accepted some of the principles of the Vienna School, yet he criticized them in his essay on "The Place and Method of the New Psychology in Philosophy," where he said that they could not entirely ignore the persistent psychological problems of metaphysical logic.[43] From the above, we may conclude, with Brière, that for many modern Chinese thinkers "metaphysics has meaning only as a foundation for ethics."[44]

Interest in Ethics and Religion

From time immemorial, the Chinese have always emphasized the necessity of a moral code, especially in times of transition. In recent years, a spate of books on ethics has appeared, some of the earlier ones bearing the same title—*Philosophy of Life* (*Jên-Shêng Chê-Hsüeh*)—but each with a differing emphasis trying to bring morals into line with scientific thought: for example, one from the pen of Shu Hsin-ch'êng (1923); one by Fung Yu-lan in 1925; that by Li Shih-ts'en in 1928; and Tu Ya-ch'üan's in 1929. When Chang Tung-sun wrote his (above-mentioned) *Philosophy of Morality* in 1930, he was interested in stressing the cultural value of virtue and in attacking the Marxist ethic.[45]

Shortly before his untimely death, Huang Fang-kang, of National Wu-Han University in Wuchang, published *A Study in Morals* (1935), largely based on the Kantian principles of the *a priori* nature of ethics which necessarily transcends experience. He felt that right and wrong could not be learned by experience; neither could standards be arrived at through self-questioning. In fact he argued that ethical standards are determined more by endowment at birth than by environmental acquirement, and, therefore, he advocated an analysis of heredity before appraising cases. On the other hand, he recognized that ethics, by suggesting an 'ought,' could be more of a determiner in human life than science. "For me," he concluded, "the real essence of morality is to recognize that any distinction between myself and others is meaningless."[46]

In addition to writing his (above-mentioned) *Outline of Ethics,* Hsieh Yu-wei continued to stimulate interest in ethics by his magazine articles on the theme of "Thought and Time," in which he proclaimed the source of happiness to lie in following the truth that gives perfect freedom.[47] Thus far we have noted only the thinkers who were strictly non-Marxist (if not anti-Marxist) in their point of view. By 1934, however, three different translations of Kautsky's *Ethics and the Materialistic Conception of History* had appeared, whose influence was clearly reflected in forthcoming books by Shen Chih-yüan (1936), Hu Sheng (1937), and Ai Ssu-ch'i in the same year.[48] Of Marxist writers, more will be said later in this chapter.

In reaction to the prevailing trend toward determinism and materialism, Lo Chia-lun wrote his *New Conception of Life* (*Hsin Jên-Shêng Kuan*) (1942) in order to help lift mankind out of the morass of current cynicism and skeptical pessimism in which it was then struggling by stressing a return to positive ethical ideals. Likewise, as Brière has pointed out, Lin Yutang's *Between Tears and Laughter* (1943) showed a similar advocacy of spiritual values in contrast to the former positivistic Epicureanism expressed in his *The Importance of Living.*[49] Following this line in his *Establishment of the Moral Self* (*Tao-Têh Tzu-Wo Chih Chien-Li*), in 1944, T'ang Chün-i sought to show how in both East and West ethics "starts in individual instinct and is developed into a transcendental moral ideal, well exemplified in the Confucian ideal of *jên*."[50]

An emergence out of the general disquietude of World War II, is also reflected in Huang Chien-chung's widely read *Comparative Ethics* (*Pi-Chao Lun-Li-Hsüeh*), published in Chungking in 1944. In his preface, he stated that his method was to look at ethical problems from two sides, test personality by direct intuition, and measure the value of conduct by 'intensive concretion,' or the synoptic method. He then made a searching analysis of Oriental and Occidental ethics, pointing out essential likenesses and showing there was little if any conflict either with ancient classical idealism or with that of Wang Yang-ming.[51] For him, morality in both East and West comes largely from instincts and habits rather than from introspection. Its essence lies in the principle of autonomy or conscience in man, which commands to do good and abhor evil. Conscience, or the voice of God, is superior to human law and is a law unto itself. Since optimists and pessimists are both extremists, Huang reasoned the only thing left for him was to become a 'meliorist,' go out to serve society in his own land and spread culture among the nations for the peace of the world.[52]

In the field of religion, modern Chinese have been formulating their ideas also more or less under the impact of the West. They came to see clearly that, if science is the attempt to see life in terms of its component, inter-related parts, and if philosophy endeavors to see life steadily and see it whole, religion is man's total response to that 'Whole.' Following the appearance of Professor Hsü Pao-ch'ien's *Talks on the Experience of Religion*, Miss Tseng Pao-sen published her *Manual of Experiential Religion*, explaining the philosophy of Christianity. About this time T. C. Chao's *Life of Christ* appeared, and, with his church hymnary, effectively aided the inspirational mood of countless Christians.

In his *Philosophy of Religion,* Hsieh Wu-hsia discussed the history, psychology, and metaphysics of religion, reflecting his interest in William James's *Varieties of Religious Experience* and certain ideas of Whitehead and Alexander as well. During World War II, in response to a request from the Chinese Philosophical Association, he undertook the translation of Josiah Royce's *The Religious Aspect of Philosophy* and completed the first volume.

To the mind of Wu Mieh, as expressed in his *Literature and Life,* all great souls from antiquity down have been based on the religious spirit. He thought it most desirable to have religion permeating government and business, because, though ancient, religion is not antiquated and is still vital to the modern need for spiritual foundations. In upholding the close relation of art to religion and by urging a return to religious attitudes in modern life, Wu Mieh was taking a position diametrically opposed to that of Ts'ai Yüan-p'ei; but for help in maintaining that position he leaned heavily upon his translations of Irving Babbitt, Paul Elmer More, and others, especially upon Hoernle's *God, Spirit, Life, Matter,* which he had translated in full with commentary.[53] If, as Ho Lin thinks, Max Weber is right in saying, in his *Protestant Ethic and the Spirit of Capitalism,* that the rise of capitalism and big business in England and America was largely the work of men in the Protestant Churches, that fact only bears out Wu Mieh's statement in reference to the influence of religion in life.[54]

Interest in Art and Comparative Literature

The Chinese people have ever been sensitive to art as expressed with brush and pen. In *The Mood of Art,* which is both poetical and philosophical, Chung Pai-hua created new interest by explaining the special beauty of Chinese art. Appreciation of art was further deepened by Teng I-chih's wartime essays entitled "Discourses on Six Methods of Chinese Art" and "Discourse on Calligraphy." Using his knowledge of art, philosophy, and religion, Wu Mieh made an illuminating interpretation of the famous old Chinese novel, *The Dream of the Red Chamber (Hung Lou Mêng),* in which he continued to stress the importance of art as complementary to religion. Both, he insisted, cause people to leave their bitterness behind and find a deep, abiding peace of soul. Where religion suggests the aim of life, art becomes a method of attaining the aim.[55]

During the second and third decades of the present century, there ran an undercurrent of controversy in China as to the relative merits of various factors in modern civilization; such as philosophy, science, art, and religion. This stemmed largely from the anti-religion movement fostered by Ts'ai Yüan-p'ei, who, in the early 1920's, advocated art and calisthenics as the best antidote for the 'artificiality' of Western religion which he openly castigated. As a student in Germany, Ts'ai had become interested in aesthetics as a substitute for religion and on his return had translated Paulsen's *System of Ethics* and soon after wrote his own *History of Chinese Ethics.* After becoming Chancellor of National Peking University, the influence he exercised in his 'back to beauty' movement assumed nation-wide proportions.[56]

The theme of the movement was well expressed in Hsü Ch'ing-yü's *Philosophy of Beauty* (*Mei-Ti Chê-Hsüeh*) (1928), in which he discussed Ts'ai's thesis that art can replace religion, but without relating beauty to ethics. He also discussed Confucius' theory of music and the aesthetic values in the Odes. It remained, however, for men like Ch'en Chu-shan in his *The Art of Living (Jên-Shêng Yi-Shu)* to lay a systematic foundation for ethics in a synthesis of truth, goodness, and beauty, which, in truth, is the Confucian ideal.[57]

Even more influential was Chu Kuang-ch'ien, who, with his *Twelve Letters to the Young,* written about 1929, sought to hold youth up to the true ideals of aestheticism. His other writings: *On Beauty* (1932), *Psychology of Literary Art* (1936), and *On Poetry* (1948) gained for him an enviable reputation and a wide following. His best claim to fame, however, rests upon his translation of Benedetto Croce's *Principles of Aes-*

thetics, rendered as *Mei-Hsüeh Yüan-Li,* and his *Critique of the Philosophy of Croce (K'ê-Lo-Ch'i Chê-Hsüeh P'ing-Shu)* (1948). As Brière summarizes his work:—"Following Croce in the main, Chu comes to the conclusion that the highest form of practical morals is artistic activity. For him, aesthetics is above ethics: the supreme good merging into absolute beauty." [58]

In recent decades, the oddly significant fact has become noticeable that scientists have made contributions to philosophy and well-known philosophers have stimulated by interpreting scientific research. A like interaction may be noted in the close relation borne between philosophy and literature. Men like Liang Chung-tai, who wrote a collection of prose called *Poetry and Truth* and translated Bosanquet's *Value and Destiny of the Individual,* or Lin T'ung-chi, who edited a magazine called *Strategy,* have done much to increase Chinese sensitivity to art, literature and philosophy.

Still another writer, Fang Chieh, has attracted many with his collection of sonnets which, though strict in form, are philosophically meditative. His popular, medium-length novel about Wu Tzu-hsi, which analyzes the contradictions of life and their resolution, has the style and flavor of philosophy. And, without a doubt, his translations of R. Steiner's *Goethes Weltanschauung,* Johann Forster's *Naturgeschichte und Philosophie des Lebens,* and Schiller's *Briefe über die ästhetische Erziehung des Menschen* have enlarged the horizons of modern China's knowledge and appreciation of art, philosophy, and literature.[59]

The Influence of Marxist Dialectical Materialism

Mention has already been made of the strong Soviet influence on Chinese republicans both before and after the founding of the Republic, of Marxist gains during the 1920's due to the writings of Chen Tu-hsiu and his collaborator, Li Ta-chao, in the very influential *La Jeunesse Nouvelle* which they edited.

Because of its plausible, political, social, and economic propaganda-promises, the influx of Marxist dialectical materialism slowly inundated North China and by 1949-50 had swept all other parties from the whole country. Placing its ultimate trust in bullets rather than in ballots, the Chinese Communist Party's so-called "People's Government" (*Jên-Ming Chêng-Fu*), like any other one-party system appears to lack reliable political machinery for unrigged elections aimed at peaceful change of government-personnel. Like all other oligarchical dictatorships, its totalitarian régime will hold sway until democratic thinking based on fundamentally religious principles can find its true expression as the will of an enlightened people.

It is not our purpose here, however, to write a critique of communism but, following Brière's *Fifty Years of Chinese Philosophy* (English edition of 1956) and Robert Payne's *Mao Tse-tung: Ruler of Red China* as guides, we wish to record very briefly how Marxism found able theoreticians among the younger Chinese in the 1930's and 1940's who, by their writings, furthered the cause of revolution in the name of the proletariat.

As early as 1923, Li Ta entered the lists for Marxism with his translations of Marx, Engels, and Lenin, and before long published his *Elements of Sociology (Shê-Hui-Hsüeh Ta-Kang)*. As an exposition of Marxist sociology, it wielded great influence, especially causing the younger generation to believe that religion is "the opiate of the people" and must be "relegated to oblivion, by force if need be."[60] The book went thru several editions, the latest, in 1947, appearing as an abridgement under the title of *Modern Sociology (Hsien-Tai Shê-Hui-Hsüeh)*. Also quite early, there appeared a definitive *Biography of Marx (Ma-K'ê-Szu Ch'uan)* in three volumes by Li Chi, which had only a limited influence.[61]

Despite the execution of Li Ta-chao as an agitator by the military in 1927, there were not lacking others to carry the torch of communism. Kuo Mo-jo first made a *Study of Ancient Chinese Society* in 1932, and later, as poet-dramatist, put new philosophical ideas into his *Ten Critiques* and *The Bronze*

Age in 1945.[62] Ai Ssu-ch'i came into prominence about 1934 as editor of a Marxist periodical, *Intellectual Life (Tu-Shu Shêng-Huo)*. Later, in 1936, he wrote "Talks on Philosophy," which were republished in book form as the very popular *Philosophy of the People (Ta-Chung Chê-Hsüeh)*, which "sets forth the Party line with clarity and forcefulness".[63]

About 1930, Yeh Ch'ing, who had studied in France, came from Szechuan to Shanghai, opened a "Thinking Bookshop" and quietly set about publishing the works of Eighteenth-Century French materialists like La Mettrie, d'Holbach, and Helvetius, as well as of known Marxists such as Déborin, Lafargue, and Plekhanov. In 1934, in his *Whither Philosophy,* he published his own reflections on the future disappearance of philosophy and science, leaving Marxism as the only workable philosophy for the human race. In reply to Chang Tung-sun's anti-Marxian essays entitled *Controversy over Dialectical Materialism,* published that same year, Yeh Ch'ing published his compilation of pro-Marxian essays under the title of *Philosophical Controversies* (1935). Again, in 1936, he followed up with his *Problems of the New Philosophy,* in which he "predicted the amalgamation of idealism and materialism in a resultant science of thought which would be Marxism."[64] Yet, as Brière relates, his critics accused Yeh Ch'ing of being as heretical as Trotsky and in 1940 severely attacked him as being "too much of a free-thinker straying from the path of orthodox Communism."[65] More palatable for the scientific materialist was Chang I-hung's *General Discourse on Philosophy (Chê-Hsüeh Kai-Lun),* published in 1936.[66]

When the Japanese invaded China in 1937, the out-and-out Marxists joined Mao Tse-tung at Yenan, while those who were content to theorize remained under the Nationalist régime as it moved from Nanking to Hankow and then on to the war-time capital of Chungking. From 1939 to 1946, Shen Chih-yüan's magazine, *Theory and Reality,* continued to serve as a forum for the airing of Marxist doctrines, while down in Shanghai books and periodicals disseminated Marxist propaganda wherever Japanese censorship could be eluded.[67]

During his incarceration by the Japanese in World War II, Chang Tung-sun shifted his interest from metaphysics to sociology; from being a neo-Kantian logician interested in "epistemological pluralism," he leaned more and more toward Marxian socialism until at war's end he was ready to publish his three essays on "Knowledge and Culture," "Thought and Society," and "Reason and Democracy" (1946)—all strongly socialistic in tone. Finally, in 1948, he swung entirely into the Marxist orbit with his *Democracy and Socialism,* which later brought him into the good graces of the Communist régime.[68] When, however, we read that Chang Tung-sun, after failing to reconcile the Kuomintang with the Communist Party line, began to preach anarchism as the best way to get rid of all forms of authoritarian control that kill the spirit of liberty in man, we begin to think that the Confucian in him was after all turning Taoist.[69]

The Wartime Philosophy of Mao Tse-tung

During World War II (in China from 1937 to 1945), Mao Tse-tung, as the acknowledged leader of the Communist Revolution, was fighting two wars at the same time: a war against the Japanese as the most hated of the representatives of imperialistic capitalism, and an internal conflict with the Kuomintang (Nationalists) as the hateful defenders of feudalistic landlordism and the upper bourgeoisie of big business bureaucrats in government circles—some of whom, like Wang Ching-wei, were openly collaborating with the Japanese invaders. In order, therefore, to bolster his own courage and the faith of his followers in the ultimate success of their cause, Mao set down in writing, either as lectures and speeches or in book form, the aims, ideals, and tactics of the dual war in which they were then engaged. As Robert Payne puts it, Mao's writings show the great strain under which he was laboring: using as he did "Chinese proverbs, classical allusions, and quotations from Marxist literature. . . . There are elements in his style which derive from Confucius and Han Yü and from the great Chinese novels, but he has also been influenced by the spare, ironical prose of the (short) story writer, Lu Hsün."[70]

In an address to the Sixth Plenum of the Chinese Communist Party delivered at Yenan on October 12, 1938, Mao Tse-tung used much material from his recently published book *On A Prolonged War,* in which he had predicted ultimate victory after a long and arduous struggle. He also declared that the invader could be driven out only if a united front were maintained by the Communists and the Nationalists and added, significantly. "The are no real differences between us, for we too desire that the *Three Principles of the People* should be put into operation."[71]

A year later, in a speech to his supporters, published in book form as *The New Democracy* in January, 1940, Mao outlined his plans for joining up with the Soviet Union in its avowed world revolution against the "imperialists of the Western world"; he also gave a preview of how he expected the new democracy to work in China through a period of experiment into a final stage of state socialism. Again, in a book composed of three lectures on *The Chinese Revolution and the Communist Party of China,* Mao elaborated his concept of the necessity of unremitting warfare against the "enemies within the country" (exploiters of the people) even more than against "international capitalism." At the same time, he revealed the tentative nature of his current thinking by stating that, while approving the nationalizing of "large capital interests," he would help "small private industries"; while approving of radical reform in land tenure, he would make "no attempt to abolish the economy of the rich farmers." This last promise was necessary because his whole enterprise depended for success on the total resources of the rural population.[72]

In February, 1941, Mao Tse-tung's fourth book came off the press under the title, *Strategic Problems of China's Revolutionary Wars,* in which he discussed the strategy of guerrilla warfare and re-affirmed his confidence in ultimate victory over the invader and over the decadent forces of Chiang K'ai-shek to win control of the whole country.[73] This confidence was again given utterance in his address to the Seventh Congress of the Chinese Communist Party at Yenan on April 24, 1945. While expressing belief that his party would sooner or later replace the Kuomintang, nevertheless, Mao stated that there was room for "peaceful coexistence," if both parties would recognize "the primacy of the popular will." When the speech appeared in book-form under the title of *Coalition Government,* it contained other bold statements, such as Mao's belief that after the war China would need foreign capital for her rehabilitation; that foreign investors would be welcomed if they were willing to "obey the laws of China" and if their investments should prove "advantageous to our economy."[74]

With these and other writings, Mao Tse-tung led his party to complete victory over the Kuomintang in 1949-1950. His outstanding helpers, to mention only a few, were Liu Shao-ch'i as his trusty adviser, Chu Tê as Commander-in-Chief of the People's Liberation Army, Lin Piao as Commander of the Fourth Field Army, and Chou En-lai as the Party's foremost negotiator and later Minister of Foreign Affairs in the Central People's Government in Peiping.[75] From 1949 until late in 1960, Mao Tse-tung served as Chairman of the People's Government and of the Central Committee (Politburo) of the Communist Party in China.

(III) *Revaluations of China's Classical Heritage in Modern Terms*

In the previous discussions of Western philosophical influences, it became clear that most of the Chinese followers of pragmatism, neo-realism, vitalism, and new-idealism, as well as Marxism, agreed that Confucianism's "old morality" held nothing for the future and that in Western philosophy lay China's only hope.[76] On the other hand, the same Western impact drove others, some younger, some older, to delve again into their ancient classical philosophies to find values suited to the modern temper. Renewed attention brought revived interest in indigenous Taoist and Confucian, as well as imported Buddhist and regurgitated Neo-Confucian ideologies—all of which were given a thorough over-hauling and revamping to fit the shape of the contemporary Chinese mind. A scrutiny of these revaluations by government educators, Christian leaders, Buddhist leaders, and contemporary Confucian philosophers, will occupy our attention for the remainder of this chapter.

A. *Revaluations by Leading Educators*

In a period largely given to debunking the 'old morality,' certain educational leaders in government-sponsored institutions showed a real concern for preserving the best in their traditional culture. One of the earliest revaluations of Confucianism was made by Monlin Chiang in his *A Study in Chinese Principles of Education* (1918).[76a] While recognizing that "the parcelling out of the universe into several spheres and the searching for facts therein . . . are wanting in Confucian philosophy," Dr. Chiang pointed out that Chu Hsi's emphasis on the 'investigation of things,' a method based on the *Doctrine of the Mean* (*Chung Yung*), was very close to the present-day scientific method. In it he found steps corresponding to the gathering and examination of data; the formulation of uniform laws; and the application of those laws.

In the second decade of the Republic, Hu Shih (1891-...), then professor in National Peking University, became famous as the leading spokesman for the Chinese "Renaissance." Through his articles in *La Jeunesse Nouvelle,* he became widely recognized as the spearhead of the literary revolution which sought to establish *Pei Hua* (spoken language) in place of the old *Wên Li* (written classical language) as the medium of current literary and journalistic production. In addition to his teaching of philosophy, Dr. Hu found time to publish the first volume of his *History of Chinese Philosophy* (*Chung-Kuo Ku-Tai Chê-Hsüeh Ta-Kang*),* in which he rejected Confucianism as too static but found some hopeful pragmatic elements in Mohism.[77] In another early volume, *The Development of Logical Method in Ancient China* (1922), he made clear his position that Confucian thought would have to be revamped if it was to live in the modern age. He stated the problem in these words:

"I am firmly of the opinion that the future of Chinese philosophy depends (not only) upon its emancipation from the moralistic and rationalistic fetters of Confucianism . . . (but also) on the revival of those great philosophical schools which once flourished side by side with the school of Confucius in Ancient China. . . .

"It is in these schools that we may hope to find the congenial soil in which to transplant the best products of occidental philosophy and science. This is especially true with regard to the problem of methodology. . . . I have the strongest desire to make my own people see that these methods of the West are not totally alien to the Chinese mind, . . . (but) . . . on the contrary, . . . are the instruments by (which) . . . much of the lost treasures of Chinese philosophy can be recovered." (78)

We are indebted to Wing-tsit Chan for enumerating Hu Shih's many achievements: his teaming up with Chen Tu-hsiu in the attack on out-moded Confucian *mores;* his espousal of pragmatic instrumentalism and contributions to the new scientific approach to Chinese philosophy—by clearing up sources and re-evaluating ancient works; his spotlighting of the social and political factors behind the shifting scenes in philosophical revolutions (of Lao Tzu, the Neo-Mohists, Huai-Nan Tzu, Shen Hui, and Tai Tung-yüan); his discovery of the place of methodology in changing Chinese thought. Possibly most revolutionary of all were Hu Shih's conception of Confucius

---

* Shanghai, The Commercial Press, Ltd., 1919 (as yet untranslated).

as a reformer giving new meaning to the *ju* or scholar class, and his interpretation of Shen Hui as a militant rebel against the older Ch'an practice of contemplative meditation.[79]

In the same article on "Hu Shih and Chinese Philosophy," Dr. Chan goes on to emphasize the great importance of Hu Shih's contribution to our understanding of Chinese philosophy by establishing three great "centers of focus" (or "watersheds") in Chinese philosophy in his *A Book on Huai-nan Tzu* (d. 122 B.C.) (*Huai-nan Wang Shu*)[80] as representative of the Ch'in-Han (221 B.C.-A.D. 220) period; his *Works by Monk Shen Hui* (d. 760) (*Shen-Hui Ho-Shêng I-Chi*)[81] as representing Chinese Buddhism; and his *Philosophy of Tai Tung-yüan* (1723-1777) (*Tai Tung-yüan Ti Chê-Hsüeh*)[82] as representative of modern Chinese philosophy.[83] In the course of his long and eminent career, Hu Shih has constantly promoted forward-looking movements in philosophical and educational thought, has served as his country's Ambassador to the United States, and, more recently as President of the *Academia Sinica,* is still much sought after as senior statesman and scholarly lecturer and writer.[84]

Another brilliant, contemporary educator to take a hand in re-sifting Chinese traditional thought has been T'ang Yung-t'ung, also a member of the philosophical faculty at "Pei Ta" University. After familiarizing himself with Eastern and Western philosophy, he even studied Sanskrit and Pali in order to familiarize himself with Buddhist philosophy. Paying considerable attention to traditional Indian Buddhism, he rather discounted Ou-Yang Ching-wu's contemporary lectures on Buddhism. After making a protracted study of the history of Buddhism in China during the Han, Wei, Liang, and Tsin (Chin) dynasties (a difficult period for Chinese philosophy), T'ang denied that the thread of Confucian thought had ever been lost. He also stoutly maintained that even during the succeeding dynasties (North-and-South, Sui, and especially T'ang), when Buddhism flourished and Confucianism was at a low ebb, China had never lost her truly indigenous racial and national spirit.[84a]

Of Professor T'ang Yung-t'ung's work available in English, may be mentioned his "Various Traditions Concerning the Entry of Buddhism into China," translated by Arthur E. Link[85] and characterized by W. T. Chan as "the most scholarly work on the subject; . . . fully documented from original . . . sources";[86] his article "On 'Ko-yi,' the Earliest Method by Which Indian Buddhism and Chinese Thought Were Synthesized," contributed to W. R. Inge (ed): *Radhakrishnan, Comparative Studies in Philosophy*[87] (1951); and his essay on "Wang Pi's New Interpretation of the *I-Ching* and *Lun-Yü*," translated by Walter Liebenthal,[88] which, according to W. T. Chan, "throws an entirely new light on this much neglected Confucianistic Neo-Taoist philosopher, definitely establishing his position as a major stage in the development of Chinese philosophy."[89]

It is T'ang Yung-t'ung's mature opinion that the infiltration of foreign Buddhism acted as a valuable stimulant to the Chinese mind which absorbed and harmonized it with indigenous Chinese philosophy. This recognition of the conservation and continuity of Confucianism made T'ang bold to declare the security of Chinese civilization in the face of recent inroads by Western modes of thought and practice. Being himself definitely idealistic, he saw in the immateriality of Chinese culture an assurance of its survival, even though it should continue to absorb a little more of Western thought.[90]

Among other educators who have contributed to our understanding of modern trends in Chinese philosophic thought are Mei Yi-pao (Y. P. Mei) with his translation of *The Ethical and Political Works of Motse* (Mo-Ti) and his own commentary on *Motse, The Neglected Rival of Confucius;*[91] Hsü Pao-ch'ien with his *Ethical Realism in Neo-Confucian Thought;*[92] Lin Mou-sheng with an excellent sketch of Chinese political thought in his *Men and Ideas;*[93] Siu-chi Huang with her fine interpretation of *Lu Hsiang-shan;*[94] Gung-hsing Wang with his brief but readable résumé of *The Chinese Mind;*[95] Cheng Chi-yü with his *Oriental and Occidental Culture Contrasted;*[96] Carsun Chang with his *The Development of Neo-Confucian Thought;*[97]

Wing-tsit Chan with his *Religious Trends in Modern China;*[98] and Liu Wu-chi with his *Confucius, His Life and Times.*[99] To these should be added Arthur W. Hummel, editor of *Eminent Chinese of the Ch'ing Period* in two volumes;[100] Herrlee Glessner Creel, of the University of Chicago, with his *Confucius, the Man and the Myth,*[101] as well as his *Chinese Thought from Confucius to Mao Tse-tung;*[102] Arthur F. Wright, of Stanford University, editor of *Studies in Chinese Thought;*[103] and John K. Fairbank, of Harvard University, as co-editor of *China's Response to the West*[104] and more recently of *Chinese Thought and Institutions.*[105] The chief value of all these works lies in the re-evaluation which they have given to Chinese classical philosophies in the light of and in the terms of modern Western thought.

Chen Li-fu's Lectures to the Central Academy of Political Science

While to most modern Chinese, Chen Li-fu (1899-...) is considered more of a politician than a philosopher or educator, nevertheless, there is to be found in his lectures to the students of the Central Academy of Political Science in Nanking the most comprehensive, contemporary presentation of Confucianism-mixed-with-Vitalism that we have seen, restated as a moral-philosophy-to-live-by. In his first series on *Life as a Metaphysical Principle, or Vitalism* (*Wei-Shêng Lun*) (1934), ranked by Homer H. Dubs as "the outstanding book of the year,"[106] Chen gave a metaphysical basis for the Kuomintang's philosophy as set forth in the *Three Principles of the People* (*San-Min Chu-I*), which had suffered much from attacks by Dr. Sun's political and philosophical opponents. In it he expressed a firm belief that, although struggle marks the life of everyone, man is steadily moving upward "in collective progress toward the refined stage of Beauty-in-Life" (—an ideal opposed to Communist ideology). Eastern culture will furnish the spiritual element and the West, the material element in a final grand International Concord.[107]

Ten years later, in 1944-45, Chen Li-fu again went into print with his second series of lectures on *Life's First Principles,* or *The Theory of Life* (*Shêng Chih Yüan-Li*), aimed at giving students and government leaders something worth fighting for—"a positive philosophy based on a genuinely Chinese view of life." Chen's *Theory of Life* revealed his re-formulation of the Confucian system in such a way as to give some place to the insights of the West in science and philosophy. This forthright defense of China's cultural heritage merits for him a place among the philosophically-minded educators of contemporary Chinese youth. The following *précis* is based on Andrew Tod Roy's translation,[108] with main ideas arranged under five topics:—

The Theory of Life

(1) *The Changing Universe and Its Evolving Existents:—*

In the beginning, there subsisted the Life-Monad (*Sheng Yüan, T'ai Chi,* or Ultimate Life-Substance), part heavenly (*ch'ien,* male), part earthly (*k'un,* female) and holding within it the principles of space and time. The *ch'ien* represented the active spiritual energy (*yang*) that creates; the *k'un,* the quiescent, material force (*yin*) that conserves. Their interaction has formed a four-dimensional, space-time continuum (which the *Book of Changes* adumbrated long before Einstein), in which have evolved the Five Elements and all the manifold things and events that make up our universe. Strictly, in what we call 'life,' there are no 'things,'—only processes; no static forms, only dynamic movement that is wave-like or spiral.

In the creative process, the forces of concretion and dissipation are fairly balanced, ever producing existents that are novel, mutually affecting and supplementing each other. . . . Man has achieved superiority over other animals through improvement of his mental capacity and self-consciousness. His ability to intuit the universe makes man the focus of the creative process, with ever-increasing responsibilities for self-realization and direction.

(*Shêng Chih Yüan-Li,* pp. 1-31; 44-56; 68-80; 81-106)

(2) *Human Life Its Own Goal:–*

The goal of life is life itself (quoting Bergson) . . . "It has value aside from the Will of God or a possible other world." Yet man finds his greatest significance (and happiness) in service rendered for the enrichment of all.

(SCYL, pp. 107-123; also quoting from the *Book of Rites, Mencius,* and the *Doctrine of the Mean*)

In the ethical life, only disinterested goodness has value. Selfless motives alone can lead men into goodness. Evil enters whenever personal desires are satisfied at the expense of others' cravings. . . . Therefore, humaneness (*jên*) finds expression in intelligent concern for and courageous work to satisfy the needs of others.

(SCYL, pp. 124-145)

Life's real motivating force is sincerity (*ch'êng*) or genuineness. As Mencius said, "There is no greater satisfaction than to be conscious of sincerity on self-examination." If completely unselfish, it can make man god-like.

(SCYL, pp. 146-161; quoting *Mencius* Bk. VII, Pt. I, Ch. IV, V-vss. 1, 2; *Doctrine of the Mean,* Ch. XX, V, 18; and *Mencius* Bk. IV, Pt. I, Ch. XII, V, 2)

(3) *The People's Livelihood in Relation to the Evolution of Culture–*

Chen Li-fu saw an interaction of politics, learning, and religion, as well as economics, in the evolution of the future culture. (To quote):

"Man's moral progress springs out of the gradual enlarging of (his understanding and expression of) love. . . . Where each seeks the good of the whole, class interest has no place. Therefore, class struggle is a symptom of social disease."

International interdependence is growing slowly on a basis of sincerity and coherence secured through book-learning and a common morality.

"Now even racial differences no longer necessarily engender hatred."

Learning would solve all problems by bringing them out into the open for free debate. Individual and social survival becomes a moral and educational question as well as depending on the people's livelihood. . . .

"Progress lies within the context of security, (but) control through courtesy (*Wang Tao*) is always better than legal control by force (*Pa Tao*)."

Only thus will men move steadily toward the "Great Commonwealth of the World." (SCYL, pp. 197-223)

At this juncture, Chen Li-fu launched into a lengthy discussion of the elements of culture inhering in the productive skills, technological sciences, legal procedures, aesthetic arts, ethical practices, *et cetera,* as they are related to man's corporate life, survival and progress. (In Dr. Roy's paraphrase): "Chen thinks *pure science* satisfies man's instinctive curiosity, extends his knowledge and understanding. *Art* and *literature* affect society because beauty . . . is not contrary to goodness. Beauty enriches the spirit and the progress of the human race depends upon such fulfilling enrichment. *Philosophy* is essential as an integrating medium. All philosophies help to attain this better corporate life, survival and progress, but no one school of philosophy has all the truth."[109]

In other words (again in Roy's paraphrase): "Chen believes that all of life's ideals can be built up out of man's life itself. . . . Religious men (he says), because they love God, advocate loving men. Chen (on the contrary), because he advocates the love of corporate life, survival, and progress, therefore loves men. . . . Still, the more religion progresses, the more it realizes that love of God must start with (or include) love of man. Thus, Chen believes the different paths come out at the same place in the end." (SCYL, pp. 224-244)

(4) *Political and Social Evolution:*—

Chen Li-fu started out by saying:

"All branches of culture rely upon government to extend their activities. . . . It is this position in culture that has made politics the battleground of all the social forces.

On the other hand, it may be said that government has no special power of its own. Politics creates government . . . but its power lies in weighing aright and deciding among the alternatives presented, i.e., in re-arranging in a new order society's demands.

Being a sort of clearing house for cultural interpenetration, government's responsibility is to advance culture and seek its harmonious development. . . .

Therefore, politics is the weighing scales of the whole social structure and the brain of the whole of society, responsible for how the social culture of the future is to develop."

As a corollary to his thesis that government and society are mutually dependent, Chen moved on to say that democracy must and can provide trustworthy personnel for good government. How the people's political power is to be effectively used in government, was clarified, according to Chen, by Sun Yat-sen in his lecture on "The Principle of Political Democracy" (in the *San Min Chu I*), as follows:—

"In the first place, by adding to the right of election also the powers of recall in relation to (government) personnel, and initiative and referendum in relation to laws, he gave the people direct participation in government.

In the second place, Dr. Sun saw that the root of politics lay in men and man's root in morality. Western governments recognized the importance of men but did not know how to get competent men into government. For this, Dr. Sun turned to the traditional Chinese theory of the equal importance of men and law and to the former Chinese use of (a) an examination-for-civil-service system, and (b) a censorship-of-officials'-conduct system. . . ."

Quoting from the *Analects, Doctrine of the Mean, Mencius,* and the *Great Learning,* to the effect that man must first be moral before he can administer government, Chen continued:

"Some think that principle applied only in the time of the monarchy but is not needed today, when all executives must obey the laws and all men may be called rulers. But . . . the Confucian position . . . retains its tremendous significance in a day when executives can get around the law or distort it.

Modern democracy has allowed (political) parties too freely to seize power regardless of capacity to rule. . . . Today's trend is toward party control (i.e. a one-party system), which is public spirited and seeks only to fulfill its duties. It is open to all citizens to contribute according to their ability (as Dr. Sun has said). The Soviet Communist Party and China's Kuo-Min-Tang are in accord with this idea. (110) Even in the case of the Democratic Party in America, with its long-extended war-time control by government personnel, the idea was similar." * (SCYL, pp. 245-257) (111)

(5) *The Road to the Great Unity, or the Realization of Peace*:—

In its interpretation of the 'spirit of peace' (*ho-p'ing*), Chen Li-fu saw the significance of Chinese culture for a world culture. From time immemorial, Chinese communal harmony has rested upon mutual respect for human personality. "Where courtesy (equity) and harmony (unity) exist, there is true co-operation in production and life." Mutual aid in creativity is better (politically) than mutual rivalry in destructive warfare. For men and nations (quoting from the *Book of Rites* and the *Record of Music*), "Mutual responsiveness makes for harmony" and "Harmony has fitting responses"—all of which are essential to corporate life, survival, and progress leading to the Great Commonwealth. (SCYL, pp. 258-278)[112]

---

* A reference is made here to Sun Fo's *China Looks Forward* (pp. 250-253), where he recognized the need for freedom of organization of political parties, provided there wasn't too much internal, factional disunity or open strife in violation of the *San Min Chu I* or Kuo-Min-Tang Party Principles. (We may add that Sun Fo, as the son of Sun Yat-sen, was writing not only as one peculiarly interested in implementing his father's "Will," but as one who, in an official capacity, had been seeking to personify in the Central Government the Confucian ideal of the disinterested public servant.)

In other words, Chen Li-fu is reminding his hearers that China has ever sought to develop moral man in a moral society as a rhythmical part of a living universe. To this end, Chinese have developed the science of *medicine;* research in physiology has paralleled the development of Chinese *"boxing"* (*kuo-shu*) as a rhythmical calisthenic exercise similar to fencing. The consciousness of man as the apex of the universal life-stream has also motivated Chinese *art* (painting), *literature,* and *calligraphy,* where everything must follow the rhythms of life itself (quoting here from the *Book of Changes).*[113]

Furthermore, Chen argued,

"In our word *'chung-ho'* (central harmony), *chung* is center of gravity; *ho* is inner and outer consistency, the expression of motivating force connecting everything with the center, fitting together, adjusting, nurturing, to make all things enduring because adapted to circumstances. . . .

But to gain permanence . . . we must . . . cultivate internal energy by withdrawal and rest. Temperance, no excess, is the Chinese ideal in life-cultivation for a lasting, durable peace.

Living in an agricultural economy, Chinese have emphasized a land-inheritance divided equally among all sons. . . . Officials came from a scholar-gentry class, which rose from agriculture and after government service returned to the land. Thus class distinctions between nobility and commoners were wiped out. Central harmony involved a balance on both sides."[114]

And, finally, Chen Li-fu concluded, Chinese culture is based on the virtues of inner integrity and outer courtesy, balancing patience and sincerity over against power and profit. (To quote):—

"China has its faults; we, therefore, need to adopt the good points of other cultures—natural science, industry, organizational abilities and administrative methods. Above all, we Chinese must have faith in ourselves, in our cultural illumination, and in our contribution to human welfare. We Chinese today, therefore, should give concrete development to our own culture and (thus) take the road to corporate life, survival, and progress—toward the world of the Great Commonwealth."

(SCYL, pp. 290-300)[115]

B. *Interpretations of the Classical Heritage by Contemporary Christian Thinkers*

Inasmuch as it has long been the contention of Chinese scholars and Western sinologues alike that Confucianism was not a religion but a system of ethics, the recent efforts of certain modern Chinese scholars to detect a religious note in the attitudes of Confucius are most significant. Even among non-Christian scholars reared in the Confucian School itself, there is what W. T. Chan would call a "trend toward the discovery of the religious position of Confucius," examples of which he finds in the writings of Hu Shih and Fu Ssu-nien.

Dr. Chan cites, for example, Hu Shih's essay "On the Literati" (*Shuo Ju*) in his larger *Recent Academic Writings* (*Hu Shih Lun-Hsüeh Chin-Chu,* 3-81), where he brings out the impression that Confucius, as a member of the *literati,* "realized that the ancient Yin (Shang) heritage had to be modified to suit the new culture of the Chou period (ca. 1027 B.C.-256 B.C.) in which he lived. . . . (He) followed certain Yin religious traditions but rejected the popular worship of spirits, and held . . . a rather abstract and rational concept of Heaven. Eventually, his religion became that of the Chinese *literati.*"[116]

Another recent Confucian scholar, Professor Fu Ssu-nien (1896-1950), according to Dr. Chan, has corroborated Hu Shih's findings in his *Critical Study of the Traditional Theories of Human Nature and Destiny* (*Hsing-Ming Ku-Hsün Pien-Cheng*). He found no cultural break between the Shang (Yin) and Chou (i.e., in the belief in Shang-ti or T'ien, as revealed in the oracle-bones) and believed that Confucius' dictum of 'waiting for Heaven's mandate' represented a middle ground between fatalism and moral determinism. Moreover, Fu Ssu-nien interpreted Confucius' remark, 'I do not murmur against Heaven,' as meaning that each one should bear his own responsibilities; that his statement, 'I have prayed for a long time,' indicated Confucius' belief that Heaven does intervene in human affairs and that human behavior can influence Heaven's mandates. But since the Way of Heaven was uncertain in its operation, Confucius chose to stress the human side in establishing that much-sought-after balance between Heaven and man.[117]

Even more remarkable has been the widespread interest evinced by philosophically-minded Christian leaders in the religious content of Confucius' mind. The problem of the meaning of God (*Shang-ti, T'ien, Tao,* or *Li*) in classical terminology as compared with Christian thought has, in recent years, occupied the minds of quite a number of leading Chinese Christian writers. In an article in *The Chinese Recorder* entitled "The Appeal of Christianity to the Chinese Mind" (May, 1918),[118] Professor T. C. Chao of Yenching University made this general, initial observation:—

"While the Chinese people are intensely ethical, they are to a much less degree religious. The (classical) Chinese mind thinks in terms of man, not of God . . . in terms of cosmic processes, not of the personal. . . . All persons and things have originated in and developed from the Absolute, which is *Tao* and is impersonal. So there can be no religion, if religion means fellowship between finite persons and the Infinite Person. Accordingly, enlightened Chinese have the conception that worship, religious rituals and ceremonies, are merely for social control. To them, religion is equivalent to superstition, necessary indeed, for the control of the unenlightened, but useless for themselves, who form China's intellectual aristocracy." (119)

A slightly differing point of view is cautiously expressed by Hsieh Sung-kao (Zia Zung-kao) of the Christian Literature Society, who hesitated to stigmatize Confucius as either atheist or agnostic. In his *The Confucian Civilization,* he stated his views thus:—

"Confucius declined to talk about death and the future. He evidently did not want to dwell upon discussions concerning God. . . . Now (this) fact does not prove that he was agnostic (or atheistic). He never denied the existence of God. . . . After most careful examination, we concede that the concept of God in Confucianism has a personal element, even though it does not give us distinctly a personal deity. . . . Confucius stopped when he reached the highest good. He educated his students to the highest pitch and held them up there, without attaching them to the highest person, or God." (120)

On the other hand, Hsieh Sung-kao found in that great Confucian virtue of *Jên* (human-heartedness) a close resemblance to the Christian virtue of *Love*. As he has collated from the *Analects* and translated what Confucius said about *jên,* we quote certain excerpts, which to his mind show how closely Confucius came to Jesus' and Paul's interpretation of *love*:—

"Clever conversation and a seemingly kind face seldom constitute *jên.*

He who does not live in *jên* can hardly be considered as wise.

I have never seen the man who loves *jên* hate the man without *jên.*

The man of *jên* does not worry.

The man of *jên* speaks with reticence.

The courageous, the enduring, the simple, and the modest are near to *jên.*

No mean man has ever possessed *jên.*

A man of *jên* will not beg for life at the cost of *jên,* but will risk his life for the accomplishment of *jên.*

To practice . . . reverence, generosity, sincerity, sagacity, and charitableness . . . will constitute *jên.*

If one be concentrated in *jên,* there will be no evil.

By *jên* is meant to love man." (121) *

D. Willard Lyon has further suggested: "Many Christian Chinese are now asking whether in this Confucian idea of *jên* we do not have a real counterpart of the word 'love,' with which Jesus summarized the commandments. They particularly point to the interpretation which Mo Ti gave to *jên* as being still closer to the Christian concept than the interpretation given by Mencius. With Mencius, *jên is founded on i* (*yi*),

---

* For a full discussion of the development of this concept, see W. T. Chan's article, "The Evolution of the Confucian Concept of *Jên*" in *Philosophy East and West,* Vol. IV, No. 4 (Jan. 1955), pp. 295-319.

which is a word usually translated 'right,' 'righteousness,' or 'justice.' But with Mo Ti, *jên* expresses itself in 'universal love' and finds its roots in the will of Heaven. . . . Because Heaven loves us with impartiality, we should love all men in the same manner. . . . Some Chinese Christians are, therefore, thinking of Mo Ti in much the same terms as the early Christians thought, for instance, of Isaiah. The Chinese are asking why the one may not be a means of introducing men to Christ as truly as the other was."[122]

Another of the harmonizing Christian philosophers, C. Y. Hsü, in his book entitled *The Philosophy of Confucius,* confidently asserted: "Confucius' idea of God is more or less similar to that of Christianity." His position is further set forth in the following excerpt:

"Confucius' whole thought is composed of two parts, *viz.,* the 'Way of Man' and the 'Way of Heaven,' the former . . . (being) the manifestation of the Way of Heaven. Were the Way of Man perfectly understood, the Way of Heaven would naturally be intelligible to us. . . .

Evidence to prove Confucius' belief in a personal God is not lacking in the *Classics*: when he was distressed by political disturbances . . . he used to comfort himself by saying that he was born of Heaven, and Heaven produced the virtue that was in him. He had the fullest confidence in Heaven, against which he never murmured, just as he did not grumble against men. . . .

In a word, Confucius understood God, believed in Him, and trusted Him. . . . Confucius, though he was not a religious founder, had paved the way for Christianity in China, as Plato had done in Greece. Thus the gulf between Confucian philosophy and Christian doctrine could be easily bridged, if both are understood thoroughly and interpreted properly." (123)

Not quite so hopeful was the attitude of Francis C. M. Wei, then President of Hua Chung College (formerly Boone University) in Wu-chang. In an article written in 1926 on "Making Christianity Live in China,"[124] while discussing the meaning of *ch'êng,* usually rendered 'sincerity,' he said:

"The idea may best be rendered by the English expression 'harmony with, or conformity to, Nature or the Universe.' But what is the Universe or Nature? At bottom, the Chinese conception is naturalistic, and therefore Confucian ethics has a naturalistic basis. To Christianize China is to change the very basis of its morality, to substitute a personal God, the Father of Jesus and of all men, for the impersonal, and at best pantheistic, Nature. In other words, the problem is how to give Chinese morality a new soul."

In a later, more hopeful utterance, President Wei gave the benefit of his maturer judgment in the following words:

"Is it possible to interpret Christian teachings in Chinese thought-forms?—to give expression to Christian faith in terms of Chinese culture? No, not adequately. . . .

To the Confucian School, . . . every man by his own efforts can develop to sainthood. This Pelagianism is found not only in Confucianism, . . . but also in Buddhism and Taoism. . . . This is contrary to the Christian teaching that man depends upon God, whether you emphasize the complete depravity of man or not. . . .

The attempt to interpret Christianity in terms of Chinese culture . . . is to read too much into Chinese ideas. . . . As instances, I may refer to Legge and Ross of the 19th century and Bruce and Rawlinson of the 20th. . . .

In interpreting the Christian teachings . . . in terms of another culture, the (first) important thing is . . . to enter into the spirit of that culture. . . . We search for a kindred spirit, and we find it in the Chinese ethical conception of the Universe. The world is a stage fit for moral struggle. . . . There is purpose and direction in history and in the universe. This is not necessarily Christian, but it is something Christianity would find congenial.". . . (125)

In his *The Spirit of Chinese Culture* (1947), Dr. Wei puts it thus:

"The Chinese classical Shang-ti is a deity of strict justice . . . a judge, not a father. . . . God as creator as well as ruler of the universe is new to the Chinese mind. . . . But Shang-ti is the fountain of man's moral sense. . . . Why should he not receive everything else from God?" (126)

In his 1930 dissertation on "The Idea of God in the Chinese

Classics,"[127] Dr. Hsü T'eng-hui (Benjamin Dung-hwe Zi) unquestionably brought several fresh insights to his painstaking interpretation of the ancient books. In support of his thesis that the belief of the Chinese people in the classical period was an ethical monotheism, Hsü made a careful, analytical survey of the Classics taken in three groups to show three earlier steps in the development of the idea of God, leaving a fourth group to reveal a fourth and final phase significantly different from the rest.

(1) A first step in the development of the idea of God is traced through the *Book of Poetry* (*Shih Ching*), the *Book of History* (*Shu Ching, Group I*), and the *Analects* (*Lun Yü*) as follows:

In the *Shih Ching,* God is clearly anthropomorphic, "playing the role of a house-mother, busily engaged . . . in the administration of all the affairs of . . . mankind." The Supreme Being was also indistinct in the minds of the people, who confused Him with the visible Heaven. There was uncertainty as to whether He was really a good or an unjust Being. There was, however, an early recognition of free access to God by all who might wish to address complaints directly to Him.

Group I of the *Shu Ching,* Hsü T'eng-hui finds very similar to the *Shih Ching* in its primitive outlook on the moral character of God and "entirely pervaded by the anthropomorphic conception of the Almighty Ruler."

In the *Lun Yü,* however, an atmosphere very different from the earlier books is noticed. Here "the conception of God which Confucius found in the belief of his forefathers was remoulded and . . . stripped of . . . (its) primitive elements. . . . The God of the *Analects* . . . discharges his functions in a quiet, kingly manner. He is the ultimate vindicator of morality . . . the judge . . . of human hearts and constantly holds himself in direct moral relationship with man."[128]

(2) A second stage in the development of the idea of God in the *Classics* is traced by Dr. Hsü through the *Book of Mencius* (the *Mêng-tzu*) and the *Book of History* (*Shu Ching,* Group II) :—

In Mencius, the idea of God is more fully developed. For him, Shang-ti (God) is still the Supreme Ruler, but does not speak directly to the person concerned. Heaven gives the imperial throne to a virtuous person through the intervention of human agencies. Heaven's will, then, is indicated by the emperor's personal conduct of affairs (*The Mêng-tzu,* V, 1, v.). "For Mencius, in other words, the sentiment of the people is a representation of the will of Heaven."

"At this stage, God is not so much a busy house-mother who attends to all affairs personally, but rather the chief of a great family assuming the dignity of his position and causing his will to be executed through the members of his family. Here we have the beginning of the conception of the divinity of the popular will."

In Group II of the *Shu Ching* (*Book of History*) dated about the same time as Mencius, Hsü T'eng-hui sees instances where rebellion rises in the name of Heaven to destroy or remove wicked rulers. Men were "fully conscious of (having) a divine mission to execute for the good of the people" . . . "It was Heaven who punished the evil and rewarded the worthy . . . but . . . it was through men that these events came about."[129]

(3) A third step, or climax, in this development of the idea of God is found by Dr. Hsü in Group III of the *Shu Ching*. Here God transcends all previously described capacities and becomes . . . "the moral, political, and religious director . . . of a well-established and systematically organized hierarchy which embraces within its scope the entire, then known universe. . . . He is the head of heads . . . sitting on the loftiest throne of glory and power (directing) . . . the vast machinery of human government in systematic fashion, through the activities of its members, acting under orders transmitted from the uppermost rank downward. . . . The ever-consistent will of Heaven is to bring about righteousness, peace, and goodwill here below. . . ."[130]

(4) There are, however, three late *Classics*—the *Doctrine of the Mean* (*Chung Yung*), the *Book of Rites* (*Li Chi*), and the *Book of Changes* (*Yi Ching*), products of the close of the

"Contending States Period" and beginning of the Han dynasty —in which, as Hsü T'eng-hui sees it, the idea of God did not conform to the patterns just outlined. Whereas "the God of the main stream of development . . . was practical, (objectively) definable, and comprehensible to the ordinary intellect, the God of this particular branch (of the *Classics*) may be characterized . . . as mystical, (subjectively) indefinable, and known only to immediate comprehension . . . or insight."

"Whence comes this mystical element?" Hsü asks, and then proceeds to show how the philosophy of Taoism as represented in the *Tao Tê Ching* (*The Lao-tzu*) had become dominant in the Ch'in period (221-207 B.C.). "It is due to this influence," he says, "that the God of these three particular *Classics* bears the stamp of (Taoist) mysticism . . . and this deviates from the main stream of development."[131]

To show Taoist influence in the *Chung Yung* (*Doctrine of the Mean*) (which is also Chapter 31 of the *Li Chi*), Hsü T'eng-hui quotes:

> "Let the states of equilibrium and harmony exist in perfection, and the happy order will prevail throughout heaven and earth and all things will be nourished and flourish." (132)
> "Sincerity is the way of Heaven. The attainment of sincerity is he who, without an effort, hits what is right." (133)

"It is no wonder," he adds, "that the God of the *Chung Yung* maintains such an . . . uncertain status, drifting from the Supreme Being of (the old) religion to the mysterious God of (the new) mysticism."

As for the rest of the *Li Chi* (*Book of Rites*), Hsü finds it much like the *Chung Yung*, although in parts of it God appears to be vividly personal. "God is Supreme Ruler of all things both animate and inanimate, and all the other deities are subordinate and subservient to Him. He is the source of all things and He is a Being of absolute goodness. He gives blessings but He also punishes those who do not walk according to His will. He accepts the sacrifice (only) of the Son of Heaven."[134]

"In the *Yi Ching* (*Book of Changes*)," so Hsü T'eng-hui discovers, "the stamp of Taoism upon the idea of God is most distinct. . . . By whatever name He is called in the *Yi Ching* (*T'ien, Ti, Shên, T'ai Chi,* or *Tao*), He is the One Principle, the Final Cause, the Ultimate Reality . . . from whom all phenomena in the universe come forth and in whom all things live, move and have their being. He works without ceasing; harmony with his working will lead one to goodness, righteousness, and prosperity. Yet, He is beyond the comprehension of (the) ordinary intellect, for He is spirit-like, inscrutable, unfathomable, vague, deep, mysterious."

"Does not this sound like a description of the *Tao* in the *Tao Tê Ching?*" remarks Hsü T'eng-hui. In contrast to the God of the *Shih Ching* or the *Shu Ching,* "who was conceived by the ordinary intellect in the fashion of an earthly ruler, sitting on a throne, wielding the mighty sceptre of his sway," (the God of the *Yi Ching* is) "rather a God within the soul of man who attains to . . . a knowledge of Him chiefly through the channel of contemplative meditation of and mystical union with Him."[135]

That the interpretations given by Hsü T'eng-hui would be acceptable to other Christian scholars, like Francis Wei or T. C. Chao, is a matter of some doubt, especially in the light of observations made by Francis Wei, in the lecture referred to above, on the difficulty of making correct translations. Interpreting the *Classics* would, in his opinion, be extremely hard, for the reason that "the inaccuracy (or indefiniteness) of some of the Chinese terms is well known. The character *tien* (*T'ien*), usually translated into English as 'Heaven' with a capital H, may mean one of several things. The Chinese language is a living language and . . . Chinese literature has a long history. Unless the word is put in its proper context, and unless we know the background of the writer who uses it, we can make the term mean almost anything, at least the thing we intend it to mean. . . ."

"By a generous interpretation of some of the terms in the Chinese language," Dr. Wei continues, "and by reading, perhaps unconsciously, some of our own ideas into some of the passages in Chinese philosophical and religious literature, we can make Chinese culture tell our own story. This is especially true when we translate Chinese into another language, particularly into one of the European languages. . . . The essential thing is to get into the spirit of the term or the passage, *die Durchsichtigkeit des Ganzen,* as the German puts it, and this can be done only by entering into the spirit of the author."[136]

From the above, it would appear that Hsü T'eng-hui very possibly was reading new (and modern Christian) meanings into the terms *T'ien* and *Shang-ti* in the *Classics* which he analyzed.

C. *Revaluations of their Classical Buddhist Heritage by Crusading Buddhist Idealists*

Throughout the three-century period immediately preceding the Republic, Buddhist philosophy had stressed the teachings of the T'ien-T'ai and Hua-Yen Schools: more specifically concentrating on two dogmas; namely, the inherent oneness of noumenon and phenomenon, and a belief that every reality (*dharma,* or element of existence) is a product of mind, which embodies the totality of truth expressed in the concept *Chen Ju* or 'Thusness.' Since humans possess an innate share of this Absolute (the Supreme Buddha), they may, therefore, confidently hope to become Buddhas.[137] While holding these metaphysical concepts in theory, the majority of Buddhists, in actual religious practice, had, nevertheless, followed closely the Pure Land School's faith in the power of Another or the Ch'an School's meditative intuition to solve the pressing problem of gaining salvation to 'eternal life.'

For those who adhered to the Pure Land School of Pietism, faith in the power of Another became all important. They found, therefore, great inspiration in *The Awakening of Faith* (*Ch'i Hsin Lun,* a treatise ascribed to Aśvaghoṣa) because of its strong emphasis upon salvation by faith. While re-stating the basic Buddhist belief in 'Thusness' as Cosmic Mind and as a synthesis of noumenon and phenomenon, it called for a perfection of faith that would create a comprehensive understanding of truth; a stock of meritorious virtue; and a compassionate desire to save others. The stepping-stones to such a faith would be a firm belief and total trust in the 'Three Refuges,' or Precious Ones: the *Buddha* (Thusness), the *Dharma* (Universal Law), and the *Sangha* (Order of Monks).[138]

During the early years of the Republic, however, China's younger Buddhist thinkers became so filled with intellectual fervor that blind faith without intellectual content seemed to them foolishness. They rejected *The Awakening of Faith* and, under the leadership of men like Ou-Yang Ching-wu, turned back to the philosophy of the *Wei Shih,* or Idealistic School.[139]

The Influence of Ou-Yang Ching-wu:—

Interest in idealism had waned during the latter years of the Ch'ing (Manchu) dynasty, until Yang Wên-hui (1837-1911) returned from a sojourn in Japan in 1880, bringing with him the monumental *Notes On The Completion of the Idealistic Doctrine* (*Ch'êng Wei-Shih Lun Shu-Chi*) by K'uei-chi (A.D. 632-682), a pupil of Hsüan-tsang. The publication of this work in 1914 attracted the attention of Ou-Yang Ching-wu (1871-1943), founder of the Institute of Inner Learning in Nanking, because these 'Notes' gave him the interpretations he needed to combat the influence of *The Awakening of Faith,* as sponsored by the T'ien-T'ai and Hua-Yen Schools.

Championing the *Wei Shih* (Mere Ideation) School, Ou-Yang declared any teaching that the phenomenal world was caused by the activity of Thusness-when-aroused to be unacceptable, inasmuch as it made a monism of the universe. On the contrary, he asserted, the universe is neither monistic nor dualistic, but pluralistic, inasmuch as causation takes place in the *ālaya*-consciousness of each individual, thereby creating the ephemeral world of multiplicity. In a word, for Ou-Yang and his group, "Thusness has nothing at all to do with causation."[140]

With this as a premise, Ou-Yang moved on to affirm that, although the *ālaya*-consciousness contains impure 'seeds' (elements derived from past *Karma*), which appear as 'dharma-characters' or 'manifestations' in the phenomenal world, yet there are also pure seeds which may be cultivated to the point of Enlightenment. Then it is that all dharma-characters become illusory and the *ālaya*-consciousness itself is transcended, as the mind enters into the Realm of True Dharma-Nature or Thusness. This doctrine gave an acceptable metaphysical basis for the new emphasis on individual freedom that was so dear to the hearts and minds of China's young patriots in the early days of the Republic.[141]

The Influence of Abbot T'ai Hsü:—

A harmonizing influence is seen in the thinking of T'ai Hsü Fa-Shih* (1889-1947), who, in 1921, had settled in Wuchang to teach in a newly established Buddhist Academy, where he became the officially recognized spokesman for liberal Chinese Buddhists. Abbot T'ai Hsü felt that Ou-Yang Ching-wu's violent attack on *The Awakening of Faith* had been due to a misunderstanding of Thusness as 'a trinity of reality, character, and function' where Thusness is absolutely transcendental. Holding Thusness to be both transcendental and immanent, T'ai Hsü differed from Ou-Yang by appealing to the principle of relativity to explain the presence in ideation of such dichotomies as being and non-being, reality and illusion, cause and effect, or life and death. In other words, by synthesizing dharma-nature and dharma-character, he declared his conviction of the oneness of reality and function—of Thusness and the phenomenal world.

* *Fa-Shih* means "Explainer of the Law."

"In this way," as Wing-tsit Chan has interpreted him, "T'ai Hsü not only synthesizes dharma-nature and dharma-character but also synthesizes Wei-Shih and Hua-Yen. This synthesis makes T'ai Hsü's system different from the traditional Wei-Shih philosophy in a very important way."[142]. . . "To T'ai Hsü, 'Mere Ideation' refers to the origination and dharma-character refers to products. One is cause and the other is effect. They are merely two phases of the same process and should not be too sharply divided. T'ai Hsü does not distinguish Idealism and Dharma-Character as two different schools, as does Ou-Yang. . . . This is the reason why he chose to call his system 'Dharma-Character Idealism.' "[143]

To understand the growth in T'ai Hsü's thought while he was developing this Dharma-Character Idealism, we must remember that for more than a decade he had been devoting himself to a sincere quest for a re-alignment of old Buddhist *Classics* with the trends of modern thought under the impact of the West. First trained under Ch'an monks at the T'ien-Tung Monastery (east of Ningpo) and in the monasteries at T'ien-T'ai Shan (south of Ningpo), T'ai Hsü had gone to Nanking (about 1910) to help Yang Wên-hui* organize his Society for Buddhist Research. In 1912, they had organized the Chinese Buddhist Association with headquarters at Nanking and branches in other centers, and T'ai Hsü had begun writing historical and critical articles for its *Monthly Review*.

Feeling the need, however, for further study, in the following year T'ai Hsü had gone to the sacred Buddhist island of Puto (in the Chusan Archipelago off the coast of Chekiang), where he spent nearly four years in seclusion, studying Buddhist and foreign philosophies (the latter in translation). At the same time, he produced several writings on current topics relating to education, evolution, and philosophy. In 1918, he had set off on a tour of Formosa and Japan and on his return had begun to lecture in Peking, Wuchang, and Canton, to arouse interest in Buddhism.

---

* Also referred to as Yang Jên-shên.

Settling finally in Wuchang in 1921, T'ai Hsü organized a new Buddhist Philosophical Society and began publishing *The Voice of the Tide* (*Hai Ch'ao Yin*), a magazine for the dissemination of Buddhist ideas among the laity.[144] By this time, therefore, his mind was ripe for sharing with other members of the Sangha not only his convictions on the truth of the Buddhist Way but also his understanding of the relation of current philosophical thought to scientific method.

Soon thereafter, at a large Buddhist Conference held in West Valley, Kuling, in 1923, which attracted delegates from all over China, as well as from Japan, India, and Thailand, T'ai Hsü gave a series of lectures that were well received.*

In them he first defined *Chen Ju* as "the undefinable Absolute Reality, the intangible emptiness, the universal unity and source of all things without beginning or end." The world as we know it has evolved from non-being in a natural process and moves toward Universal Being. Since Reality is intangible, therefore, the tangible, visible Universe is unreal. Men and things are a dream, yet there is an underlying unity in everything, as the sea underlies the individual waves.

Chen Ju, however, as conceived by T'ai Hsü, precludes the idea of individual personality. This concept is the mother of all unrest, strife, and desire; so there is no salvation from these until we get rid of the delusion of personality. There can be no such thing as individual personality because heaven and earth and all things are Unity. We, being one with all living and inanimate things, are on absolute equality as parts of the great Reality. So *Chen Ju* cannot be thought of as having

---

* An interesting sidelight on this gathering of Oriental Buddhists is found in the late Karl Ludwig Reichelt's report of it in *The Chinese Recorder* (Shanghai, Nov., 1923). In an article entitled "A Conference of Chinese Buddhist Leaders," the well-known Director of the Mission to Buddhists at Tao Fêng Shan (in the hills near Kowloon, Hong Kong) tells how he was invited by T'ai Hsü Fa-Shih to lecture to the hundred or more monks assembled at Ta Ling Ssŭ (in West Valley, Kuling) on "The Relation of Christianity to Buddhism." He responded with an interpretation of "The Word" (Logos) in John 1:1-18 (which in Chinese is translated "*Tao*"). After he had finished, T'ai Hsü thanked him saying, "Jesus Christ is the incarnated *Tao*. This I now understand. But for us the chief thing is that *Tao* can also be incarnated in us."

personality. It is more of an impersonal Nature, sometimes called Mind (Hsin). As the summation of all Buddhas, it is the True Essence into whose Universal Being we all are to be re-absorbed.

At this point, T'ai Hsü found it necessary to distinguish the impersonal *Chen Ju* from the personal *Ju Lai* (*Fo*) in this way, as Frank R. Millican has pointed out:—[145] (In brief) "*Ju* (Sameness) means that . . . definite quality . . . in any . . . thing or event, which never . . . changes. . . . Because of the changelessness of this quality, *Ju* is also *Chen* (Truth). . . . In short, that quality of changelessness or sameness in all things, places, and events, is given the name *Chen Ju* (Thusness)."

"*Ju Lai* is another name for Buddha (Šākyamuni) : He who, one with this true *Ju,* has already appeared (*Lai*) amidst things, ceaselessly revolving according to principle, is called *Ju Lai.* (Again), He who continually comes (*lai*) into the revolving feelings and senses (of men) and, through testimony to the True Sameness (*Ju*), frees them from the superstition (illusion) which is their cause is called *Ju-Lai.* In the first appearance, *Ju-Lai* is spoken of as 'the true Buddha'; in the second, as 'the transforming Buddha.'"[146] To this, T'ai Hsü would add that *Chen Ju* is a kind of ever-flowing and never-resting consciousness filling all things just as ether fills all space. . . . In other words, Reality may be taken as Truth, Goodness, and Beauty, but if taken as Life and Power of Motion it is called Buddha. As the Christians' God is revealed in Jesus of Nazareth, so in Buddhism *Chen Ju* has been manifested in Šākyamuni (Gautama), or as Amitābha (*O-Mi-T'o Fo),* and will appear in the future as the Buddhist Messiah—Maitreya (*Mi-Lê*-Fo*).[147]

Passing on from the metaphysical to the soteriological aspects of Buddhist teachings, T'ai Hsü reminded his hearers that by following Śākyamuni, they and all men might, like him, become Buddhas. As the *Sangha* is a collective unity of *some* of his true disciples, *Chen Ju* may be taken as the col-

* Written and pronounced variously as *Lê, Lei,* or *Lo.*

lective unity of *all* true disciples. As Buddhist cenobites they had all vowed to take refuge in the Three Precious Ones: the *Buddha (Fo-pao* or Buddha-Body), the *Dharma* (*Fa-pao,* or Law-Body), and the *Sangha* (*Seng-pao,* or Body of Monks).* Mahāyānists, however, had gradually put the Dharma first and said that Buddha was the emanation of its creative energy and the Sangha was the organized universe in its final, perfected state. Therefore, T'ai Hsü stressed the importance of understanding and giving full obedience to the Buddhist Dharma (Law), interpreting it as the law of cause and effect running through all existence. Our future, he said, is determined by our own good or bad life. Knowledge of sure retribution should deter evil-doers. As each man determines his own destiny, anyone who lives an upright, honest life can hope to be reborn into a higher order, but everyone should give as much time as possible to quiet meditation.[148]

Up to this point, T'ai Hsü had confined himself to orthodox Buddhist reasoning on which both Ch'an and Wei-Shih monks could pretty well agree. Then he launched into an exposition of the newest trend his mind had taken as a result of his studies of Western thought—a trend we shall call 'critical harmonization.' He revealed how his mind had been attracted toward Western science, not so much to the physical sciences as to Western psychology. Here his harmonizing mind found no conflict with Buddhist thought and he reminded his hearers that the Buddhist Hall of Meditation could be their laboratory for an advanced type of scientific research, using as materials the things of their environment presented to the mind through their bodily senses.

While rejecting any 'Thing-in-Itself' as beyond possible human knowledge, he, nevertheless, believed anyone could have direct experience of the universe through a proper psychological approach. While in his psychology he denied soul as a distinct entity, yet he favored the concept of "a universe

---

* Probably reflecting early Brāhmanism with its Trimūrti:—Brahma, Vishnu, and Śiva.

radiating outward from a self-acting soul or mind-center." To such a universe, the Buddhist could move beyond the science based on the senses into a higher study of thought-processes and still higher into "the more profound science of direct, intuitive acquaintance or enlightenment."

In passing, the learned Abbot intimated that Confucianism was on the right track as far as it went in its emphasis on right conduct and making the best possible adjustment to environment, but was only in the kindergarten stage as compared with Buddhist philosophical thought. The philosophy he (T'ai Hsü) advocated must be based on a psychological rather than a speculative approach. It would normally move from a direct, conscious experience of environmental objects into an understanding of the law of growth, change, and decay operating in the environment. Finally, one would see beyond the changing phenomena of existence and become conscious of and be in harmony with that Ultimate Reality in which are no distinctions of this or that, good or evil, self or non-self. This final stage would indeed be salvation—the goal of life. This he called the New (Agnostic) Idealism.[149]

These ideas were clearly set forth in book-form about 1925 under the title of *Jên-shêng-kuan ti k'o-hsüeh* (*A Scientific Philosophy of Life*), which Millican reviewed in *The Chinese Recorder* in an article entitled "Buddhism in the Light of Modern Thought as Interpreted by the Monk T'ai Hsü."[150] In this period, T'ai Hsü Fa-Shih was at the peak of his career.* Without a doubt, he had become the most widely accepted modern interpreter of Buddhist philosophy, at least from the Chinese point of view.

After serving as Chinese Buddhism's chief delegate and spokesman at a Buddhist Conference in Japan in 1925, T'ai Hsü accepted the invitation of the German Ambassador to lecture at the German Academy of Oriental Research in Berlin.

---

* The writer recalls the standing ovation given (in the spring of 1926) to T'ai Hsü Fa-Shih by the students of Hangchow (Christian) University at the close of his memorable address to their Student Assembly on "The Harmonies of Buddhist and Christian Thought."

He lectured also in Frankfurt, Paris, London and New York.[151] From an English translation of these lectures made by "Kuen-Lun" and published in Paris in 1928,[152] we glean a few of the salient points of his more fully developed Dharma-Character Idealism as he presented it to Western audiences.

In the introduction to his *T'ai Hsü: Lectures in Buddhism,* T'ai Hsü gave a condensed definition of Buddhist philosophy, taken from such Mahāyāna scriptures as the *Hua-Yen Ching* and the *Fa-Hua Ching,* as follows:

"The essence of the Buddhist doctrine consists in an eternal, unlimited, and absolute conception of the spiritual and material phenomena of the Universe. . . . It considers that the principles underlying all phenomena are the same as those underlying the human personality, which is the 'spiritual body' of substance. This teaching should be brought to all (men), who have the possibility in them of some day becoming Buddha and who, by their perfectly enlightened conscience are able to bring about the unity of substance and create such 'spiritual bodies'." (153)

After giving a lengthy statement of the historical background of the Buddhist faith, T'ai Hsü stated his belief that Buddhist metaphysics could answer questions which Western Science and Western Philosophy could not, and then launched into an elucidation of general Buddhist principles, followed by discussion of particular phases of Buddhist belief.

1. *General Principles of Chinese Mahāyāna Buddhism:—*

(A) *The Universe and Its Laws.*

"Buddhist doctrine teaches that the universe is endless, incalculable, and has never had a beginning. . . . The atoms which go to compose it have always existed, whether manifested or not, and all of them contain the possibilities of conscious life. . . . All that exists is bound up with the law of cause and effect, which is the fundamental law of life. . .

"The Universe is a reservoir of forces constantly manifesting themselves through this chain of cause and effect, and their variations are infinite. . . .

"The elements that compose the life of the body are in course of time decomposed, until they again enter into the composition of another form, and so on *ad infinitum*. . . . Thus we see how life is continuous not only for the body, but also for the spirit. . . . The Buddhist doctrine, therefore, lies in its conception of the unity of existence and the continuity of life. . . ."

(B) *The Oneness of Organic Life.*

"All animals evolve by degrees, until eventually they reach the level of human consciousness. . . . It is only by following the Buddhist doctrine that humanity can remain on the higher plane of existence. . . . Since often human souls are re-incarnated in animal forms, we should show compassion for all living things.". . .

(C) *Man Evolves Upward Toward Buddhahood.*

"The Buddhist doctrine springs from the heart of life itself, and by its union of Science and Morality throws light on the deepest truths of existence, and guides and assists us in our evolution. . . . By a gradual . . . development of the inner life, we come to control ourselves, until, at last, we enter on the steep and rocky way that leads to Nirvāṇa. . . ."

"According to the teaching of the Buddha, we are all destined to become Buddhas, . . . and our one object in life should be to reach this perfect enlightenment, by avoiding the stormy oceans of passion and desire. . . . First of all, we have to develop moral character, detach ourselves from the denser bodies of desire and learn to open the inner eye of the mind. . . ."

T'ai Hsü then turned to more particular topics:—e.g.

2. *On Science, Philosophy, and Buddhism:—*

In this chapter, T'ai Hsü makes clear that what Science has revealed, Buddhism knew twenty-five centuries ago . . . The disciple will seek the wisdom of Buddha by the five ways of enlightenment—language, art, logic, philosophy, and by the comparative methods of science. . . .

"When we go beyond these methods we find that Science is unable to grasp the reality of the Buddhist doctrine. . . . For this, (one) must have attained the wisdom of Buddha himself; it is not, however, by the use of Science or Logic that we can expect to acquire such wisdom. Science, therefore, is only a stepping-stone in such matters."

T'ai Hsü then went on to express the belief that the different European systems of philosophy had failed to register much progress in real knowledge of the "noumena of the Universe" because of inability to grasp the doctrine of the "Ego and the Law."

"Philosophy," he said, "is derived from false perceptions. . . . All these theories of mind, matter, and energy are based upon law, which is erroneously supposed to be part of the noumenon itself. . . . In the Buddhist doctrine, the truth about the noumena is made self-evident, and all error is eliminated from the very start. . . .
"By prolonged meditation, by intelligence and wisdom, a sudden awakening may be brought about which in the end will lead to an enlightened understanding of the Creation. Such an entrance into the realms of the Buddha would be a revelation for the philosopher, who would come to see that Buddhism is a clear perception of things freed from all illusion.". . . (In short):—
"If life . . . were founded on the six *pāramitās*—the six perfect virtues of the Bodhisattvas—we then might hope to enter into the pure realms of Buddha and emerge from the chaos of fire and brimstone into which we have fallen. . . ."

The topic of T'ai Hsü's next lecture was

3. *The Union of Eternal Truth, Conduct, and Power:—*

T'ai Hsü's discussion of the possibility of arriving at an understanding of Eternal Truth is epitomized in his statement that the 'holy one' (or Bodhisattva)* has progressed far beyond the knowledge of the scientist . . . that, although his (Mahāyāna) state of knowledge is still partial, he has "emerged from contact with the world and entered the Buddhist dharma," where he can (ultimately) attain unto the fullest truth known to the Fully Conscious One (Buddha) himself. (To quote):—

"Some unite knowledge and conduct, but are without power; others have power and good conduct but lack knowledge and wisdom. . . . Buddha is the embodiment of that wisdom whereby we may hope to reach the realm of 'supreme, absolute, and universal knowledge' . . . Since Buddha is the incarnation of Great Mercy, his conduct must be virtuous, and his influence strong enough to lead all sentient beings. These three qualities: knowledge, conduct, and power, (therefore), cannot be united by ordinary persons, but only by the Enlightened and Conscious One, that is, by Buddha."

T'ai Hsü concluded his discourse by saying that where for most people there is only a cycle of life, moving through four stages of achievement, rest, destruction, and emptiness, the Buddhist Bodhisattvas . . . by self-discipline, have attained a state of real evolution whereby they become detached from the mundane sphere and enter upon "a state of Eternity which is free from all limits . . . disentangled from the world." [154]

In 1938, T'ai Hsü published his *Dharma-Character Idealistic Philosophy (Fa-Hsiang Wei-Shih Hsüeh),* in which he maintained (as had Ou-Yang Ching-wu) that all *dharmas* (objects) manifested in ideation . . . are devoid of self-nature, being merely 'aggregates conditioned by many causes.'. . . But in an effort to avoid one-sidedness, . . . he attempted to combine Western subjective idealism (which reduces reality to individual consciousness) and Western objective idealism (which recognizes a Universal Mind), by holding that transformations occurring in the 'eight consciousnesses' may be either particulars or universals.[155]

---

* A Bodhisattva is a human being who has taken the vow to enter upon and follow the Way to becoming a Buddha.

Again, in 1940, in *The True Realism (Chen Hsien-Shih Lun),* T'ai Hsü summed it all up by saying that anyone who wishes to become a true Follower of the Way must follow Buddha as an example of one who attained illumination—not worship him as a Creator-God. One has only to follow the true essence of his own mind to find perfect illumination:—an illumination that will involve an understanding of the origin of being in consciousness, and of the eternal flux of all being; the total negation of self; as well as the total denial of the objective existence of the universe. He then went on to show how one may achieve this state of illumination by developing self-control, by mental concentration, and by achieving knowledge through instruction.[156]

As Neo-Buddhism's greatest theoretician, T'ai Hsü sought to harmonize all modern scientific and philosophical views, including Einstein's Theory of Relativity, as well as the rival T'ien-T'ai and Hua-Yen points of view—to synthesize them in alignment with the thinking of the Wei-Shih School of Chinese Buddhism. Of all this, W. T. Chan makes the final comment: "In spite of all his efforts at synthesis, . . . (T'ai Hsü) . . . is not free from philosophical denominationalism. This is the reason why Hu Shih condemns T'ai Hsü's activities as a 'stubborn effort to outlive historical usefulness.' "[157]

D. *Revaluations of Confucianism by Outstanding Confucian Philosophers*

(1) *The Development of Idealistic Neo-Confucianism* (Lu-Wang School)

Liang Shu-min:—

In 1921, Liang Shu-min attracted wide attention by his lectures on *The Civilizations of the Orient and Occident and Their Philosophies (Tung Hsi Wên-Hua Chi Ch'i Chê-*

Hsüeh),* in which he insisted that the ancient Confucian philosophy—(i.e., of Reason as the principle of existence and of Change as the principle of production and reproduction) —was entirely suited to modern life. Brière suggests that he may have been influenced by Liang Ch'i-ch'ao's *Recollections of a Trip to Europe,* which had criticized the failures of Western science as "inhuman" and over-mechanized.[158]

At first, Liang Shu-min had been a Buddhist ascetic and vegetarian, but later, after he had turned to Confucianism, he married and began to eat meat. He pointed out that material environment had a certain relation to consciousness, but couldn't say that it was a deciding factor. Differences in culture, he felt, were due to subjective attitudes to life and could not be explained by material differences. In his lectures he stressed the saner Chinese ideal of the Middle Way—the harmonizing of passions—over against the Western excessive satisfaction of desire and the excessive suppression of desires by the Hindu philosophers. In this he was turning back to Wang Yang-ming in an effort to purge materialism of its utilitarianism.[159]

Feeling that Hu Shih and others had gone completely overboard into a welter of European or Western ideas, Liang felt it his duty to make an adequate re-statement of China's own cultural contribution. His seven main "Articles of Faith" may here be summarized as follows:**

(a) The Chinese cultural attitude is one of adjustment to circumstance, of harmony with and enjoyment of Nature, and of accommodation to authority. (To quote):—(***)

> "The thought of the Chinese is to do one's duty, be content, reduce desires, and order one's life, without any thought of stimulating material enjoyment (enrichment); at the same time without the Indian idea of repressing desires (the celibacy and poverty of Buddhist and Taoist monks being an imitation of

---

* Published in book-form in Shanghai, 1922 and 1926.

** Following Andrew Tod Roy's paraphrasing (condensed). (160)

*** Using one paragraph from Warren H. Stuart's translation. (161)

Indian customs, not originally Chinese). Whatever the environment, the Chinese can be content, and accept it quietly, without necessarily trying to change conditions. . . ."

"Where Indian and Western philosophies discussed the nature of being or the problem of substance, Chinese philosophers have thought of the universe in terms of ceaseless flux (*pien hua*), not so much of any substance, or entity, or being (at rest). They have used abstract 'ideational flavors' caught by intuition, rather than fixed concepts rationally arrived at.

"Taking the *Book of Changes (Chou I,* as he called it) as the basis of his theory of change, with its central idea of *'blending and adjustment' (t'iao ho),* Liang felt that Chinese metaphysics, in thinking of all phenomena as relative by reason of the mutual opposition and interpenetration of dualistic forces, was very close to Einstein's theory of relativity." (162)

(b) The Confucian philosophy of life grew out of *this root idea of blended change.* . . . Since life is ever on the move, *it is unpredictable, with no arbitrary rules.* . . . The way of the universe is one of reconciliation and compromise, in which *there is no place for the absolute,* the extreme, or the prejudiced. . . . Therefore, one could not follow Mo Tzu's law of universal love, as being too fixed, not resilient or discriminating enough. (163)

(c) (We do well to follow) Confucius (who) placed complete trust in *intuition,* saying that man will find no external signposts for what is right. If he proceeds without weighing advantage . . . then everything will work out all right. . . . This . . . he summed up in *jên* (humaneness, or the sensitivity of intuition), saying, "When reason enters, it becomes calculating for selfish ends and, therefore, will be less humane than *jên.*" (164)

(d) Confucius believed in *the cultivation of the inner life* in order to have one's normal, regular routine of living to be in accordance with the universe's own changes. . . . Confucius was, therefore, non-utilitarian, (lacking any calculating) desire for profit . . . Calculation started with the idea of making certain of what was ahead, (but) certainly lost the equilibrium of the Mean." (165)

(e) Conversely, the 'princely way' (*Wang Tao*) is entirely disinterested. Confucius' joy in living came from within, was not attached (by emotion) to any object. Nor did he worry about *T'ien ming* (the Will of Heaven as a fixed fate), but took environmental circumstances as *the opportunity offered by Nature for his self-realization.* (166)

(f) Confucius held . . . religion (to be) summed up in filial and fraternal affection, combined with etiquette (*li*) and music (*yüeh*) —all giving expression to emotions, which are the basis of *jên* (humaneness). . . .

By its emphases, Confucianism had the effects of religion without being a religion itself. . . . Through sacrifices to ancestors, men's emotions were linked to the past and their desires linked to the future, thus giving life's unstable existence more weight, with the flavor of satisfying continuity. (167)

(g) (Finally), Liang called attention to the need for reflective thinking upon the experience to which intuition was adapting itself. . . . (He) reminded his readers that any adaptation to circumstances must be positive, not negative; (it must be done) with resoluteness, giving expression to action from 'tremendous resources of inner strength' rather than any supine yielding to external forces. . . .

"Any renaissance movement," Liang said, "must represent the advancing revival of China's own distinctive (Confucian) way of life." (168)

"(These and) similar ideas find an echo in the writings of Chen Li-fu," comments Andrew T. Roy. "They represent a consistent interpretation in the tradition of the Wang Yang-ming intuitional school." While warmly accepting the theories of the Lu-Wang School and agreeing that we can understand Reason and Change only as we possess *jên,* at the same time Liang Shu-min felt that as *jên* was both the principle and the spring of action, it was incumbent upon him to leave his chosen field of teaching and pioneer in the reconstruction of rural economic life as a prelude to political reform. Without an economic plan, he argued, there is no use to talk politics. As Ho Lin has added: "Although heartily approving the benefits of Western science and democracy, Liang Shu-min nevertheless reverted to Confucian sensitivity to the spiritual values for the energizing core of his welfare activities. . . ."[169]

The results of Liang Shu-min's economic pioneering have been described in his two (privately published) reports: *Rural*

Reconstruction in Tsouping, Shantung (December, 1935) and *Five Years of Rural Work in Tsouping* (December, 1936).[170] A decade later, in 1947, Liang Shu-min's voice was again heard reiterating the age-old Confucian thesis that political and social problems would find their solution only insofar as personal cultural problems were finding adequate solution.[171]

Ma I-fu:–

Less influenced by the West and for that very reason perhaps winning wider acclaim in the revival of Idealistic Confucianism, was Ma I-fu, learned scholar and poet of the first rank, who before World War II was living in quiet retirement at West Lake, Hangchow. Steeped in ancient, classical lore and renowned as an exponent of traditional Chinese culture, he was best known for his *Conversations at T'ai Ho (T'ai-Ho Hui-Yü),* his *Conversations at I-Shan (I-Shan Hui-Yü),* and his *General Meaning of the Four Books (Ssu-Shu Ta-I),* in which latter he expounds the *Analects, Great Learning, Doctrine of the Mean,* and *Mencius* in a synthesizing treatise.[172]

In these writings, Ma I-fu expressed a confident belief that the teaching of poetry, etiquette, common knowledge, music, the *Yi Ching* and the *Ch'un Ch'iu* constituted an amply complete curriculum for modern youth. While admitting that a little Western knowledge might be included in these "Six Arts," he insisted that they summed up the three basic values of truth, goodness, and beauty. Etiquette and music belong to 'beauty;' poetry and common knowledge belong to 'goodness'; while the *Yi Ching* and *Ch'un Ch'iu* belong to 'truth.' These are not to be estimated materially but spiritually, as stemming from the heart, for all true civilization streams from the heart; if the heart doesn't die, civilization will not die.[173]

Hsiung Shih-li:–

In his *Contemporary Chinese Philosophy,* Professor Ho Lin has traced the revival of Lu-Wang Idealism in the twentieth century from K'ang Yu-wei through his pupil T'an Ssu-t'ung, and thence through Chang T'ai-yen, Ou-Yang Ching-wu, Liang Shu-min, and Ma I-fu to Hsiung Shih-li. The close connection of this movement with contemporary Buddhist trends is seen in the fact that Hsiung Shih-li (ca. 1883–) became a brilliant scholar under Liang Ch'i-ch'ao in the Institute for Inner Learning (*Nei-Hsüeh Yüan*) at Nanking and ultimately succeeded Ou-Yang Ching-wu as its president.[174]

Despite his strong Buddhist leanings, Hsiung Shih-li may still be included among those who have contributed to the development of Idealistic Neo-Confucianism in the present age. His *New Exposition of Pure Idea (Hsin Wei-Shih Lun)** (1944), discloses his main theses in which he attempted a cosmic philosophy by adding Buddhist concepts to Lu-Wang idealism, under the certain influence of Henri Bergson. Guided by Wing-tsit Chan's recapitulation,[175] we may present Hsiung's philosophy in six paragraphs, as follows:—

(1) The Great Unchanging Reality manifests itself in a running current of countless phenomena which is not illusory (as Buddhists would say). By an interdependent, alternating contraction and expansion, the universe differentiates the One into the Many, withal continuously opposing any concretion that would resist Reality's own self-nature of change.

(2) Contraction is the congealing operation that produces apparently concrete objects of matter ever under the directing activity of 'expansion' or mind. Thereby, this universal flux of seemingly contradictory tensions becomes an orderly, constant transformation rather than a static equilibrium of interacting forces.

(3) Reality, then, is function or process, never completely passive but ever producing and reproducing a harmonious synthesis of Heaven, Earth, and Man, recognized by all Confucian men of *jên* from Confucius down to Wang Yang-ming.

(4) By stating that phenomenon (matter) is a product of noumenon (mind), having independent existence, Hsiung exhibited considerable agreement with Buddhist idealism. On the other hand,

---

* Published by The Commercial Press, Ltd., Shanghai, 1947. Reviewed by Clarence H. Hamilton in *Far-Eastern Quarterly,* Vol. 9, No. 2, February, 1950.

he rejected the theory of causation by 'perfumed seeds' upheld by Ou-Yang Ching-wu and T'ai Hsü Fa-Shih because of its inherent separation of cause and effect.

The Buddhists' postulation of seeds in the *ālaya*-consciousness as causing all *dharmas* (phenomena) Hsiung felt to be a bifurcation of Nature, inasmuch as it left Thusness (Reality) and 'seeds' entirely unrelated. He insisted that ideation is, itself, an expression (or form) of voluntary energy, like electricity, which, running in waves through sense-organs and nerves, unites the internal and external worlds in one real, indivisible unity of mind.

(5) In other words, Thusness and energy are one and the same reality. Hsiung's world is not pluralistic, its seeming multiplicity being merely a function of the reality that is energy. Hsiung's critics, (like Chou Ku-ch'eng and Yin Shun) (176), nevertheless feel that he is closer to the intuitive school of Buddhism than he will admit.

(6) As Reality (Being) has no tangible form, yet is absolute and eternally self-sufficient, so man's Mind-Heart partakes of these qualities as the quintessence of Nature.

As *I* (meaning or intention), it is the thought-control of Nature, while as (man's) body it is only a part of Nature. This power of direction is 'life-force,' ever developing its inner, essential nature in harmony with environment.

As *Shih* (understanding or discernment), the active intellect understands and interprets Nature, without necessarily being cognizant of all its forms. There is change, but personality persists. Thus, Mind-Heart unifies the material world. *I* directs, *Shih* interprets. Mind-Heart thereby inspires and infuses all subjective, moral idealism. (177)

In short, Hsiung Shih-li, while recognizing that Being (Spirit) subsisted before matter, held that, once Being had manifested itself in the movement of evolution, it was irrevocably immanent in and inseparable from its phenomenal manifestations. The reality of being and its activities, however, lies in the process of change—a process, perceivable only by intuition, whereby objective and subjective life can be continually in flux as two aspects of one indivisible whole.[178] Throughout all his philosophizing, Hsiung Shih-li placed *jên* at the center and thoroughly believed in the capacity of all men to possess a share of it, thereby proving himself truly Confucian in spirit.[179]

(2) *The Development of Rationalistic Neo-Confucianism* (Ch'eng-Chu School)

Fung Yu-lan:—

"The most influential philosophers today are those who are trying to reconstruct Neo-Confucianism in the light of Western philosophy or combine it with Western objectivism." So writes Professor Wing-tsit Chan of Dartmouth College in *Essays in East-West Philosophy*[180] and goes on to declare in his *Religious Trends in Modern China:* "There is no doubt that Fung Yu-lan has been the most outstanding and the most creative of contemporary Chinese philosophers." [181] As early as 1922, Fung showed himself to be a keen critic of the classical philosophers in an article, "Why China Has No Science," published that year in the *International Journal of Ethics*.[182] There he discussed Taoism, Mohism, and Confucianism as to their differences on the relative value of 'nature' and 'art' (or 'nurture'). If China had followed Mo Tzu with his emphasis on the useful, or Hsün Tzu with his stress on controlling nature, she might ultimately have produced science. But Taoism and Confucianism won the day with their stress on the development of the inner man rather than the development of things external.

It was his book, *A Comparative Study of Life Ideals* (1924), that first brought Fung Yu-lan to the attention of the English-reading public.[182a] By 1934, his reputation as a teacher in China won for him an invitation to read a paper on "Philosophy in Contemporary China" before the Eighth International Philosophy Congress, held that year in Prague.[182b] The first volume of his monumental *History of Chinese Philosophy,* as translated by Professor Derk Bodde of the University of Pennsylvania, was published by Henri Vetch in Peking in 1937. More recently, Volume I has been re-published (1951) and Volume II published in 1953, both by Princeton University Press,[182c]

The rendering of this great work into English has laid us all under a great debt of gratitude to the author and his translator. While its insights and interpretations may not be accepted by some of the other Chinese scholars, yet all will agree that Fung Yu-lan's work merits for him the name of "greatest living historian of Chinese philosophy."

Our interest here, however, is not so much in Fung the historian as in Fung the philosopher. For his own philosophizing, therefore, we must turn to a fairly recent series of ("pre-communist") writings which collectively make up his systematic presentation of "The New Rational Philosophy." They are:—*The New Rationalism (Hsin Li-Hsüeh)**; *On The Nature of Man (Hsin Yüan-Jên)***; *The Development of Philosophy (Hsin Yüan-Tao)****; *The Methodology of Metaphysics (Hsin Chih-Yen)*; *On the Way of Life (Hsin Shih-Hsün)*; and *On Practical Affairs (Hsin Shih-Lun)*. Of these "New Treatises,' W. T. Chan comments: "Significantly, he (Fung) calls his system 'The New Rational Philosophy' *(Hsin Li-Hsüeh)*, which is the name for the Neo-Confucian philosophical tradition of the Ch'eng-Chu School. . . . What is new is that he incorporates into his rationalistic Neo-Confucianism the Western elements of realism and logic, as well as the Taoist elements of negativism and transcendentalism." [183] In his *A Short History of Chinese Philosophy,*[184] Fung Yu-lan gave a brief account of his philosophy as "following in part the Rationalistic School of Neo-Confucianism," though trying to avoid its "elements of authoritarianism and conservatism," and as applying "the fruits of his study of Western philosophy." [185]

The Development of Philosophy (Hsin Yüan-Tao) gives Fung's criticism of the older Confucianism and his own restatement of the basic concepts of the later (or 'Neo-') Confucianism. Translated into English by Professor E. R. Hughes of the University of Oxford and published under the title of *The Spirit of Chinese Philosophy,*[186] it enables us the more

---

* Published in Shanghai by the Commercial Press, Ltd., 1939.
** Published in Shanghai by the Commercial Press, Ltd., 1943.
*** Published in English translation in London by Kegan Paul, 1947.

readily to present two sections which best reflect the range of Fung Yu-lan's thought:—(A) his "Appraisal of the Older Confucian Concepts" and (B) his "Re-statement of the Later Confucian Metaphysics." *

A. *Fung Yu-lan's Appraisal of the Older Confucian Concepts*

After discussing Confucius and Mencius in Chapter 1, Yang Chu and Mo Ti in Chapter 2, Fung Yu-lan went on, in Chapter 3, to describe the theories of the early Dialecticians *(Pien Che)* and Logicians *(Ming Chia)* of the fourth and third centuries B.C., especially Hui Shih and Kung-sun Lung, whose ideas were discussed in the "Chiu Hsüeh" and "T'ien Hsia" Chapters of *The Chuang-tzu*. Inasmuch as they seemed to be trying to prove that "things are not what they seem" in this "world of shapes and features," they were strongly opposed not only by the Taoists but by Mo Tzu and Hsün Tzu as well.[187]

In succeeding comments, Fung expressed the opinion that Hsün Tzu, though strongly influenced by Taoists, was unable either to rightly appreciate or correctly criticize other philosophies, especially the Taoistic tenets in regard to the 'world beyond shapes and features.' On the other hand, whenever Confucianists were sufficiently stimulated by Taoists, it raised the level of their philosophical thinking. Hence the *Amplifications of the Yi Scripture (Yi Ching* or *Book of Changes)* and the *Chung Yung* (or *Doctrine of the Mean)*, though attributed to Confucius, undoubtedly came from the pens of a later group of (Confucian) writers—all of whom were influenced by Taoist thought, even though "they accepted the Confucianist tradition and emphasized a concern for the common task." [188] Fung then proceeded to give his own appraisal of those two parts of the *Classics*.

---

* As has been the case with other translators from the Chinese, Professor Hughes found paraphrase usually more effective, making for smoother reading, than any attempt at word-for-word translation. This will be noticeably true of the passages here selected.

(1) *Appraisal of the Yi Amplifications:—*

After pointing out that the *Yi Ching* was originally a book of divination, offering formulae for fortune-telling, Fung went on to explain how its symbols could be taken to represent any known combination of circumstances in human affairs and its appended judgments, for good or for ill, could be accepted as fairly reliable answers to individual and state problems. When understood, these symbols (viz., the *Pa Kua* or Eight Trigrams, and Sixty-four Hexagrams) are simple and their variability makes possible a complete coverage of all situations and the principles governing them.[189]*

Moreover, Fung added, the "Hsi Tz'u" chapter of the *Yi Amplifications* explains in great detail the workings of the *Yang* and *Yin* principles in Nature under the names *'Ch'ien'* and *'K'un,'* respectively, as the originating movement and the responding quiescence complementing each other in the continuous process of production and reproduction. The theme of the book (as of Nature itself) is 'unceasing change' . . . 'All things emerge from the *Tao* and return to it.'[191] . . . Fung Yu-lan felt, however, that whereas the *Tao* of the later *Yi Amplifications* could produce things in the 'world of shapes,' his own interpretation of the *Tao-concept* differed from both of them. (To quote):

"We may say that the Taoists' *Tao* is an unclear version of the concept which figures in the *Hsin Li-Hsüeh* as *ch'i;* and that the *Tao* of the *Yi Amplifications* is an unclear version of the concept which figures in the *Hsin Li-Hsüeh* as *li.*" (192)

---

* *Note:* A further word of explanation needed here is supplied by Dr. Andrew Tod Roy: "According to Ku Chieh-kang, in his *Ku-Shih Pien* (pp. 43-44), the *Book of Changes* was originally a book of divination with no Confucian moral teachings—possibly written before Confucius. The *Appendices* (showing Taoist influence) (which Fung calls the *Yi Amplifications*) were probably written by an unknown philosopher between the Period of Contending States and the middle of the Han dynasty. It was not until after the *Appendices* were added that the *Book of Changes* became a Confucian sacred book. Thus it could be held that the *Changes* represented a separate tradition." (190)

In other words, Fung would not admit that *Tao* can have anything directly to do with the 'world of shapes and features.' He further observed that

Where the Taoists tended to stress the return to quiescence (or Non-Being), the Confucians emphasized the endless going and coming (or Being). It is needful, they said, for the sage-man to remember the law of transformations that makes everything at the peak of its flourishing to begin a reversal of direction toward its lowest phase. (The sage, being ever aware of Nature's flux, is consequently able to meet both prosperity and adversity with equanimity), maintaining throughout (perfect) rectitude of conduct (i.e., not seeking any profit or avoiding any injury). (193)

And again:

The Yi Amplifications (Hsi Tz'u Chapter), therefore, concludes that "the sage attains to the highest sphere because he has the highest form of knowledge" (i.e., of the mysterious working of the *Tao* of Heaven, Earth, and Man). . . . "He occupies a high position and is not arrogant; is low in the social scale and is not distressed." If he is truly modest and humble, proves himself one whose head is not turned by knowledge, he will truly find that "the sphere in which he lives is the transcendent sphere." (194)

(2) *Appraisal of the Chung Yung (Doctrine of the Mean):—*

Here Fung Yu-lan observes that the *Chung Yung* is, in ideas and even phraseology, very similar to the *Yi Amplifications.*

"(Like the *Book of Mencius*), they both stress man's affinity to Heaven through the working of his mind at the highest possible level. . . . By cultivating his Heaven-given *tao* through learning, the sage-man becomes real and is able thereby to . . . live in the transcendent sphere. . . .
(As Chu Hsi says): 'Achieving the Mean is the name for not erring to one side or the other, for being neither too much nor too little.' (195)
(And as the *Chung Yung says*): 'How perfect is the Mean in ordinary

action!' . . . (and again) . . . '(It is conceivable that) men might refuse noble station and the wealth that goes with it. They might trample the naked sword underfoot. But to achieve the Mean in ordinary action, it is (well-nigh) impossible . . . for them to do that.' (Only the sage-man could do that).' (196)

(Again), "To have the emotions welling up and yet in due proportion is also a state of the Mean; (as the *Chung Yung* says): . . . 'This is to be described as being in a state of harmony. This state of equilibrium is the chief foundation of the Great Society' . . . (Yet) harmony is not to be confused with sameness. . . . 'Sameness has no offspring'. . . . (As Yen Tzu said in the *Tso Chuan*): 'If the harp and the lute were the same, who would delight in them. . . . A harmony includes differences, with all the differences harmonized to produce a state of harmony.'" (197)

Developing further the 'achieving the Mean in ordinary action,' Fung Yu-lan added that the sage-man walks with his feet in the sphere of ordinary life but with his head in the clouds of the transcendent sphere, ever bent on uniting the twain by his spirit of self-dedication. (To quote):

The sage-man being fully enlightened and real, will be "assisting the transforming and nourishing work of Heaven and Earth." (As the *Chung Yung* says): 'It is only the man who is completely real in the world who can weave the fabric of the great basic strands in human society . . . and . . . understand the transforming and nourishing work of Heaven and Earth.'. . . (198)

"The Taoists constantly said: 'To thing things, but not to be thinged by things' . . . (meaning that the completely real man) . . . may quite well . . . be, in point of action, engaged 'in the deeds of ordinary virtue and devote himself to ordinary speech'. But in regard to his sphere of living, it is one with the universe. . . . (It) is that described by Mencius as 'the marriage of righteousness and the *Tao*'.

"But the difference in the sphere attained to lies in the kind of *Tao* to which righteousness is 'married,' (for) there are higher and lower kinds of *tao*. . . . The man who lives in the moral sphere is without selfishness, as also is the man who lives in the transcendent sphere. . . . It follows, then, that the sphere in which he lives depends on the loftiness of the *tao* to which he is devoted." (199)

By way of concluding these two appraisals, Fung Yu-lan made this significant, final observation: "The authors of the *Yi Amplifications* and the *Chung Yung* knew that the nameable can also transcend shapes and features. But they did not know that, for a perfect discussion of what transcends shapes and features, it is necessary that the unnameable should also be considered. It is not necessary that what transcends shapes and features should be unnameable, but *it is necessary that what transcends shapes and features should not be restricted to the nameable.* Arguing from this, we maintain that the philosophical system in the two books with which this chapter has dealt is entirely in accord with the criterion of 'performing the common task,' but it is still not entirely in accord with the criterion of 'attaining to the sublime.' Thus, the kind of life attained through this philosophy is still inadequate for 'absorption in the Abstract and ferrying over into the Beyond.' "[200]

It might be added here, as Fung has elsewhere noted, that he would recognize the Hexagrams as representing fluctuations in Nature that correspond to changes in human life and as, therefore, models for the conduct of society and government. Moreover, that, although *Amplifications* I and II reflect ideas from *The Lao-tzu,* yet their stress on a choice of the Middle Way between the extremes (as already expressed in the *Chung Yung)* may be accepted as reflecting true Confucian opinion.[201]

(3) *A Re-Appraisal of the Ancient Mystical School:—*

While he was casting a critical eye on the older concepts in China's classical heritage, Fung Yu-lan could not resist the temptation to pass judgment on the ancient Mystical School by saying:—

"It remained for the philosophers of the Mystical School of the Wei and Chin era (3rd and 4th centuries A.D.) to recognize the philosophy of the transcendent as enabling men (really) to 'reach the sphere of the Abstract and ferry over into the Beyond.' They took pleasure in the discussions of the 'mystery of all mysteries' and called the *Lao-tzu,* the *Chuang-tzu,* and the *Yi Amplifications* the 'Three Mystical Books'. . . . The Mystical School was the (lineal) descendant of the Lao-Chuang School of philosophy. Its members followed the dialectical logic of the Logicians (Hui Shih and Kung-sun Lung) and became immersed in 'distinguishing terms and analyzing logical principles'." (202)

"Where the Han scholars had raised Confucius even to the rank of a god, the Mystics (Hsiang Hsiu and Kuo Hsiang) regarded him (simply) as the greatest sage. They felt (as I have expressed it in my *Hsin Yüan-Jên*) that 'Chuang Chou's (i.e., Chuang Tzu's) sphere of living consisted in knowing (about) Heaven, (whereas Confucius' sphere of living consisted in (actual) identification with Heaven. . . . Chuang Chou knew only *about* this kind of identification, but was unable to actualize it. . . . Thus, although his sphere of living was a transcendent one, yet *his sphere was one of knowing and not of doing* (and was, therefore, not equal to Confucius' sphere)'." (203)

"In the Early Taoists, the (unmanifested) *Tao* occupied the important position; in the Hsiang-Kuo system, Heaven (or *Tao* manifested) occupied the important position. Heaven is the Great Whole, and the sage is the one who identifies himself with the Great Whole . . . and . . . wanders in spirit beyond the confines of shapes and features. This wandering, however, does not entail being 'a contemplative in the midst of the hills and woods'. . . . Although the sphere of the sage is so exalted, yet his action may be completely ordinary. . . . (Therefore), the distinction between being outside or inside the world does not exist for the sage." (204)

Thus the Mystics sought to turn the early Taoist philosophy of the solitary into "a philosophy of this world and the ordinary beings in it.". . . They were also much influenced by the Buddhist philosophy, and Seng Chao attempted a synthesis of Taoist and Buddhist thought, "resolving the antithesis between mutability and immutability, between real knowledge and ordinary knowledge, between *wu-wei* and *yu-wei,* between action and inaction." (205)

By making these and many other appraisals throughout the long task of writing the history of his people's cultural heritage, Fung Yu-lan found his own mind coming to rest in certain interpretations which he felt approximated 'identification with the Great Whole.' These new insights, in what might be termed 'a modern Confucian metaphysic,' he shared with his contemporaries in the series of writings mentioned above, which comprised his New Rational Philosophy. The core of his thought is summarized in the following section.

B. *Fung Yu-lan's Re-Statement of the Later Confucian Metaphysics*

In Chapter Ten of *The Spirit of Chinese Philosophy (Hsin Yüan-Tao),* a section entitled "A New System" is devoted to a recapitulation of Fung's "New Rationalism" as it had appeared earlier in his *Hsin Li-Hsüeh.*[206] Here we find his sober judgment of his predecessors' understanding of 'Reality' and his own re-statement of the Neo-Confucian philosophy as he thought it should be made in the light of his own studies and mature reflections.

By way of preliminary introduction, Fung outlined early Taoist religious philosophy[207] and said: (a) "The cosmology held by the earlier Neo-Confucianists was derived from this Taoistic religion." [208] *. . . The philosophy of Chou Tun-yi, Shao Yung, and Chang Tsai also had stemmed from it and, therefore, was unavoidably affected by 'shapes and features.'" (b) "The Ch'eng-Chu (*Li-Hsüeh*) thinkers, (influenced by the Taoistic religion), did not transcend 'shapes and features,' though moving closer to the abstract. Their conception of *li* still savored of the actual. Even in the *Hsin-Hsüeh* School (of Lu Hsiang-shan and Wang Yang-ming), influenced as it was by the Buddhist 'Inner-light' dictum, there was still a touch of the 'shapes and features' point of view, when they emphasized 'being mind, being Buddha' rather than 'not mind, not Buddha.' In other words, they were never able completely to attain to the sphere of the sublime or abstract." [209]

---

* Referring to Sung Neo-Confucianists and a Taoistic religion formed of an amalgam of the primitive religion and science of the *Yin-Yang* School and early philosophical Taoism.

Bringing the discussion of his own philosophical point of view to a focus, Fung Yu-lan went on to elucidate his new *Li-Hsüeh* (pure metaphysics) as stemming from "pre-Chin Taoists, the Wei-Chin Mystics, and the T'ang Inner-light thinkers; as seeking to avoid reference to the actual, and, therefore, it says nothing positive." He was also inspired by the *Li-Hsüeh* of the Sung and Ming eras. In short, Fung's New System of *Li-Hsüeh* consists of the elucidation of four sets of formal propositions from which are derived four formal concepts: *Li* (principle or ideal form; reason or law), *Ch'i* (matter), *Tao-Ti* (the evolution of the *Tao*), and *Ta Ch'üan* (the Great Whole).[210]

Proposition Set I—The Meaning of LI

"Any and every thing (or event-thing) cannot but be a certain thing, and being such cannot but belong to a certain class of thing. If a certain class of thing is, then there is *that by which* that class of thing is (what it is). . . . In other words, that which all mountains have in common is *that by which* mountains are mountains (though they are different in size and shape). That which all rivers have in common is *that by which* rivers are rivers. This is what the new *Li-Hsüeh* designates as the *li* of mountains and the *li* of rivers."

(Fung here states two corollaries to this first formal proposition, *viz.*):

(1) "It is possible there is (subsists) *that by which* a certain class of thing is that class of thing without there being (actually existing) that class of thing."

(2) "There being *that by which* a certain class of thing is that class of thing is logically prior to the *be*-ing of the things in that class. In other words, real *be*-ing or subsistence comes before actual being or existence (a logical priority, not priority in time). So we can say, 'That being so, *that by which* mountains are mountains can subsist without there being any mountains in existence'."

(Going on from here, therefore),

"we can infer from the non-subsistence of a certain *li* (principle, ideal form) that no such thing exists, but we cannot infer from the non-existence of the thing the non-subsistence of the *li*. For this reason, we are warranted in saying there are more *li* than there are classes of things."
"(Furthermore), the *li* taken as a whole are designated in the new *Li-Hsüeh* as the *T'ai Chi*, or alternatively as the world of *li*. This world of *li*, logically speaking, has precedence of the actual world. As has been said, 'it is empty and silent, without a sign, and yet with all forms there' . . . Thus, from a formal explanation of the actual, we discover a new world, 'a world which is pure and empty of actual content'." (211)

. . . .

Proposition Set II—The Meaning of CH'I

"Things cannot but exist. Those things which exist cannot but be *able* to exist. Those things which are able to exist cannot but have *that by which* they are *able* to exist.
"Here the subject of consideration is the individual thing; we can, however, neither infer nor derive the actual (thing) from the *li*. . . . A *li* cannot actualize itself. . . . Since things must have *that by which* they can exist before they do exist, we, therefore, maintain that if there is *li*, there must be *ch'i*, by which we mean that if there be actualization of a *li*, there must be the *ch'i* which actualizes the *li*.
"*Ch'i* may be used in a relative sense where it has reference to a class of things; for example, the constituent parts of the body, which exist by reason of *ch'i*. But if we extend the inquiry, we arrive at something which is after all *that by which* all things can exist and (yet) in itself is only a potentiality of existence. This is the true, primordial *ch'i*, which we use to express an abstract meaning. In my own terminology (in the new *Li-Hsüeh*), the term *ch'i* always has an absolute meaning. The *ch'i* is something about which we cannot say what it is, nor can we ask what that is *by which* it can exist (subsist), for it is not in the sphere of shapes and things. It is not a 'what,' but is unnameable 'non-being'." (212)

. . . .

Proposition Set III—The Meaning of Becoming, or Evolution of TAO

"Existence is a continuous process. All existences are existences of things. *The existence of a thing is the process of actualization of a certain li by means of its ch'i.* Existence viewed as a whole is the (continuous) process of actualization of the *T'ai Chi* (the Supreme Point of Perfection) by means of the primordial *ch'i.* (This may) be called 'the Evolution of the Tao' (*Tao Ti*). . . .
"In my *Hsin Li-Hsüeh* book, this (bare process of actualizing the *li* of change and movement by means of the primordial *ch'i*) is called 'the changing and moving ch'i', and later on it is spoken of as *Ch'ien Yüan* (the First Mover). This name . . . may appear to mean what in pictorial thought is thought of as (God or) the Creator, but in my thought it may be described as the pure activity of *ch'i*. . . . To speak of a *Ch'ien Yüan* is only to make a formal explanation of the actual. Hence, to speak of there being a *Ch'ien Yüan* does not entail any assertion about the actual. To speak of God or a Creator is in the nature of an assertion about the actual." (213)

. . . .

Proposition Set IV—The Meaning of the "Great Whole"

"In the new *Li-Hsüeh* metaphysic, the sum total of beings is the Great Whole. . . . There is that which has actual being; there is that which has only real being (the actual being included in the real but not necessarily vice-versa): and all these taken together are what is called the Great Whole (or the universe). . . .This which I call the universe, is not the universe of physics or astronomy. That is the physical universe (which) . . . may be said to be a whole but is only a sectional whole; it is not the supreme whole beyond which there is no other.
"The Great Whole may be named the One . . . (as did pre-Ch'in philosophers). . . . The new *Li-Hsüeh,* (however), in speaking of the One as the All and the All as the One, makes no assertion that there are inner connections, (as emphasized by Buddhists), or internal relations, (as emphasized by Bradley and other idealists), between things; there is no assertion about the actual." [214]

. . . .

Recapitulation:–

In his concise summation, Fung Yu-lan stated: "From the above four sets of analytical propositions, we get four formal concepts: *Li* and *Ch'i*–(from speculative *analysis* in regard to *things),* and the *Evolution of the Tao* and the *Great Whole*–(from speculative *synthesis* in regard to *things*)." . . .

"The concept of *li* bears a resemblance to the concept of 'being' in Greek philosophy, notably in Plato and Aristotle, and in modern philosophy, notably in Hegel."

"The concept of *ch'i* also bears a resemblance to the concept of 'non-being' in these philosophers."

"The concept of the *Evolution of the Tao* bears a resemblance to their concept of 'becoming' or 'change.' "

"The concept of the *Great Whole* bears a resemblance to their concept of 'the Absolute' . . ."

"The four concepts in the new *Li-Hsüeh* are . . . derived by the formal method and, therefore, are entirely formal concepts. In them, there is no positive element . . . and (they, therefore,) contain no assertion about the actual."

Taking refuge in Wang Yang-ming's dictum: ". . . The way to become a sage is nothing more than (by) restoring the original essence of the mind, which is common to all men, and leaving knowledge and skill out of account". . . , Fung confesses that his philosophy has no practical suggestions to give on how to shoot a gun or pilot an airplane; that he is close to the Mystics and the Buddhist Inner-light point of view, and, therefore, may be considered utterly useless. Yet he defends his position by saying:

"(While) positive knowledge and practical ability . . . is outside the purview of the new *Li-Hsüeh,* yet the concepts of *li* and *ch'i* can enable men's minds to wander in that which is prior to things, and the concepts of the *Evolution of the Tao* and the *Great Whole* enable men's minds to wander in the wholeness of being. . . . Since these four concepts represent what transcends shapes and features, . . . the sphere to which we attain with their aid is the sphere of the empty beyond. . . .

"Although men in this sphere have thus become 'ferried over into the beyond,' yet the business in which they are engaged may be the discharge of the daily duties in human relations. They are (sage-men) mysteriously remote and yet not divorced from actual utility." . . . *"If philosophy can enable men to become sage-men* (the reaching to the height of what it means to be a man), *then this is the usefulness of philosophy's uselessness."* [215]

(And, finally): "Philosophy cannot make a man an expert in a certain profession . . . (but) it can make a perfect man (or sage) who is supremely suited to be a 'king,' i.e., a man who has the highest quality of leadership in (any) society. . . . The supreme leader does not do things himself but gets all the talents in the country to do their best; in that way everything will get done. . . . The man who lives in the transcendent sphere identifies himself with, and sees things from the standpoint of, the *Great Whole.* He can be the supreme leader whose mind is open and impartial and all-embracive—in which all things follow their own course and do not conflict with each other. Thus the new *Li-Hsüeh* upholds 'sageness within and kingliness without,' which is the goal of true philosophy." [216]

. . . .

Estimate of Fung Yu-lan:—

In his reconstruction of Ch'eng-Chu philosophy, Fung Yu-lan has followed a modern, strictly scientific point of view:—that we live in a world of evolutionary change; that life is part of that unfinished process; that the aim of life is the working out of one's own destiny by developing one's nature to the utmost by systematic, objective study, by induction and experimentation rather than by speculation (like Chu Hsi). As Professor Chan has pointed out, Fung has purposely sought to avoid the Buddhist mysticism which had crept into the Ch'eng Brothers and Chu Hsi; he also undermined the Ch'ing (Manchu) philosophers' argument that Reason (*Li,* Principle) is immanent in things and is (taken as) the basis of their practical, this-worldly spirit. Likewise, Fung felt that Chu Hsi was wrong in assuming that all entities (including the human mind) embodied all the principles of Reason (*Li*), for the reason that, as the *yin* principle (of passivity and destruction) is so strong in life, nothing can be either perfect or permanent.[217]

Although at first Fung Yu-lan criticized the Lu-Wang School as not being metaphysical enough, later he came to recognize and appreciate the values in Lu-Wang intuitionism.[218] In the end, he undeniably and admittedly arrived at a transcendentalism which is unmistakably realistic and logical, yet which, perhaps unadmittedly, leans favorably toward the mystical. In a special chapter in his *Hsin Li-Hsüeh,* Fung outlined a philosophy of religion in which he arrived at the concept of 'the unity of man and Heaven' as the most acceptable core of human morality. This being a central Confucian concept, as well as one that is basically religious, (as W. T. Chan has reminded us),[219] Fung's attitude toward 'religion,' being slightly skeptical, was thoroughly Confucian; perhaps reflecting Santayana's theory of religion as poetry, he looked upon Confucian 'etiquette' more or less as a poetic form of religious philosophy.[220] However that may be, any estimate of Fung Yu-lan must regard him as the most outstanding critic and interpreter of rationalistic Neo-Confucianism that contemporary China has produced. No estimate can as yet be final, however, inasmuch as, since 1950, he has been living under the Communist régime and is subject to its directives—aimed at 'brain-washing' his mind of all independent thought.

In a small paragraph dealing with "Confucianism under Communism" in his *Religious Trends in Modern China* (1953), Professor Chan reported: "With the Communist triumph in China, Hsiung (Shih-li) has entered into voluntary silence, and Fung (Yu-lan) has repudiated himself."[221] Referring to certain retractions appearing in the Chinese press, Chan went on to explain: "In a recent article (in English) in *People's China,* entitled 'I Discovered Marxism-Leninism,' Fung, confessing his past mistakes, says that his *New Rational Philosophy (Hsin Li-*

Hsüeh) is but a twilight of old Chinese philosophy. . . . He regrets that he has emphasized the eternal and neglected the concrete. He now realizes that Marxism-Leninism is comparable to modern medicine, whereas old Chinese philosophy is comparable to medieval medicine." [222]

Moreover, according to Chan, "In a still later article, in the *Bright Light Daily* (in Chinese),[223] entitled 'Self-Appraisal about *Hsin Li-Hsüeh,'* Fung specifically rejects the main thesis of each of the five books . . . (in which he expounds) . . . his system. He says that the main point of his *Hsin Yüan-Jên (On the Nature of Man),* to become a 'citizen of Heaven' is, in the final analysis, escapism. As to his chief work, *Hsin Li-Hsüeh,* he says his great mistake was to have emphasized the contrast between the particular and the universal instead of stressing their unity. According to his self-appraisal, the book is too strongly influenced by Taoism and Buddhism and reflects the crumbling old (feudal) society (of Confucianism)." [224]

Some comfort, however, is found by Professor Chan in the belief that Confucianism cannot be entirely dead in China if even Chairman Mao Tse-tung, while attacking Confucianism as semi-feudal in his *China's New Democracy,*[225] at the same time, in his *On Entering the New Stage,*[226] advised his party-members to learn from Confucius and Sun Yat-sen, as well as from Marx and Lenin. Finally, Mao conceded: "The new culture of China is developed from the old culture of China. Therefore, we must respect our own history!" [227]

More recent reports indicate a continuing "cold war" between "rightist" and "leftist" elements within the Communist fold and between professors and students of philosophy in Peiping. Under pressures generated by the "Double-Anti Movement," Fung Yu-lan was compelled to publish another self-denunciation. In the *Cheng Ming* ("Contending") No. 6, June 6, 1958, he admitted failure to recognize the leadership of the Party in all things, a tendency in himself to cherish ancient rather than modern ideas, and an effort to compromise by "revisionist" methods, such as distinguishing between the abstract and concrete meaning of a subject under discussion. He likewise confessed to showing ambition for himself and favoritism in the choice of personnel for his philosophy department at Tsing Hua University; also to having consorted with Professor Ho Lin of Peking University, whose "ideological style" was idealistic like his own. After these and other confessions, Fung Yu-lan concluded with a declaration of firm determination to "lay down his arms and surrender, and once more be a common soldier in the ranks of Marxist-Leninist philosophers under the banner of the Party and Marxism." [228]

Yet the third-year students in the Department of Philosophy of Peking University evidently were still not satisfied with even so clear a statement as the above-mentioned. In a subsequent issue of their new organ, "New Red Army"—(a "wall-newspaper" in their dining-hall)—they took strong exception to the idealist and reactionary viewpoints of philosophers Fung Yu-lan, Ho Lin, and Hung Ch'ien. As reported in the Peking *Kuang Ming Jih Pao* for June 25, 1958, one of the articles in the student paper criticized Fung especially for "holding on firmly to his old reactionary viewpoints" . . . for . . . "deliberately trying to obliterate the essential difference between materialism and idealism" . . . and for "adopting the stand of the bourgeoisie." [229]

Despite the fact that he is, apparently, still a controversial figure, Fung Yu-lan, nevertheless, has won the respect and confidence of the leaders of both professional and political circles to the extent of being made Director of the History of Chinese Philosophy Seminar in Peking University, Member of the Academic Committee of the Academy of Science, and a member of the National Political Consultative Council in Communist China.[230]

. . . .

Chapter 14

Recapitulation and Conclusion

Recapitulation:—

In the course of this necessarily rather cursory study of Chinese philosophic thought, we have followed the long, winding stream of indigenous philosophy, which has mingled at times with confusing yet enriching waters from tributary streams of foreign ideologies. These, Chinese philosophy has absorbed and utilized in its triple task of bearing on its broadening current the multifarious craft of conflicting ideas, of fertilizing the fields of creative Chinese thinking, and of turning the turbines of dynamic energy required for the building of an empire and a great modern state.

Yin-Yang Naturalism

We have briefly noted China's ancient, primitive, *Yin-Yang* naturalism, with its concept of the primordial Universe (*T'ai Chi*) working silently through the Primary Modalities (*Yin* and *Yang*) and the Five Elements (*Wu Hsing*). Changes in Nature and in human history were explained as the result of the action of these hidden forces; while governmental affairs were controlled by each elemental power during its period of ascendancy in the cycle of the year. Interpretive cosmologies and philosophies of history came into being at an early date; one by Tsou Yen early in the third century B.C., and one by Tung Chung-shu, elaborated toward the middle of the second century B.C., being noted as especially significant.

Early Taoist Harmony With Nature

Attention was given to the early Taoist philosophy, which embraced the basic concept of an eternal, self-subsisting, unchanging Principle (*Tao*) behind and in the phenomenal world, yet working through an individuating principle (*Tê*) to create the myriad entities in the world of things. The quietness and apparent effortlessness of the *Tao's* working was matched only by the inner harmony of that evolutionary change which is called "Life." To conform to it with quiet non-activity was the Taoist ideal for individual and social (including political) living. Where action was called for in human relationships, it was to be characterized by complete freedom and equality, by spontaneity and tranquillity. Identification with the "Great Flux' called for utter simplicity and humility as the hallmarks of perfect personality.

Confucian Training For Social Responsibilities

We have seen how Confucius elaborated a this-worldly philosophy based upon virtuous character, in which *jên* or benevolent concern for others grew out of a primary inner integrity. Love for home and family, respect for parents, spelled harmony with cosmic law. True relationships resting on and maintained by personal integrity could provide good government, as well as a true social order. No one is "born to rule," and those who occupy positions of power bear a double responsibility for reverence toward Heaven and for wisdom in administration. Only education of the right kind could provide virtuous men and wise rulers.

Mencius and Hsün Tzu now stand out for us more clearly as the great commentators and moulders of Confucian principles-in-practice. Believing in the goodness of human nature, Mencius stressed filial piety as the keynote of character and the education of youth as the prime requisite of good government. Opposing all graft and intriguing for private gain, he campaigned for a better equalization of land-distribution as the first step toward a more stable economic order. Without sincerity of mind and heart, nothing permanent can be accomplished. More of a disciplinarian than Mencius, Hsün Tzu likewise saw the necessity of sincerity in the teaching end as well as the learning side of the educative process. Holding youth with a tight rein, he was able to instill into them some of his own great ideas, not the least of which was that the forces of Nature were to be harnessed for the benefit of mankind.

The philosophers of this period saw a naturally close relationship between man and the universe, the nature of one embodying the principles of the other, as indicated in the *Book of Mencius* and in the *Doctrine of the Mean.* If man will live up to his true spiritual inheritance, he may aspire to forming a trinity with Heaven and Earth.[1]

We found Mo Tzu standing on high ground, prophetically insisting that love exists only when it has included everyone in its scope. All transactions must benefit *both parties*! Love is not weak, but will ever defend its rights and the cause of true justice. Heaven is on the side of all who live abstemiously and who altruistically seek to establish true relationships in a spirit of "mutual profitableness." Where Mo Ti envisioned a universal application of love as "peace on earth good will toward men," Yang Chu expressed interest chiefly in "self-realization" as a worthy, though confessedly private, objective in human living, provided the passions of desire were moderated somewhat by reason.

We have seen how persistently the problem of good and evil presented itself to the minds of philosophers in each generation. Long before the Buddhist infiltration, Chinese minds had grappled with the question of whether man was born good or with an innate tendency to evil. Attempts were made to find the real cause of evil, and both Taoists and Confucianists in general held it to lie in desires-born-of-ignorance, or in unwitting deviation from the Golden Mean. All man had to do was to study to be good and thus win through to the freedom vouchsafed by his own Heaven-born nature.[2]

Pre-Han and Han Period Revisionary Changes

In the Warring States Period (fifth to second centuries B.C.), we found legalism becoming prominent in philosophical thinking. The principle of *"Fa,"* or a code of laws, replaced government by *"Li"* * as a regulator of civilian life. In this, and in the succeeding Han Period, the supposed harmony between human nature and the heavenly order was not to be depended upon for satisfactory results in actual situations involving a conflict of interests. Yet in the applied *Yin-Yang* philosophy of Tung Chung-shu, if the ruler lived scrupulously by "Heaven's decrees," a virtuous social order would automatically follow. Wang Mang's daring, though unsuccessful, experiment in state socialism only proved him far ahead of his age. Throughout this period the pendulum swung to and fro, sometimes favoring Neo-Taoistic notions of personal freedom and forward-looking self-development and again swinging toward a greater emphasis on society's control over the individual.

In this period, came one of those great "Syntheses in Chinese Metaphysics" to which Professor Wing-tsit Chan has called our attention. For it was during the Han dynasty that "the Taoist ideal of the Great Unit (or Oneness), the *Yin-Yang* theory of the interaction of the positive and negative cosmic principles, and the Confucian philosophy of *ch'êng,* or truth, in the *Doctrine of the Mean* were synthesized into one philosophy (of change) that was to dominate Chinese thought for centuries and form a firm basis for Neo-Confucianism." [3]

Post-Han Buddhist Indoctrination and Reaction

The influence of Buddhist philosophy, as we have learned, was indeed powerful and far-reaching. With a wide range of interpretations as to reality and the goal of life, Buddhism made

---

* The Chinese ideograph used (as here) for the *"Li"* meaning ceremony, ritual, or social "etiquette" is different from the *"Li"* used for cosmic principle, reason, law, or ultimate reality.

its appeal to scholars and peasants alike. For the intellectual, it offered the contemplative life of reflection on the illusoriness of this self-centered existence compared to the glorious gain of the selfless, supersensory world of Great Mind. For the common man, it offered an easy salvation to Paradise by simple faith in the power of Buddha and his assisting Bodhisattvas, without the need for knowledge gained by exhaustive study of scriptures or by flagellant asceticism. For all alike there must come a "saving" of the mind, for eternal reality is to be found only in the rarefied atmosphere of clarified consciousness and in total commitment to the Buddhist principle of "non-attachment" to worldly things. Here lay the hope of instantaneous enlightenment, the confident expectation of a salvation interpreted as re-absorption into Universal Being or as entering into the blissful Non-Being of Nirvāṇa.

Here again, the harmonizing mind of the Chinese grappled with problems of synthesis presented by the invasion of Buddhist thought. Even among the Buddhists themselves there was no unanimity of opinion on problems such as "Being and Non-Being," and "The One or the Many." We have seen how Fa-tsang in the Hua-Yen School resolved the apparent conflict by taking refuge in a doctrine of interpenetrating oneness of gold and lion, of non-discrimination, of the inclusiveness of the "Great Norm." Where for other schools like the Ch'an (south of the Yangtze River), being and non-being were taken as illusion and negated in the Void, for the Hua-Yen (north of the Yangtze), being was accepted as complementary to its opposite in one great synthesis of the noumenal and the phenomenal, the one and the many.[4]

When the Taoists faced these problems, they accepted all existences as coming from non-being and, therefore, as self-transforming. Yet, if they held to the equality of all things, as manifestations of the Great Oneness, they, like the Buddhists, faced the difficulty of finding any specific individuality in discrete objects. The Neo-Confucianists resolved the difficulty by affirming both being and non-being in the continuous process of production and reproduction. For them, change was harmonious and all-embracing. Declaring that reality is one and never upholding pluralism, they, paradoxically enough, affirmed the co-existence of the one and the many. But, as Chan points out, "even their dualism of *li* and *ch'i* was weak, since the *T'ai Chi* includes both *li* and *ch'i*. . . . The effect of *ch'i* (for Chou Tun-yi and Chang Tsai) was to pervade all things in such different ways as to create opposites that are not isolated but included in a universal, infinite harmony."[5]

Adverse reaction to Buddhism's other-worldly monasticism and Taoism's cosmological symbolism came slowly but surely. After a long period of fraternizing appreciation and mutual borrowing, exemplified in Li Ao and others, there came the critical re-appraisal and inevitable recusancy exemplified by Chang Tsai and the Ch'eng Brothers. With a resiliency characteristic of Chinese philosophizing, came the rebound of their Confucian minds, re-asserting belief in the time-honored Confucian convictions of the worthwhileness of life, of the dependability of human nature if educated correctly, and of the objective reality of Heavenly Principle.

In the Ch'eng Brothers, however, (as we discovered), the stream of Neo-Confucian philosophy struck the submerged rock of divergence in reasoning as to the epistemological value of the "investigation of things." This caused it to separate and thenceforth to flow in two main channels: that of Ch'eng-Chu objective rationalism and that of Lu-Wang subjective idealism.

In Chu Hsi, we found Ch'eng-Chu rationalistic Neo-Confucianism reaching a high level of metaphysical analysis. Typically interested in establishing a philosophical basis for belief in human capacities, Chu Tzu furnished both motivation and direction to the application of Confucian principles. For him and his followers, the human mind can clearly embrace the realities of the phenomenal world; moreover, human nature can conceivably produce character sufficiently fortified to stand the strains and stresses of social and political responsibilities.

Under the guidance of Lu Hsiang-shan and Wang Yang-ming, the Lu-Wang School was seen to develop a monistic idealism that pleaded for trust in the capacity of mind to intuit the universe. Wang Yang-ming's sixteenth century emphasis on the mutuality of knowing and doing came to fruition centuries later in its appeal to all insurgent youth to be "up and doing" and gave the courage-for-action needed by twentieth century revolutionary leaders.

Through the Sung-Ming period, traditional Confucianism so assimilated Taoism and Buddhism as to form the great synthesis in Chinese metaphysics known as "Neo-Confucianism." Here again, the harmonizing mind of Neo-Confucian thinkers tackled the imposing problems of relating the cosmic forces of Principle or Energy (*Li*) and Ether or Matter (*Ch'i*) and the perennial correlation of knowledge and conduct. Openly borrowing from the Hua-Yen School its dichotomy of a realm of principles separate from a realm of facts, they argued that *"Li"* is the Great Ultimate (*T'ai Chi*) that unites everything and is "fully embodied in mind"; that "Ch'i" (like *Tê*) is the differentiating energy of *Li,* producing and ultimately destroying and re-creating all things. Yet, as Professor Chan has pointed out, even the Neo-Confucianists differed in regard to their interpretations of *Li* and *Ch'i.* From Ch'eng Yi to Tai Chen they wrestled with the problem of the relation of energy to matter. (Following W. T. Chan's analysis) :—

The Sung philosophers of the Ch'eng-Chu School held the *Li* in all things to be incorporeal and transcendent, in contrast to *Ch'i.* Existence is not necessary to *li,* but is essential to *ch'i;* yet *li* cannot be known except as manifested in *ch'i.* Mind can embrace all *li,* though *li* can subsist without becoming known. True knowledge consists in "extending the mind to all things." But, whereas Ch'eng Yi stressed investigating one thing thoroughly, Chu Hsi urged the investigation of all things. Yet Chu Hsi departed from the orthodox path when he described *ch'i* as corporeal matter rather than a force, as Taoists and other Neo-Confucianists had maintained.[6]

The Sung-Ming philosophers of the Lu-Wang School, in opposition to the Ch'eng-Chu School, insisted that mind is *li;* that the universe is embraced in mind; hence mind possesses all *li.* To understand *li,* therefore, one has merely to understand *mind*. In this way the "Mind School" sought to overcome the "Reason School's" bifurcation of reality. But they in turn met opposition from the later Ch'ing period philosophers, especially Yen Yüan and Tai Chen, who held *li* to be the principle of a thing and *ch'i* its substance. Where there is *li,* they said, there is *ch'i* and, conversely, where there is no *ch'i,* there can be no *li*. *Li,* for them, is immanent in all things and to know it one must "observe and analyze things." It is to be noted, however, that in all their attempts to synthesize energy (*li*) and matter (*ch'i*), never did the philosophers in these three periods claim that only one of them was real and the other a mere abstraction.[7]

As for the "perennial correlation of knowledge and conduct," in Professor Chan's view, they have been identified as a unity by most Neo-Confucian thinkers. The knower must become identified with the known; although the Buddhists stressed 'higher' and 'lower' forms of knowledge of truth, the Taoists talked of 'great' and 'small' knowledge, and the Neo-Confucianists spoke of a distinction between knowledge through one's moral nature (intuition) and knowledge through information (by study). Though Neo-Confucianists did not distrust the latter, they have always put first the attainment of understanding of *li* and the fulfillment of one's nature through knowledge obtained through one's own moral nature. Therefore, the Neo-Confucians did not direct their quest to knowledge of a transcendental Absolute or consider the self to be dissolved into nothingness, as the Taoists and Buddhists did.[8]

Moreover, the Neo-Confucianists believed that one could extend knowledge by first realizing the *li* of one's own mind. If one's whole personality was morally sound, one could attain the worth-while knowledge of the universal *Li*. Intellectual effort and actual practice always went hand in hand for the Ch'eng Chu School. In fact, Chu Hsi combined rational, intuitive, and empirical methods. While deploring meditation or introspection, his "intuition" was "rationally arrived at." In other words, both deductive and inductive methods were used by Neo-Confucianists, although not in the Western sense of 'scientific method.' Their search for knowledge was a personal one and the mind made its own discoveries, not depending on any "revelation" of truth. This was true for Taoist, Buddhist, and Confucian philosophers alike and, in Dr. Chan's opinion, was an important contribution of Chinese philosophy to world philosophy.[9]

Return to Realism Born of Practical Experience

We watched with growing interest the late Ming and early Ch'ing reaction against Sung-Ming, Buddhist-tinged speculation, which came in the form of a return to "empirical realism" with the slogan of "Back to the Han" for pure, unalloyed Confucianism. We saw how patriotic Chinese (both those who had survived the Ming debacle and those growing up under the Manchu régime), smarting under the sting of defeat, had delved into their ancient heritage to find true principles on which to build a new life.

Leaders in this quest arose in the persons of Yen Yüan in the seventeenth century and Tai Chen in the eighteenth; the former eschewed book-knowledge in favor of pragmatic participation in affairs; the latter argued for the immanence of Principle as actualized in affairs, for the release of pent-up desires in wholesome activity, and for "joint-planning" in the administration of government. Release of repressed desires through wholesome activity for a host of Ch'ing scholars took the form of editing the *Classics,* in making historical and textual criticism of all the major works, and in detailed philological and semantic studies.

Reconstructed and Diversified Modern Thought

Toward the end of the nineteenth and during the first decade of the twentieth century, came the movement for democratic reforms in society and government. We were initiated into the intricacies of that movement: how one wing, led by K'ang Yu-wei and Ku Hung-ming, moved cautiously toward a constitutional monarchy guided by pure Confucian principles; how the center, personified in Liang Ch'i-ch'ao, called for a strong resolution in establishing a republican form of government, but a resolution tempered with moderation born of a firm conviction in the ultimate rightness and cohesive power of Confucian morality; and, finally, how the other wing, represented by Sun Yat-sen and Chiang K'ai-shek, as men of action, by-passed Confucianism as a total framework of thought, yet accepted the Lu-Wang dictum that "doing is proof of knowing" as the philosophical basis of their revolutionary procedures. It was this wing that furnished the leadership that successfully launched the new ship of state and piloted it for well-nigh forty years under the aegis of the Kuomintang.

We have been guided into an understanding of how, in those four decades—roughly from 1910 to 1950—the minds of modern Chinese thinkers, under manifold influences from abroad, have been vitally concerned with the varied and persistent problems of the new order. We have been observing how the modern, philosophically inclined mind has been running in two chief, more or less inter-related, channels of thought: the politico-socio-economic and the educational-religious-philosophical. Those who were particularly interested in national issues saw the necessity for revision in political theory and practice. Those whose minds were absorbed with a passion for the Western sciences saw that it was important to harness the Chinese capacity for endurance in mental effort to scientific methods of study. Those who were giving themselves to the solution of China's educational problems felt convinced that the best psychology must be applied to the making of new textbooks. Those who were chiefly concerned with China's moral and social problems saw from another angle how essential it was that there should be revision and adaptation in China's ethical practices. But all in common held the feeling that such radical changes could not be brought about too suddenly without courting disaster. Words to this effect were written in 1927 by the late David Willard Lyon, life-long friend of the Chinese people and close student of their language, customs, and culture.[10]

Our chief concern, however, has been with the effect of political and social revolution on the philosophical bent of the Chinese mind in the republican period. The impact of Western (and particularly of Marxist-Leninist dialectical) materialism, of vitalism and logical empiricism, pragmatism, idealism, and neo-realism, as well as the influence of Western science, religion, art, economics, and education-in-theory-and-practice—all had a profound effect on the philosophic Chinese mind, causing a renascence in and revamping of classical, Chinese reflective concepts. A certain synthesizing process is still going on (both behind the "Bamboo Curtain" and outside of it) in the attempt of contemporary philosophers to harmonize or combine Western with traditional Chinese philosophy.[11]

Finally, we have observed the way in which the traditional cultural heritage has been placed in the crucible of historical and textual criticism by the eager, questing minds of its own inheritors. We have seen how they have re-examined its every facet, weighed every ounce of its pure substance and found it not wanting. When regarded in a modern setting, placed in the right light of appreciative comparison and restated in modern terms, it has stood the test and won the approval of China's leading contemporary philosophers. They have found the wonder of their classical heritage to be the fact that, like a great crown jewel in a circular, glass case, its many facets could be viewed from all sides. By so doing, they have made the discovery that truth is many-sided; that beauty is found in the harmonization of colorful differences; and that goodness emerges from the resolution of diverse viewpoints in the all-embracing magnitude of the One Ultimate Reality.

Concluding Estimates by Chinese Critics

Of Oriental philosophy in general and Chinese philosophy in particular, Fung Yu-lan has this to say: "Chinese philosophy is inferior to Western and Indian philosophies in demonstration and explanation; it is not systematic in form but is systematic in content; it does not contrast man and the universe, but has subordinated metaphysics to human affairs. (Moreover), it has not developed a system of logic, nor has it attached much importance to epistemology, for it is not interested in knowledge for its own sake. (Furthermore), on the other hand, it has always emphasized what man *is* rather than what man *has,* and has extensively discussed the problem of how to live."[12]

To this opinion, Wing-tsit Chan would add it as his mature judgment that Chinese philosophy has been "primarily devoted to the quest for the final solution of human problems. The ultimate goal is . . . 'long life and lasting vision' for Taoism, 'individual perfection and a harmonius social order' for Confucianism and Neo-Confucianism, and 'general welfare' for Mohism. These are not set up as high and remote ideals incapable of realization. On the contrary, they are firmly believed to be attainable and, what is even more significant, attainable in this world. . . . In all indigenous Chinese philosophies, the symbols of perfection, namely the sage and the moral order, do not transcend this world."[13] *

Many Chinese writers have sought to put into a nutshell the total contribution of China to modern world thought. Uppermost in Professor Ho Lin's mind, however, has been the seething ferment caused by the impact of modern world thought upon contemporary Chinese thinking. Writing in *Contemporary Chinese Philosophy,* he summarizes the situation thus:

'(Modern) Chinese philosophy has been looking largely for those points where East and West could be harmonized and the best of both be applied to social life and its changes. . . . Through the study of Western philosophy, the development of a republican spirit, and a new interest in the study of Buddhist philosophy, our contemporary thought has been heightened

* Here Dr. Chan has (probably intentionally) omitted mention of the imported Buddhist philosophy; he might also wish to make an exception of Fung Yu-lan's pre-Communist position, as stated in his *Hsin Yüan-Tao,* Chapter 10.

and deepened. As a result, the Lu-Wang School of thought has been broadened; a new reconciliation has been made between Confucian and Buddhist thought; a new harmonizing of the Ch'eng-Chu and Lu-Wang Schools has been achieved; and a re-study has been made of the history of Chinese philosophy, with a consequent re-systematization and revaluation of it for the new age."[14]

As for China's contribution to the world, one Chinese writer has phrased it in these simple words (in effect) :—China from her long experience has a three-fold heritage which she would willingly share with the rest of the world. *First* of all, is her age-old emphasis on a stable family life. *Second,* is her stress on the "personal equation" or "group conscience" over against the Western conception of "law and order." In the *third* place, is her accentuation upon the use of enlightened reason in settling differences between people and between states.

In writing of the "Outstanding Traits and Contributions of Chinese Civilization," Chen Li-fu describes them thus: "Chinese civilization upholds the life of the people as its center which rests upon benevolence. . . . Chinese civilization takes cosmopolitanism as its ultimate aim, which is built upon the foundation of complete fairness. . . . Chinese civilization aims at the attainment of centralizing harmony which is realized through indefatigable performance. . . . Because of this principle, there was no class war in China. . . . Since there is no permanent system of nobility, the political workers all emerge from among the common people. . . . Chinese civilization upholds propriety and righteousness, which come out of complete sophi-conscience:—The spirit of Chinese civilization lies in the Mean. . . . Sophi-conscience is self-accomplishment . . . (or) . . . the motivating power that brings forth . . . (the) . . . latent organic power (of Nature) . . . (that) . . . "centralizes (or unifies) the multifarious energies of the universe and the individual."[15]

Wing-tsit Chan's concluding estimate of Chinese philosophy is that, no matter how much the newer philosophy of China may be influenced by the West, it will still preserve the old

Chinese ideals: "We refer particularly to the ideals of central harmony, of cordial relationship between Nature and man, of the 'both-and' attitude, of the Golden Mean, of humanism, of the preservation of one's life and the full realization of one's nature, of mental tranquility, of incessant transformation and spontaneous creation, of the interaction of the active and passive universal principles, of the harmony of the One and the Many, and of the (fundamental) goodness of human nature."[16]

NOTES AND REFERENCES

NOTES
to Chapter 1

1 Consult James M. Menzies' *The Culture of the Shang Dynasty* or his *Prehistoric China,* Part 2, on *The Oracle Bones of Yin* and H. G. Creel's *Sinism, Studies in Early Chinese Culture,* and *The Birth of China.* See also my article, "Religious Origins in China" in *The Chinese Recorder,* Shanghai, May, 1940; also my *Chinese Peasant Cults,* pp. 175-178.

2 Joseph Needham: *Science and Civilization in China,* II, p. 300f. Cf. also Vol. I, p. 154.

3 Consult Henry C. Fenn's chart "China-in-Brief" facing p. 44 of Goodrich and Fenn: *Syllabus of the History of Chinese Civilization and Culture.*

4 Cf. Y. L. Fung, *History of Chinese Philosophy,* I, p. 163.

5 Cf. Y. L. Fung: *Short History of Chinese Philosophy,* pp. 18-19.

6 Part V, Book 4 of the *Book of History* (*Shu Ching*).

7 Cf. Fung: *Short History,* p. 131.

8 Cf. Fung: *History,* I, p. 165 and footnote.

9 *Ibid*., p. 169. In his art. "The First Hundred Schools" in *China Reconstructs* (Mar., 1958), p. 29, Yang Hsiang-kwei calls Tsou Yen "the unifier of the Yin-Yang School," but adds, "though its ideas had existed in China since the most ancient times."

10 Cf. Fung: *Short History,* pp. 135-8 (referring to the *Yüeh Ling, passim*). For an extended discussion of the *Yüeh Ling,* see W. E. Soothill: *The Hall of Light,* pp. 22-51.

11 Cf. Needham, Op. Cit., II, p. 243f.

12 Cf. Fung: *History,* I, p. 164 (referring to the *Hung Fan,* pp. 147-8).

13 *Ibid.,* p. 166f, (quoting *The Kuan-tzu,* XXXIX, *chüan* 14, pp. 1-3).

14 Wing-tsit Chan, art., "The Story of Chinese Philosophy" in Charles A. Moore (ed): *Philosophy East and West,* Chapter III, p. 37 (referring to the *Tao Tê Ching,* chapters 8, 42, 55).

15 As translated by W. T. Chan in his art., "Syntheses in Chinese Metaphysics" in Charles A. Moore (ed) : *Essays in East-West Philosophy,* p. 165.

16 As interpreted by Y. L. Fung: *Short History,* p. 141f; Cf. Needham, *Op. Cit.,* II, p. 274.

17 As interpreted by Y. L. Fung: *Short History,* p. 140f.

18 Cf. Fung: *History,* I, p. 390f.

19 *Ibid.,* p. 33, quoting *The Kuo-Yü* (*Yüeh Yü,* II, 1).

20 Cf. Fung: *Short History,* p. 138, quoting *The Kuo-Yü* (*Chou Yü,* I, 10).

21 *Ibid.,* p. 32.

22 *Ibid.,* p. 139f.

23 Cf. Fung: *History,* I, p. 379.

24 *Ibid.,* I, p. 383; 159-ftn. 1; also *Short History,* p. 131.

25 Cf. Fung: *History,* I, p. 165.

26 *Ibid.,* I, p. 33; cf. p. 24.

27 Cf. Yang Ch'ing-k'un (C. K. Yang), art., "The Functional Relationship between Confucian Thought and Chinese Religion" in John K. Fairbank (ed): *Chinese Thought and Institutions,* pp. 272-273.

28 *Ibid.,* p. 275.

29 *Ibid.,* p. 275; Cf. also W. T. Chan, art., "The Story of Chinese Philosophy" in Charles A. Moore (ed) : *Philosophy East and West,* p. 48.

30 Cf. Fung Yu-lan (E. R. Hughes tr.) : *The Spirit of Chinese Philosophy,* p. 116.

NOTES
to Chapter 2

1 Cf. W. E. Soothill: *Hall of Light,* pp. 113, 118.

2 Cf. W. T. Chan, art., "Basic Problems in the Study of Chinese Philosophy" in *Philosophy East and West,* IV, 2 (July, 1954), p. 164.

3 Cf. Fung: *History,* I, p. 172.

4 *Ibid.,* I, p. 178, quoting *The Lao-tzu,* chapter 1.

5 *Ibid.,* p. 180, quoting *The Kuan-tzu,* Chap. XXXIX, *chüan* 13, p. 3.

6 *Ibid.,* p. 180; cf. p. 225.

7 *Ibid.,* p. 181, quoting *The Lao-tzu,* chapter 37.

8 *Ibid.*, p. 180, quoting *The Lao-tzu,* chapter 51.

9 *Ibid.*, pp. 182, 183, quoting *The Lao-tzu,* chapters 25, 40, 65.

10 *Ibid.*, p. 183, quoting *The Lao-tzu,* chapter 23.

11 *Ibid.*, p. 183, quoting *The Lao-tzu,* chapter 43.

12 *Ibid.*, p. 183, quoting *The Lao-tzu,* chapter 30, italics mine.

13 *Ibid.*, p. 188, quoting *The Lao-tzu,* chapters 3, 37; cf. chapter 19.

14 *Ibid.*, p. 188, quoting *The Lao-tzu,* chapters 59, 44, 46.

15 *Ibid.*, pp. 189, 188, quoting *The Lao-tzu,* chapters 20, 19.

16 *Ibid.*, p. 189, quoting *The Lao-tzu,* chapters 48, 20, 18.

17 *Ibid.*, pp. 189-190, quoting *The Lao-tzu,* chapters 20, 48.

18 Needham: *Op. Cit.,* II, pp. 61-63 (referring to Arthur Waley's translation of the *Tao Tê Ching,* chapter 7).

19 W. T. Chan's translation in his art., "The Story of Chinese Philosophy" in Charles A. Moore (ed): *Philosophy East and West,* p. 37, quoting the *Tao Tê Ching,* chapter 16.

20 Cf. Fung, *History,* I, p. 186, quoting *The Lao-tzu* (*Tao Tê Ching*), chapter 57.

21 *Ibid.*

22 *Ibid.*, quoting *The Lao-tzu,* chapters 29, 75.

23 Cf. W. E. Soothill: *A Mission in China,* p. 258.

24 Cf. Fung: *History,* I, p. 225, quoting *The Chuang-tzu,* p. 138.

25 *Ibid.*, p. 225f, quoting *The Chuang-tzu,* p. 15.

26 *Ibid.*, p. 226, quoting *The Chuang-tzu,* p. 209.

27 *Ibid.*, p. 226, quoting *The Chuang-tzu,* p. 365.

28 *Ibid.*, p. 231, quoting *The Chuang-tzu,* p. 31.

29 *Ibid.*, p. 233, quoting *The Chuang-tzu,* p. 21.

30 Cf. W. T. Chan, art., "The Story of Chinese Philosophy" in Charles A. Moore (ed): *Philosophy East and West,* p. 46, referring to the *Tao Tê Ching,* chapter 7; Cf. Fung: *History,* I, p. 34.

31 Cf. Fung: *History,* I, p. 234, quoting *The Chuang-tzu,* p. 205f (with the order of ideas here slightly altered).

32 *Ibid.*, p. 228f (slightly altered).

33 *Ibid.*, p. 237, quoting *The Chuang-tzu,* p. 223f.

34 *Ibid.*, p. 238f, quoting *The Chuang-tzu,* pp. 79-80.

35 *Ibid.*, p. 240f. This passage may be compared with strangely similar expressions by Ch'eng Hao on p. 192, by Chu Hsi on p. 204, by Wang-Yang-ming on p. 217, by Hsiung Shih-li on pp. 328-9, and by Fung Yu-lan on p. 342 of this text.

36 *Ibid.*, p. 241, quoting *The Chuang-tzu,* IV, p. 43.

37 *Ibid.*, p. 241, quoting *The Chuang-tzu,* VI, p. 89.

38 *Ibid.*, p. 243, quoting *The Chuang-tzu,* II, p. 27.

39 *Ibid.*, p. 244.

40 Cf. W. T. Chan, art., "The Story of Chinese Philosophy" in Charles A. Moore (ed) : *Philosophy East and West,* chapter III, p. 45.

41 Cf. W. E. Soothill: *A Mission in China,* p. 258.

42 *Ibid.*, pp. 259-260.

NOTES
to Chapter 3

1 For Fung Yu-lan's modern appraisal of the *Yi Ching, vide supra* pp. 333-334.

2 Cf. W. E. Soothill: *Hall of Light,* p. 148; also p. 17f, where he declares: ". . . neither Confucius nor any of his immediate disciples could have seen this book (the *Li Chi*) in its present form—nor indeed, any of the books on which we are mainly dependent for our knowledge of the doctrine attributed to him. All these books, as we know them, are redactions of the Han period, when they were 'edited.' Confucius may possibly have seen part of the *Book of Changes,* and the ancient *Shu,* or *History,* part or all of the *Odes,* possibly the (source) text of Lü's *Spring and Autumn Annals,* and perhaps the archetypal ritual manuals from which part of the material for the three ritual books (*I Li, Chou Li,* and *Li Chi*) was drawn. . . . But, as Chu Hsi asserts, it is possible that part of the *Li Chi* may actually consist of 'treatises composed by the disciples of the disciples of Confucius'. . . . These treatises . . . had never existed as a book; they were the unassembled presentation of various subjects as recorded by different writers (in the succeeding schools of Confucian thought)."*Author's note:* In the above-mentioned process certain elements of the *Record of Music* (*Yüeh Chi*) became incorporated in Book XVII and other parts of the *Li Chi.*

3 —The dating of the *Ch'un Ch'iu* presents a problem. These "Annals of the State of Lu" must have existed in some form in the time of Confucius but in what 'archetypal' form is difficult if not impossible to say. Of the several commentaries on it, the *Kung-yang Chuan* by Kung-yang Kao at the beginning of the Han dynasty, was much studied until the influence of Liu Hsin (d. A.D. 23), cataloguer of the Han Imperial Library, swung interest to the older *Tso Chuan* of Tso Ch'iu-ming. (Cf. Fung, I, 16, 16-ftn 3, 417).

Further Note on the Tso Chuan

In his *Criticism on Ancient History,* p. 78, a modern Chinese commentator, T. K. Koo, writes: "As to the *Tso Chuan,* or commentary of Tso Ch'iu-ming, it was originally an *'Episodes of the States,'* commonly known as *Kuo Yü,* compiled by a scholar of the Contending States Period (3rd century, B.C.?). It had not the least . . . connection . . . with the book *Ch'un Ch'iu.* (Later) it was handed down to Liu Hsin and through his recompilation and addition to it of the mysterious and obscure words (known as the 'Fifty Huan'), it became finally a commentary on the *Ch'un Ch'iu.* To the unused portion of materials, he re-applied the old name *Kuo Yü.*"

After quoting the above statement, another modern commentator, Hsü T'eng-hui (in an unpublished doctoral dissertation, Hartford Seminary Foundation, March, 1930, pp. 36[a], 33) has this to say: "The work (*Ch'un Ch'iu*) appeared in Liu Hsin's catalogue with two collections of the text of the classic. . . . Hence we know that at this early time the text of the classic was known, and that there were writings of five different masters commenting on it. . . . Of the three (extant) ones, the *Chuan of Tso* was incomparably the most important. Of the writer himself . . . next to nothing is known . . . except that he was a disciple of Confucius; but his glowing narrative remains, and is likely to continue to remain, one of the most precious heirlooms of the Chinese people. What he did was this:

"He (Tso Ch'iu-ming) took the dry bones of these annals (*Ch'un Ch'iu*) and clothed them with life and reality by adding a more or less complete setting to each of the events recorded. He described the loves and hates, the heroes and their battles, their treaties, their feasting and their deaths in a style which is always effective and often approved as to grandeur. Circumstances of apparently the most trivial character are expanded into interesting episodes, and every now and then some quaint conceit or scrap of proverbial literature is thrown in to give a passing flavor of its own."

(Used by permission of the author. For a résumé of Dr. Hsü's thesis: "The Idea of God in the Chinese Classics," *vide supra,* pp. 307ff).

Hu Shih favors the theory that the *Tso Chuan* was a forged

'classic' of the Han dynasty, written probably at the end of the first century, B.C., or else during the régime of Wang Mang in the first century, A.D. (*Vide supra*, p. 88 for his opinion of the *Chou Li* as also one of those 'forged classics' of the Han dynasty.)

Further Note on the Ch'un Ch'iu

The first prime minister of the House of Ch'in, Lü Pu-wei, "is said to have assembled a number of scholars who . . . compiled the *Ch'un Ch'iu*, or *Spring and Autumn*—i.e., Annals. The work, published in 238 B.C., is styled the *Lü Shih Ch'un Ch'iu*, and a book still exists with that title (whose authenticity is questioned). The contents of its first 12 sections, however, styled the *Yüeh Ling*, or 'Monthly Observances' (Commands), have formed part of the *Li Chi* since the 1st century, A.D." (Cf. W. E. Soothill, *Hall of Light*, p. 20). This work must have been based on a source handed down from the time of Confucius.

A further word on Lü Pu-wei (d. 235 B.C.) is of interest here. When the Ch'in prince whom he was serving died, Lü was made guardian of his master's son. As regent, he may have substituted his own son; at any rate, when the boy grew up he became China's first unifier—the famous Ch'in Shih Huang Ti. It was he who followed the suggestion of his prime minister, Li Ssu, and decreed the "Burning of the Books" in 213 B.C., which may have included any copies of the *Lü Shih Ch'un Ch'iu* and other classical books found outside the imperial archives. (Cf. Fung, I, p. 13-ftn 2).

4 For Fung Yu-lan's modern appraisal of the *Chung Yung, vide supra*, pp. 334-336.

5 Cf. Y. L. Fung: *History*, I, pp. 19-21, for a further discussion of the chronology of the *Classics*. Cf. J. B. Noss: *Man's Religions*, p. 344-ftn; 345 and ftn; 346-ftn, and 347 for résumé of critical opinion on the *Classics* and the *Four Books*.

6 Cf. Hu Shih: *Development of Logical Method in Ancient China*, p. 22.

7 Cf. Fung: *History*, I, p. 59f, quoting *Lun Yü*, XIII, 3.

8 *Ibid.*, p. 68.

9 *Ibid.*, p. 66f.

10 *Ibid.*, p. 69-ftn 2.

11 *Ibid.*, pp. 69-71, quoting *Lun Yü,* XVI, 27; XII, 22; XII, 1, 2; VI, 28.

12 *Ibid.*, I, p. 71, quoting *Lun Yü,* IV, 15.

13 *Ibid.*, I, p. 72.

14 *Ibid.*, I, p. 74f, quoting *Lun Yü,* XVIII, 7; XIV, 41; IX, 1; IV, 16.

15 Cf. W. T. Chan art., "The Story of Chinese Philosophy" in Charles A. Moore (ed): *Philosophy East and West* (Chap. III), pp. 27-29, 31.

16 *Ibid.*, p. 26. (W. T. Chan quotes the Introduction to the *Great Learning* as "the finest passage from Confucius").

17 Cf. Lin Yutang: *The Wisdom of Confucius,* p. 94, *Chung Yung,* sec. 1—"Central Harmony" (using Ku Hung-ming's translation).

18 *Ibid.*, p. 95 (*Chung Yung,* sec. 2—"The Golden Mean").

19 *Ibid.*, p. 97 (*Chung Yung,* sec. 2—"The Golden Mean").

20 *Ibid.*, pp. 99-101 (*Chung Yung,* sec. 4—"Humanistic Standard").

21 *Ibid.*, p. 113, 112 (*Chung Yung,* sec. 8—"Absolute True Selves").

22 *Ibid.*, p. 110 (*Chung Yung,* sec. 7—"Being One's True Self").

23 *Ibid.*, p. 173 (*Lun Yü,* sec. 7—"Superior and Inferior Man").

24 *Ibid.*, p. 164 (*Lun Yü* sec. 5—"Wit and Wisdom").

25 *Ibid.*, p. 179 (*Lun Yü, sec.* 8—"The Mean as the Ideal Character").

26 *Ibid.*, p. 169 (*Lun Yü,* sec. 6—"Humanism and True Manhood").

27 *Ibid.*, p. 216f (with order of ideas altered) (*Li Chi,* IX, sec. 5—"Method of Cultivating Li"); Cf. also Leonard S. Hsü: *The Political Philosophy of Confucianism,* pp. 90-104 on "The Principle of Li."

28 Cf. Lin Yutang, *Op. Cit.*, p. 215 (*Li Chi,* IX, sec. 4—"Li Based on Heaven").

29 *Ibid.*, p. 206f (*Li Chi,* IX, sec. 1—"Two Orders of Human Society"); Cf. also M. M. Dawson: *The Ethics of Confucius,* pp. 299-303, where Chen Huang-chang's translation rather puts the 'Golden Age' in the future.

30 Cf. Lin Yutang, *Op. Cit.*, p. 126 (*Ta Hsüeh,* sec. 1—"General Idea").

31 *Ibid.*, p. 164 (*Lun Yü,* sec. 5—"Wit and Wisdom").

32 *Ibid.*, pp. 133f, 136 (*Ta Hsüeh,* sec. 8—"Relation between National Life and World Peace").

33 *Ibid.,* p. 132 (*Ta Hsüeh,* sec. 7—"Relation between Family and National Life".

34 *Ibid.,* p. 194 (*Li Chi,* XXVI—"First Discourse on Education").

35 *Ibid.,* p. 181 (*Lun Yü,* sec. 9—"Government by Moral Example").

36 *Ibid.,* p. 136f (*Ta Hsüeh,* sec. 8—"Relation between National Life and World Peace").

37 *Ibid.,* p. 129 (*Ta Hsüeh,* sec. 3—"On Achieving True Knowledge").

38 *Ibid.,* p. 180 (*Lun Yü,* sec. 9—"Moral Ideal of Government").

39 *Ibid.,* pp. 105-110 (*Chung Yung,* sec. 6—"Ethics and Politics").

40 *Ibid.,* p. 125 (*Ta Hsüeh,* sec. 1—"General Idea").

41 *Ibid.,* p. 107 (*Chung Yung,* sec. 6—"Ethics and Politics").

42 *Ibid.,* p. 105 (*Chung Yung,* sec. 5—"Certain Models"). For a discussion of the political intrigues of Confucius' day, see Shigeki Kaizuka: *Confucius,* pp. 126-170 (Chap. V, "Confucius the Statesman," especially sec. 4. "Confucius the would-be revolutionary," pp. 148-158, and following sections).

43 Cf. Lin Yutang, *Op. Cit.,* p. 125 (*Ta Hsüeh,* sec. 1—"General Idea").

44 *Ibid.,* p. 219 (*Li Chi,* XVIII, sec. 1—"Need for Education").

45 *Ibid.,* p. 184 (*Lun Yü,* sec. 10—"On Education, Ritual, and Poetry").

46 *Ibid.,* p. 223 (*Li Chi,* XVIII, sec. 3—"Extra-Curricular Studies").

47 *Ibid.,* p. 162 (*Lun Yü,* sec. 5—"Wit and Wisdom")

48 *Ibid.,* p. 223 (*Li Chi,* XVIII, sec. 3—"Extra Curricular Studies" and sec. 4—"The Ideal Teacher"); Cf. also Liu Wu-chi: *Confucius, His Life and Time,* pp. 122-124, sec. 3, on "Individualized Tutorship."

49 Cf. Lin Yutang, *Op. Cit.,* p. 223 (*Li Chi,* XVIII, sec. 3—"Extra-Curricular Studies").

50 Cf. Y. L. Fung: *History,* I, p. 47f.

51 Cf. W. T. Chan, art., "Hu Shih and Chinese Philosophy" in *Philosophy East and West, VI,* 1 (April, 1956), p. 11.

52 See the late D. Willard Lyon's unpublished manuscript "Confucianism Today" (Shanghai, 1927), Chap. 2, p. 11 (Used by permission of the author before his death).

53 Cf. Lin Yutang, *Op. Cit.*, p. 184 (*Lun Yü*, sec. 10—"On Education, Ritual and Poetry").

54 *Ibid.*, p. 220 (*Li Chi*, XVIII, sec. 1—"Need for Education").

55 *Ibid.*, p. 224 (*Li Chi*, XVIII, sec. 4—"The Ideal Teacher").

56 *Ibid.*, p. 226f (*Li Chi*, XVIII, sec. 5—"Process of Learning").

57 *Ibid.*, p. 224 (*Li Chi*, XVIII, sec. 3—"Extra-Curricular Studies").

58 *Ibid.*, p. 225 (*Li Chi*, XVIII, sec. 4—"The Ideal Teacher").

59 *Ibid.*, p. 227 (*Li Chi*, XVIII, sec. 5—"Process of Learning").

60 *Ibid.*, p. 225 (*Li Chi*, XVIII, sec. 4—"The Ideal Teacher").

61 *Ibid.*, p. 182 (*Lun Yü*, sec. 10—"On Education, Ritual, and Poetry").

62 *Ibid.*, p. 182 (*Lun Yü*, sec. 10—"On Education, Ritual, and Poetry").

63 *Ibid.*, p. 183 (*Lun Yü*, sec. 10—"On Education, Ritual, and Poetry").

64 *Ibid.*, p. 208 (*Li Chi*, IX, sec. 2—"Evolution of Li or Social Order").

65 *Ibid.*, p. 193 (*Li Chi*, XXVI, "First Discourse on Education").

66 *Ibid.*, p. 194 (*Li Chi*, XXVI, "First Discourse on Education").

67 *Ibid.*, p. 194 (*Li Chi*, XXVI, "First Discourse on Education").

68 *Ibid.*, p. 188 Introductory note.

69 *Ibid.*, p. 146f (*Lun Yü*, sec. 1—"Descriptions of Confucius").

70 *Ibid.*, p. 147f (*Lun Yü*, sec. 1—"Descriptions of Confucius"); quoted also by Christopher Storrs in *Many Creeds, One Cross*, p. 109.

71 Cf. Evan Morgan: *Guide to Wenli Styles and Chinese Ideals*, p. 164.

72 Cf. Lin Yutang, *Op. Cit.*, p. 149.

73 *Ibid.*, p. 115 (*Chung Yung*, sec. 9—"Eulogy on Confucius").

74 *Ibid.*, pp. 117, 119 (*Chung Yung*, sec. 9—"Eulogy on Confucius").

75 *Ibid.*, p. 151 (*Lun Yü*, sec. 2—"Emotional Life of Confucius"); also pp. 166, 184 (*Lun Yü*, sec. 6—"Humanism and True Manhood").

76 *Ibid.*, pp. 165, 162, 164 (*Lun Yü*, sec. 5—"Wit and Wisdom").

77 Cf. John K. Shryock: *Origin and Development of the State Cult of Confucius*, p. 206.

78 Cf. Y. L. Fung: *History*, I. p. 48 (*Lun Yü*, VII, 33).

79 *Ibid.*, p. 48; Cf. p. 106. Space will not permit our going into the controversy started by Hu Shih's essay "On the Ju" (*Shuo*

Ju, 1934), as to the real status of the *ju* or scholar class before and during Confucius' lifetime. *Vide* W. T. Chan's art., "Hu Shih and Chinese Philosophy" in *Philosophy East and West,* VI, 1 (April, 1956), pp. 10-11; also his art., "Basic Problems in the Study of Chinese Philosophy" in *Philosophy East and West,* IV, 2, (July, 1954), pp. 160-162.

80 Cf. Y. L. Fung: *History,* I, pp. 49, 53 (*Lun Yü,* VII, 7).

81 *Ibid.,* p. 51 (*Lun Yü,* XVIII, 7; Cf. also p. 136.

82 *Ibid.,* p. 51 (*Mem. Hist.,* V, 308).

83 *Ibid.,* p. 51 (*Chuang-tzu,* p. 389).

84 *Ibid.,* p. 52 (*Han-fei-tzu, chüan,* 19, p. 3f).

85 *Ibid.,* p. 51 (*Lun Yü,* XIII, 4 and XI, 18).

86 *Ibid.,* p. 52 (*Lun Yü,* XIX, 13).

87 Cf. W. T. Chan, art., "The Story of Chinese Philosophy" in Charles A. Moore (ed): *Philosophy East and West,* Chap. III, p. 29.

88 Cf. Y. L. Fung: *History,* I, p. 108 (*Mencius,* VII-b, 38).

89 Cf. Lin Yutang, *Op. Cit.,* pp. 252, 250 (*Mencius,* VI, Pt. I, Introductory note).

90 Cf. Liang Ch'i-ch'ao: *History of Chinese Political Thought,* p. 53f.

91 Cf. Y. L. Fung: *History,* I, p. 121f (*Mencius,* VI-a, 6).

92 Cf. Lin Yutang, *Op. Cit.,* pp. 276-282 (*Mencius,* VI, Part I; Cf. also Fung, I, p. 123).

93 Cf. Y. L. Fung: *History,* I, p. 120 (*Mencius,* I-a, 7).

94 *Ibid.,* p. 120.

95 Cf. W. T. Chan, art., "The Story of Chinese Philosophy" in Charles A. Moore (ed): *Philosophy East and West,* Chapter III, p. 30f.

96 Cf. Lin Yutang, *Op. Cit.,* pp. 264, 263, 262, 260f (*Mencius,* VI, Pt. III—"The Higher Life and the Greater Self").

97 Cf. Y. L. Fung: *History,* I, p. 126 (*Mencius,* IV-b, 6); also p. 127 (*Mencius,* VII-b, 33).

98 *Ibid.,* p. 129 (*Mencius,* VII-a, 13, 4).

99 *Ibid.,* p. 131 (*Mencius,* II-a, 2-par. 13).

100 *Ibid.,* p. 117f.

101 *Ibid.,* p. 118.

102 *Ibid.,* p. 118 (*Mencius,* I-a, 3).

103 *Ibid.*

104 *Ibid.,* pp. 114, 117f.

105 Cf. Lin Yutang, *Op. Cit.,* p. 251f (*Mencius,* VI, Part I, Introductory note).

106 Cf. Homer H. Dubs: *Hsüntze, The Moulder of Ancient Confucianism,* pp. 22, 25.

107 *Ibid.,* Preface xviii, xvii.

108 Cf. Y. L. Fung: *History,* I, p. 285 (*Hsün-tzu,* Chapter 17, pp. 173-175).

109 *Ibid.,* p. 285 (*Hsün-tzu,* Chapter 17, p. 183).

110 Cf. W. T. Chan, art., "Syntheses in Chinese Metaphysics" in Charles A. Moore (ed): *Essays in East-West Philosophy,* p. 176.

111 Cf. Y. L. Fung: *History,* I. p. 286f (*Hsün-tzu,* Ch. 19, p. 234; Ch. 23, p. 301).

112 *Ibid.,* p. 287 (*Hsün-tzu,* Ch. 23, p. 312f).

113 *Ibid.,* p. 288 (*Hsün-tzu,* Ch. 8, p .115f). *Note:* a penetrating analysis of this phase of Hsün Tzu's thinking may be found in Andrew Chih-yi Cheng: *Hsüntzu's Theory of Human Nature and Its Influence on Chinese Thought.*

114 Cf. Homer H. Dubs, *Op. Cit.,* Foreword, xiii-xiv.

115 *Ibid.,* pp. 177-179.

116 *Ibid.,* p. 179f.

117 *Ibid.,* p. 171f (*Hsün-tzu,* XXI, 8).

118 *Ibid.,* p. 173 (Dubs's paraphrase).

119 Cf. Y. L. Fung: *History,* I, p. 290.

120 Cf. Dubs, *Op. Cit.,* p. 188f (*Hsün-tzu,* I, 7).

121 Cf. W. T. Chan, art., "The Story of Chinese Philosophy" in Charles A. Moore (ed): *Philosophy East and West,* Chap III, p. 32.

122 Cf. Dubs, *Op. Cit.,* p. 191f (*Hsün-tzu,* I, 9f).

123 *Ibid.,* p. 193 (*Hsün-tzu,* I, 9).

124 *Ibid.,* p. 195 (*Hsün-tzu,* II, 20).

125 Cf. Y. L. Fung: *History,* I, p. 293 (*Hsün-tzu,* III, *chüan* 2, pp. 6-7).

126 Cf. Dubs, *Op. Cit.,* p. 84.

127 Cf. W. T. Chan, art., "The Story of Chinese Philosophy" in Charles A. Moore (ed): *Philosophy East and West,* Chapter III, pp. 32-33.

NOTES
to Chapter 4

1 Cf. Hu Shih: *Development of Logical Method in China,* p. 57.

2 Cf. Y. L. Fung: *History,* I, p. 83 (referring to *Lü-Shih Ch'un Ch'iu,* XIX, 3, p. 327f.)

3 *Ibid.,* p. 84 (*Lü-Shih Ch'un Ch'iu,* I, 5, p. 12).

4 Cf. Liang Ch'i-ch'ao: *History of Chinese Political Thought,* p. 93f (quoting *Mo-tzu:* "On Impartial Love," sec. 1, 2).

5 *Ibid.,* p. 94 (Mo-tzu, "On Observing Little Things").

6 Cf. Y. L. Fung: *History,* I, pp. 91-93 (*Mo-tzu,* XVI, pp. 87ff—slightly altered).

7 *Ibid.,* p. 94.

8 *Ibid.,* p. 85f (*Mo-tzu,* XXXV, p. 182f).

9 Cf. Yi-pao Mei (Y. P. Mei): *Motse, The Neglected Rival of Confucius,* pp. 61-68; 68-9; 69; 84.

10 Cf. Y. L. Fung: *History,* I, p. 87 (*Mo-tzu,* XX, pp. 117-119).

11 *Ibid.,* p. 88f (*Mo-tzu,* XXI, pp. 120-122; XXV, p. 126f).

12 *Ibid.,* p. 89f (*Mo-tzu,* XXXII, p. 176f).

13 Cf. Liang Ch'i-ch'ao, *Op. Cit.,* p. 98 (*Mo-tzu,* "On the Classics," 1; "On Impartial Love," 2, 3; "On Law and Form").

14. Cf. Yi-pao Mei, *Op. Cit.,* p. 130, quoting James Legge's translation, Vol. IV, p. 179.

15 Cf. W. T. Chan, art., "The Story of Chinese Philosophy" in Charles A. Moore (ed): *Philosophy East and West,* Chapter III, p. 39.

16 Cf. Yi-pao Mei, *Op. Cit.,* pp. 128-135.

17 *Ibid.,* pp. 129-130, 135.

18 *Ibid.,* p. 131.

19 Cf. Y. L. Fung: *History,* I, p. 94f (*Mo-tzu,* XVIII, pp. 101-104).

20 *Ibid.,* p. 95f (referring to *Mencius,* IV-a, 14).

21 Cf. Yi-pao Mei, *Op. Cit.,* p. 97 (*Mo-tzu,* p. 115).

22 *Ibid.,* p. 97 (*Mo-tzu,* p. 128f).

23 Cf. Y. L. Fung: *History,* I, p. 81 (*Mo-tzu,* L, pp. 257-259).

24 Cf. Yi-pao Mei, *Op. Cit.,* p. 99.

25 Cf. Y. L. Fung: *History,* I, pp. 100-103 (*Mo-tzu,* XI, p. 55f; XIII, pp. 72-75).

26 *Ibid.,* p. 102 (*Hsün-tzu,* p. 184f).

27 *Ibid.,* p. 101 (referring to Hobbes: *Leviathan,* Pt. I, Ch. 17, and Pt. II, Ch. 29).

28 *Ibid.,* p. 96f (*Mo-tzu,* XXVI, pp. 137-139).

29 *Ibid.,* p. 98f (*Mo-tzu, XXXI,* p. 160).

30 *Ibid.,* p. 100 (ref. to *Mo-tzu,* XXXV, p. 135f).

31 Cf. W. T. Chan, art., "The Story of Chinese Philosophy" in

Charles A. Moore (ed): *Philosophy East and West,* Chapter III, p. 41.

32 Cf. Y. L. Fung: *History,* I, p. 103f (*Chuang-tzu,* XXXIII, p. 440f).

33 Cf. H. G. Creel: *Chinese Thought From Confucius to Mao Tse-tung,* pp. 56, 66.

34 Cf. Y. L. Fung: *History,* I, p. 104 (*Hsün-tzu,* p. 263f).

35 Cf. Liang Ch'i-ch'ao, *Op. Cit.,* pp. 111, 102-105.

36 Cf. Y. L. Fung: *History,* I, pp. 125, 133-4 (*Mencius,* III-b, 9, par. 9; VII-a, 26).

37 *Ibid.,* p. 133 (*Han-fei-tzu,* 50, *chüan* 19, p. 8); also p. 134 (*Huai-nan-tzu,* Ch. 13, p. 155).

38 *Ibid.,* pp. 133-137 (referring to *The Lieh-tzu,* Chapter on "Yang Chu").

39 *Ibid.,* p. 137f; 139; 143. Cf. also Fung: *Short History,* pp. 60-67. On *The Lieh-tzu, vide supra* pp. 91-2.

40 *Ibid.,* p. 203 (Tr. note).

41 Cf. E. R. Hughes: *Chinese Philosophy in Classical Times,* pp. 122-128.

42 Cf. *Harvard Journal of Asiatic Studies,* Vol. 16 (1953), pp. 404-437.

43 Cf. Y. L. Fung: *History,* I, pp. 192-194; 305-6; 323-325.

NOTES
to Chapter 5

1 Cf. Y. L. Fung: *History,* I, p. 335.

2 Cf. E. R. Hughes: *Chinese Philosophy in Classical Times,* Preface, p. xlii; also Henry C. Fenn's chart—"China in Brief" (revised, 1950), facing p. 44 in Goodrich and Fenn: *A Syllabus of the History of Chinese Civilization and Culture* (N. Y., 6th edition, 1958).

3 Cf. J. J. L. Duyvendak: *The Book of Lord Shang, passim.*

4 Cf. Elbert Duncan Thomas: *Chinese Political Thought,* p. 20.

5 Cf. Y. L. Fung: *History,* I, p. 321 (*Kuan-tzu,* Ch. 46, *chüan* 21, p. 10); *vide supra* footnote, p. 76.

6 *Ibid.,* p. 320 (*Shih Chi,* Ch. 63, pp. 5-6); also Cf. pp. 321-323; Cf. Hu Shih, *Op. Cit.,* pp. 181-184.

7 *Ibid.,* pp. 325f; 321-323 (*Han-fei-tzu,* Chaps. 27, 38, 6, 41, 49, 28, 7 and 48).

8 Cf. Leonard Tomkinson art., "The Early Legalist School of Chinese Political Thought" in *Open Court,* Vol. 45 (1931), pp. 357-369.

9 Cf. Y. L. Fung: *History,* I, p. 323 (Fung paraphrase).

10 *Ibid.,* pp. 15-17.

11 *Ibid.,* pp. 325-327; 330 (especially *Han-fei-tzu,* Ch. 50, *chüan* 19, p. 9f).

12 *Ibid.,* pp. 330-335 (especially *Chuang-tzu,* Ch. 13, pp. 160f, 163f; Cf. *Han-fei-tzu,* Chaps. 20, 21; also *Chuang-tzu,* Ch. 11, p. 133f; Cf. *Kuan-tzu,* Chaps. 38, 49).

13 *Ibid.,* pp. 327-336, *passim;* Cf. p. 286f (*Hsün-tzu,* Ch. 23, p. 301).

14 *Ibid.,* p. 328.

15 *Ibid.,* p. 322.

16 Cf. Leonard Tomkinson, *Op. Cit.,* p. 365f.

NOTES
to Chapter 6

1 Cf. John K. Shryock: *Origin and Development of the State Cult of Confucius,* pp. 113ff.

2. Cf. Y. L. Fung: *History,* I, p. 399; see also 395-398.

3 Cf. Evan Morgan: *Tao, the Great Luminant,* pp. 1-242, *passim;* especially pp. 184, 186.

4 Cf. W. T. Chan, art., "The Story of Chinese Philosophy" in Charles A. Moore (ed): *Philosophy East and West,* pp. 48-50.

5 Cf. Yao Shan-yu, art., "The Cosmological and Anthropological Philosophy of Tung Chung-shu" in *J.R.A.S.* (N.C.B.), 1948, Vol. LXXIII, pp. 40-68. Cf. Fung: *History,* I, p. 17.

6 Cf. Yao Shan-yu, *Op. Cit.,* p. 45 and footnote. (Translator's note: "Tung's philosophy may be called 'Theistic Naturalism', but he does not seem to conceive Heaven in anthropomorphic terms. His Heaven is essentially Nature possessing moral principle, purpose, will, and intelligence"). Cf. Fung: *History,* II, pp. 9, 26ff, where he notes the originality of Tung's thinking.

7 Cf. Yao Shan-yu, *Op. Cit.,* pp. 45-47.

8 *Ibid.,* p. 58.

9 *Ibid.,* pp. 48, 49, 50.

10 *Ibid.,* p. 52f.

11 Cf. Y. L. Fung: *History,* Vol. II, p. 42f; Cf. p. 37, where Fung notes that "in thus stressing the importance of nurture in the cultivation of the goodness of the nature, Tung Chung-shu seems to be harmonizing the views of Confucius, Mencius and Hsün Tzu."

12 *Ibid.,* pp. 53, 54, 69 (referring to Tung Chung-shu: *Ch'un Ch'iu Fan Lu,* Ch. 23 and *History of the Former Han* (*Ch'ien Han Shu*), 56:18).

13 *Ibid.,* pp. 58-60.

14 *Ibid.,* p. 131.

15 *Ibid.,* pp. 131, 18, 19, 129.

16 *Ibid.,* Preface xx; also p. 131.

17 Cf. Hu Shih, art., "Wang Mang, the Socialist Emperor of Nineteen Centuries Ago" in *J.R.A.S.* (N.C.B.), 1928, Vol. LIX, pp. 224-225 (referring to *Han Shu,* Bk. 99b; Cf. Bk. 24a). Cf. also H. G. Creel: *Chinese Thought from Confucius to Mao Tse-tung,* p. 179.

18 Cf. Hu Shih, *Op. Cit.,* pp. 226-228, 229, 228 (*Han Shu,* Bk. 24a, 24b; Bk. 99b).

19 *Ibid.,* pp. 229, 228, 223.

20 Cf. Y. L. Fung: *History,* II, p. 134f.

21 Cf. Hu Shih, *Op. Cit.,* pp. 229, 220f.

22 Cf. Y. L. Fung: *History,* II, pp. 134ff; 150ff. Cf. also W. T. Chan, art., "The Story of Chinese Philosophy" in Charles A. Moore (ed): *Philosophy East and West,* pp. 48-51; Cf. also H. G. Creel, *Op. Cit.,* p. 183.

23 Cf. Y. L. Fung: *History,* II, p. 134f.

24 *Ibid.,* II, p. 9.

25 *Ibid.,* II, pp. 146, 150, 137.

26 Cf. Warren H. Stuart: *The Use of Material from China's Spiritual Inheritance in the Christian Education of Chinese Youth,* p. 112. Cf. also W. T. Chan, *Op. Cit.,* p. 51.

27 Cf. Y. L. Fung: *History,* II, pp. 158-161.

28 *Ibid.,* II, pp. 162-167; also 168-175, 190f.

29 *Ibid.,* II, p. 156f.

30 Cf. W. T. Chan, art., "Syntheses in Chinese Metaphysics" in Charles A. Moore (ed): *Essays in East-West Philosophy,* p. 176.

31 Cf. W. T. Chan, art. "The Story of Chinese Philosophy" in Charles A. Moore (ed.): *Philosophy East and West,* Ch. III, p. 50f.

32 Cf. Y. L. Fung, *Op. Cit.*, II, Preface xxii; Cf. also W. T. Chan, art., "Syntheses in Chinese Metaphysics," *Loc. cit.*, p. 176.

33 Cf. Y. L. Fung: *History,* II, pp. 190-194; Cf. W. T. Chan, art., "The Story of Chinese Philosophy," *Loc. cit.*, p. 51, where Dr. Chan speaks of the vogue which the *Lieh-tzu* had in Taoist circles, because of its "fatalistic mechanism."

34 Cf. Y. L. Fung, *Op. Cit.,* II, p. 196 (referring to the *Lieh-tzu,* Ch. 7, entitled "Yang Chu," but probably not written by him, p. 41).

35 *Ibid.,* II, pp. 196-200, 203.

36 *Ibid.,* II, pp. 202-204.

37 *Ibid.,* II, pp. 216, 235f.

38 Cf. Y. L. Fung: *Chuang-tzu,* pp. 147-156; Cf. Fung: *History* II, pp. 210-219, 236.

39 Cf. W. T. Chan, art., "The Story of Chinese Philosophy," *Loc. cit.,* p. 51.

40 Cf. W. T. Chan's review of A. C. Graham: *Two Chinese Philosophers* in *J.A.O.S.,* Vol. 79, No. 2, April-June, 1959, p. 151. Cf. also Y. L. Fung: *History,* II, p. 174f.

NOTES

to Chapter 7

1 Cf. John B. Noss: *Man's Religions,* pp. 151-152 (quoting phrases from the Majjhima Nikaya 1.22 in Lord Chalmers: *Further Dialogues of the Buddha* I, p. 15; also Majjhima Nikaya 1.22 as found in Sir Charles Eliot: *Hinduism and Buddhism,* Vol. I. p. 139; and Majjhima Nikaya 1.24 in *Further Dialogues of the Buddha* I. p. 17).

2 Cf. Noss, *Op. Cit.,* p. 153f (condensed from Edward J. Thomas (tr) : *Buddhist Scriptures* (Wisdom of the East Series), p. 52 (*Khuddaka Patha* 2) .

3 Cf. W. T. Chan, art. "Buddhism" in Ferm (ed): *Encyclopedia of Religion,* p. 96, where Dr. Chan dates it as early as 383 B.C.

4 Cf. Edward J. Thomas: *History of Buddhist Thought,* pp. 37f, 41, 168-170, 212f; also App. II-pp. 288-292. Cf. Albert Schweitzer: *Indian Thought and its Development,* pp. 56-74. I am indebted to Schweitzer for much of the material presented in succeeding para-

graphs. Cf. P. T. Raju: *Idealistic Thought of India,* pp. 208-218 (on Sarvāstivādins) and p. 218 (on Mahāsāṅghikās).

5 Cf. P. T. Raju, *Op. Cit.,* pp. 93-96, 97-103.

6 *Ibid.,* pp. 117-119, 121f.

7 For a brief résumé of this philosophy, see M. Hiriyanna: *Essentials of Indian Philosophy,* pp. 106-128.

8 Cf. P. T. Raju, *Op. Cit.* pp. 173-176.

9 Cf. Eliot: *Hinduism and Buddhism,* Vol. II, pp. 76-79.

10 Cf. K. L. Reichelt: *Truth and Tradition in Chinese Buddhism,* p. 204f; also John B. Noss: *Op. Cit.,* pp. 180-182.

11 Cf. Reichelt, *Op. Cit.,* p. 30, ftn.; also Herbert A. Giles: *Confucianism and Its Rivals,* p. 169.

12 Cf. Eliot, *Op. Cit.,* II, pp. 82-84; also Charles S. Braden: *The Scriptures of Mankind,* pp. 198, 196. More extravagant than either the *Buddha Carita* or the *Jātaka Tales* of Buddha's miraculous birth and life, was the *Lalita-Vistara,* translated into Chinese about A.D. 300.

13 Cf. W. T. Chan, art. "Aśvaghoṣa" in Ferm (ed): *Enc. of Relig.,* p. 92.

14 Cf. T. R. V. Murti: *The Central Philosophy of Buddhism,* Preface, p. vii.

15 *Ibid.,* p. vii.

16 *Ibid.,* p. 6.

17 *Ibid.,* pp. 329-332.

18 *Ibid.,* pp. 212f, 217f, 223f.

19 *Ibid.,* pp. 224-226.

20 Cf. S. Radhakrishnan: *India and China,* p. 122ff; also Eliot: *Op. Cit.,* II, pp. 84-86.

21 Cf. T. R. V. Murti, *Op. Cit., passim,* for a detailed analysis of the rise and influence of the Mādhyamika System of Dialectic.

22 Cf. Reichelt, *Op. Cit.,* p. 31; also Radhakrishnan, *Op. Cit.,* pp. 124-128.

23 Cf. Eliot, *Op. Cit.,* II, p. 86; also W. T. Chan, art. "Vasubandhu" in Ferm (ed), *Op. Cit.,* p. 109.

24 Cf. C. H. Hamilton, art. "Buddhist Philosophical Systems" in Ferm (ed): *A History of Philosophical Systems,* Chap. III, pp. 39, 41; also T. R. V. Murti, *Op. Cit.,* pp. 586, 587.

25 Cf. Murti, *Op. Cit.,* pp. 588, 587.

26 Cf. W. T. Chan, art., "Buddhist Terminology: Idealistic School" in Ferm (ed): *Enc. of Relig.,* pp. 99-100.

27 Cf. S. Radhakrishnan: *Indian Philosophy,* Vol. I, pp. 624, 625.
28 Cf. Murti, *Op. Cit.,* p. 587.

NOTES
to Chapter 8

1 Cf. Y. L. Fung (Derk Bodde, tr.): *History of Chinese Philosophy,* Vol. II, p. 239f.

2 Cf. Arthur F. Wright: *Buddhism in Chinese History,* p. 56f.

3 See W. T. Chan, art. "Buddhism" (Sec. II, "Buddhism in China") in Vergilius Ferm (ed): *Encyclopedia of Religion,* p. 96.

4 Cf. Carsun Chang: *Development of Neo-Confucian Thought,* pp. 116, 113.

5 Cf. W. T. Chan, *Op. Cit.,* p. 97.

6 Cf. T. R. V. Murti, art. "Radhakrishnan and Buddhism" in Paul A. Schilpp (ed): *The Philosophy of Sarvepalli Radhakrishnan,* p. 579.

7 Cf. W. T. Chan, art. "Transformation of Buddhism in China" in *Philosophy East and West,* Vol. VII, Nos. 3/4 (Oct. 1957/Jan. 1958), p. 109f.

8 Cf. K. L. Reichelt: *Truth and Tradition in Chinese Buddhism,* pp. 33, 40, 141-2, 216, 277 (A translation of the *Amitābha Sūtra* by Kumārajīva, ca. A.D. 401-2, was given the title "The Sayings of Buddha About Amitābha" (*Fu-Shuo O-Mi-T'o Ching*). Cf. also Blofeld: *The Jewel in the Lotus,* pp. 141ff; and Cf. Sir Charles Eliot: *Hinduism and Buddhism,* Vol. III, p. 313f.

9 Cf. *Ibid.,* p. 313, where Eliot states that the *Amitāyurdhyāna Sūtra* was retranslated by Kalyaśas ca. A.D. 424. Evidently earlier translations had been destroyed in recurring warfare. See S.B.E., Vol. XLIX for English translation of Pure Land Sutras by E. B. Cowell, F. Max Müller, and J. Takakusu.

10 Cf. W. T. Chan, art. "Pure Land School" in Ferm (ed): *Encyclopedia of Religion,* p. 106.

11 Cf. Timothy Richard: *New Testament of Higher Buddhism (The Awakening of Faith)*, Chapter 4, quoted by Reichelt: *Truth and Tradition in Chinese Buddhism,* pp. 127-8.

12 Cf. Sir S. Radhakrishnan: *India and China,* pp. 128f, 131, where he uses the same kind of Christian trinitarian terminology as does Reichelt in his comments on the Pure Land School in his

Truth and Tradition in Chinese Buddhism, especially pp. 2, 179f. Cf. C. B. Day, art. "The Cult of Amitābha" in *China Journal of Arts and Sciences,* Dec. 1940, pp. 235-248.

13 Cf. Clarence H. Hamilton (ed): *Buddhism, A Religion of Infinite Compassion,* pp. 113-15, quoting the *Prajñā-pāramitā Hridaya Sūtra,* as translated by Shao-chang Lee in *Popular Buddhism in China,* pp. 23-26.

14 Cf. Hamilton, *Op. Cit.,* 107-9 (in Part III, Chapter 22, entitled "The Bodhisattva Ideal"), quoting *The Mahāvastu,* I, 133-4, as translated by J. J. Jones in S.B.E., Vol. XVII, p. 105f. *Note: The Mahāvastu* is reputedly the product of the Mahāsāṅghikā or "Great Community" liberals who broke away from the conservative Theravādins at the Second Council, at Vesali in 377 B.C. Cf. also E. J. Thomas: *History of Buddhist Thought,* p. 201. Cf. also W. T. Chan, art. "Buddhist Terminology: Buddhism" in Ferm (ed): *Encyclopedia of Religion,* pp. 97, 93, and 366 (on "incarnations").

15 Cf. Pi-cheng Lee: *Two Buddhist Books in Mahayana,* pp. 34-45.

16 *Ibid.,* pp. 105-118—translation made from the text of Saṇghavarman. [*Note: The Aparimitāyur Sūtra*—(*Fu-Shuo Wu-Liang-Shou Ching,* or "Sayings of Buddha About Amitāyus, Buddha of Everlasting Life"—another name for Amitābha)—was translated into Chinese by Saṇghavarman ca. A.D. 252, according to Soothill and Hodous: *A Dictionary of Chinese Buddhist Terms,* p. 229-b.]

17 Cf. Pi-cheng Lee, *Op. Cit.,* pp. 119-132—originally translated from Sanskrit into Chinese by Kalayaśas in A.D. 424, this *Amitāyurdhyāna Sūtra* has been rendered into English by J. Takakusu in Vol. 49 of the S.B.E.

18 Cf. Pi-cheng Lee, *Op. Cit.,* pp. 133-141—*The Greater Sukhāvatī-Vyūha Sūtra* was originally translated from Sanskrit into Chinese by Kumārajīva in A.D. 384, or possibly later.

19 Cf. Pi-cheng Lee, *Op. Cit.,* pp. 85, 90, 91-93, 104.

20 See P. T. Raju: *Idealistic Thought of India,* pp. 242-251 for a brief résumé of this school of thought. Carsun Chang, *Op. Cit.,* p. 114f, lists the *Śata-śāstra,* the *Mādhyamika-śāstra,* and the *Dvādaśanikāya-śāstra* as the three basic scriptures for this school.

21 Cf. W. T. Chan, art. "Middle Doctrine School" in Ferm (ed): *Encyclopedia of Religion,* p. 104.

22 Cf. John Blofeld: *Op. Cit.,* p. 167; cf. also Wing-tsit Chan: *Religious Trends in Modern China,* p. 102 and ftn 18; 103.

23 Cf. E. J. Thomas, *Op. Cit.*, pp. 214-217.

24 Cf. Y. L. Fung: *History,* II, pp. 239-406 (note p. 245).

25 *Ibid.*, pp. 260-264 (referring to Walter Liebenthal: *The Book of Chao,* Peiping, Catholic University, 1948, especially pp. 46-53).

26 Cf. Y. L. Fung: *History,* II, pp. 260-264.

27 *Ibid.*, p. 264, ftn 1.

28 *Ibid.*, pp. 264-5, *passim* (quoting Liebenthal, *Op. Cit.*, pp. 64-65, with comment).

29 *Ibid.*, pp. 266-7.

30 *Ibid.*, p. 269 (note).

31 *Ibid.*, p. 274.

32 *Ibid.*, pp. 274, 276, 282.

33 *Ibid.*, p. 388. Cf. W. T. Chan, art. "Tao-sheng" in Ferm, *Op. Cit.*, p. 108; also "Transformation of Buddhism" in *Philosophy East and West,* VII, 3/4 (Oct., 1957/Jan., 1958), p. 110f.

34 *Ibid.*, p. 289 and ftn 3.

35 *Ibid.*, pp. 294-298, especially 294 and ftn 2 (referring to Taishō Edition of the *Tripiṭaka,* No. 1854, Vol. 45, pp. 77-115).

36 As schematized by Derk Bodde in Fung, *History,* II, p. 295.

37 Cf. *Ibid.*, p. 286, ftn 1.

38 *Ibid.*, p. 298f; cf. p. 164; also Reichelt: *Truth and Tradition in Chinese Buddhism,* p. 307f.

39 Cf. W. T. Chan, art. "Middle Doctrine School" in Ferm, *Op. Cit.*, pp. 104, 107.

39-A Cf. Pratt: *Pilgrimage of Buddhism,* p. 407.

40 *Ibid.*, p. 104.

41. *Ibid.*

42 See Hu Shih, art. "Ch'an (Zen) Buddhism in China, Its History and Method" in *Philosophy East and West,* Vol. III, No. 1, (April, 1953), pp. 3-24.

43 Cf. Blofeld, *Op. Cit.*, pp. 126-129; also Eliot, *Op. Cit.*, III, pp. 304-309.

44 Cf. W. T. Chan, art. "Transformation of Buddhism in China" in *Philosophy East and West,* VII, 3/4 (Oct., 1957 / Jan., 1958), p. 112f.

45 Cf. Kenneth Chen, art. "Anti-Buddhist Propaganda during the Nan-Ch'ao" in *H.J.A.S.*, Vol. 15 (1952), pp. 166-192, especially pp. 184-192.

46 Cf. Reichelt: *Truth and Tradition in Chinese Buddhism,* p. 222; also p. 211f. (*Note:*—The *Diamond Sūtra* was first printed

in A.D. 868, each page carved in relief on a wooden block. Somewhat later, movable wooden type were used, thus antedating by several hundred years the printing from movable type of the Gutenburg Bible in Mainz in 1450 or 1452). Cf. Thomas F. Carter: *The Invention of Printing in China,* N. Y., Columbia University Press, 1925, *passim* (2nd ed. Ronald Press, 1955). [The Chinese *Tripiṭaka* (*San Ts'ang*—or "Three Baskets") came into print in A.D. 972 in the reign of T'ang Tai Hsü and was officially re-published under the Ch'ing Emperor, Ch'ien Lung (A.D. 1736-1796), with the number of canonical scriptures fixed at 1662. The "Hardoon Edition" appeared in 1913.]

47 Cf. Reichelt: *Ibid.,* p. 215f.

48 (Translator's note continued) :—The "Noble Eight-fold Path" (Aṣṭa-mārga) consists of (1) correct views or ability to discern the truth; (2) correct thought, or absence of evil thought; (3) correct speech; (4) correct conduct; (5) correct livelihood or occupation; (6) correct energy or zeal; (7) correct memory; (8) correct meditation, abstraction or concentration. This Way leads to Nirvāṇa, extinction of the phenomenal and, therefore, of sorrow (which results from desires for phenomenal objects, perceived through phenomenal sense-organs).

49 Cf. A. F. Price (tr): *The Jewel of Transcendental Wisdom* (*The Diamond Sūtra*)—Selections are from pp. 23-71.

50 Cf. Hamilton: *Op. Cit.,* pp. 116f, quoting Sections 31 and 32, as typical of the *Diamond Sūtra,* using Shao-chang Lee's translation taken from Kumārajīva's Chinese version of the *Vajracchedika.*

51 Translation by Charles Johnston in his *The Bhagavad-Gītā,* New York, Quarterly Book Department, 1908.

52 Cf. Wong Mou-lam (tr): *The Sūtra of Wei Lang* (*Hui Neng*), published for the Buddhist Society of London by Luzac & Company Ltd., 1947.

53 Cf. Chinese Buddhist Association (ed): *Buddhists in New China* (Peking, Nationalities Publishing House), 1956, p. 101.

54 Cf. Wong Mou-lam: *Sūtra of Wei Lang,* pp. 27-31.

55 *Ibid.,* pp. 39-44; 88, 81-ftn.

56 *Ibid.,* p. 46f, quoting from the *Vimalakīrti-Nirdeśa Sūtra.*

57 *Ibid.,* p. 51f.

58 *Ibid.,* p. 53f.

59 *Ibid.,* pp. 54-63.

60 *Ibid.*, pp. 48-50.

61 *Ibid.*, pp. 31-38.

62 *Ibid.*, p. 96f.

63 *Ibid.*, pp. 78, 80-81.

64 Cf. Chang Chen-chi art. "The Nature of Ch'an (Zen) Buddhism" in *Philosophy East and West*, Vol. VI, No. 4 (Jan., 1957), p. 343f.

65 Cf. Wong Mou-lam: *Sūtra of Wei Lang*, pp. 71, 74-75, 78.

66 *Ibid.*, pp. 101-104.

67 *Ibid.*, p. 102-ftn.

68 *Ibid.*, p. 102-ftn.

69 D. T. Suzuki: *The Zen Doctrine of No-Mind* (The Significance of the Sūtra of Hui Neng or Wei Lang), published for The Buddhist Society of London by Rider & Company, 1949.

70 Cf. H. G. Creel: *Chinese Thought From Confucius to Mao Tse-tung*, pp. 201-202.

71 Cf. W. T. Chan, art. "Buddhist Terminology: Meditation School" in Ferm (ed) : *Op. Cit.*, p. 104; Cf. Fung, II, p. 338.

72 Cf. Hu Shih, art. "Ch'an (Zen) Buddhism in China" in *Philosophy East and West*, Vol. 3, 1953, pp. 3-17.

73 Cf. Chang Chen-chi, art. "The Nature of Ch'an (Zen) Buddhism" in *Philosophy East and West*, Vol. VI, No. 4, Jan. 1957, p. 336.

74 Cf. D. T. Suzuki: *The Zen Doctrine of No-Mind*, pp. 37, 36-7, 49, 48, 31, 32, 39f, 54, 48, 55, 52-3, 55.

75 *Ibid.*, pp. 71-72—ftn.

76 *Ibid.*, pp. 57, 101, 124, 126, 58-60.

77 *Ibid.*, pp. 60, 72-ftn, 60, 62.

77-A *Ibid.*, pp. 76, 78, 80, 130, 134f, 145.

78 Cf. Chang Chen-chi, *Op. Cit.*, pp. 346ff.

79 Cf. Chang Chen-chi, *Op. Cit.*, pp. 339, 355.

80 Cf. D. T. Suzuki,*Op. Cit.*, pp. 63, 64, 66.

81 *Ibid.*, pp. 70, 73-ftn, 58, 81, 42, 45, 83f.

82 *Ibid.*, pp. 102, 84f, 87.

83 Cf. Carsun Chang, art. "Reason and Intuition in Chinese Philosophy" in *Philosophy East and West*, Vol. IV, No. 2, July, 1954, p. 110f.

84 See Sir Charles Eliot: *Japanese Buddhism*, pp. 6-7, for a brief and lucid account of them.

85 Cf. D. T. Suzuki, *Op. Cit.,* p. 66f.

86 Cf. Walter Liebenthal: "Song of Enlightenment" in the *Journal of Oriental Studies* (of the Catholic University of Peiping), Vol. VI, 1941.

87 Published by Sidgwick and Jackson, Ltd., London, 1948.

88 Cf. S. Radhakrishnan: *India and China,* p. 130f.

89 Cf. Y. L. Fung: *History,* II, pp. 390-406.

90 *Ibid.,* p. 406.

91 Cf. W. T. Chan: *Religious Trends in Modern China,* p. 102-ftn 17; Cf. P. T. Raju: *Idealistic Thought of India,* p. 225.

92 Cf. Reichelt: *Truth and Tradition in Chinese Buddhism,* p. 307f.

93 Cf. Radhakrishnan, *Op. Cit.,* p. 134.

94 Cf. W. T. Chan, art. "Buddhist Terminology: Kośa School" in Ferm (ed) : *Op. Cit.,* p. 101.

95 *Ibid.,* p. 101; Cf. also Eliot: *Hinduism and Buddhism,* III, p. 314f, and Reichelt: *Op. Cit.,* p. 307f.

96 Cf. Hu Shih: art. "Ch'an (Zen) Buddhism in China" in *Philosophy East and West,* Vol. III, 1953, pp. 19-24; Cf. also Reichelt: *Op. Cit.,* p. 308; cf. his *Religion in Chinese Garment,* p. 129.

97 Cf. Charles S. Braden: *The Scriptures of Mankind,* p. 200, where he suggests the earlier date of A.D. 223 for its translation into Chinese. Cf. also Radhakrishnan, *Op. Cit.,* p. 135; Blofeld, *Op. Cit.,* p. 163f; and W. T. Chan, art. "Buddhist Terminology: Lotus Sūtra" in Ferm (ed) : *Op. Cit.,* p. 102, where he places the translation date at ca. A.D. 255—he also states that the version in common use today is, however, Kumārajīva's translation of A.D. 406.

98 See Wing-tsit Chan's detailed description in his "The Lotus Sūtra," a paper read at the Conference On Oriental Classics in General Education, Columbia University, Sept. 12-13, 1958.

99 Cf. E. J. Thomas, *Op. Cit.,* p. 179.

100 *Ibid.,* p. 185f.

101 Cf. Blofeld, *Op. Cit.,* p. 153f.

102 Cf. Eliot, *Op. Cit.,* II, p. 310.

103 Cf. W. T. Chan, art. "Neo-Confucianism" in H. F. MacNair (ed) : *China,* p. 255.

104 Cf. W. T. Chan, art. "Buddhist Terminology: T'ien-t'ai School" in Ferm (ed) : *Op. Cit.,* p. 108f.

105 Cf. W. T. Chan, art. "Transformation of Buddhism in

China" in *Philosophy East and West,* Vol. VII, Nos. 3/4 (Oct., 1957/Jan., 1958), p. 112.

106 Cf. Y. L. Fung: *History,* II, p. 360 and ftn 6.

107 Cf. W. T. Chan: *Religious Trends in Modern China,* p. 63-ftn 19.

108 Cf. Y. L. Fung: *History,* II, pp. 360-386.

109 *Ibid.,* pp. 177-ftn, 369.

110 *Ibid.,* pp. 380-383 (Sec. vii—The order of ideas has been somewhat rearranged).

111 *Ibid.,* pp. 384f, 386.

112 Cf. Reichelt: *Religion in Chinese Garment,* p. 123; Blofeld, *Op. Cit.,* p. 165; Eliot, *Op. Cit.,* III, pp. 316, 322; Chan: *Op. Cit.,* pp.63, 68f.

113 Cf. Pratt: *Pilgrimage of Buddhism,* p. 285.

114 Cf. Y. L. Fung: *History,* II, p. 300-ftn 1.

115 Cf. Reichelt, *Truth and Tradition in Chinese Buddhism,* pp. 63-76, for a synopsis of its highly fantastic plot.

116 Cf. Radhakrishnan and Moore (ed): *Source Book in Indian Philosophy,* p. 328-ftn 2.

117 Cf. C. H. Hamilton: *Wei-Shih Erh-Shih Lun,* pp. 43-65, *passim.* Cf. also Y. L. Fung, *Op. Cit.,* II, pp. 320-323, commenting on Hamilton's *Wei-Shih Erh-Shih Lun,* pp. 22, 23, 25, and the *Ch'êng Wei-Shih Lun,* pp. 428-435. Cf. also Radhakrishnan and Moore (eds): *A Source Book in Indian Philosophy,* pp. 328-333.

118 Cf. Y. L. Fung, *Op. Cit.,* II, pp. 301-302, quoting K'uei-chi's Commentary, known as *Ch'êng Wei-Shih Lun Shu-Chi* (T. T. #1830, Vol. 43, pp. 229-606).

119 Cf. Y. L. Fung, *Op. Cit.,* II, p. 314.

120 *Ibid.,* p. 312f.

121 Cf. Blofeld, *Op. Cit.,* pp. 161, 163; also Fung, *Op. Cit.,* II, p. 328.

122 Cf. Fung, *Op. Cit.,* II, pp. 304-307, 325f.

123 *Ibid.,* pp. 310-312.

123-A Cf. Pratt: *Pilgrimage of Buddhism,* p. 409.

124 *Ibid.,* pp. 302-3, especially 303-ftn 1.

125 *Ibid.,* pp. 328-338.

126 *Ibid.,* p. 340-ftn 7.

127 Cf. Reichelt, *Op. Cit.,* p. 215.

128 Cf. Radhakrishnan, *Op. Cit.,* p. 135; also Reichelt, *Op. Cit.,* p. 215.

129 Cf. Carsun Chang: *Development of Neo-Confucian Thought,* p. 123.

130 Cf. Blofeld, *Op. Cit.,* p. 161; also W. T. Chan: *Religious Trends in Modern China,* p. 64 and ftn 20.

131 Cf. W. T. Chan, art. "Neo-Confucianism" in H. F. MacNair (ed) : *China,* p. 255f.

132 Cf. Y. L. Fung: *History,* II, 339-359.

133 *Ibid.,* p. 359.

134 Cf. W. T. Chan, art. "Buddhist Terminology: Mystical School" in Ferm (ed) : *Encyclopedia of Religion,* p. 105.

135 *Ibid.,* p. 105; also W. T. Chan: *Religious Trends in Modern China,* p. 72-ftn.

136 Cf. W. T. Chan, art. "Buddhist Terminology: Mystical School" in Ferm (ed) : *Op. Cit.,* p. 105 (wording and punctuation slightly altered for smoothness) .

137 Cf. *Ibid.,* p. 104f, especially p. 105-col. 1; Cf. also p. 102 (art. "Lamaism") ; p. 94 (art. "Buddhahood") ; p. 92 (art. "Bodhisattva") ; p. 100-col. 2 (art. "Idealistic School") .

138 Cf. Reichelt: *Religion in Chinese Garment,* pp. 106, 108.

139 Cf. W. T. Chan, art. "Buddhist Terminology: Mystical School" in Ferm (ed): *Op. Cit.,* p. 105.

140 Cf. Blofeld: *The Jewel in the Lotus,* pp. 150-152.

141 *Ibid.,* pp. 152-153.

142 Cf. Sir Charles Eliot: *Hinduism and Buddhism,* Vol. III, p. 318-ftn.

143 Cf. W. T. Chan, art. "Transformation of Buddhism in China" in *Philosophy East and West,* Vol. VII, Nos. 3/4 (Oct., 1957/Jan., 1958) , p. 115.

144 Cf. Carsun Chang, *Op. Cit.,* pp. 117-120.

NOTES
to Chapter 9

1 Cf. Y. L. Fung: *History of Chinese Philosophy,* Vol. II, pp. 407-8. (*Note*) :—Before the publication of Vol. II in complete form, the translator (Dr. Derk Bodde) submitted the material covering this period to the editors of the *Harvard Journal of Asiatic Studies,* who published the article under the title "The Rise of Neo-Confucianism and Its Borrowings From Buddhism and Taoism" in

HJAS, Vol. 7, No. 2 (July, 1942), pp. 89-125. Cf. Fung, II, pp. 407-433; Cf. also A. C. Graham: *Two Chinese Philosophers,* Preface, pp. xiii, xiv.

2 Cf. W. T. Chan, art. "The Story of Chinese Philosophy" in Charles A. Moore (ed): *Philosophy East and West* (A Symposium), p. 51; W. Theodore de Bary, art. "A Re-Appraisal of Neo-Confucianism" in Arthur F. Wright (ed): *Studies in Chinese Thought,* p. 83f, where he notes the strength of Han Yü's crusading for Confucian orthodoxy; also Cf. Fung: *History,* II, 408-413 on Han Yü; and Carsun Chang: *Development of Neo-Confucian Thought,* pp. 84-100, especially pp. 92-97 on Han Yü.

3 Cf. Carsun Chang, *Op. Cit.,* p. 106.

4 Cf. Fung, *Op. Cit.,* II, pp. 413-424, esp. 416, 421, 419.

5 Cf. K. L. Reichelt: *Truth and Tradition in Chinese Buddhism,* p. 18.

6 Cf. Fung: *History,* II, pp. 424, 433.

7 Cf. Carsun Chang, *Op. Cit.,* pp. 146, 153-158.

8 Cf. A. C. Graham, *Op. Cit.,* General Introduction, p. xxx.

9 Cf. Fung: *History,* II, pp. 434-451, esp. 443-4, 445-6.

10 Cf. W. T. Chan in *Journal of the American Oriental Society,* Vol. 79, No. 2 (1959), p. 154, reviewing A. C. Graham's *Two Chinese Philosophers: Ch'êng Ming-tao and Ch'êng Yi-ch'uan.*

11 Cf. A. C. Graham: *Two Chinese Philosophers,* p. 153; also Cf. Fung: *History,* II, pp. 454-476, esp. 454-9, 465-9.

12 Cf. *Ibid.,* p. 466-ftn 2.

13 Cf. *Ibid.,* p. 466.

14 Cf. *Ibid.,* p. 468, quoting Shao Yung's *Treatise On The Observation of Things,* Part I, p. 17—the *Kuan Wu P'ien,* a section of his *Huang-Chi Ching-Shih* or *"Cosmological Chronology."*

15 Cf. Fung: *History,* II, p. 473-ftn, giving translator's note.

16 *Ibid.,* p. 474, quoting Shao Yung's "On the Observation of Things," Pt. II-pp. 12-b, 13.

17 Cf. Carsun Chang, *Op. Cit.,* p. 167.

18 Cf. W. T. Chan, review of A. C. Graham: *Two Chinese Philosophers, JAOS,* 79, 2 (1959), p. 152.

19 Cf. Carsun Chang, *Op. Cit.,* p. 171.

20 Cf. Fung: *History,* II, pp. 477-493, *passim.*

21 Cf. Carsun Chang, *Op. Cit.,* pp.172-176; 181f.

22 *Ibid.,* pp. 171; 178-180.

23 Cf. Fung: *History,* II, p. 493.

24 Cf. Carsun Chang, *Op. Cit.,* p. 178.

25 Cf. Fung: *History,* II, pp. 492, 495.

26 Cf. *Ibid.,* II, p. 492, referring to *The Mêng-tzu,* VIIa, 15—i.e., "The knowledge possessed by men without the exercise of thought is their 'good' (i.e., intuitive) knowledge."

27 Cf. *Ibid.,* p. 500.

28. Cf. W. T. deBary, art. "A Re-Appraisal of Neo-Confucianism" in Wright (ed): *Studies in Chinese Thought,* p. 89.

29 Cf. Carsun Chang, *Op. Cit.,* p. 169f.

30 Cf. A. C. Graham, *Op. Cit.,* p. 176.

31 *Ibid.,* p. xviii.

32 Cf. *Ibid.,* p. xvi and C. Wilfrid Allen: *Makers of Cathay,* p. 101.

33 Cf. Fung: *History,* II, pp. 500ff, esp. 507-8.

34 Cf. *Ibid.,* pp. 518, 520-527, *passim.*

35 Cf. A. C. Graham, *Op. Cit.,* pp. 95, 99.

36 Cf. Fung: *History,* II, pp. 524, 525 (slightly altered).

37 Cf. W. T. Chan, review of A. C. Graham: *Two Chinese Philosophers, JAOS,* 79, 2 (1959), p. 151.

38 Cf. A. C. Graham, *Op. Cit.,* Gen. Introd., p. xvi.

39 Cf. *Ibid.,* Part I, p. 3.

40 Cf. Carsun Chang, Op. Cit., p. 208 (*Note*):—His whole book is an excellent re-interpretation of T'ang-Sung philosophy, with many criticisms of Fung Yu-lan's interpretations.

41 Cf. Fung: *History,* II, pp. 502ff, 511ff.

42 Cf. W. T. Chan, review of A. C. Graham: *Two Chinese Philosophers, JAOS,* 79,2 (1959), p. 152.

43 Cf. Fung: *History,* II, pp. 516-520, *passim.*

44 A problem raised by W. T. Chan, *Op. Cit., J.A.O.S.,* 79, 2 (1959), p. 153.

45 Cf. Fung: *History,* II, pp. 527-532, *passim.*

46 Cf. W. T. Chan, *Op. Cit., JAOS,* 79, 2 (1959), p. 151.

47 Cf. Fung, *Op. Cit.,* II, pp. 501f, 505 ff.

48 Cf. A. C. Graham: *Op. Cit.,* Preface, p. xviii.

49 Cf. W. T. Chan, *Op. Cit., JAOS,* 79, 2 (1959), p. 153.

50 Cf. Fung, *Op. Cit.,* II, pp. 514-520, 520-527, esp. 527-531, *passim;* also W. T. deBary, *Op. Cit.,* in Wright (ed): *Studies in Chinese Thought,* pp. 98-100, 103-5.

51 Cf. A. C. Graham: *Op. Cit.*, Preface, p. xviii.

52 Cf. W. T. Chan, review of A. C. Graham: *Two Chinese Philosophers, JAOS*, 79, 2 (1959), p. 151.

53 Cf. Fung, *Op. Cit.*, II, pp. 527-532, *passim;* also Carsun Chang, *Op. Cit.*, Chap. 11, pp. 231-241—"The Period of Transition Between Ch'eng Yi and Chu Hsi" (esp. pp. 236-241). (*Note*) :—The spelling of *"Li"* as *"Ri"* is due to the failure in some areas of China, especially Hunan, to distinguish in pronunciation the consonants l, r, and n.

54 Cf. John C. Ferguson, art. "Wang An Shih" in *JRAS* (N.C.B), V, 35, pp. 65-75.

55 Cf. C. Wilfrid Allen: *Makers of Cathay*, p. 101.

56 Cf. H. R. Williamson: *Wang An-Shih* (2 vols.) Vol. II, pp. 297, 372-4, 342-4.

NOTES
to Chapter 10

1 Cf. A. C. Graham: *Two Chinese Philosophers: Ch'êng Ming-tao and Ch'êng Yi-ch'uan*, Introduction, pp. xix, xxx.

2 Cf. Y. L. Fung: *History of Chinese Philosophy*, Vol. II, p. 534.

3 Cf. *Ibid.*, p. 538f; also J. Percy Bruce: *The Philosophy of Human Nature by Chu Hsi*, pp. 16-55, 269-290. (See also his *Chu Hsi and His Masters: Introduction to Chu Hsi and the Sung School*).

4 Cf. Y. L. Fung, *Op. Cit.*, II, pp. 539-541, 542-6, 546-551.

5 Cf. J. P. Bruce, *Op. Cit.*, p. 291f.

6 *Ibid.*, p. 291.

7 Cf. Carsun Chang: *Development of Neo-Confucian Thought*, pp. 254, 258f, 269.

8 Cf. Y. L. Fung, *Op. Cit.*, II, p. 542

9 *Ibid.*, p. 543.

10 Cf. *Ibid.*, p. 545-ftn.

11 Cf. W. T. Chan, art. "Neo-Confucianism" in H. F. MacNair (ed): *China*, p. 257.

12 Cf. W. T. Chan, art. "Neo-Confucianism and Chinese Scientific Thought" in *Philosophy East and West*, VI, 4 (Jan., 1957), pp. 319-329, esp. p. 320.

13 Cf. Joseph Needham: *Science and Civilization in China,* Vol. II, p. 292.

14 Cf. Y. L. Fung, *Op. Cit.,* II, pp. 546-8.

15 Cf. *Ibid.,* II, p. 550, quoting *Classified Conversations of Chu Hsi* (*Chu-tzu Yü-Lei*), pp. 94, 15.

16 Cf. J. P. Bruce, *Op. Cit.,* pp. 142-145.

17 Cf. *Ibid.,* p. 146.

18 *Ibid.,* p. 146.

19 Cf. *Ibid.,* p. 147.

20 *Ibid.,* p. 147 (ref. to *Shu Ching,* p. 185).

21 Cf. Y. L. Fung, *Op. Cit.,* II, p. 551, quoting *Classified Conversations of Chu Hsi,* pp. 4, 10.

22 Cf. Y. L. Fung, *Op. Cit.,* II, pp. 554, 552f; also Carsun Chang, *Op. Cit.,* pp. 260-263; 265f.

23 Cf. Y. L. Fung, *Op. Cit.,* II, pp. 556-7, 567, 571.

24 Cf. Carsun Chang, art. "Reason and Intuition in Chinese Philosophy" in *Philosophy East and West,* Vol. IV, No. 2 (July, 1954), p. 101.

25 Cf. J. Percy Bruce, *Op. Cit.,* p. 59.

26 Cf. Y. L. Fung, *Op. Cit.,* II, p. 557; also Bruce, *Op. Cit.,* pp. 169, 174f.

27 Cf. W. T. Chan, art. "Syntheses in Chinese Metaphysics" in Charles A. Moore (ed): *Essays in East-West Philosophy,* p. 176.

28 Cf. J. P. Bruce, *Op. Cit.,* pp. 191, 209ff, 250f, 253f.

29 Cf. *Ibid.,* p. 260.

30 *Ibid.,* pp. 261, 260.

31 Cf. *Ibid.,* p. 61.

32 *Ibid.,* p. 48.

33 Cf. *Ibid.,* p. 128.

34 *Ibid.,* p. 86f.

35 Cf. Y. L. Fung: *History,* II, pp. 560-562, quoting Chu Hsi's *Commentary on the Great Learning* (*Ta Hsüeh Chang-Chü*), section on "The Investigation of Things."

36 Cf. *Ibid.,* p. 562-ftn 1.

37 Cf. J. P. Bruce: *Philosophy of Human Nature by Chu Hsi,* pp. 262f; Cf. pp. 264-266.

38 Cf. *Ibid.,* p. 316 and ftn 1; also p. 263.

39 Cf. *Ibid.,* p. 11.

40 *Ibid.,* pp. 292, 286-291, 270-279.

41 Cf. *Ibid.,* pp. 304, 306.

42 *Ibid.*, p. 317f.

43 Cf. *Ibid.*, pp. 311, 312, 313.

44 Cf. *Ibid.*, p. 316.

45 *Ibid.*, p. 380 (Cf. *Analects* VI, lx, p. 52 and ftn; also VI, xxi, p. 56).

46 *Ibid.*, p. 328.

47 Cf. *Ibid.*, p. 330.

48 *Ibid.*, pp. 415, 419, 421-424.

49 Cf. *Ibid.*, pp. 425; 425-ftn 3; 428; 426; Cf. 410, 421, 431; Cf. 387ff, 289; Cf. pp. 320f, 336, 337, 436.

50 Cf. Y. L. Fung: *History*, II, p. 562ff, quoting *The Collected Writings of Chu Hsi*, Ch. 36, pp. 27, 29, 25.

51 Cf. W. T. Chan art. "Neo-Confucianism" in H. F. MacNair (ed) : *China*, pp. 254-256.

52 Cf. Y. L. Fung, *Op. Cit.*, II, p. 569; also J. P. Bruce, *Op. Cit.*, p. 301f.

53 Cf. Carsun Chang: *Development of Neo-Confucian Thought*, pp. 268, 272-4, 277.

54 Cf. Y. L. Fung, *Op. Cit.*, II, p. 571. (*Note*) :—Fung Yu-lan's treatment of Chu Hsi, translated with introduction and notes by Derk Bodde, appeared in the *HJAS*, Vol. 7, April, 1942, pp. 1-51, under the title "The Philosophy of Chu Hsi."

NOTES
to Chapter 11

1 Cf. W. T. Chan, art. "The Story of Chinese Philosophy" in Charles A. Moore (ed) : *Philosophy East and West*, pp. 61-4.

2 Cf. David S. Nivison, art. "The Problem of 'Knowledge' and 'Action' in Chinese Thought Since Wang Yang-ming," in Arthur F. Wright (ed): *Studies in Chinese Thought*, pp. 112-145, esp. p. 117.

3 Cf. Y. L. Fung: *History of Chinese Philosophy*, II, pp. 574-9.

4 Cf. *Ibid.*

5 *Ibid.*, p. 577f.

6 Cf. Siu-chi Huang: *Lu Hsiang-shan*, pp. 45-46; Cf. pp. 25-26.

7 Cf. Leonard Tomkinson, art. "The Sung Philosophers On Character Culture" in *The Chinese Recorder*, Oct., 1941, p. 551.

8. Cf. *Ibid.*, p. 552.

9 Cf. Siu-chi Huang, *Op. Cit.*, pp. 29, 34.

10 Cf. *Ibid.*, p. 37, quoting Lu's *Conversations*, pp. 35, 290; Cf. also pp. 30, 34-36.

11 Cf. Carsun Chang: *Development of Neo-Confucian Thought*, p. 292f.

12 *Ibid.*, pp. 297-301.

13 Cf. Siu-chi Huang, *Op. Cit.*, pp. 79-86.

14 Cf. *Ibid.*, p. 44, quoting Legge, p. 79—the *Mêng-tzu*, IIa, 6.

15 Cf. *Ibid.*, p. 44.

16 Cf. *Ibid.*, p. 26.

17 Cf. Y. L. Fung, *Op. Cit.*, pp. 595, 594.

18 Cf. Fung: *Ibid.*, p. 596; also Siu-chi Huang, *Op. Cit.*, p. 87.

19 Cf. Fung: *Ibid.*, p. 596 and ftn 2.

20 Cf. F. G. Henke: *The Philosophy of Wang Yang-ming*, p. 481-485; Cf. p. 15.

21 Cf. Carsun Chang, *Op. Cit.*, p. 303.

22 Cf. Siu-chi Huang, *Op. Cit.*, p. 93.

23 Cf. Y. L. Fung: *History*, II, pp. 600-601, quoting Wang Yang-ming's *Ta Hsüeh Wên*, pp. 204-208; also Henke, *Op. Cit*, pp. 205-210.

24 Cf. Fung, *Op. Cit.*, p. 602, quoting Wang Yang-ming: *Record of Instructions* (*Ch'uan-hsi Lu*), p. 154.

25 Cf. F. G. Henke, *Op. Cit.*, pp. 167f, 171-2; also Fung, *Op. Cit.*, pp. 599, 600-603, *passim*.

26 Cf. F. G. Henke, *Op. Cit.*, pp. 288ff, replying to Ou-Yang Ch'ung-i.

27 Cf. *Ibid.*, pp. 154f, 152.

28 *Ibid.*, pp. 168, 152.

29 Cf. Y. L. Fung: *History*, II, p. 602, quoting Wang's *Questions on the Great Learning* (*Ta Hsüeh Wên*), p. 213; Cf. Henke, *Op. Cit.*, p. 167f.

30 Cf. F. G. Henke, *Op. Cit.*, pp. 216, 59, 284f.

31 Cf. Y. L. Fung: *History*, II, pp. 606-607, quoting Chu Hsi: *Letters*, pp. 303-5; Cf. Henke, *Op. Cit.*, pp. 215-217, 260.

32 Cf. F. G. Henke, *Op. Cit.*, p. 177f; Cf. Fung, *Op. Cit.*, p. 607.

33 As Carsun Chang has suggested in his art. "Wang Yang-ming's Philosophy" in *Philosophy East and West*, Vol. V, No. 1 (April, 1955), p. 14.

34 Cf. Y. L. Fung, *Op. Cit.*, II, pp. 608-610, quoting Chu Hsi:

Letters, p. 298 and *Record of Instructions,* pp. 168f, 184f; Cf. also Henke, *Op. Cit.,* p. 202f.

35 Cf. Y. L. Fung, *Op. Cit.,* II, p. 604 (slightly altered).

36 Cf. David S. Nivison, *Op. Cit.,* p. 118f.

37 Cf. Y. L. Fung, *Op. Cit.,* p. 619f, quoting Wang's *Letters,* p. 387f (here slightly altered).

38 Cf. *Ibid.,* p. 620, quoting Wang's *Letters,* p. 260.

39 *Ibid.,* p. 614.

40 *Ibid.,* pp. 614-617, *passim.*

41 Cf. F. G. Henke, *Op. Cit.,* p. 110.

42 Cf. *Ibid.,* pp. 125, 92f, 155.

43 Cf. *Ibid.,* pp. 122f, 245-8, 73, 78f; Cf. also pp. 115, 121, 147f, 158f, 167; also pp. 234, 238f, 240-243, 387.

44 Cf. *Ibid.,* pp. 186, 139f, 212-214, 82f; Cf. also pp. 130-133, 244-6, 108, 84, 111f, 127, 239, 78-84, 117-119.

45 Cf. *Ibid.,* p. 258; Cf. also pp. 234, 243-6, 255; Cf. pp. 98-102.

46 Cf. *Ibid.,* p. 262.

47 Cf. Carsun Chang, art. "Wang Yang-ming's Philosophy" in *Philosophy East and West,* Vol. V, No. 1 (April, 1955), p. 10.

48 Cf. Y. L. Fung: *History,* II, pp. 612-614, esp. 614, quoting Wang's *Record of Instructions,* pp. 106-108.

49 Cf. F. G. Henke, *Op. Cit.,* p. 327.

50 Cf. *Ibid.,* p. 138, referring to *Chung Yung,* Ch. 20, par. 4, 8, 12.

51 Cf. *Ibid.,* pp. 49, 52, referring to *Lun Yü,* Bk. XIV.

52 Cf. *Ibid.,* p. 176; Cf. also pp. 180, 184f, 199.

53 Cf. *Ibid.,* pp. 193-4; Cf. also pp. 271-280, esp. 278f.

54 Cf. *Ibid.,* p. 181.

55 Cf. *Ibid.,* pp. 100-102, 113, 327f, 330.

56 Cf. *Ibid.,* p. 363f.

57 Cf. *Ibid.,* pp. 89, 168.

58 Cf. *Ibid.,* pp. 85, 87f.

59 *Ibid.,* p. 202.

60 Cf. *Ibid.,* p. 105.

61 *Ibid.,* p. 197.

62 Cf. *Ibid.,* p. 342.

63 *Ibid.,* p. 343.

64 Cf. *Ibid.,* p. 348.

65 *Ibid.,* pp. 117, 83f, 105, 104.

66 Cf. *Ibid.,* pp. 119f, 185, 198, 474f.

67 Cf. *Ibid.,* pp. 369, 421; Cf. also pp. 163, 199, 74, 465.

68 Cf. *Ibid.*, p. 73.
69 *Ibid.*, p. 182.
70 Cf. *Ibid.*, p. 189.
71 *Ibid.*, pp. 156, 306.
72 Cf. *Ibid.*, p. 320.
73 *Ibid.*, p. 165; Cf. also pp. 320, 356, 139f.
74 Cf. *Ibid.*
75 Cf. *Ibid.*, pp. 152, 197. (Cf. Leonard Tomkinson, *Op. Cit.*, pp. 546-553, *passim*).
76 Cf. *Ibid.*, pp. 161, 71.
77 *Ibid.*, p. 91.
78 Cf. *Ibid.*, pp. 115, 227.
79 *Ibid.*, pp. 139f, 223, 224-6; Cf. Tomkinson, *Op. Cit.*, *passim*.
80 Cf. O. Brière (S. J.) : *Fifty Years of Chinese Philosophy*, p. 14.

NOTES
to Chapter 12

1 Cf. W. T. Chan, art. "Philosophies of China" in Dagobert D. Runes (ed) : *Twentieth Century Philosophy*, p. 543; Cf. also Y. L. Fung: *History of Chinese Philosophy*, II, p. 630f.
2 Cf. Mansfield Freeman, art. "Ch'ing Dynasty Criticism of Sung Politico-Philosophy" in *J.R.A.S.* (North China Branch), Vol. LIX, 1928, *passim* (pp. 78-110).
3 Cf. W. Theodore de Bary, art. "A Re-Appraisal of Neo-Confucianism" in Arthur F. Wright (ed) : *Studies in Chinese Thought*, pp. 100-101. See above (p. 88) for Hu Shih's dating of the *Chou Li* and its influence on Wang An-shih.
4 Cf. Freeman, *Op. Cit.*, p. 84.
5 Cf. *Ibid.*, p. 85.
6 *Ibid.*, pp. 85f, 97.
7 Cf. *Ibid.*, p. 87.
8 *Ibid.*, pp. 87ff.
9 Cf. *Ibid.*, pp. 89ff.
10 *Ibid.*, p. 92.
11 Cf. David S. Nivison, art. "The Problem of 'Knowledge' and 'Action' in Chinese Thought Since Wang Yang-ming" in Arthur F. Wright, *Op. Cit.*, p. 125; also W. Theodore de Bary, *Op. Cit.*,

p. 82, where he notes Huang Tsung-hsi and Ku Yen-wu as 17th century Confucianists who "went on grappling with the problems of government"; also Arthur W. Hummel (ed): *Eminent Chinese of the Ch'ing Period,* Vol. I, pp. 421-425.

12 Cf. *Ibid.,* II, pp. 817-819; also Y. L. Fung, *Op. Cit.,* II, p. 641-ftn 3; also W. T. Chan, art. "Neo-Confucianism" in H. F. MacNair (ed) : *China,* p. 261.

13 Cf. Hummel, *Op. Cit.,* II, pp. 817-819.

14 Cf. Y. L. Fung, *Op. Cit.,* II, p. 640-ftn 3.

15 Cf. Hummel, *Op. Cit.,* Vol. I, pp. 351-354.

16 Cf. Andrew Tod Roy: "Modern Confucian Social Theory and its Concept of Change" (Princeton University Ph.D. dissertation, July, 1948, pp. 8-15 (quoting Tu Lien-chê in Hummel. *Op. Cit.,* Vol. I, pp. 351-354) .

17 Cf. Lin Mou-sheng: *Men and Ideas,* p. 187.

18 Cf. A. T. Roy, *Op. Cit.,* p. 14.

19 Cf. Hummel, *Op. Cit.,* Vol. I, p. 45.

20 Cf. Freeman, *Op. Cit.,* p. 95, quoting *Hung-Tao Shu, Pt. II...*

21 Cf. *Ibid.,* p. 97f, quoting *Hung-Tao Shu,* Pt. III.

22 Cf. *Ibid.,* p. 100, quoting *Hung-Tao Shu,* Pt. I.

23 Cf. *Ibid.,* pp. 98, 95f.

24 Cf. Hummel, *Op. Cit,* Vol. I, p. 335f.

25 Cf. A. T. Roy, *Op. Cit.,* p. 31.

26 Cf. Mansfield Freeman, art. "Yen Hsi-chai—A Seventeenth Century Philosopher" in *J.R.A.S.* (North China Branch), LVII, 1926, p. 70.

27 Cf. *Ibid.,* p. 104f.

28 Cf. Hummel, *Op. Cit.,* II, p. 914.

29 Cf. Freeman, art. "Yen Hsi-chai," *loc. cit.,* pp. 71-74.

30 Cf. *Ibid.,* pp. 74- 78, 81.

31 *Ibid.,* pp. 84f, 76f.

32 Cf. Warren H. Stuart: *The Use of Material from China's Spiritual Inheritance in the Christian Education of Chinese Youth* (Yale University Ph.D. dissertation), p. 133f, quoting from Wang Feng-chieh's *History of Education* (*Chung-Kuo Chiao-Yü Shih Ta-Kang*), pp. 263ff.

33 Cf. Freeman, art. "Yen Hsi-chai," *loc. cit.,* pp. 85, 107.

34 Cf. *Ibid.,* p. 106, quoting *T'sun Hsüeh,* sec. 2.

35 Cf. *Ibid.,* p. 88f, quoting *Ts'un Hsüeh,* part II.

36 Cf. *Ibid.,* pp. 70, 91.

37 Cf. Hummel, *Op. Cit.*, II, p. 915.

38 Cf. Y. L. Fung: *History,* II, pp. 636-9; also Hummel, *Op. Cit.*, II, pp. 912-915; also Nivison, art. "The Problem of 'Knowledge' and 'Action' in Chinese Thought Since Wang Yang-ming," *loc. cit.*, p. 124, where he thinks Yen Yüan not so significant as some have suggested, although influential in stressing the importance of experience as the acid test of knowledge.

39 Cf. Y. L. Fung: *History,* II, p. 644f.

40 Cf. Freeman, art. "Ch'ing Dynasty Criticism of Sung Politico-Philosophy," *loc. cit.*, p. 109.

41 Cf. Y. L. Fung: *History,* II, p. 647.

42 Cf. *Ibid.*, p. 650 (slightly altered).

43 Cf. Andrew Tod Roy, *Op. Cit.*, p. 32.

44 Cf. Mansfield Freeman, art. "The Philosophy of Tai Tung-yüan" in *J.R.A.S.* (North China Branch), Vol. LXIV, 1933, p. 55f.

45 Cf. H. G. Creel: *Chinese Thought from Confucius to Mao Tse-tung,* p. 226f; also Fang Chao-ying, art. "Tai Chen" in Hummel, *Op. Cit.*, II, pp. 695-9, esp. 697; also W. T. Chan, art. "Story of Chinese Philosophy" in Charles A. Moore (ed): *Philosophy East and West,* Chap. III, p. 65.

46 Cf. Y. L. Fung: *History,* II, pp. 652-672, *passim;* also Freeman, art. "Philosophy of Tai Tung-yüan," *loc. cit.*, pp. 55-67.

47 Cf. *Ibid.*, p. 56f; also Fung, *Op. Cit.*, II, p. 652f.

48 Cf. Hummel, *Op. Cit.*, II, pp. 695-699.

49 cf. Freeman, art. "Philosophy of Tai Tung-yüan," *loc. cit.*, p. 56f.

50 Cf. Hummel, *Op. Cit.*, II, p. 698f (selected and slightly paraphrased).

51 Cf. Freeman, art. "Philosophy of Tai Tung-yüan," *loc. cit.*, p. 68, referring to *Yüan Shan,* Pt. III, 8.

52 Cf. *Ibid.*, p. 68, referring to *Mêng-Tzu Tzu Yi Shu Chêng,* 41.

53 Cf. W. T. Chan, art. "Story of Chinese Philosophy," *loc. cit.*, p. 67; also W. T. Chan, art. "Philosophies of China" in D. D. Runes, *Op. Cit.*, p. 543f.

54 Cf. Y.L. Fung: *History,* II, p. 659.

55 Cf. *Ibid.*, p. 663; cf. 660f.

56 Cf. *Ibid.*, pp. 661-3.

57 Cf. Freeman, art. "Philosophy of Tai Tung-yüan," *loc. cit.*, p. 61, referring to *Yüan Shan,* Pt. I, 6; cf. also Y. L. Fung, *Op. Cit.*, II, pp. 661-3.

58 Cf. W. T. Chan, art. "Philosophies of China," *loc. cit.*, p. 544 (Chan's paraphrase).

59 Cf. Y. L. Fung, *Op. Cit.*, II, p. 666f; also Freeman, art., "Philosophy of Tai Tung-yüan," *loc. cit.*, p. 58.

60 Cf. *Ibid.*, p. 62.

61 Cf. H. G. Creel, *Op. Cit.*, p. 231.

62 Cf. Freeman, art. "Philosophy of Tai Tung-yüan," *loc. cit.*, p. 62.

63 Cf. Fang, art. "Tai Chen" in Hummel, *Op. Cit.*, II, p. 699.

64 Cf. Y. L. Fung, *Op. Cit.*, II, p. 664f.

65 *Ibid.*, p. 662; cf. 660.

66 Cf. Freeman, art. "Philosophy of Tai Tung-yüan," *loc. cit.*, p. 63f, quoting *Mêng-Tzu Tzu Yi Shu Chêng, 5.*

67 Cf. *Ibid.*, p. 65f; also H. G. Creel, *Op. Cit.*, p. 230f.

68 Cf. Fang, art. "Tai Chen" in Hummel, *Op. Cit.*, II, p. 699 (paraphrased somewhat).

69 Cf. Y. L. Fung, *Op. Cit.*, II, p. 672.

70 Cf. Hummel, *Op. Cit.*, II, p. 982.

71 Cf. Freeman, art. "Philosophy of Tai Tung-yüan," *loc. cit.*, p. 70f.

72 Cf. Hummel, *Op. Cit.*, II, p. 699.

73 Cf. Gung-hsing Wang: *The Chinese Mind*, p. 156f.

74 Cf. Hummel, *Op. Cit.*, II, p. 698.

75 Cf. Andrew Tod Roy, *Op. Cit.*, p. 39f.

76 *Ibid.*

77 Cf. Joshua W. K. Liao, art. "Chinese Philosophy and Politics" in *China Weekly Review*, Dec. 25, 1948, pp. 90-92; also on Yu Yüeh, see Hummel, *Op. Cit.*, II, p. 944f; on Sun I-jang, see Vol. II, pp. 677-9.

78 Cf. Lin Mou-sheng: *Men and Ideas*, pp. 223-226.

79 Cf. Y. L. Fung: *History*, II, p. 678f. *Note*: for a detailed discussion of the six phases of the long-drawn-out controversy over the "New"—and "Old"—Text literature, see Fung, II, pp. 705-721. Cf. also Joshua W. K. Liao, art. "Chinese Philosophy and Politics," *loc. cit.*, pp. 90-92, for K'ang Yu-wei's and Liao Ping's studies in "The New and Old Text Literatures." Cf. also J. R. Levenson;—*Liang Ch'i-ch'ao and the Mind of Modern China*, Appendix, pp. 221-223, for an extended discussion of the controversy over "New" and "Old" Texts in Chinese Literature. Cf. also W. T. Chan, art. "Neo-Confucianism" in H. F. MacNair (ed): *China*, p. 263.

80 Cf. Y. L. Fung: *History,* II, pp. 679-681, *passim,* quoting K'ang's *Commentary on the Analects* (*Lun-Yü Chu*) 2, 10.

81 Cf. *Ibid.,* p. 683.

82 Cf. *Ibid.,* p. 683, quoting K'ang's *Commentary on the Doctrine of the Mean* (*Chung-Yung Chu*), p. 36.

83 Cf. O. Brière (S. J.): *Fifty Years of Chinese Philosophy,* (English Edition), p. 18, ftn 4.

84 Cf. Y. L. Fung, *Op. Cit.,* II, p. 687, quoting *Ta-T'ung Shu,* I, 13.

85 Cf. *Ibid.,* p. 689 (Fung's comment).

86 Cf. Lin Yutang: *The Wisdom of Confucius,* p. 95, quoting *Chung Yung,* Ch. 1.

87 Cf. W. T. Chan, art. "Philosophies of China" in Dagobert D. Runes (ed): *Twentieth Century Philosophy,* p. 545f.

88 Cf. Andrew Tod Roy, *Op. Cit.,* p. 83, quoting *Tsing Hua Journal,* Vol. XI, No. 3, Peiping, July, 1936, pp. 583ff.

89 Cf. Y. L. Fung, *Op. Cit,* II, p. 691 (see translator's note on the total contents of the *Book of the Great Unity*).

90 Cf. *Ibid.,* p. 689f.

91 *Ibid.,* p. 690 (translator's note).

92 Cf. *Ibid.,* p. 693f.

93 *Ibid.,* p. 694, quoting *Jên Hsüeh,* p. 4.

94 Cf. *Ibid.,* pp. 693, 698.

95 Cf. *Ibid.,* p. 691 (translator's note); 703.

96 Cf. *Ibid., p.* 703.

97 Cf. Andrew Tod Roy, *Op. Cit.* p. 94f, quoting Ch'ien Mu in *Tsing Hua Journal, loc. cit.* p. 624.

98 Cf. *Ibid.,* p. 96, quoting Reinsch: *Intellectual and Political Currents in the Far East,* pp. 143-4; original source: Liang Ch'i-ch'ao's *Biographies of the Six Martyrs of 1898* (*Wu-Hsü Liu-Chün-Tzu Chuan*).

99 Published by Kelly & Walsh, Ltd., Shanghai, 1898.

100 Published by *Peking Daily News,* Peking, 1915.

101 Published by John Murray, London, 1920.

102 Cf. Ku Hung-ming: *The Conduct of Life,* p. 9, quoted by D. Willard Lyon in his unpublished MS, "Confucianism Today," written in Shanghai, 1927, p. 60. (Used by permission of the author before his death).

103 Cf. Andrew Tod Roy, *Op. Cit.,* pp. 62-65.

104 Cf. *Ibid.,* pp. 68-75.

105 Cf. W. T. Chan, art. "Neo-Confucianism," *loc. cit.*, p. 264f; see also Hummel, *Op. Cit.,* Vol. I, pp. 351-354.

106 Cf. Ho Lin: *Tang-Tai Chung-Kuo Chê-Hsüeh (Contemporary Chinese Philosophy)*, pp. 5-8; cf. also O. Brière, *Op. Cit.*, pp. 16-17.

107 Cf. Benjamin Schwartz, art. "The Intellectual History of China" in John K. Fairbank (ed): *Chinese Thought and Institutions,* p. 26.

108 Published by Harcourt, Brace & Company, N. Y., and by Kegan Paul, London, 1930.

109 Cf. Ho Lin, *Op. Cit.,* p. 4; also Liang Ch'i-ch'ao: *History of Chinese Political Thought,* pp. 150-152—"On Democratic Ideals"; 196-9—"On People's Rights"; 139-140—"On the Problem of Harmonizing the Spiritual and the Material Life."

110 Cf. W. T. Chan, art. "Philosophies of China," *loc. cit.,* p. 557; cf. also Liang's *History of Chinese Political Thought,* Conclusion, pp. 139-142.

111 Cf. J. R. Levenson, *Op. Cit.,* pp. 205-206.

112 Cf. Andrew Tod Roy, *Op. Cit.,* pp. 131-8.

113 Cf. *Ibid.,* Chapter I, p. 39.

114 Cf. Hu Shih: *The Chinese Renaissance,* Chap. III, "The Chinese Renaissance," pp. 44-62; Chap. IV, "Intellectual Life, Past and Present," pp. 63-77.

NOTES
to Chapter 13

1 Cf. D. Willard Lyon: (MS) "Confucianism Today" (Shanghai, 1927), p. 122, quoting Wang Ching-dao: *Confucius and Modern China.* Used by permission of the author.

2 *Ibid.,* p. 59, quoting Chen Huang-chang: *Economic Principles of Confucius and His School,* Vol. I, p. 47; Vol. II, pp. 727, 729, 730.

3 *Ibid.,* pp. 59,116.

4 Cf. Ho Lin: *Contemporary Chinese Philosophy* (in Chinese), p. 19f.

5 *Ibid.,* pp. 117f, 120ff.

6 Cf. O. Brière, S.J.: *Fifty Years of Chinese Philosophy,* p. 58.

7 Cf. Andrew Tod Roy: (MS) "Modern Confucian Social Theory and Its Concept of Change" (Princeton University, 1948);

pp. 264-268, especially footnotes 84 and 85 on p. 266, where Dr. Roy calls attention to the very anti-Sun Yat-sen translation of and commentary on the *San Min Chu I* by Father Paschal D'Elia entitled *The Triple Demism of Sun Yat-sen,* published in Wuchang in 1931.

8 Cf. Ssu-yü Teng and John K. Fairbank (eds): *China's Response to the West,* pp. 258-267.

9 Cf. Andrew Tod Roy, *Op. Cit.,* pp. 261-263.

10 Cf. W. T. Chan, art. "Philosophies of China" in D. D. Runes (ed): *Twentieth Century Philosophy,* pp. 550f; also cf. Teng and Fairbank, *Op. Cit.,* pp. 240-246, 249-251.

11 Cf. O. Brière, *Op. Cit.,* p. 23; also W. T. Chan's article "Philosophies of China" in D. D. Runes, *Op. Cit.,* p. 551, referring to Li Ta-chao: "My Views on Marxism" in *La Jeunesse Nouvelle,* Vol. VI, nos. 5, 6.

12 Cf. Ho Lin, *Op. Cit.,* p. 72f.

13 Cf. Andrew Tod Roy, *Op. Cit.,* pp. 186, 223.

14 Cf. Ho Lin, *Op. Cit.,* pp. 125, 128ff.

15 *Ibid.,* pp. 128f, 131ff; also cf. Chiang K'ai-shek: *A Philosophy of Action,* pp. 7-20.

16 Cf. W. T. Chan, art. "Philosophies of China" in D. D. Runes, *Op. Cit.,* p. 562.

17 Cf. O. Brière, *Op. Cit.,* p. 59f.

18 Cf. Robert Payne: *Mao Tse-tung,* p. 183.

19 Cf. Ho Lin, *Op. Cit.,* p. 120ff.

20 *Ibid.,* Chapter 2, "The Harmonization of Western Philosophy with Chinese Thought," p. 25ff.

21 Cf. W. T. Chan, art. "Hu Shih and Chinese Philosophy" in *Philosophy East and West,* Vol. VI, No. 1 (Apr. '56), p. 3; also cf. Brière, *Op. Cit.,* p. 20.

22 Cf. Ho Lin, *Op. Cit.,* p. 26f; also cf. O. Brière, *Op. Cit.,* p. 37.

23 Cf. O. Brière, *Op Cit.,* p. 20.

24 *Ibid.,* p. 21.

25 Cf. O. Brière, *Op. Cit.,* p. 26; also cf. W. T. Chan, art. "Philosophies of China" in D. D. Runes, *Op. Cit.,* pp. 551-2, ref. to *La Jeunesse,* Vol. VI, 1919, No. 4, pp. 342-358.

26 Cf. W. T. Chan, *Ibid.,* p. 552.

27 Cf. Ho Lin, *Op. Cit.,* pp. 28-31.

28 Cf. O. Brière, *Op. Cit.,* pp. 85-87.

29 *Ibid.,* p. 88.

30 Cf. Ho Lin, *Op. Cit.,* pp. 39-47.
31 *Ibid.,* pp. 48-51.
32 Cf. O. Brière, *Op. Cit.,* p. 72.
33 Cf. Ho Lin, *Op. Cit.,* pp. 28-31; also Brière, *Op. Cit.,* p. 75.
34 Cf. O. Brière, *Op. Cit.,* p. 73f.
35 Cf. Ho Lin, *Op. Cit.,* p. 51.
36 *Ibid.*
37 Cf. O. Brière, *Op. Cit.,* pp. 38, 53-54.
38 *Ibid.,* pp. 54-55.
39 Cf. O. Brière, *Op. Cit.,* pp. 29-31.
40 Cf. Ho Lin, *Op. Cit.,* pp. 52-55.
41 Cf. O. Brière, *Op. Cit.,* p. 100.
42 Cf. Ho Lin, *Op. Cit.,* pp. 52-55.
43 *Ibid.,* pp. 52-55.
44 Cf. O. Brière, *Op. Cit.,* p. 88.
45 Cf. O. Brière, *Op. Cit.,* pp. 90-91.
46 Cf. Ho Lin, *Op. Cit.,* pp. 60-62; also O. Brière, *Op. Cit.,* p. 91.
47 *Ibid.* p. 56.
48 Cf. O. Brière, *Op. Cit.,* p. 90.
49 *Ibid.,* p. 93.
50 Cf. *Ibid.,* p. 92.
51 *Ibid.,* pp. 91-92.
52 Cf. Ho Lin, *Op. Cit.,* pp. 57-59.
53 Cf. O. Brière, *Op. Cit.,* p. 99.
54 Cf. Ho Lin, *Op. Cit.,* p. 62.
55 Cf. Ho Lin, *Op. Cit.,* pp. 64-66.
56 Cf. O. Brière, *Op. Cit.,* p. 31.
57 Cf. *Ibid.,* p. 95f.
58 Cf. *Ibid.,* p. 97; also cf. Ho Lin, *Op. Cit.,* p. 63.
59 Cf. Ho Lin, *Op. Cit.,* pp. 64-66.
60 Cf. O. Brière, *Op. Cit.,* p. 76f.
61 *Ibid.,* p. 77f.
62 Cf. *Ibid.,* p. 32.
63 *Ibid.,* p. 78f.
64 Cf. *Ibid.,* pp. 81-83.
65 *Ibid.,* p. 84.
66 Cf. *Ibid.,* p. 85.
67 *Ibid.,* pp. 36, 80.
68 Cf. *Ibid.,* p. 39.
69 *Ibid.,* pp. 70-72.

70 Cf. Robert Payne: *Mao Tse-tung* (*Ruler of Red China*), p. 172. (Copyright 1950 by Robert Payne) (pub. by Henry Schuman, Inc. New York).

71 Cf. *Ibid.*, p. 177.

72 Cf. *Ibid.*, p. 188f.

73 *Ibid.*, pp.. 190-194.

74 Cf. *Ibid.*, pp. 194-197.

75 Cf. Nym Wales: *Red Dust*, Appendix A, pp. 221-224.

76 Cf. W. T. Chan, art. "Philosophies of China" in D. D. Runes, *Op. Cit.*, p. 547.

76-A Cf. Monlin Chiang: *A Study in Chinese Principles of Education* (1918), pp. 71, 52-56, and 57-ftn 16a.

77 Cf. O. Brière, *Op. Cit.*, pp. 24-26.

78 Cf. Hu Shih: *The Development of Logical Method in Ancient China* (1922), p. 8f.

79 Cf. W. T. Chan, art. "Hu Shih and Chinese Philosophy" in *Philosophy East and West*, Vol. VI, No. 1 (Apr. '56), pp. 5-12, esp. pp. 6-7.

80 Published Shanghai, Commercial Press, Ltd., 1931.

81 Published Shanghai, Ya-Tung Book Co., 1930.

82 Published Shanghai, Commercial Press, Ltd., 1932.

83 Cf. W. T. Chan, art. "Hu Shih and Chinese Philosophy," *Loc. Cit.*, pp. 6-7.

84 Cf. Teng & Fairbank (eds): *China's Response to the West*, pp. 251-258; also Hu Shih: *Recent Sinological Treatises* (*Hu Shih Lun-Hsüeh Chin-Chu*) (first series) (Shanghai, Commercial Press, Ltd., 1935), *passim*.

84-A Cf. Ho Lin, *Op. Cit.*, pp. 23-25.

85 Published in *Phi Theta Annal*, No. 4 (1953) pp. 31-93, and listed in W. T. Chan: *Outline & Bibliography of Chinese Philosophy*, p. 117—from which quotation is made.

86 *Ibid.*, p. 117.

87 Pub. London, Allen & Unwin, 1951, pp. 276-286, and listed in Chan, *Op. Cit.*, p. 117.

88 Pub. in *HJAS*, No. 10 (1947), pp. 124-161, and listed in Chan, *Op. Cit.*, p. 117—from which quotation is made.

89 *Ibid.*, p. 117.

90 Cf. Ho Lin, *Op. Cit.*, pp. 23-25.

91 Pub. London, Probsthain & Co., Ltd., 1929 and 1934, respectively.

92 Pub. privately, 1933; by Yenching University, Peiping, 1937.
93 Pub. N. Y., John Day Co., 1942.
94 Pub., New Haven, Amer. Oriental Soc'y, 1944.
95 Pub. New York, John Day Co., 1946.
96 Pub., Berkeley, Gillick Press, 1943.
97 Pub., N. Y., Bookman Associates, 1957.
98 Pub., N. Y., Columbia University Press, 1953.
99 Pub., N. Y., Philosophical Library, 1955.
100 Pub., Wash., D. C., U. S. Gov't Printing Office, 1943, 1944.
101 Pub., N. Y., John Day Co, 1949.
102 Pub., Chicago, University of Chicago Press, 1953.
103 Pub., Chicago, University of Chicago Press, 1953.
104 Pub., Cambridge, Mass., Harvard University Press, 1954.
105 Pub., Chicago, University of Chicago Press, 1957.
106 Cf. Homer H. Dubs, art. "Recent Chinese Philosophy" in *Journal of Philosophy,* No. 35 (1938), p. 35.
107 Cf. O. Brière, *Op. Cit.,* pp. 36f, 60-62.
108 Cf. *Ibid.,* p. 37; also see Andrew Tod Roy: (MS.) "Modern Confucian Social Theory and Its Concept of Change," *passim;* (*Note*: See report of an interview with Chen Li-fu by Frederick Gruin in *Time,* May 26, 1947).
109 Cf. Andrew Tod Roy, *Op. Cit.,* pp. 395-398.
110 Cf. *Ibid.,* pp. 413-415, quoting the *Book of Rites,* Sec. II, par. 18; also the *Mêng-tzu,* Bk. II-A, VIII, vss. 3-5.
111 Cf. *Ibid.,* pp. 404, 421ff.
112 Cf. *Ibid.,* pp. 413-415.
113 Cf. *Ibid.,* p. 429, ftn 65, 66, quoting *Book of Changes* (Great Appendix—"Hsi-tz'u," Sec. II, Ch. 2, vs. 15; also Appendix I—"T'uan," Sec. II, Hexagram 32, vs. 4).
114 Cf. *Ibid.,* pp. 421-437.
115 *Ibid.,* pp. 421-437.
116 Cf. W. T. Chan: *Religious Trends in Modern China,* p. 25f.
117 Cf. *Ibid.,* pp. 27-30.
118 Cf. T. C. Chao, art. "The Appeal of Christianity to the Chinese Mind," Shanghai, *The Chinese Recorder,* May, 1918, p. 295.
119 Cf. *Ibid.,* p. 295; also cf. Y. L. Fung: *History,* II, p. 638.
120 Cf. Hsieh Sung-kao (Z. K. Zia): *The Confucian Civilization,* (1925), pp. 39, 21, 60.
121 Cf. *Ibid.,* pp. 30-33, quoted in D. Willard Lyon: (MS) "Confucianism Today," p. 82.

122 Cf. D. Willard Lyon, *Op. Cit.*, p. 82f. (Used by permission of the author). *Note*: F. G. Henke (*Op. Cit.*, p. 267) states that when Wang Yang-ming was discussing *"ai"* and *"jên,"* he is quoted as having said: "Why should not the word *'ai'* . . . be considered as having the same meaning as *'jên'* "?

123 Cf. C. Y. Hsü: *The Philosophy of Confucius*, pp. 57, 58, 60, 63, (quoted by D. Willard Lyon in "Confucianism Today").

124 Cf. *The Chinese Recorder*, Shanghai, Feb., 1926, pp. 119ff.

125 Cf. Francis C. M. Wei: *Rooting the Christian Church in Chinese Soil*, an address inaugurating the Henry W. Luce Visiting Professorship of World Christianity in Union Theological Seminary, New York City, delivered on October 24, 1945. (Privately printed and distributed by Union Theological Seminary) —pp. 9-14.

126 Cf. Francis C. M. Wei: *The Spirit of Chinese Culture* (1947), p. 175f.

127 Cf. Hsü T'eng-hui (Benjamin Dung-hwe Zi): "The Idea of God in the Chinese Classics" (Hartford Seminary Foundation, Ph. D. dissertation, March, 1930), q.v. *passim*.

128 Cf. *Ibid.*, pp. 314-316.

129 Cf. *Ibid.*, p. 319f.

130 Cf. *Ibid.*, p. 321f.

131 *Ibid.*, pp. 324-326.

132 Cf. *Ibid.*, p. 330f, quoting *Chung Yung*, Chap. 1, p. 4.

133 Cf. *Ibid.*, p. 331, quoting *Chung Yung*, Chap. 20, p. 18.

134 Cf. *Ibid.*, p. 331.

135 Cf. *Ibid.*, p. 334.

136 Cf. Francis C. M. Wei: "Rooting the Christian Church in Chinese Soil," p. 10.

137 Cf. W. T. Chan: *Religious Trends in Modern China*, p. 94f, and p. 95-ftn 2, where Dr. Chan quotes Junjiro Takakusu's definition of *"dharmas"* as "ideals" in the mind; as different in different persons (referring to his *The Essentials of Buddhist Philosophy*, edited by Wing-tsit Chan and Charles A. Moore, Un. of Hawaii Pr., 2nd ed. 1949, p. 57).

138 Cf. W. T. Chan, *Op. Cit.*, pp. 94-100, *passim* (ref. to D. T. Suzuki's translation of Aśvaghoṣa's *Discourse on the Awakening of Faith in the Mahāyāna*, Chicago, Open Court, 1900, pp. 113, 116, 128). Cf. Timothy Richard and Yang Wên-hui (tr): *The Awakening of Faith in the Mahāyāna Doctrine*, Edinb., T. & T. Clark, 1894.

139 Cf. W. T. Chan, *Op. Cit.*, p. 101.

140 Cf. *Ibid.*, p. 117; cf. pp. 105-8, 112-118, giving quotations from Ou-Yang's pupils which support this point of view and referring to Suzuki's translation of *The Awakening of Faith.*

141 Cf. W. T. Chan, *Op. Cit.*, pp. 111-118.

142 Cf. *Ibid.*, p. 122f.

143 *Ibid.*, p. 123, quoting T'ai Hsü: *Fa-Hsiang Wei-Shih Hsüeh*, pp. 2, 10, 425, 16.

144 Cf. Kuen-Lun (tr): *T'ai Hsü: Lectures in Buddhism*, Introd.

145 Cf. Frank R. Millican, art. "Chen Ju" in *The Chinese Recorder*, Shanghai, Feb., 1924, p. 115ff.

146 Cf. *Ibid.*, pp. 115ff, *passim.*

147 Cf. *Ibid.*, referring to T'ai Hsü 's art. in *The New Buddhism*, No. 10, published in Ningpo in 1920.

148 Cf. Frank R. Millican, art. "T'ai Hsü and Modern Buddhism" in *The Chinese Recorder*, Shanghai, June, 1923, pp. 326-334—quoting *The Voice of the Tide* (*Hai Ch'ao Yin*), Vol. I, No. 10.

149 Cf. Frank R. Millican, art. "Buddhism in the Light of Modern Thought—As Interpreted by the Monk T'ai Hsü," in *The Chinese Recorder*, Shanghai, 1926, pp. 91-94.

150 *Cf. Ibid., passim.*

151 Cf. O. Brière: *Fifty Years of Chinese Philosophy*, p. 46.

152 Cf. Kuen-Lun (tr): *T'ai Hsü: Lectures in Buddhism*, Introd.

153 Cf. *Ibid.*, p. 6.

154 Cf. *Ibid.*, pp. 90-92.

155 Cf. W. T. Chan, *Op. Cit.*, pp. 119-125, *passim.*

156 Cf. O. Brière, *Op. Cit.*, pp. 45-48; cf. pp. 39-42.

157 Cf. W. T. Chan, *Op. Cit.*, p. 125, quoted in A. E. Haydon: *Modern Trends in World Religions*, Un. of Chicago Pr., 1934, p. 248.

158 Cf. O. Brière, *Op. Cit.*, p. 27f.

159 *Ibid.*, p. 28.

160 Cf. Andrew Tod Roy, *Op. Cit.*, pp. 297-304, referring to Liang Shu-min: *Civilizations of the Orient and Occident*, pp. 117-144.

161 Cf. Warren H. Stuart, *Op. Cit.*, p. 76, quoting from Liang Shu-min: *Civilizations of the Orient and Occident* (*Tung Hsi Wên-Hua Chih Ch'i Chê-Hsüeh*).

162 Cf. Andrew Tod Roy, *Op. Cit.*, pp. 297-304, quoting Liang, *Op. Cit.*, pp. 117ff.

163 *Ibid.*

164 Cf. *Ibid.*, quoting Liang, *Op. Cit.*, pp. 121ff, referring to *The Mêng-tzu,* Bk. VI, Pt. I, Ch. VI, Sec. V, vs. 7.

165 Cf. *Ibid.*, quoting Liang, *Op. Cit.*, pp. 125ff.

166 Cf. *Ibid.*, quoting Liang, *Op Cit.*, p. 130f.

167 Cf. *Ibid.*, quoting Liang, *Op. Cit.*, pp. 133-137.

168 Cf. *Ibid.*, p. 304, quoting Liang, *Op. Cit.*, p. 143f, referring to the *Ta Hsüeh, Commentary,* Chap. VI, Sec. V, vs. 1.

169 Cf. Ho Lin: *Contemporary Chinese Philosophy,* pp. 9-13; cf. also W. T. Chan: *Religious Trends in Modern China,* pp. 31-33.

170 Cf. Rural Reconstruction Series, Nos. 1 and 2.

171 Cf. O. Brière, *Op. Cit.*, p. 28.

172 *Ibid.*, p. 56.

173 Cf. Ho Lin, *Op. Cit.*, p. 16f.

174 Cf. O. Brière, *Op. Cit.*, p. 42.

175 Cf. W. T. Chan, *Op. Cit.*, pp. 33-42, 126-135.

176 Cf. *Ibid.*, p. 133 and ftn; pp. 125, 127, 128—referring to Chou Ku-ch'eng's *Chung-Kuo Shih-Hsüeh Chih Chin-Hua* (*Development of Chinese Historiography*), pp. 30-41; also to Yin Shun's *P'ing Hsiung Shih-li ti Hsin Wei-Shih Lun* (*Criticism of Hsiung Shih-li's New Idealism*), pp. 16-17, 45.

177 Cf. *Ibid.*, pp. 33-43; 126-134.

178 Cf. O. Brière, *Op. Cit.*, p. 49f.

179 Cf. Ho Lin, *Op. Cit.*, p. 13.

180 Cf. W. T. Chan, art. "Syntheses in Chinese Metaphysics" in Charles A. Moore (ed): *Essays in East-West Philosophy,* p. 176.

181 Cf. W. T. Chan: *Religious Trends in Modern China,* p. 43.

182 Cf. *International Journal of Ethics,* Vol. XXXII, No. 3, April, 1922 (included in Fung's *Chung-Kuo Chê-Hsüeh Shih Pu—Supplement to Chinese Philosophy,* pp. 9-40.)

182-A Published by The Commercial Press, Ltd., Shanghai, 1924.

182-B Also included in Fung's *Supplement to Chinese Philosophy,* n.d. ca. 1940, by The Commercial Press, Ltd., Shanghai.

182-C Vol. I published by Henri Vetch, Peking, and by Allen and Unwin, Ltd., London, in 1937; republished by Princeton University Press in 1951, with identical pagination. Vol. II published by Princeton University Press in 1953. In each case, the translation, with notes, was made by Dr. Derk Bodde, Chairman, Department of Oriental Studies, University of Pennsylvania.

183 Cf. W. T. Chan: *Religious Trends in Modern China,* pp. 43-45 (slightly altered).

184 (Derk Bodde, tr.), published by The Macmillan Co., 1950; Cf. Chap. 28.

185 Cf. Fung: *History,* II, p. 721 (translator's footnote).

186 Pub. London, Kegan Paul, Trench, Trübner & Co., Ltd., 1947, q.v., *passim.*

187 Cf. E. R. Hughes (tr): *The Spirit of Chinese Philosophy,* pp. 45-58.

188 Cf. *Ibid.,* p. 82f.

189 *Ibid.,* pp. 86-90.

190 Cf. Andrew Tod Roy, *Op. Cit.,* Chap. 10, p. 6; Cf. H. G. Creel, *Op. Cit.,* p. 172.

191 Cf. E. R. Hughes (tr), *Op. Cit.,* pp. 91-102.

192 Cf. *Ibid.,* p. 86.

193 *Ibid.,* pp. 91-102.

194 Cf. *Ibid.,* p. 102f.

195 Cf. *Ibid.,* p. 106.

196 *Ibid.*

197 *Ibid.,* p. 107f, *passim.*

198 Cf. *Ibid.,* p. 110.

199 Cf. *Ibid.,* p. 110f.

200 *Ibid.,* p. 111.

201 Cf. Y. L. Fung, *History,* I, pp. 391-393.

202 Cf. E. R. Hughes (tr), *Op. Cit.,* p. 130f.

203 Cf. *Ibid.,* pp. 134, 135, 136.

204 Cf. *Ibid.,* pp.143, 144, 145.

205 Cf. *Ibid.,* pp. 146-154.

206 Cf. *Ibid.,* pp. 202f; Cf. Author's Preface, vii; Cf. also W. T. Chan: *Religious Trends in Modern China,* pp. 45-51; Cf. also W. T. Chan, art. "Philosophies of China" in D. D. Runes, *Op. Cit.,* pp. 563-567 for condensed summary of Fung's "New Rational Philosophy"; also rendered in condensed form in W. T. Chan's art. "Trends in Contemporary Philosophy" in H. F. MacNair (ed): *China.*

207 Cf. E. R. Hughes (tr), *Op. Cit.,* pp. 112-129.

208 Cf. *Ibid.,* p. 202.

209 Cf. *Ibid.,* p. 202f.

210 *Ibid.,* pp. 205-212.

211 *Ibid.*, pp. 205-207.
212 *Ibid.*, pp. 207-209
213 *Ibid.*, pp. 209-211.
214 Cf. *Ibid.*, p. 211f.
215 Cf. *Ibid.*, p. 219.
216 Cf. *Ibid.*, pp. 212-220.
217 Cf. W. T. Chan, art. "Philosophies of China" in D. D. Runes, *Op. Cit.*, p. 565.
218 Cf. Ho Lin, *Op. Cit.*, p. 23; Cf. O. Brière, *Op. Cit.*, pp. 50-53.
219 Cf. W. T. Chan: *Religious Trends in Modern China*, pp. 50f, 247f.
220 Cf. *Ibid.*, p. 52; Cf. also Ho Lin, *Op. Cit.*, p. 23.
221 Cf. W. T. Chan, *Op. Cit.*, p. 52.
222 Cf. *Ibid.*, p. 52-ftn 206, ref. to *People's China*, Vol. I, No. 6, March 6, 1950.
223 Cf. *Ibid.*, p. 52-ftn 207, ref. to *Bright Light Daily* (in Chinese: *Kuang-Min Jih-Pao)*, Oct. 8, 1950.
224 Cf. *Ibid.*, p. 52.
225. *Ibid.*, p. 53, referring to Mao's *New Democracy*, pub. in Chinese and English, Shanghai, 1940.
226 Cf. *Ibid.*, p. 53, ref. to Mao's *On Entering the New Stage (Lun Hsin Chieh-Tuan)*.
227 *Ibid.*, p. 53.
228 From a reliable source in Hong Kong.
229 From a reliable source in Hong Kong.
230 As reported from a reliable source.

NOTES
to Chapter 14

1 Cf. W. T. Chan, art. "Syntheses in Chinese Metaphysics" in Charles A. Moore (ed): *Essays in East-West Philosophy* (1951), p. 170f.
2 Cf. *Ibid.*, p. 171f.
3 Cf. *Ibid.*, p. 163.
4 Cf. *Ibid.*, p. 164f, 169.
5 Cf. *Ibid.*, pp. 165-167, 170.

6 Cf. *Ibid.,* pp.164, 168.
7 Cf. *Ibid.,* pp. 168, 169.
8 Cf. *Ibid.,* p. 172.
9 Cf. *Ibid.,* p. 173f.
10 Cf. D. Willard Lyon: (MS) "Confucianism Today" (1927), p. 61.
11 Cf. W. T. Chan, art. "Syntheses in Chinese Metaphysics," p. 164.
12 Cf. Charles A. Moore (ed): *Philosophy East and West (A Symposium),* p. 144f (order and wording slightly altered). Cf. Fung: *History* I, pp. 1-6.
13 Cf. *Ibid.,* p. 145.
14 Cf. Ho Lin: *Contemporary Chinese Philosophy* (in Chinese), pp. 1-2.
15 Cf. Chen Li-fu (Jen Tai, tr.): *Philosophy of Life,* pp. 125-130; pp. 74-76.
16 Cf. Charles A. Moore (ed): *Philosophy East and West,* p. 68.

Appendix I

CHINESE HISTORY IN OUTLINE

Dynasties	Approximate Dates	No. of Rulers	Men and Events
I. *LEGENDARY PERIOD* (ca. 2852-2197 B.C.)		(9)	Period of "Five Rulers"
Fu Hsi (ca. 2852-2738); Yao (ca. 2357-2255); Shun (ca. 2255-2205)			The Great Yü (ca. 2205-2197)
II. *PRIMITIVE DYNASTIES* (2197-221 B.C.)			
Hsia (1994-1523)		(17)	Casting of Bronze
Shang (Yin) (1523-1027)		(28)	Oracle Bones of Yin
Chou (1027-256)		(34)	Lao Tzu, Confucius, Mo Tzu, Yang Chu, Mencius, Chuang Tzu, Hsün Tzu, Shang Yang, Han Fei Tzu
Warring States Period (ca. 403-221 B.C.)			
III. *ANCIENT DYNASTIES* (221 B.C.-A.D. 618)			
Ch'in (221-207 B.C.)		(5)	Building of Great Wall Tung Chung-shu
Han (207 B.C.-A.D. 220)		(26)	Buddhism introduced Confucianism established
Three Kingdoms (220-265)		(11)	"Age of Chivalry"
Chin (Tsin) (265-420)		(15)	China Under One Ruler
North and South (420-589)		(58)	Country Again Divided Buddhism Well Established
Sui (589-618)		(4)	Country United Again

IV. *MEDIEVAL DYNASTIES* (A.D. 618-1368)		Buddhism flourishing
T'ang (618-905)	(22)	Arts and literature develop; printing invented
Five Dynasties (905-960)	(13)	Neo-Confucian Philosophy
Sung (960-1279) (So. Sung, 1127-1279)	(18)	and Poetry flourish; Ch'eng Brothers, Chu Hsi, Lu Hsiang-shan
Yüan (Mongol) (1280-1368)	(9)	Marco Polo to China Drama developed
V. *MODERN DYNASTIES* (A.D. 1368-1911)	(17)	Poetry, Painting, Industry
Ming (1368-1644)		Wang Yang-ming
Ch'ing (Manchu) (1644-1911)	(10)	All arts flourish T'aiping Rebellion
VI. *REPUBLIC OF CHINA* (A.D. 1912-)		
Sun Yat-sen (1912) (First Republic)		Prov'l President, Nanking
Yüan Shih-k'ai (1912-1916)		First President, Peking
Series of Presidents		
Chiang K'ai-shek (1927-) (Second Republic)		Nationalist Revolution (Kuomintang Government established Nanking; moved to T'aiwan, 1949)
Mao Tse-tung (1949-) (People's or Third Republic)		(People's Communist Government established in Peking)

Note:—See Henry C. Fenn's chart—*"China in Brief,"* facing p. 44 in Goodrich and Fenn: *A Syllabus of the History of Chinese Civilization and Culture* (6th ed.), N. Y., The China Society of America, Inc., 1958.

Appendix II

A SUGGESTED READING LIST

Blofeld, John. *The Jewel in the Lotus.* London, Sidgwick & Jackson, Ltd., 1948.

Brière, O. (S. J.). *Fifty Years of Chinese Philosophy* (1898-1950). French edition. Shanghai, Aurora Press, ca. 1950. (Laurence G. Thompson, tr.) Eng. ed. London, Allen & Unwin, Ltd., 1956.

Bruce, J. Percy (tr.): *Chu Hsi—The Philosophy of Human Nature.* London, Arthur Probsthain, 1922.

Chan, Wing-tsit. *Religious Trends in Modern China.* N. Y., Columbia University Press, 1953.

———. *An Outline and An Annotated Bibliography of Chinese Philosophy.* New Haven, Far-Eastern Publications, 1959.

———. *A Source Book in Chinese Philosophy.* Princeton University Press, 1961.

Chang, Carsun. *The Development of Neo-Confucian Thought.* N. Y., Bookman Associates, 1957.

Chen, Li-fu. *Philosophy of Life* (Jen Tai, tr.). N. Y., Philosophical Library, 1948.

Chu Ch'an (tr.): *The Huang Po Doctrine of Universal Mind.* London, The Buddhist Society, 1947.

Creel, Herrlee Glessner. *Chinese Thought From Confucius to Mao Tse-tung.* University of Chicago Press, 1953.

Day, Clarence B. *Chinese Peasant Cults.* Shanghai, Kelly & Walsh, Ltd., 1940.

Dubs, Homer H. *Hsüntze, The Moulder of Ancient Confucianism.* London, Arthur Probsthain, 1927.

Fairbank, John K. (ed.): *Chinese Thought and Institutions.* University of Chicago Press, 1957.

Fung, Yu-lan. *A History of Chinese Philosophy* (2 vols.), (Derk Bodde, tr.). Princeton University Press, Vol. I, 1951; Vol. II, 1953.

Fung, Yu-lan. *The Spirit of Chinese Philosophy (Hsin Yüan Tao),* (E. R. Hughes, tr.). London, Kegan Paul, Trench, Trübner & Co., Ltd., 1947.

Graham, A. C. *Two Chinese Philosophers: Ch'êng Ming-tao and Ch'êng Yi-ch'uan.* London, Lund Humphries, 1958.

Hamilton, C. H. (ed.): *Buddhism, A Religion of Infinite Compassion.* N. Y., Liberal Arts Press, Inc., 1952.

Henke, Frederick G. (tr.): *The Philosophy of Wang Yang-ming.* Chicago, Open Court Publishing Co., 1916.

Huang, Siu-chi. *Lu Hsiang-shan: A Twelfth Century Chinese Idealist Philosopher.* New Haven, Amer. Oriental Soc'y (Series Vol. 27), 1944.

Hu Shih. *Development of Logical Method in Ancient China.* Shanghai, Oriental Book Company, 1922.

Hughes, Ernest R. *Chinese Philosophy in Classical Times.* London, J. M. Dent & Sons, Ltd., 1924, ("Everyman's"). N. Y., E. P. Dutton & Co., 1942.

———. (tr.): *The Great Learning and the Mean in Action* (Translations of the *Ta Hsüeh* and the *Chung Yung*). N. Y., E. P. Dutton & Co., 1943.

Hummel, Arthur W. (ed.): *Eminent Chinese of the Ch'ing Period* (2 vols.). Washington, D. C., U.S. Gov't Printing Office, 1943-1944.

Levenson, J. R. *Liang Ch'i-ch'ao and the Mind of Modern China.* Cambridge, Harvard University Press, 1953.

Liang, Ch'i-ch'ao. *A History of Chinese Political Thought.* London, Kegan Paul, Trench, Trübner & Co., Ltd., 1930. N. Y., Harcourt, Brace & Co., Inc., 1930.

Liao, W. K. (Joshua). *The Complete Works of Han Fei Tzu* (Vol. I), (A Classic of Legalism). London, Arthur Probsthain, 1939.

Lin, Mousheng. *Men and Ideas.* N. Y., The John Day Company, 1942.

Lin, Yutang (tr.): *The Wisdom of Confucius.* N. Y., Random House (Illus. Mod. Libr.), 1943.

Liu, Wu-chi. *A Short History of Confucian Philosophy.* Harmondsworth, Middlesex, England, 1955. Baltimore, Penguin Books, Ltd., 1955.

Maverick, Lewis (ed.): *Economic Dialogues in Ancient China—Selections from the KUAN TZU.* Carbondale, Ill., Privately published, 1954.

Mei, Yi-pao. *Motse, The Neglected Rival of Confucius.* London, Arthur Probsthain & Co., 1934.
Moore, Charles A. (ed.): *Philosophy East and West* (A Symposium). Princeton University Press, 1944.
———. (ed.): *Essays in East-West Philosophy.* Honolulu, University of Hawaii Press, 1951.
Murti, T. R. V. *The Central Philosophy of Buddhism* (A Study of the Mādhyamika System). London, George Allen & Unwin, Ltd., 1955.
Pratt, James B. *The Pilgrimage of Buddhism.* N. Y., The Macmillan Company, 1928.
Price, A. F. (tr.): *The Perfection of Transcendental Wisdom* ("The Diamond Sūtra"). London, The Buddhist Society, 1947.
Radhakrishnan, Sir Sarvepalli. *India and China* (*Lectures in China,* 1944). Bombay, Hind Kitabs, Ltd., 1944, 1947.
———. *Indian Philosophy* (2 vols.), (2nd Rev. ed.). London, Allen & Unwin, Ltd., 1951. N. Y., The Macmillan Company, 1951.
Reichelt, Karl L. *Religion in Chinese Garment.* (Joseph Tetlie, tr.). N. Y., Philosophical Library, 1951.
Soothill, W. E. (tr.): *The Lotus of the Wonderful Law* (A Selected Translation of the *Miao-Fa Lien-Hua Ching* or *Saddharma-Puṇdarika Sūtra).* Oxford, Clarendon Press, 1930.
Stuart, Warren H. *The Use of Material from China's Spiritual Inheritance in the Christian Education of Chinese Youth.* Shanghai, Kwang Hsüeh Publishing House, 1932.
Sun Yat-sen. *San Min Chu I* (*Three Principles of the People*), (Frank W. Price, tr.). Shanghai, The Commercial Press, Ltd., 1928.
Suzuki, Beatrice Lane. *Mahāyāna Buddhism.* London, David Marlowe, Ltd., 1948.
Suzuki, D. T. (tr.): *Aśvaghoṣa's Discourse on the Awakening of Faith in the Mahāyāna,* Chicago, Open Court Pub. Co., 1900.
———. *The Zen Doctrine of No-Mind* (The Significance of the Sūtra of Hui Neng). London, Rider & Co., 1949.
T'ai Hsü (Abbot). *Lectures in Buddhism* (Kuen Lun, tr.). Paris, Imp. Union, 1928.
Takakusu, Junjiro. *Essentials of Buddhist Philosophy* (W. T. Chan & C. A. Moore, eds.). University of Hawaii Press (2nd ed.), 1949.
Teng, Ssu-yü and Fairbank, John K. (eds.): *China's Response to the West.* Cambridge, Harvard University Press, 1954.

Thomas, Edward J. *A History of Buddhist Thought.* Lond., Kegan Paul, Trench, Trübner & Co., Ltd., 1933. N. Y., Alfred Knopf, 1933. N. Y., Barnes and Noble (2nd ed.), 1951.

Tomkinson, Leonard. *The Social Teachings of Meh Tse* (Mo Tzu.). Lond., Kegan Paul, Trench, Trübner & Co., Ltd., 1927.

Wei, Francis C. M. *The Spirit of Chinese Culture.* N. Y., Charles Scribner's Sons, 1947.

Wong, Mou-lam (tr.): *The Sūtra of Wei Lang* (Hui Neng). London, Luzac & Co., 1947.

Wright, Arthur F. (ed.): *Studies in Chinese Thought.* University of Chicago Press, 1953.

———. *Buddhism in Chinese History.* Palo Alto, Stanford University Press, 1959.

ACKNOWLEDGMENTS

Acknowledgment is here gratefully made to those persons or publishers who have granted permission to quote from copyrighted publications:—

Mrs. James B. Pratt—J. B. Pratt: *The Pilgrimage of Buddhism.*

Mrs. Robert Redfield—John K. Fairbank (ed.): *Chinese Thought and Institutions* and Arthur F. Wright (ed.): *Studies in Chinese Thought.*

Abelard-Schuman Ltd., New York—Robert Payne: *Mao Tse-tung, Ruler of Red China.*

George Allen & Unwin Ltd., London—T. R. V. Murti: *The Central Philosophy of Buddhism;* O. Brière: *Fifty Years of Chinese Philosophy;* S. Radhakrishnan: *Indian Philosophy,* Vol. I.

American Oriental Society, New Haven—C. H. Hamilton (tr.): *Wei-Shih Erh-Shih Lun (Treatise in Twenty Stanzas on Representation Only)*—(A. O. S. Series Vol. 13. 1938). Siu-chi Huang: *Lu Hsiang-shan—A Twelfth Century Chinese Idealist Philosopher* (A. O. S. Series Vol. 27, 1944). W. T. Chan: Review of A. C. Graham's *Two Chinese Philosophers* in J. A. O. S., Vol. 79, No. 2, 1959.

Edward Arnold (Publishers) Ltd., London—Sir Charles Eliot: *Hinduism and Buddhism* (3 vols.).

Barnes and Noble, Inc., New York—Edward J. Thomas: *A History of Buddhist Thought* (2nd ed., 1951).

Bookman Associates, Inc., New York—Carsun Chang: *Development of Neo-Confucian Thought.*

The Buddhist Society, London—Chu Ch'an (tr.): *Sutra of Forty-two Sections; Doctrine Bequeathed by the Buddha; Eight Awakenings of the Great Ones* (1947); *Huang Po Doctrine of Universal Mind* (1947); A. F. Price (tr.); *Perfection of Transcendental Wisdom.*

University of California Press, Berkeley—H. F. MacNair (ed.): *China.*

University of Chicago Press, Chicago—H. G. Creel: *Chinese Thought from Confucius to Mao Tse-tung.*

Columbia University Press, New York—W. T. Chan: *Religious Trends in Modern China;* Chen Huang-chang: *Economic Principles of Confucius and His School* (2 vols.).

The John Day Company, Inc., New York—Lin Mousheng: *Men and Ideas.*

Harcourt, Brace and World, Inc., New York—Liang Ch'i-ch'ao: *History of Chinese Political Thought.*

Harvard University Press, Cambridge—Joseph R. Levenson: *Liang Ch'i-ch'ao and the Mind of Modern China.*

University of Hawaii Press, Honolulu—Charles A. Moore (ed.); *Essays in East-West Philosophy* (1951); also from *Philosophy East and West,* V, No. 1 (April, 1955); VI, No. 1, (April, 1956); VI, No. 4, (Jan. 1957); VII, No. 3/4 (Oct. '57/Jan. '58).

David Higham Associates, Ltd., London—E. R. Hughes (tr.): *Spirit of Chinese Philosophy* (Fung Yu-lan's *Hsin-Yüan Tao*).

Hillary House Publishers Ltd., New York, and Hutchinson & Co. (Publishers) Ltd., London—D. T. Suzuki: *The Zen Doctrine of No-Mind.*

Hind Kitabs, Ltd., Bombay—Sir S. Radhakrishnan: *India and China.*

Luzac & Company Ltd., London—Wong Mou-lam: *Sutra of Wei Lang.*

The Macmillan Company, New York—John B. Noss: *Man's Religions;* Sir S. Radhakrishnan: *Indian Philosophy,* Vol .I; O. Brière: *Fifty Years of Chinese Philosophy;* T. R. V. Murti: *The Central Philosophy of Buddhism.*

John Murray, London—Ku Hung-ming: *The Conduct of Life.*

Open Court Publishing Company, La Salle, Illinois—F. G. Henke: *The Philosophy of Wang Yang-ming.*

Philosophical Library (Publishers), New York—D. D. Runes (ed.): *Twentieth Century Philosophy;* Vergilius Ferm (ed.): *Encyclopedia of Religion;* Chen Li-fu (Jen Tai, tr.) *Philosophy of Life;* Karl L. Reichelt (Joseph Tetlie, tr.): *Religion in Chinese Garment;* W. E. Soothill: *Hall of Light;* and Ferm (ed.): *History of Philosophical Systems.*

Princeton University Press, Princeton, New Jersey—Fung Yu-lan (Derk Bodde, tr.): *History of Chinese Philosophy* (2 vols.); Charles A. Moore (ed.): *Philosophy East and West* (A Symposium).

Arthur Probsthain (Publisher), London—J. P. Bruce: *Chu Hsi: Philosophy of Human Nature;* H. H. Dubs: *Hsüntze, Moulder of Ancient Confucianism;* Mei Yi-pao: *Motse, The Neglected Rival of Confucius.*

Random House, Inc., New York—Lin Yutang (tr.): *The Wisdom of Confucius* (Copyright 1938 by Random House, Inc.)

Fleming H. Revell Company, Westwood, New Jersey—W. E. Soothill: *A Mission in China.*

Routledge and Kegan Paul Ltd., London—Liang Ch'i-ch'ao: *History of Chinese Political Thought;* Evan Morgan: *Tao, The Great Luminant.*

Charles Scribner's Sons, New York—Francis C. M. Wei: *Spirit of Chinese Culture.*

Sidgwick & Jackson Ltd., London—John Blofeld: *Jewel in the Lotus.*

Paul A. Schilpp, Editor, Library of Living Philosophers, Northwestern University, Evanston, Illinois—T. R. V. Murti, art. "Radhakrishnan and Buddhism" in Paul A. Schilpp (ed.): *The Philosophy of Sarvepalli Radhakrishnan* (N. Y., Tudor Pub. Co., 1952).

Union Seminary Quarterly Review, New York—Francis C. M. Wei: *Rooting the Christian Church in Chinese Soil.*

INDEX

INDEX